Natural Language Computing

An English Generative Grammar in Prolog

Ray C. Dougherty
New York University
Linguistics Department

 LAWRENCE ERLBAUM ASSOCIATES, PUBLISHERS
1994   Hillsdale, New Jersey   Hove, UK

Etching by Michael Burke.
Photograph by Jonathan Smith.

Lawrence Erlbaum Associates, Inc., Publishers
365 Broadway
Hillsdale, New Jersey 07642

Library of Congress Cataloging-in-Publication Data

Natural language computing : an English generative grammar in
Prolog / Ray C. Dougherty.
    p. cm.
    Includes bibliographical references and index.
    ISBN 0-8058-1525-2 (cloth). -- ISBN 0-8058-1526-0 (pbk).
    1. English language--Grammar, Generative--Data processing.
    2. Natural language processing (Computer science) I. Title.
    PE1074.5.D68 1994
    425'.0285--dc20   94-5269
                                                        CIP

Books published by Lawrence Erlbaum Associates are printed
on acid-free paper, and their bindings are chosen
for strength and durability.

Printed in the United States of America

10 9 8 7 6 5 4 3 2 1

To my wife

Claudia Leacock

Contents

PREFACE

I have, notwithstanding discouragement, attempted a Dictionary of the English Language, which, while it was employed in the cultivation of every species of literature, has itself been hitherto neglected; suffered to spread, under the direction of chance, into wild exuberance; resigned to the tyranny of time and fashion; and exposed to the corruptions of ignorance, and caprices of innovation.

When I took the first survey of my undertaking, I found our speech copious without order, and energetic without rule; wherever I turned my view, there was perplexity to be disentangled and confusion to be regulated; choice was to be made out of boundless variety, without any established principle of selection; adulterations were to be detected, without a settled test of purity; and modes of expression to be rejected or received, without the sufferages of any writers of classical reputation or acknowledged authority.

Samuel Johnson, 1755/1938
Preface to the English Dictionary

From the time he could pick up a crayon, Pablo Picasso had the ability to sketch pictures that accurately depicted the things he saw. He was exceptional. Most of us spent our early years following the dots, painting by numbers, and drawing on tracing paper held over some else's picture. If you are a Pablo Picasso of the computer, and if computational linguistics comes easy to you, this book may not be for you. But if you would like a follow–the–dots approach to natural language processing, linguistic theory, artificial intelligence, and expert systems, you will like this presentation. The basic idea is to present meaningful answers to significant problems involved in representing human language data on a computing machine. My main focus is on the grammatical devices underlying constructions of English, French, and German. I use the absolute minimum required from any computer hardware or from either of the computer languages discussed: Prolog and UNIX.

This book, which perhaps should be subtitled *start here*, offers a hands–on approach to anyone who wishes to gain a perspective on **natural language processing**, the computational analysis of human language data. All of the examples in this book are illustrated using computer programs that run. The optimal way for a person to get started is to run these existing programs to gain an understanding of how they work. After gaining such familiarity, you can start to modify the programs and eventually start to write your own. The optimal way to learn to create programs is to operate on live ones by modifying existing code. All programs discussed, and a shareware version of Prolog to execute them, are available on a disk (see Appendix I) or from the New York University public domain bulletin board (see Appendix II). All programs run on free versions of Prolog–2 (IBM) and Open–Prolog (Apple). See *How to Use This Book* for a pictorial representation of the book's organization. If you have a computer, you have no excuse for not running these programs as you work through the book.

My main goal is to show the reader how to use the linguistic theory of Noam Chomsky, called **Universal Grammar**, to represent some of the grammatical processes of English, French, and German on a computer using the Prolog computer language. I assume the reader knows very little about Prolog and less about Chomsky's linguistic theories. The Introduction, *What is Computational Linguistics?*, presents an overview of the problems and problem areas I discuss.

Prolog, short for *PROgramming in LOGic*, differs from most computer languages in that the programmer usually does not need to tell the computer the procedural steps to follow in order to find an answer. A Prolog program consists of a database, relations among items in the database, and a set of boundary conditions that identify correct, or acceptable, answers. Although the operation of Prolog initially appears counterintuitive, and although the basic concepts underlying Prolog reflect the arcana of formal logic, Prolog is remarkably easy to learn for beginners if it is presented using simple examples and lots of diagrams. This introduction to Prolog offers simple examples and figures to illustrate most Prolog operations.

Chomsky's linguistic theories (generative grammar, universal grammar, principles and parameters, etc.) do not lend themselves to simplification because the theoretical significance of them derives from their logical "tightness." That is, from a small number of general principles that can be formalized in terms of logic and computer processes (hence, the relevance of Prolog in the exposition), it is possible to derive many of the seemingly exceptional and irregular properties of human language structure. Unfortunately, the diagrams offered to clarify ideas basic to sentence analysis in Chomsky's system often frighten people away.

Rather than plunge directly into the basic assumptions of Chomsky's system and attempt to derive the properties of human language by Cartesian deduction from the basic principles of Universal

Grammar, I first discuss the types of problems that arise in Chomsky's system, and then turn to formal linguistic theories. My view of Chomsky's system has more in common with the methodological views of Gertrude Stein than of Descartes and Pascal.

Gertrude Stein wrote:

> When you are at school and learn grammar grammar is very exciting. I really do not know that anything has ever been more exciting than diagraming sentences. I suppose other things may be more exciting to others when they are at school but to me undoubtedly when I was at school the really completely exciting thing was diagraming sentences and that has been to me ever since the one thing that has been completely exciting and completely completing. I like the feeling the everlasting feeling of sentences as they diagram themselves. (Stein 1935: 81)

Following Stein's ideas, my goal is to use the computer language Prolog to diagram sentences using the types of diagrams that Chomsky has developed.

Chomsky and his group select human languages (English, Walpiri, etc.) and structures in human languages (questions, passives, relative clauses, etc.) because these languages and structures bear on the correctness or incorrectness of their linguistic descriptions and theories of mind. In selecting problems I depart from this strategy and follow the guidelines of Ms. Stein. Abandoning concerns of description and explanation, she focused on the interesting and ignored the boring. She claimed:

> Now in that diagraming of the sentences of course there are articles and prepositions and as I say there are nouns but nouns as I say even by definition are completely not interesting, the same thing is true of adjectives. Adjectives are not really and truly interesting... Beside the nouns and the adjectives there are verbs and adverbs. Verbs and adverbs are more interesting. In the first place they have one very nice quality and that is that they can be so mistaken. It is wonderful the number of mistakes a verb can make and that is equally true of its adverb... In that way any one can see that verbs and adverbs are more interesting than nouns and adjectives. (Stein 1935: 82)

Diagraming sentences in 1935 was fun for Ms. Stein when the diagrams fit on the back of an envelope and could be sketched with a pencil. But Ms. Stein's smile would soon yield to a frown with Chomsky–

type diagrams. Even for a simple sentence like *Tess tried to go*, Chomsky's structural descriptions rapidly inflate – according to general principles, of course – to cover pages. This study shows how to program Chomsky's grammar into a computer using Prolog to diagram sentences using diagrams (structural descriptions) of the type developed by Chomsky's studies in theoretical linguistics. In terms of computer processes (derivations) and data structures (representations) I follow the theories of Noam Chomsky closely. In terms of problem selection and presentation, I follow the insights of Gertrude Stein.

I attempt to communicate Stein's enthusiasm for diagramming sentences by relegating to Prolog the boring job of drawing the giant Chomsky–type structural representations. I focus on phenomena, such as ambiguity, that Stein felt enabled verbs and adverbs to make mistakes. But there are other sources of enthusiasm for this study. Stein said:

> One of the things that is a very interesting thing to know is how you are feeling inside you to the words that are coming out to be outside of you. Do you always have the same kind of feeling in relation to the sounds as the words come out of you or do you not. All this has so much to do with grammar and with poetry and with prose. (Stein 1935: 93)

Although not quite the way Chomsky would say it, Stein's point echoes a tenet underlying Chomsky's study.

According to Chomsky's **universal grammar**, human language structure directly reflects the structure of human intellectual capacities. The phonetic, phonological, morphological, lexical, syntactic, and semantic structures found in language reflect the pattern–recognition abilities, problem–solving skills, and memory–storage capacities of the human intellect. There are three main reasons for studying **linguistics**, the science of the formal structures of human languages and the computational mechanisms internal to the human brain that underlie those structures.

- Language is as much a part of any human culture as are religion, politics, and rituals of birth, marriage, and death.
- Human language in its outline and in its details has structures that can be formalized in terms of logic and mathematics and that are sufficiently rigid to support or refute formal theories that describe those structures. One of the main contributions made by Noam Chomsky to the development of linguistics as a science consists of his methodological perspective, which shows in detail how aspects of mathematical logic can be used to develop formal

theories of human language structures.

- The human capacity to learn, know, and use a language reflects a genetically based species' specific biological endowment. In studying how language is acquired by children, linguistics focuses on the nature–nurture debate: To what extent is human knowledge part of the inborn structures of the human brain? What is the role of experience in learning? What data are necessary and sufficient to enable a child to acquire a human language?

My main hope is that I can communicate some of Gertrude Stein's excitement for diagraming sentences, even though the diagrams reflect an intricate Cartesian sort of deduction from Chomsky's tightly knotted formal theories of language. For the most part, I focus on the language problems and the diagrams. I develop Prolog as a tool to handle the intricate deducing.

The diversity of the technological frontiers is one of the main hurdles facing anyone trying to get a handle on the linguistic and computational problems involved in getting a computer to learn, read, write, and perhaps understand sentences in English, French, and German. I have adopted the lifeboat approach as opposed to the steamship view. You would pack a lifeboat with only essentials, but you could stuff a steamship with things you might need on a rainy day. My approach shows the reader where to focus attention and concentrate efforts. I try to present only those terms that constitute benchmarks for defining problems and solutions. Some such selection is necessary for a reader trying to keep his or her head above the sea of linguistic terminology, computer jargon, and general technobabble that has emerged from some artificial intelligence, expert systems, and knowledge engineering approaches that try to implement human languages onto a computer.

In the text, any term in SMALL CAPITALS is a basic concept you will need to learn, hence, I define it in the text and illustrate it using a Prolog program that encodes some aspect of English grammar. Any term in *italics* is a technical term in the background literature that underlies this study and can be referenced in linguistics and computer science textbooks. It would be nice to learn, but you might postpone it until you have mastered more basic concepts. Technical terms that are neither italicized or small capitals you can learn if you want to, but they are not essential. Any term in **boldface** is a definition or the name of a program. The goal here is to use Noam Chomsky's UNIVERSAL GRAMMAR to develop a GENERATIVE GRAMMAR to describe issues in the *syntax*, *semantics*, and *morphology* of English, German, and French using the NONPROCEDURAL language Prolog.

All of the examples run in C–Prolog on a UNIX VAX. The syntax of C–Prolog is the same as DEC–10 Prolog. Almost all universities, colleges, and junior colleges have a machine capable of running C–Prolog. The programs also run on Quintus Prolog. If you have no access to a DEC–10 or a VAX, I show how you can obtain a shareware copy of Prolog–2 and Open–Prolog via E–mail from New York University's Public Domain Bulletin Board. With some (usually slight) modifications, all programs will run on an IBM PC or Macintosh in Public Domain Prolog. Some students have run the programs using Arity Prolog and Microlog Prolog. All of the examples follow the definitions, style, and punctuation in the book by Clocksin and Mellish (1981).

If you intend to run the programs in Prolog–2 on an IBM PC, you might refer to Dodd (1990). Dodd is the developer of Prolog–2 for the IBM. He stated in his preface: "Readers with access to an IBM PC or equivalent with 512K of memory or more are welcome to a free copy of the simplest version of Prolog–2, a smallish Prolog that will execute most of the examples in Dodd (1990). Write the author c/o Oxford University Press." (Dodd: vi) This simple version of Prolog–2 also runs most of the programs in this book. Dodd's book is complementary to this one in that he provides a detailed analysis of the complexities of Prolog, but his book contains, as he stated, "no serious presentation of natural language systems." (p. vii)

The uninitiated person who wishes to gain hands–on experience with natural language processing, artificial intelligence, Chomsky's linguistic theories, and expert systems is beset with a cornucopia of materials. This book serves both as a prism and a lens between you and the huge stack of literature on these subjects. The book functions as a prism by breaking the basic ideas of natural language processing into the component parts and illustrating each of them using a simple example. The book is a lens in that it focuses on the most relevant and interesting parts of natural language processing and ignores the extremely important, but less interesting, questions concerned with the elegance, efficiency, speed, and machine–specific implementation of the solutions. If I can illustrate some point very clearly by having an understandable 2 page program, then I present the 2 page program even if the program could be replaced by a logically equivalent smaller program that is intellectually opaque because it presents the problem obliquely.

If any program could be made more understandable by changing it in some way, then the change was made even if it led to redundancy, inefficiency, wasted memory space, misuse of computer resources, excessive CPU time, or worse. As you gain an understanding of the operation of Prolog, you will see alternatives to the programs presented in this book.

Almost all of the examples encoded into Prolog come from current research in linguistics. When I focus on nonlinguistic data, it is to drive home a point. In Chapter 1 I discuss *intelligence* in several domains in order to clarify a basic issue. In Linguistics, the term *human intelligence* is understood as a species specific biological endowment that is common to all humans, just as binocular vision, binaural hearing, and other like properties are common to human beings. The concept of *human intelligence* that underlies IQ testing, which aims at exaggerating the differences among humans, is not the concept being explored. Chapter 5, in which I encode a bibliography into Prolog, serves as a flu shot against the two most common errors that frustrate beginning Prolog programmers. Most neophytes use capital letters when they are prohibited, and even worse, they forget to use the period. A bibliography has lots of capitals and punctuation and serves as an ideal training ground to learn the two most misused Prolog conventions: A capital is always a variable. All statements must end in a period, and a period anywhere but at the end of a statement is usually bad news.

The material in the *Foreword* derives from an interdisciplinary course funded by the New York University Humanities Council, *The Cultural History of Computers, Robots, and Artificial Intelligence.* I first offered the course to undergraduates in 1986. Given its favorable response, the Humanities Council funded research to develop an interdisciplinary graduate course of the same name, offered in 1990. The course was cross–listed and offered for credit in several departments. Comparative literature students showed that Hamlet's reflective indecision was limited by the fact that he spoke English. Some art history students pointed out that it seemed to them natural for the exceptions and irregularities of English to be considered "simpler" than the regular forms. The ideas from this class led to the organization of this book and, in particular, to the order of the presentation of material.

The material in Chapter 1, *Natural Intelligence, Linguistics, and Prolog,* derives from an interdisciplinary faculty seminar, *The Information Society: Artificial Intelligence, Robotics, and Expert Systems,* funded by the Humanities Council from 1985 until the present. Each term we establish a schedule of speakers, one every two weeks. The speakers are from diverse fields in various universities; from IBM, Bell Labs, and various other corporate research facilities. Each speaker sends us materials that we read and discuss at a meeting the week before they speak. This guarantees each speaker a live audience that will understand his or her ideas. It was at these meetings that I was forced to develop answers to the questions: What is the *information society*? What is *artificial intelligence*? What is an *expert system*? What is *computer power*? Why study Prolog? Why study natural language computing in Prolog? How does research on generative grammar in the Linguistic theories of Noam Chomsky have any bearing on the productivity of workers in sector III, *the services sector,* of the economy? Insofar as this essay is eclectic, it derives its eclecticism from my attempts to clarify and justify my work to the heterogeneous array of friendly, but not necessarily sympathetic, participants at the faculty seminars.

The computational linguistics material in this book has been used in various Linguistics courses at New York University for three years. Although there may be some glitch that has snuck through, several generations of students have ironed out most of the kinks and wrinkles in the programs. I am quite certain that each program will execute precisely as indicated if you are using C–Prolog on a UNIX VAX. I am less certain about the possible outcome if you are running the programs in the shareware version of Prolog, which executes on an IBM PC. In this case, the results will depend on the properties of your specific IBM PC. For one term I had a dozen students testing the materials using the shareware version of Prolog on whatever computer they had at home. Most of the problems encountered were minor and easily remedied, even by a novice. The main difference between C–Prolog and the shareware Prolog is speed. When you run some programs on a 286 IBM PC, you will have lots of time to go get a drink of water, stretch your legs, or read the papers. Shareware Prolog on a 486 PC can sometimes outperform C–Prolog on the VAX.

Some of the terminology used in this book diverges from that one might find in a standard linguistics text or in a book devoted to Prolog and symbolic languages. In particular, the use of the terms *top–down parsing, bottom–up parsing, inflectional morphology, derivational morphology,* and *word–formation morphology* might strike seasoned linguists and hardened Prolog programmers as unusual. I try to indicate those places where I differ from others and show why there are differences.

One major concern has been to provide a perspective internal to which one can conceptualize the aims and goals of linguistics in relation to the aims and goals of other sciences. To accomplish this, each of Chapters 6–8 has been written to define a perspective as well as illustrate the theories and methods of linguistic research.

Chapter 6 covers the type of material that was discussed in **taxonomic linguistics.** The goal of taxonomic linguistics, which basically refers to work prior to the ideas of Chomsky, is to obtain a redundancy–free catalog of the elements that function in a language and to indicate the restrictions on distribution of each element. All methods are designed to isolate and define the basic elements that function in a language.

Chapter 7 introduces the idea of **level,** which is basic to all varieties of linguistic analysis. The definitions of various types of morphology derive from the computational model presented here, which assumes that some morphemes (e.g., *be+en* of the passive, *wh*–elements of questions and relatives, etc.) are instructions to the parser about how to build the sentence. These morphemes are part of the logical relations of Prolog that define the combinations of elements at the level of syntax. Elements like *be+en, who, what, why,* and *how,* are instructions to the parser about how to access the lexicon for information about structure. These elements are only minimally represented in the lexicon (dictionary).

My view of the lexicon draws heavily on the work of Gross (1989a, 1989b, 1991, 1992, 1993), most of which describes complexities in French. I have followed his finite state model of the lexicon as closely as this presentation allowed. The lexicon for complement constructions (*expect, persuade, promise, want, seem...*) is essentially that presented in Leacock (1990, 1991). I also relied on insights provided in M. Baker (1988) and Stabler (1993).

In addition, Chapter 7 defines terms to facilitate exposition of basic Prolog tools (*append, recursion,* and *parallel processing*) to provide uninitiated readers with sufficient technical terms so that they can access traditional grammars (Jespersen, Curme, etc.) for more examples and to lead into my view of parsing. The parser considered here requires us to think of the elements (words, morphemes, formatives, stress levels, intonation patterns, etc.) in a sentence as having two functions: An element can be an instruction to the parser about how to access the lexicon. An element can be an item that does not contain specific instructions to the parser about the organization of the lexicon. Some elements are both. My definitions are consistent with my theory of lexical structure and model of parsing, but readers wedded to another framework may charge me with fitting morphology unhappily into a Procrustean bed.

O'Grady, Dobrovolsky, and Aronoff (1993) and Fromkin and Rodman (1993) provide excellent introductions to morphology. Aronoff (1976) gives a detailed analysis of morphology. Sproat (1992) presents a computational analysis of morphology. A unification, or Prolog, approach to morphology is presented in Gazdar (1985), Koskenniemi (1983), and Tzoukerman and Liberman (1990).

Chapter 8 tackles what Chomsky has called Humboldt's problem: How can a human being make infinite use of finite means? I focus on **recursion** – a basic computational process that enables a Prolog program to call itself to define sentences. A grammar, represented as a **lexically driven parser**, assigns structures to sentences by projecting information about words (morphemes and formatives) given in the lexicon (dictionary).

Excellent textbooks covering the basic terminology of Chomsky's model include: C. Baker (1978), Freidin (1992), Lightfoot (1984, 1991), Radford (1985), and van Riemsdijk and Williams (1986). At a more advanced level, Lasnik and Uriagereka (1988) is excellent. These books do not cover computational models. Books that cover unification and Prolog in some detail, but that skimp on linguistic theory, include Pereira and Shieber (1987), Pereira and Warren (1980), and Shieber (1986, 1992). Those interested a detailed analysis of complex noun phrases should refer to Bains (1994), who presents a grammar of Hindi-Urdu. Meyers (1994) presents an analysis of various grammatical frameworks, including government and binding, in a unification framework. I rely heavily on his work.

Our study mainly presents Prolog grammars to encode Chomsky's ideas about the internal structure of simple sentences, that is, sentences containing only one verb, although I do present some Prolog grammars to describe complex structures. Dougherty (in preparation) presents Prolog grammars to describe complex coordinate sentences, for example, *Tess danced and Tracy sang, Neither when he was wise nor when he was unwise was Socrates ever boring*, and subordinate/complement constructions, for example, *Tess seems to be happy, Tracy is easy to please, Sean promised to be home on time, Tracy was expected to win*. To analyze these sentence structures one must understand how Prolog employs pointers to structure the memory, which is beyond this present study.

Semantics – which includes sense–disambiguation, ambiguity, synonymy, and so on – is discussed by Leacock et al. (1993a, 1993b), Miller (1991), and Miller et al. (1993, 1994) in the framework developed on the Word–Net Project (see Miller). I accept their concepts and definitions.

The text has been written to accord with three basic rules of style. Winston Churchill's dictum, "A preposition is something you should never end a sentence with," has been strictly observed. Bertrand Russell's insight: "And should only be used to begin a sentence," caused early drafts to be revised. The hardest rule has been that set by Charles S. Peirce: "Write for people who are intelligent, but who know nothing about your subject matter."

I want to thank all those students and colleagues who helped me with this project. I feel particularly indebted to the following for their ideas, advice, and criticisms: Angel Arzan, Gurprit S. Bains, Scott Browne, Robert Corre, Lyle Jenkins, Peter Jeong, David Johnson, Thomas Kramer, Ira Langen, Gerald McCullum, Susanna Michalska, Dennis Perzanowsky, Amy Pierce, Paul Postal, Marc Schwarz, Steve Seegmiller, Linda Susman, George Thompson, Amy Weinberg, and Arthur Williamson. I thank Adam Meyers for his useful insights. Many of the ideas underlying my approach were developed while I was a Fullbright Scholar at the University of Salzburg (1976–1977) working with Gaberel Drachman, see Dougherty (1979). I thank Maurice Gross for introducing me to the use of finite state models in the lexical representation of natural language and for explaining to me many of the ideas of Zellig Harris. I thank David Halitsky for discussing all aspects of the book at length with me. I am especially indebted to Claudia Leacock for ideas, advice, and encouragement at every stage of the book's development.

I am grateful to Praxis International Inc. for funding research into the cross–point switch model of human language. The research into the cultural history of computers, robots, and artificial intelligence was funded by the New York University Humanities Council and by Exxon. I thank the New York University Academic Computing Facility for supplying the advice, information, and resources that made this project possible. I am especially indebted to David Ackerman, Ed Friedman, and Estelle Hochberg.

INTRODUCTION
WHAT IS COMPUTATIONAL LINGUISTICS?

The study of generative grammar developed from the confluence of two intellectual traditions: traditional and structuralist grammar, and the study of formal systems. Although there are important precursors, it was not until the mid–1950s that these intellectual currents truly merged, as ideas adapted from the study of formal systems came to be applied to the far more complex systems of natural language in something approaching their actual richness, and in subsequent years, their actual variety, thus making it possible, really for the first time, to give some substance to Humboldt's aphorism that language involves "the infinite use of finite means," the "finite means" being those that constitute the I–language.

Noam Chomsky, 1986
Knowledge of Language

Why must we learn a computer language in order to interact with a computer? Why can we not simply type in the information in English sentences and get the machine to respond in English sentences? What difficulties block the construction of an English–French–German translation program? The goal of this book is to make explicit some of the main problems facing any project to develop a computing machine that can read and write in English or that can translate among English, German, and French. This work is a chapter in **computational linguistics**, the general study of the problems involved in representing human language data on digital computers.

Problems in computational linguistics fall into two classes: *Conceptual problems*: What is a language? What is meant by English? What does it mean to understand English? What is a grammar of English? How does a human being know that a certain sound evokes a specific meaning? What constitutes knowledge of language? How is knowledge of language acquired? How is knowledge of language put to use? *Technical problems*: How can we represent English words, phrases, and sentences on a computing machine? How can we encode information about sentence types (indicative, question, imperative, etc.), parts of speech (nouns, verbs, adjectives, etc.), endings (plural, tense, etc.), and a myriad of other grammatical information in a notation that a computer can digest? At the end of this study, you will not have all the answers, but you will understand the questions better.

For this study, the ideas of Noam Chomsky provide a basic conceptual framework and linguistic terminology: *grammar, language, morphology, derivation, sentence,* and *syntax*. I discuss the technical problems involved in representing English on a computing machine in a Chomsky–type generative grammar framework using Prolog. Hence, this book serves as an introduction to the concepts of Noam Chomsky's linguistic theory and as a primer for mastering the fundamentals of logic–based programming in general and Prolog in particular. Most books on the Chomsky perspective rarely discuss computational implementations, and even rarelier, present a grammar encoded in a computer language.

Because the goal is to motivate the two technical terms *explanation* and *intelligence*, my presentation is selective and not encyclopedic. In linguistics, I focus on simple lexical and syntactic facts that are glaringly obvious and anyone can understand, such as the use of *rarelier* in the above paragraph. Clearly the correct form is *more rarely*. English grammar contains *friendly/friendlier* and *early/earlier*, but not *rarely/*rarelier*. One assumes that an English speaker can differentiate between *more rarely*, a *well–formed* (*grammatical*) expression and **rarelier*, an *ill–formed* (*ungrammatical*) expression. Some researchers have directed attention to the fact that many sentences exist that are sort of in between grammatical and ungrammatical. They argue that this middle ground of semigrammatical sentences renders useless the distinction between *grammatical* and *ungrammatical*. My position is that the grammatical versus ungrammatical distinction remains useful despite the disputed middle territory and the people like e.e. cummings who live there. I simply base all decisions on obvious cases and let the computational model divide the middle ground as it will. I cannot let the obvious fact that there is a twilight obscure the fundamental difference between day and night.

In computation, I concentrate on two basic data structures. Chapter 4, on irregular verbs, shows how to represent *tables of data* in Prolog. Chapter 5 indicates how to represent a bibliography in Prolog and introduces *files with records containing variable length fields*. In these Prolog formulations, I consider almost all linguistic structures to be either tables of data or files of records with variable field length. I follow the approaches of Maurice Gross, Dominique Perrin, and Max Silberztein by assuming that the organization and structure of the lexicon can be optimally formulated as a *finite state grammar*. The linguistic data and the computational mechanisms discussed here enable me to show that UNIVERSAL GRAMMAR provides a context that enables one to see that

EXPLANATION IN THEORETICAL LINGUISTICS correlates directly with ROBUSTNESS IN COMPUTATIONAL LINGUISTICS. This study also suggests how linguistic research on the four aspects of INTELLIGENCE that underlie normal human acquisition and use of language can provide the basis for the development of *artificial intelligence* and *expert systems* in sector III (services) of the economy.

It is assumed that the reader has little understanding of the science of linguistics and no acquaintance with the universal grammar theories of Noam Chomsky. It is presupposed that the reader understands English well enough to recognize the basic facts I represent in Prolog: AMBIGUOUS SENTENCES: *You can't take religion too seriously*, for instance, is ambiguous between opposite readings. I draw on the intuitions about WELL–FORMEDNESS in English, that is, things that one can and cannot say. Consider contractions: *are not* in *You are not tall* can contract to *aren't* to yield *You aren't tall*. But *am not* in *I am not tall* cannot contract to **I amn't tall*. The contraction of *am not* is *ain't*, as in *I ain't tall*. One can say: *I am just that kind of guy*, *I'm just that kind of guy*, and *That's just the kind of guy I am*, but not **That's just the kind of guy I'm*. There are HOLES in the English orthography, and some sentences can be spoken but not written. One can say or write: *I want to go. You said too much. She is two.* One can say, but not write: *There are three to/two/too's in English.* It would be incorrect to write: *There are three too's in English. There are three two's in English.* Or, *There are three to's in English.* One can say and write: *There are three ways to write two in English: 2, II, and two.*

It is assumed that the reader has no acquaintance with symbolic programming languages such as Prolog and Lisp and has not encountered nonprocedural logic–based programming concepts such as *symbolic programming, unification, subsumption, backtracking, goal–directed searching, recursion, variable binding,* and *parallel processing.* I will define all the necessary terms and offer natural language examples to illustrate them in real data situations.

For those familiar with linguistics and Prolog, the goal of this study is to show how a parser (written in Prolog) can assign the representations (*syntactic structures, logical forms,* and linguistic objects at each level) developed by Chomsky and his school to sentences (*strings*). The derivations that assign structure to a string at each level are formulated as nonprocedural logic–based Prolog relations that are well–formedness conditions on representations. In brief, the REPRESENTATIONS are those offered by Chomskyian universal grammar, but the DERIVATIONAL PROCESSES that assign (or justify the assignment of) a structure to a string are expressed in terms of the nonprocedural processes of unification and subsumption and formulated as Prolog facts and relations. I sketch how to formulate a generative grammar as a

Prolog program that will relate a string to its representation at the levels defined by Chomskyian linguistics.

In all cases, this presentation is expository and not polemical. I assume the version of linguistic theory offered by Chomsky (1975b, 1986b, 1987, 1992b) and Chomsky and Lasnik (1991). I accept the definitions of UNIFICATION and SUBSUMPTION offered by Shieber (1986), and Pereira and Shieber (1987). I use the term PURE PROLOG in the sense of Sowa (1987). The Prolog relations offered here are formulated to resemble those discussed in Clocksin and Mellish (1981). This study presents only the linguistic theory of Noam Chomsky. Covington (1993), Gazdar and Mellish (1989), and Walker, McCord, Sowa, and Wilson (1987) present a variety of linguistic theories in Prolog formulations.

The best single book for those who wish to learn more about the intricacies of Prolog than is covered here is *Prolog: A Logical Approach* by T. Dodd (1990). The book presents clear and concise answers to most of the basic issues that arise in Prolog programming. One advantage is that all of the examples in Dodd's book run in Prolog–2. Not an unexpected fact given that Dodd is the designer of Prolog–2.

The organization of material here is rhetorical and moves from the simplest Prolog mechanisms to the most difficult. From the linguistic point of view, this might seem odd since it leads to treating irregular verbs (*have, be, go*) and nouns (*woman/women*) before treating the regular cases (*look, print, girl/girls*). From the Prolog point of view it makes sense because I can initially present the linguistic data structures as simple tables and the linguistic processes as simple relational database operations on memory structures. This enables me to formulate all problems in terms of searching for information in tables and to utilize only pure Prolog. Hence, I can describe problems of lexical structure in terms of relational database mechanisms that are handled by the Prolog interpreter. From the user's point of view, this means that I do not introduce any nonbuilt–in Prolog functions until the seventh chapter, and, even better, it means that the material in the first six chapters should run on any Prolog machine with no modifications except for minor punctuation. From this Prolog point of view, regular processes in language, such as verbs that add *–ed* to form the past and nouns that add *–s* for the plural, are more complicated than the irregulars because they lead to formulating Prolog relations and to defining functions.

The fact that I present a pure Prolog implementation can be important for the reader on a shoestring budget. One can download a copy of *Prolog–2 shareware Prolog* from the New York University (NYU) E–mail Public Domain Bulletin Board for free. Prolog–2 on an IBM PC, either under DOS or windows, will run all the examples in this book. Appendices I and II contain instructions on how to obtain Prolog–2 (IBM) and Open–Prolog (Apple) by ftp from NYU or on a disk via the postal service, how to set it up, and how to run the examples.

Why try to represent English, French, and German on a computer? If successful, then one will not have to learn to program in computer languages (C, Fortran, Cobol). Instead one could simply type in English sentences. If human languages were represented on a computer, then one could translate from one language to another automatically. On a more profound note, any problem that can be posed in any formal notation or in any formal language can be posed in English. If there was a computer that could correctly interpret English sentences, then it would correctly interpret any problem and give answers in unambiguous grammatical English sentences.

Prolog is optimally suited to characterizing complex sets of interrelations among large numbers of facts, especially when some facts follow one rule, some another, and some no rule at all. Authors have illustrated Prolog concepts by selecting complex databases, including the succession of the monarchy in England, the English vocabulary indicating family relations (*mother, father, sister, uncle, ancestor,* etc.), states and countries that border on each other, the Fibbonacci numbers, and the factorial function. Most, if not all textbooks, select a variety of problems taken from various data domains. My approach is different.

One of my goals is to show that the most complex database available to any person is one's knowledge of one's native language. This often becomes clear when a student starts to learn a foreign language. The amount of data that is instantly available to a speaker of English is staggering. With rare exceptions, the only problems discussed in this text are problems of implementing the data structures of English, French, and German in Prolog. I focus on problems linguists discuss under the rubrics of SELECTION and AGREEMENT in areas traditionally called DERIVATIONAL MORPHOLOGY, INFLECTIONAL MORPHOLOGY, SYNTAX, and SEMANTICS. I define these terms in the text, but in a nutshell, I assume that readers have intuitions of GRAMMATICALITY: that is, they know the following sentences preceded by an asterisk are odd, whereas those with no asterisk are well–formed. I program a computer in Prolog to be able to make these distinctions. *John gave a book me. John gave a book to me. *Mary explained us how to go. Mary explained to us how to go. *How many advices did Sue give you? How much advice did Sue give you? *A collie is intelligenter and more tall than a doberman. A collie is more intelligent and taller than a doberman. *This door is more tall than you are. This door is more tall than wide. *This door is taller than wide. *Each of the children outnumbered the adults. The children outnumbered the adults. *Some in the group is from New Jersey. Some of the group is from New Jersey. Some in the group are from New Jersey. *I bought the book who you recommended. I bought the book that/which you recommended.

*Alice is a bird of a feather. *I stacked up the book. I stacked the books up.

I assume the reader has intuitions about semantics. In particular, intuitions about AMBIGUITY, that is, the following sentences have two or more interpretations: *John decided on the boat. Flying planes can be dangerous.* And intuitions about PARAPHRASE, that is, either two sentences have the same meaning, or if one sentence is true, then another must also be true. For instance, in a lotto game, one could imagine describing a bonus plan like this: *If the number you pick is even, you win double if it is six or eight.* But it is odd to say: *If the number you pick is six or eight, you win double if it is even.* If *The number is six or eight* is true, then *The number is even* must be true. If *The number is even is true*, then *The number is six or eight* may be true.

If everything proposed in this study came true, and all the processes of human language discussed were implemented on the largest, fastest computer available, there would still be an enormous amount of work to do to make the computer understand every English sentence one might throw at it. If one were a 100% successful in one's endeavor, it would still require considerably more work before one could feed the computer all of Shakespeare's plays and then ask: *Was "to be or not to be" really the question?* On the other hand, consider the problems that constrained Hamlet to say what he said the way he said it. For instance, Hamlet said: *To be or not to be, that is the question.* If we think of Hamlet looking down from heaven with hindsight, he might reflect: *To have been or not to have been, that was the question.* But if we think of Hamlet in heaven before his birth obtaining information about his future life from an angel, Hamlet could not say: *To will be or not to will be, that will be the question.* Hamlet's reflective indecision was both limited and constrained by the fact that he pondered in English. In German, Hamlet's question is well–formed in the past, present, and future: *Gewesen sein oder nicht gewesen sein, das ist die Frage gewesen. Sein oder nicht sein, das ist die Frage. Sein werden oder nicht sein werden, das wird die Frage sein.*

The Prolog machine programmed with English, German, and Chinese might never know what it is to be or not to be; it might never pose a question; and it might not be able to answer some questions, but it would know that the grammatical rules of English, German, and Chinese constrain the questions that can be asked and answered in these languages. The machine would know which questions are well–formed in each language and which sentences in one language can be translated readily into the other.

There are strong reasons for programming in Prolog if the goal is to obtain a theoretical understanding of the computational processes that underlie the constructions found in English, the principles of word formation, dictionary construction, sentence parsing, morphology, and translation. The basic operations of the pure Prolog machine (SUBSUMPTION and UNIFICATION) suffice to express many of the agreement and selection phenomena of human language, in particular, those represented by the italicized sentences earlier. Prolog is nonprocedural and pure Prolog lends itself to parallel processing. Insofar as the conditions defined in Chomsky's grammar are independently applied to determine the properties of a sentence (i.e., *modular*), they can be formulated as nonprocedural and parallel processing mechanisms.

This book derives from courses taught over five years in which students learned to encode the principles of sentence construction of human languages into Lisp, C, Awk, Pascal, Setl, Fortran, and other programming languages. Experience has shown that students produce useful programs on their own in a very short time when taught Prolog. With other languages it can take considerable time before anything interesting emerges. I believe this follows from the NONPROCEDURAL nature of Prolog. Students do not have to learn how to formulate algorithms to obtain results; instead, they learn to express the facts of the language in an explicit terminology. For instance, in programming agreement phenomena into Prolog, one need not indicate *how* the agreement is assigned, that is, whether the verb must agree with the subject or the subject with the verb. Instead, one simply writes a Prolog biconditional statement that states that there is agreement between the subject and verb.

Prolog is not so much a programming language as it is a logical notation for expressing what you already know (the *database*) and what you want to find out (the *query*). Prolog provides a special way and specific notation for conceptualizing, organizing, and presenting problems. Programming is essentially formatting the data. It is very easy to get started and to get meaningful results quickly. Naturally, it takes time to get good and write efficient programs. For the reader interested in optimizing Prolog code and in mastering the intricacies of Prolog, there are many excellent books: Bratko (1990), Clocksin and Mellish (1981), Dodd (1990), Malpas (1987), Mueller and Page (1988), and Sterling and Shapiro (1987).

This book differs from all of these above in attitude, approach, and material covered. Most Prolog textbooks offer a solution in search of a problem. They primarily cover the complex mechanisms and data structures of Prolog and secondarily apply these tools to illustrative problems. I offer a problem in search of a solution. This study is *data driven* in that I try to program information about language structure into the computer, using as few instructions as possible. I do not present some Prolog mechanism and then try to show how it can be used to describe some data. Rather, I discuss some data structure of a human language and try to encode it into pure Prolog as one or more tables of data with complex interactions among the elements of the table and between different tables. If the human language data structure cannot be encoded as relations among table entries, that is, if it cannot be considered a problem in *relational database* management, I reluctantly define a new function.

This approach leads to neglecting some often discussed Prolog functions, such as *reverse*, that converts a string like *abcdef* to *fedcba*, and *purge*, that inputs an element and a string and removes that element from the string, for example, *purge(c,abcde,X)* returns *X = abde*. I neglect many such traditionally discussed functions for two reasons: mainly because they seem to play no role in describing the structures one finds in human languages, and second, because they are abundantly discussed in most Prolog textbooks.

One point about my labeling of programs and figures might cause some confusion. The programs and figures in this book are labeled by chapter, g0803 is the 3rd program in Chapter 8, Figure 8.13 is the 13th figure in Chapter 8. The NYU CWIS bulletin board is a main source of information for students in classes at NYU. Most graduate classes meet 14 times. Most undergraduate classes meet 28 times. Materials labeled for courses can be numbered up to 28, for example, g2805 would be the 5th program in the 28th meeting of a course currently being taught at NYU. If you download Figure 9.8 or Figure 17.3, these are course materials from the 9th and 17th meeting of a current class. There is some material on the included disk which is not in this book. This is NYU course materials from a graduate class in which this book was used.

Chomsky (1986b) defined Plato's Problem and Orwell's Problem:

> For many years, I have been intrigued by two problems, concerning human knowledge. The first is the problem of explaining how we can know so much given that we have such limited evidence. The second is the problem of explaining how we can know so little, given that we have so much evidence. The first problem we might call "Plato's Problem," the second, "Orwell's Problem,"... (p. xxv)

Chapters 1-8 indicate the basic thrust of Chomsky's approach to answering "Plato's Problem" by offering a computational model of generative grammar.

A linguistic version of "Orwell's Problem" might be stated: Why are the enormous resources of the Internet – most of which are free – not widely used by researchers in natural language? To the extent that the answer is, "I do not know where to start," the next section, *How to Use*

This Book, will be useful (see Appendix III for information about the Internet). This is where you start. These materials are rhetorically organized to enable researchers who do not know where to begin to take their first steps without wasting time learning arcane computer formalisms and terminology. The next section describes the facilities of the computer laboratories at New York University and shows how these facilities relate to research and teaching in computational linguistics.

I agree wholeheartedly with one of the basic ideas presented by J. Weizenbaum (1976). Weizenbaum pointed out that,

> apart from such minor, though possibly not unhelpful, phenomena as the flashing of the computers' lights and the occasional motions of their tape reels, the only evidence of their structures that the computers provide is, after all, linguistic. They accept strings of linguistic inputs in the form of the texts typed on their console typewriters, and they respond with linguistic outputs written on the same instrument or onto magnetic media....If we strive to explain computers when bounded by the restriction that we may not break the computer open, then all explanations must be derived from linguistic bases. (p. 135)

The question asked is simple:

If all interaction with the computer is linguistic, then why must humans give up their natural languages (English, French, etc.) and learn artificial languages (Fortran, Cobol, C, Awk, etc.) in order to interact with the computer?

Currently, the tail seems to be wagging the dog. Why not bring the computer around to read and write in human languages? As computer memory becomes cheaper and faster, as the speed of central processing units increases, and as parallel processing becomes available, one may reasonably expect that one of the imminent major breakthroughs in the computer culture will be computers that read, write, and translate human languages. What integrations of software, firmware, and hardware are 25, or even 10, years away we can only guess at. But, as I hope to show, any machines that read and write in English in the next few years will probably be programmed in a nonprocedural language, like Prolog, using the universal grammar ideas introduced by Noam Chomsky. Whatever the eventual outcome, **computational linguistics** is the discipline that will integrate the computer technology with linguistic theory.

HOW TO USE THIS BOOK
PICTORIAL CONTENTS

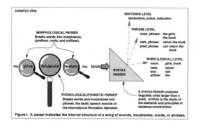

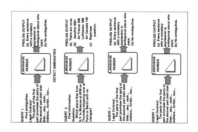

Figure 2. What problems do we hope to solve with prolog?

Figure 4. What practical applications exist for a parser?

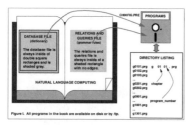

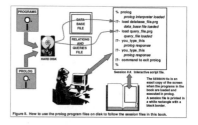

Figure 5. How does this book present the solution to natural language problems?

Figure 6. How can you use our programs to solve linguistic problems?

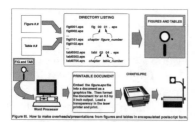

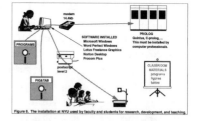

Figure 8. How can a teacher make transparencies of all tables and figures?

Figure 9. An overhead projection environment for teaching, research, and development.

HOW TO USE THIS BOOK

A PICTORIAL ESSAY

> If you want to convince people of something, the fact that it is correct counts among the least of its recommendations.
>
> Antoine Arnauld, 1662/1964
> *The Art of Thinking*

These three hurdles confront us at the outset.

- **Linguistics**, defined by Chomsky as the scientific study of human language, remains a mystery to many people. Some scholars have contended that there is no problem in analyzing language.

- **Logic**, in general, and the first order predicate calculus in particular, cannot count among the most popular courses in a university. Rarely does a logic textbook hit the bestseller list, although exceptions, like Arnauld's (1662/1964) book, do spark courage in authors.

- **Prolog** and logic–based nonprocedural languages seldom appear outside of university classrooms or research centers. One can safely say most people have never heard of Prolog.

Why should one learn an obscure computer language and solve logical problems in first–order predicate calculus in order to provide detailed analyses of English grammar and solve problems in natural language analysis? Hopefully, the figures can communicate the scope and content of this study and thereby provide the rationale.

Here, I discuss some practical applications for this project. One is to replace the mouse with a natural language processor. (See Figure 1.) In Chapters 6–8, we discuss the theoretical significance of this analysis.

What problems do we hope to solve with Prolog?

Figure 2 illustrates that a parser shows the structure of a sentence. I offer Prolog programs (on disk or by ftp, see Figure 3) that can analyze words into their component parts (phones and morphemes), represented by the magnifying glasses. I mainly discuss a **syntax parser**, represented by the prism, that indicates how a sentence is composed of words and phrases.

Just as a prism can scatter sunlight into its spectrum, it can also combine a spectrum of colors back to form sunlight. Although I will usually discuss how a syntax parser scatters a sentence into words and phrases, this is for heuristic reasons to facilitate the

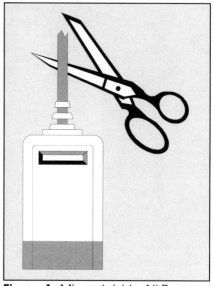

Figure 1. Mice yield to NLP.

presentation. A syntax parser is neutral between "decomposing" a sentence into words and phrases and "composing" words and phrases to form a sentence. I return to this important point in Chapters 7 and 8. (See Figures 7.6 and 8.12.)

What practical applications exist for a parser?

Just as a dictionary relates a sound with a meaning at the word level, a parser relates a sound string with a meaning at the sentence level. If we had a language parser that could analyze sentences, it could serve as the interface between a human and a computer. Figure 4 indicates four applications for a natural language processor, labeled Query1 to Query4.

A parser can **detect ambiguities** in text (see query 1). One can develop a parser that would read documents and indicate all ambiguous sentences. If we incorporate a lexicon (see Gross 1989a, Miller 1991), it could flag sentences to indicate the general semantics involved in the sentences containing the ambiguities.

A parser could process **information retrieval** requests. The sentences indicated in Queries 2 and 3 are quite straightforward and could be implemented into a Prolog parser used as a natural language interface to a database.

xxx

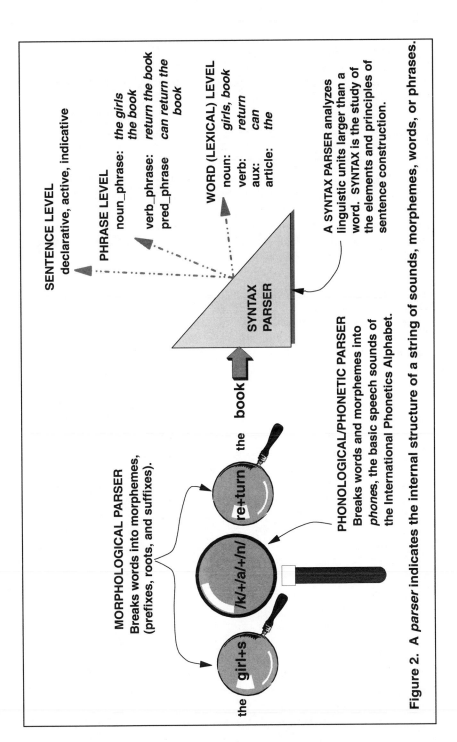

SENTENCE LEVEL
declarative, active, indicative

PHRASE LEVEL
noun_phrase: *the girls*
the book
verb_phrase: *return the book*
pred_phrase: *can return the book*

WORD (LEXICAL) LEVEL
noun: *girls, book*
verb: *return*
aux: *can*
article: *the*

SYNTAX PARSER

A SYNTAX PARSER analyzes
linguistic units larger than a
word. SYNTAX is the study of
the elements and principles of
sentence construction.

MORPHOLOGICAL PARSER
Breaks words into morphemes,
(prefixes, roots, and suffixes).

PHONOLOGICAL/PHONETIC PARSER
Breaks words and morphemes into
phones, the basic speech sounds of
the International Phonetics Alphabet.

the girl+s   /k/+/a/+/n/   re+turn   the   book

Figure 2. A *parser* indicates the internal structure of a string of sounds, morphemes, words, or phrases.

Query 4, my favorite problem, would be to design a **natural language interface** to word processing, text editing, layout and design, and graphics presentation programs. Then one could permanently unplug the mouse. Some of the grammar was developed as a natural language interface for a multi–layer three dimensional graphics program. The problem posed in this query – move the text lower, center it, change the fonts, check spelling, and so on – are basic problems that arise in any graphics program. The main way of interacting with the programs at present is with a mouse. The mouse, a manual instrument, requires all of your ideas to be formatted to flow through your hand. This has enormous disadvantages in two areas: selecting the objects to modify and positioning the objects to match common sense desires. One basic problem is that the mouse can select an object when the cursor touches it or when the object is inside or touching a box. If the desired object is under an undesired object, problems abound.

It would be straight-forward, but not simple, to develop a natural language interface that would enable a user to construct, format, and modify graphics images using natural language, for example: *Move the shaded triangle up so it almost touches the top of the box.* Most of the technical problems could be solved by allowing the user to assign words to represent selected objects and by carrying along the properties of items (groupings, sub–groupings, line thickness color, etc.) as property lists. The hardest part would be to get a natural language processor to "understand" the sentences input by the users.

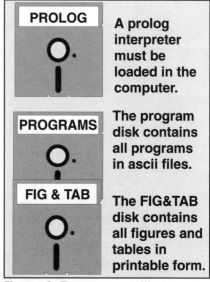

Figure 3. Three necessities.

Semantics, the study of the meanings of sentences, could be developed for the limited world of the computer screen and graphics images. The natural language processor would "understand" the sentence, *Move the text lower and center it*, if it performed the appropriate actions on the correct objects. The semantic world would be the drawn objects and the instructions to draw them.

The natural language interfaces, one of which could replace or

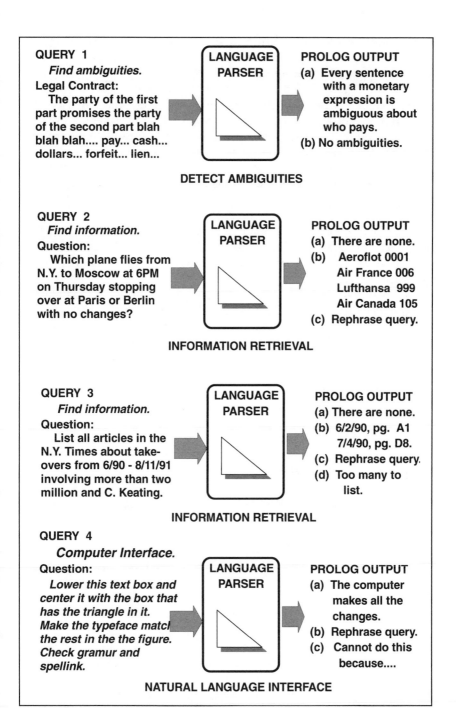

Figure 4. A natural language parser is an intelligent machine.

supplement the mechanical mouse, are artificial intelligence machines. They are adequate to the extent their response parallels that of the natural language capacities of a human.

The solution of these problems requires us to delve into the problems of syntactic and semantic analysis and specify the computational processes that define the operation of the syntax prism in Figures 2 and 4. The main focus of this book is to formulate the internal structure and contents of the syntax prism in Prolog.

How does this book present the solution to the problems?

The Prolog programs that analyze a sentence as a set of phrases and words, represented as a prism in Figures 2 and 4, are formulated into two types of programs. A **database program** is essentially the dictionary of a language. The **relations and query program** basically contains what most people would call grammatical rules.

You will probably not change any of the entries in the database (dictionary) file, although you may add new entries. Most of your modifications will be to the relations file. Most of the programs you write will be like the relations and query files presented here.

There are three disks that contain all of the relevant materials (see Appendix I). In compressed format, the Prolog and programs fill one disk. The figures formatted as overheads are available from the publisher.

The **Prolog Disk** contains shareware Prolog–2. If you are doing everything on a single PC, then you must install a copy of the Prolog language on your machine. See Appendix I for information about obtaining and installing shareware Prolog–2 on a PC. If you are using a university computer system, you cannot install Prolog yourself. (See Figure 9 for a recommended installation on a larger computer using Quintus or C–Prolog.)

The **Programs Disk** contains all programs in the book in ASCII. Every program printed in this book is available on a disk or by ftp over internet. The programs are named, as indicated in Figure 5, to show their chapter and order in the chapter, for example, program *g0511.prg* is the 11th program in Chapter 5.

The **Figures and Tables Disk** contains every table and figure in this book as an encapsulated postscript file. There are no headers so each file is in ASCII. Any word processor, for example, WordPerfect, can read an eps file and print it as a graphic object.

How can you use the programs to solve linguistic problems in Prolog?

This book is a cookbook of programs to illustrate the mechanisms of Prolog and the properties of natural language that are amenable to computational analysis. The quickest way to gain an understanding of Prolog is to modify existing programs that you can understand. The simplest way to grasp the ideas underlying Chomsky's grammar is to learn to add words to the lexicon in the existing Prolog grammars.

The disks available contain the program, figure, and table files from this book. No disks contain the session files. Your objective is to sit in front of a computer and follow the instructions in the session files. Your eventual goal is to master the recipes in this book and develop your own (see Figure 6).

If you are using a PC, install the Prolog interpreter onto the hard disk. Load the programs onto the hard disk. Call up Prolog, as discussed in Chapter 3, *How to Load, Run, and Edit a Prolog Program.* For each problem solved, the book contains a **session file**, that is, a white rectangle with a black border that contains an exact copy of the screen when the programs in the book are loaded and executed in Prolog. After following these cookbook recipes, you will be able to modify the programs and generate your own results.

How can a teacher make transparencies of all figures and tables?

Figure 7 indicates three alternatives for presenting the materials in this book to a class.

 A teacher might try to use a blackboard and chalk in order to sketch the relevant diagrams and to present programs and session files to students. While possible, there is no reason for such austerity. When drawing, the teacher faces away from the class for a large chunk of the lecture. Time spent writing and drawing is wasted time.

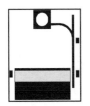 Using the **figures & tables disk**, the teacher can make transparencies of all figures and tables, as indicated in Figure 8. Each figure is on the disk as an Encapsulated Postscript Level 2 file with the extension *.eps*, for example, *fig0501.eps* is Figure 1 in Chapter 5. To make a classroom transparency, follow these steps.

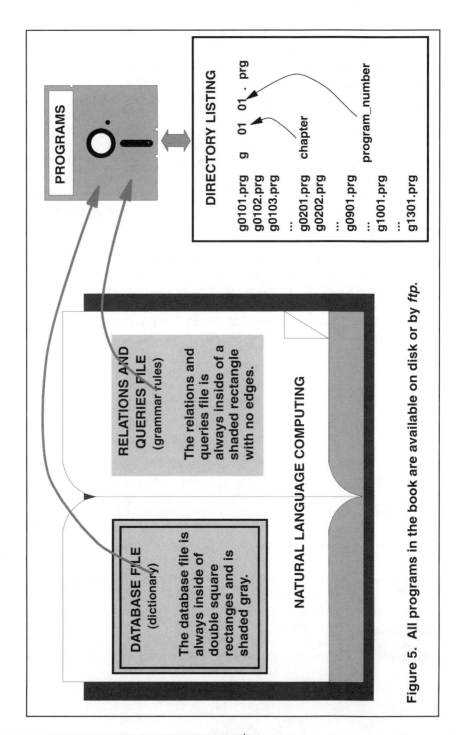

Figure 5. All programs in the book are available on disk or by *ftp*.

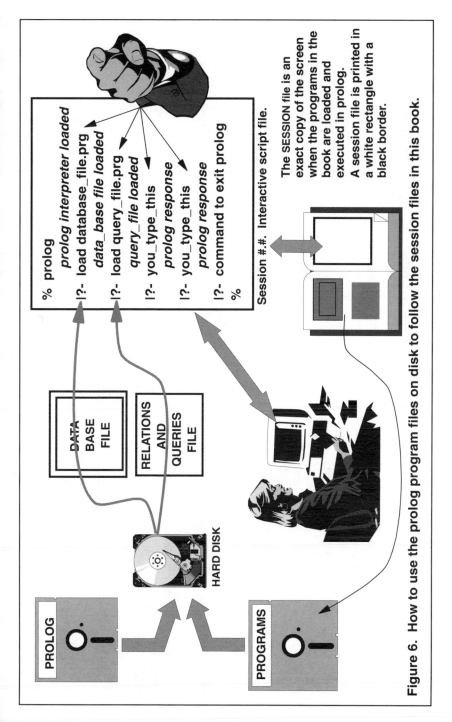

% prolog
prolog interpreter loaded
|?- load database_file.prg
data_base file loaded
|?- load query_file.prg
query_file loaded
|?- you_type_this
prolog response
|?- you_type_this
prolog response
|?- command to exit prolog
%

Session #.#. Interactive script file.

The SESSION file is an exact copy of the screen when the programs in the book are loaded and executed in prolog.
A session file is printed in a white rectangle with a black border.

DATA BASE FILE

RELATIONS AND QUERIES FILE

HARD DISK

PROLOG

PROGRAMS

Figure 6. How to use the prolog program files on disk to follow the session files in this book.

SCREEN PROJECTION
(system 509)

The teacher
* has all materials on the computer hard disk in the form of presentation files (Lotus Freelance Version 2).
* can show any graphic by typing in the filename or by clicking a mouse.
* can run any program at any time to illustrate issues raised during the class
* can edit any file anytime from anywhere.

OVERHEAD PROJECTION

The teacher
* has a big stack of foils for the course, a small stack for each lecture.
* has to shuffle through foils to find the right one.
* must physically carry the foils to the presentation.

BLACKBOARD WRITING

The teacher
* tries to draw relevant figures and tables.
* writes programs and session files on the blackboard with chalk.
* must redraw what has been erased.

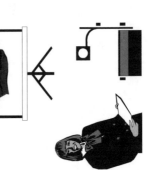

Figure 7. Three ways for a teacher to present the materials to students: screen projection, overheads, blackboard.

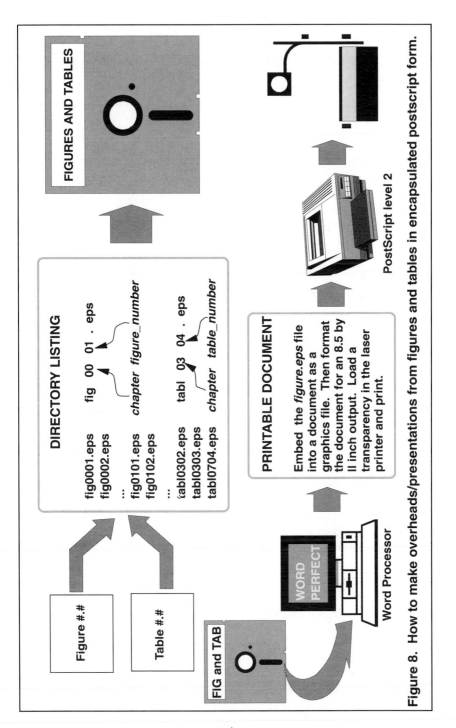

Figure 8. How to make overheads/presentations from figures and tables in encapsulated postscript form.

Call up WordPerfect, or any similar product, on the PC, Mac, etc.
Open a document and set the margins, 8.5 by 11 inches.
Open a Figure Box as a Graphic.
Retrieve one of the files, *e.g., fig0301.eps*, from the FIG&TAB disk.
Close the Graphic Figure Box.
Load a transparency into the laser printer and print.

This will print Figure 1 in Chapter 3.

Figure 9 sketches the teaching resources in a classroom with an overhead projector.

Postscript is a computer language used to describe pictures, images, and text on a page. A **postscript file** is a set of instructions to a hardware device to display the file.

To display a postscript file on a computer screen requires a *visual postscript* interpreter. These are currently quite expensive and exist only on higher level machines from IBM, DEC, SUN, and so on. The NeXT machine incorporates a visual postscript display.

To print a postscript file is relatively inexpensive and requires only a printer capable of *display postscript*. Currently one can purchase the printer we use, a NEC 95 postscript level 2 laser printer, for much less than a thousand dollars. Using Adobe Type Manager (ATM), a postscript file can be printed on just about any type of dot matrix printer. In brief, this means that you can print the *.eps* files if you have a laser printer, but you cannot see the pictures on a computer screen unless you invest in a visual postscript interpreter.

An **encapsulated postscript file** is a totally self–contained set of instructions to draw a single page. At present, most personal computers cannot display an *eps* file on the screen and it will appear as a big box that fills the screen. The box will have written across it a message, such as *This figure can only be printed*. Although you cannot see it on the screen, any word processor can read the *eps* file as a graphic (a drawing) and print it as a drawing.

All the *eps* files use only Helvetica font, grayscale and no color, and no patterns. Any polygon is either solid or no fill. In other words, these files should print on just about anything that can handle postscript.

The NeXT computer is exceptional. It contains high–resolution visual and display postscript interpreters. This means that what you see on the screen is identical to what will print on the printer. It is ideally suited for developing, editing, and presenting classroom materials of the type we are discussing. The closest alternative is more than double the price and does not provide the image quality and control of the NeXT.

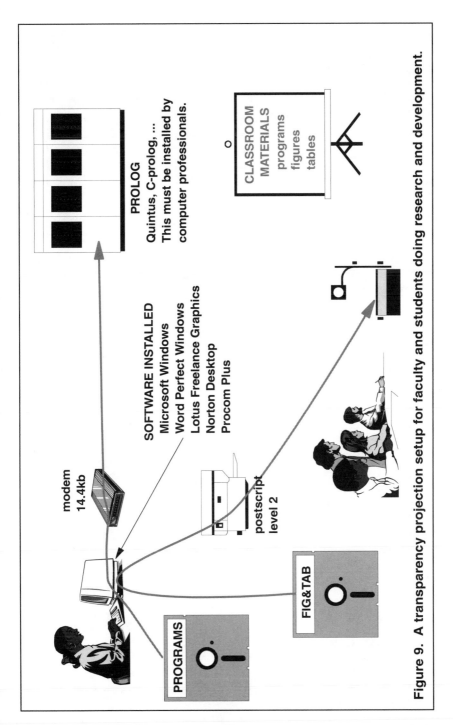

Figure 9. A transparency projection setup for faculty and students doing research and development.

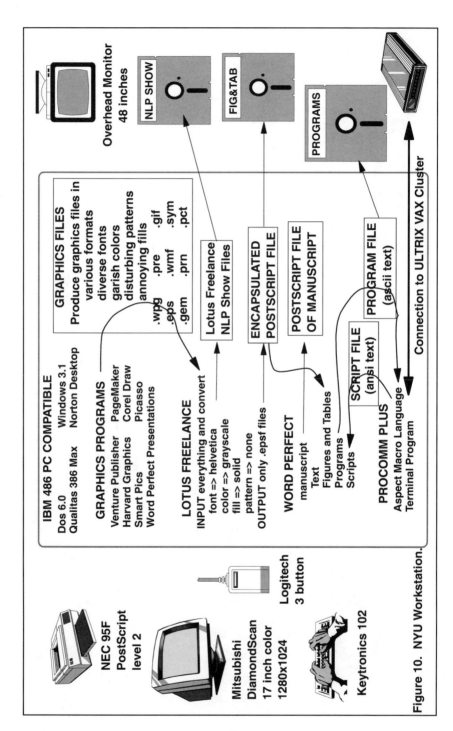

Figure 10. NYU Workstation.

The Linguistics Department at NYU uses mainly IBM PCs and DEC Ultrix machines. Much of the research of Maurice Gross at the University of Paris has utilized the NeXT machines.

By using an IBM PC or a Mac, you cannot easily edit or modify any of the figures, but using commands in WordPerfect, you can scale, crop, rotate, lighten or darken, and title the *eps* picture before sending it to the printer. To print the *eps* files is trivial. If you have the chutzpa to learn Prolog in order to tackle problems in Chomsky–type grammars, you should find printing the *eps* files a breeze.

The installation at New York University

NYU System 509, a computerized classroom at NYU, permits a teacher to control a large (classroom size) overhead projection computer monitor using an IBM PC, a Macintosh, or a NeXT machine. (See Figure 10 for an overview of the system 509 classroom computer installation at NYU.) All of my discussion centers around IBM PC–compatible equipment, but it applies equally to Apple and NeXT machines.

A teacher in a system 509 classroom essentially has all of the materials in this book on the hard disk of a personal computer. Using the commercial product, **Lotus Freelance Version 2,** the

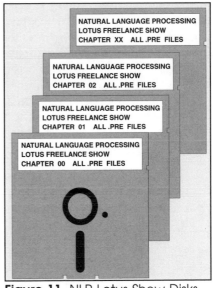

Figure 11. NLP Lotus Show Disks.

teacher can instantly project on the screen any of the images. (See Figures 11 and 12.) The teacher avoids the shuffling of overheads, the frustration of not finding the correct one, and the humiliation of dropping them all on the floor. The teacher is spared the labor of carrying all the overheads around campus. No more packing overheads into carry on luggage so they are not lost on the way to a conference. More than 50 Lotus Presentation Pages fit on one floppy disk.

Perhaps the single most valuable aspect of having the materials on the computer is *availability* and *editability*. If the teacher must clarify a point to a student, the computer files can be brought up and displayed anywhere: in class, in the lab, in the student workroom, at home, while

xliii

visiting colleagues in Paris, while lecturing in Rome. If the teacher finds something is unclear or wrong in a file, it can be instantly modified. No more writing notes on the side of the overhead so that it can be modified later, usually after you forgot what modification was required.

At any point in the lecture, the teacher can present any figure, run any existing program, enter a new program and run it, print anything, call up the network, and so on. Using windows, the teacher in New York can run a program in one window and in another window obtain information about how to run the program over e–mail from the program's author in Paris. Student's can bring their materials to class, and the teacher can run their programs and discuss them with the class.

A **presentation package** is a program, usually directed at the business community, for organizing graphics presentations at business meetings. Most of them contain elaborate instructions to make complicated charts, graphs, and tables. Currently, leading examples are **Lotus Freelance**, Harvard Graphics, WordPerfect Presentations, and CorelDraw. For our purposes, anything you can do with one of these programs you can do with another. Materials can be imported and exported from any one of them to any other.

Details aside, the figures in this book were made by a variety of programs, and then all loaded into Lotus Freelance. Each figure, program, session, and table is a *presentation page* in a *Lotus Show*. This means that

any page can be edited
any page can be printed as a transparency
any page can be projected on a projection computer monitor
all pages can be reordered
any page can be incorporated into a WordPerfect document

A **Lotus presentation page** is like a slide in a slide show. A **Lotus Show**, a computer file with the extension *.pre*, is like a set of slides in a carousel projector. To show the slides, you load the **Lotus Freelance program**. Then Lotus reads a *.pre* file (a show) and projects the slides (presentation pages) to the overhead monitor in any order you want.

If any teacher has access to a system 509 computerized classroom, they should take advantage of it, particularly if the class being taught involves student projects and research.

All of the figures, tables, programs, and session files are available from Lawrence Erlbaum Associates in the form of *Lotus Freelance Show Graphics, level 2*. These are on a set of disks, and each file has the extension *.pre*. For instance, all of the figures in this section are in the file *ch00fig.pre*. All of the figures in Chapter 4 are in *ch04fig.pre*, all tables in *ch04tab.pre*, all programs in *ch04prg.pre*, and all scripts in *ch04scr.pre*.

The **Natural Language Processing, Lotus Freelance Show Package**, contains detailed instructions on how to set up various computer installations to utilize the material to full advantage in a system 509 classroom. To utilize the NLP Lotus Presentation Pack, one must have a PC and a copy of Lotus Freelance Graphics, available from Lotus.

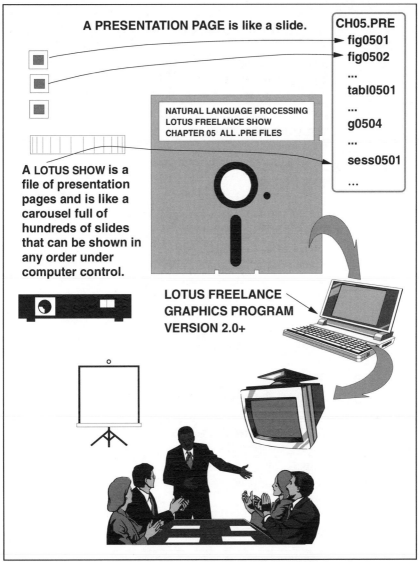

Figure 12. Presenting the *NLP Lotus Show* files on a big monitor.

The following lists some of the main sources of information, Prolog interpreters, and programs available to researchers in computational linguistics via E-mail or ftp (file transfer program).

To obtain information about this book, connect to this gopher site:
CWIS@nyu.edu

To be added to the **Quintus user's group** mailing list, send mail to:
quintus-users-request@quintus.com

To join the **Association for Logic Programming**, send mail to:
csa@doc.ic.ac.uk

To obtain a copy of **Open-Prolog** by ftp, connect to:
grattan.cs.tcd.ie

To obtain a copy of **Prolog–2** by ftp, connect to:
ai.uga.edu

To obtain an **announcement message** from the server of the **Computation and Language Electronic Preprint Server**, send a message to:
cmp-lg@xxx.lanl.gov
with the subject *'get announce.txt'* and empty body.

To retrieve information about **how to subscribe to and use** the server, send a message to:
cmp-lg@xxx.lanl.gov
with the subject *'help'* and empty body.

To **subscribe to linguist**, send a message to:
        listserv@tamvm1.tamu.edu   (on the Internet)
or
        listserv@tamvm1   (on Bitnet)
The message should consist of the following line only:
    subscribe linguist firstname lastname
Ex: *subscribe linguist Marlene Dietrich*

To obtain all sorts of useful information via ftp, connect to:
archive.umich.edu

chapter 1

NATURAL INTELLIGENCE, LINGUISTICS, AND PROLOG

The old phrase "stop and think" is sound psychology. For thinking is stoppage of the immediate manifestation of impulse until that impulse has been brought into connection with other possible tendencies to action so that a more comprehensive plan of activity is formed.... Thinking is thus a postponement of immediate action, while it effects internal control of impulse through a union of observation and memory, this union being the heart of reflection.... What has been said explains the meaning of the well–word phrase "self–control".... The method of intelligence manifested in the experimental method demands keeping track of ideas, activities, and observed consequences. Keeping track is a matter of reflective review and summarizing, in that there is both discrimination and record of the significant features of a developing experience. To reflect is to look back over what has been done so as to extract the net meanings that are the capital stock for intelligent dealing with further experiences. It is the heart of intellectual organization and of the disciplined mind.

John Dewey, 1938/1969
Experience and Education

1.1. The Information Society

Table 1.1 presents information about the distribution of the workforce in various countries since 1900 between three segments of the economy. **Sector I** includes agriculture, forestry, and fishing. **Sector II** includes manufacturing, mining, and construction. **Sector III** includes service, education, and medicine.

A society that is predominantly sector I might be called *pre-industrial*. A society that is predominantly sector II is called an *industrial society*. A population mainly employed in sector III is often called a *service society*, in which the service industries include education, medicine,

	Sector I agriculture forestry mining	Sector II manufacturing mining construction	Section III service education medicine
Table 1.1. Change in the Distribution of Employment in Three Sectors (percentage of total workforce)			
France			
1901	42	30	28
1959	23	38	38
1979	9	35	56
United States			
1900	38	28	34
1960	9	34	57
1981	3	29	68
Turkey			
1927	82	8	10
1960	75	10	15
1975	64	11	25
Sweden			
1965	12	42	46
1969	9	40	51
1979	9	32	62
India			
1901	72	12	16
1971	71	12	17
Japan			
1920	54	25	21
1950	48	27	25
1980	10	35	55

repairs, shipping, data management, insurance, computer programming, inventory control, and delivery and postal services. Insofar as much of the service consists of information–based services, the service society can be called an **information society**.

The charts in Figure 1.1 indicate that the United States moved from a society mainly occupied in sectors I and II in 1900 to an information society in which 68% of the workforce was occupied in sector III by 1981. At present, less than 3% of the workforce in sector I generates all of the agricultural and forest products in the United States. The chart labeled *Tomorrow* is based on recent U.S. government statistics.

Baumol and Wolff (1992), in their article considering the latest data on comparative U.S. productivity and the state of manufacturing, discussed the shift of the labor force into sector III in these terms:

> [Consider] the service economy "deindustrialization" argument, that claims that because the share of the U.S. labor force employed in the services is growing, we can infer that U.S. manufacturing exports are losing out to foreign competitors. [The data] indicate that the share of service jobs in the U.S. did grow about 20 percent in the 23 years between 1965 and 1988, for which figures are available. But [data] also show that this growth rate of service job share was higher than ours in all of the leading industrial economies. If we are becoming, increasingly, a service economy, other countries are moving in that direction far faster than we.
>
> Actually, there is good reason to believe that the share of service employment in every industrial country is growing for the same reason the share of manufacturing jobs grew earlier. The previous intersectoral shift of the labor force out of agriculture and into manufacturing is attributable primarily to the sensational growth of agricultural productivity. In the 18th century it took about 90 percent of the population to produce enough farm products to feed the nation poorly; today a mere 3 percent of the labor force produces unmanageable surpluses of farm products. In its turn, rapid growth of productivity in manufacturing is reducing the share of the labor force needed to meet demands for manufactured goods, and so is driving workers to the services - and predominantly to the burgeoning information industries, not to mere hamburger flipping and dishwashing.
>
> None of this proves that our country is immune from long run threats to retention of its economic leadership of the world, and that it faces no problems in this arena. But, evidently, it is in a far better state than is widely believed. (pp. 2-3)

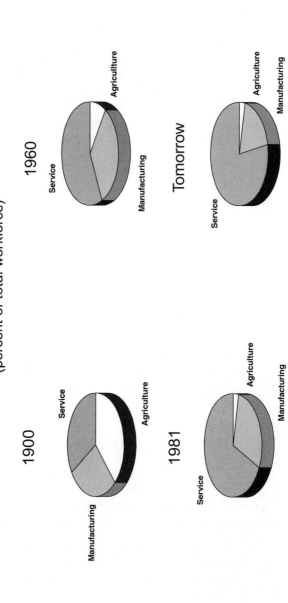

Figure 1.1. Change in the Distribution of Employment in Three Sectors (percent of total workforce)

The change from section I to II was based on the use of tools and machines to replace or amplify human efforts. *Natural power* – *natural* in that sense that it occurs in nature independent of human invention (human beings, horses, oxen, elephants, etc.) – was replaced by *artificial power* – *artificial* in that it is a human construct (tractors, bulldozers, factory ships, chainsaws, etc.). *Natural energy* sources (sun, wind, water) were replaced by *artificial energy* sources (electricity, coal, oil, atomic energy). Concepts such as *power* and *energy* are essential to understanding sectors I and II. The concepts *information* and *intelligence* play a crucial role in understanding sector III.

Shannon and Weaver (1949) developed *information theory* in which information is defined in terms of selection among a given set of alternatives. Any communication we receive that helps us make a selection by reducing the number of possible alternatives contains **information.** Shannon and Weaver differentiate *information* from *data.* Consider two different telephone books. The *alpha–book* contains an alphabetical list of all subscribers by last names. Each entry consists of the subscriber's last name, first name, address, and telephone number. The *num–book* contains a sequential list of all telephone numbers, smallest to largest. Each entry consists of the telephone number, the subscriber's last name, first name, and address. These books contain the same *data* but different *information.*

Information relates to how data are structured for answering questions. A **datum** provides the answer to a question. One book is suited to answer: *What is the telephone number of Jane Doe?* The other is suited to answer: *What is the name of the person with the number 998–7950?* Consider the alpha–book. If the datum for Bob Steigler incorrectly lists his telephone number as 998–7950 when it is actually 777–3010, and Bob Steigler is listed in the correct alphabetical order of names, then the book has the correct information structure but the wrong datum. If the datum for Bob Steigler correctly lists his phone number as 777–3010, but incorrectly has placed Steigler out of alphabetic order among the Bs, then the book has the correct datum but an incorrect information structure. This type of technical terminology is rarely discussed in this book, but we have been consistent in differentiating the data structures (record structure) from the information structure of the database (that structure relating to the questions to be answered).

When we program in Prolog, we decide the information structure of the data. To rephrase John Dewey, the method of intelligence manifested in Prolog demands keeping track of ideas, activities, and observed consequences. Programming so that Prolog can keep track of the data is a matter of reflective review and summarization, in which there is both discrimination and record of the significant information structures of the data.

Intelligence that occurs in nature is **natural intelligence**. Intelligence that does not occur except through human intervention and artifice is **artificial intelligence**. Our attempt to program human language structures onto a computing machine assumes it is possible to construct an artificial intelligence that in some significant sense duplicates a fragment of natural intelligence, particularly, some specific aspects of human intelligence.

Our usage of **natural** versus **artificial** accords with that of Darwin. *Artificial selection* is that practiced by animal breeders who select males and females from one generation to produce specific properties in the males and females of the next. Darwin (1962/1859), in his *Origin of Species*, argued that the same evolution of properties that occurs through artificial selection occurs in nature through a process of *natural selection.* I follow Darwin's usage because I believe that *intelligence* is part of the biological world and should be studied scientifically, just as one would study any other biological object. It is possible to research the structure, function, development, growth, and evolution of the heart, liver, kidneys, thumb, binocular vision, binaural hearing, hand–eye coordination, memory, pattern–recognition abilities, and problem–solving skills. In this study we follow the perspective of Noam Chomsky and focus on those species–specific aspects of human intelligence that make language possible.

For a considerable time after Darwin theorized that the principles of heredity that regulate artificial selection also regulate natural selection, people argued that he was confusing two fundamentally different processes. They maintained that the principles of heredity that work in artificial farm breeding situations do not operate in nature. A current debate concerning intelligence parallels the debates of Darwin's time, but in the other direction. Some people argue that the principles of *natural intelligence* that regulate natural human behavior and functions do not bear much relation to the principles of *artificial intelligence* that are invoked to explain the functions of a machines (for an interesting discussion, see Chomsky, 1966; Descartes 1964/1911; and Searle , 1984).

Most people associate *natural intelligence* with animals and not plants or inanimate objects. Also, since the work of Descartes in the 1600s, most people – insofar as they even think about such things – associate *artificial intelligence* with machines and not undifferentiated lumps of matter.

What have been the major factors in causing the shift from sectors I and II to III? The obvious reason for the shift is the rise in the

productivity of a worker. The shift of workers out of agriculture, forestry, and mining has not resulted in a decrease in sector I products.

What has led to the increase in worker productivity? Any answer will include these three major factors:

> There is a *theory of problem types* and *job tasks* for the workers in sectors I and II.
>
> Science and technology enabled us to understand, harness, shape, and transform *power* and *energy* in order to channel it into job tasks.
>
> There is a (relatively) well–defined idea of *worker productivity* for sectors I and II: bushels of wheat per worker, tons of steel per worker, worker hours per car, and so on.

Most people grasp the changes that have taken place in farming, fishing, and mining, although they might not glorify their understanding with terms such as *theory of problem types*. The problems confronting a farmer or forester involve moving heavy things, cutting things down, bundling things up, shipping things long distances, and avoiding rodents. Insofar as a horse had any sense, it would have seen the writing on the wall as the steam tractor chugged its way into the farmer's heart by greatly increasing his productivity while decreasing his maintenance expenditures. A *theory of job tasks* led to the invention of specific tools (chainsaw, reaper, hydraulic winch, etc.), each of which increased worker productivity. In sector I one can easily visualize the problem types that led to specific job tasks and the natural sources of labor (horse, ox, farmer) that were replaced by tools and machines.

In sector II, the theory of job tasks – formulated in some cases by "efficiency experts" and industrial engineers – led to assembly lines, automation, robotics, and sophisticated machines whose operation was governed by photosensors and computer programs. Technical innovations led to very high productivity per worker and a high output with a decreased workforce.

What about worker productivity in sector III? Three problems confront us immediately:

> There is no *theory of problem types* and *job tasks* for the workers in sector III.
>
> Science and technology have not enabled us to understand, harness, shape, and transform *information* and *intelligence*

into job tasks.

There is no well–defined idea of *worker productivity* for sector III.

Consider sector III *productivity*. The debate concerning doctors in private practice versus those in health maintenance organizations often focuses obliquely on *doctor productivity*. Is doctor productivity measured by prevention or cure? Is a health maintenance organization, in which each patient represents a loss of income, likely to be more or less productive than a doctor in private practice in which each patient represents increased income? What is *teacher productivity*? How does it relate to class size? Individual versus group lessons?

How can we utilize our scientific and technological understanding of *information* and *intelligence* in order to produce intelligent tools and machines that will increase worker productivity on specific job tasks? Before any progress can be made, we must understand what is meant by *information* and *intelligence*. To my mind, the most interesting discussion of *intelligence* (in particular, human intelligence) and its relation to animal intelligence and artificial intelligence is offered by Noam Chomsky in his analysis of the structure of human languages. I will discuss some of his ideas later. In this study, I do not discuss information theory. I simply adopt the definitions and approach of Shannon and Weaver (1949).

1.2. An Old Theory of Computer Power and Intelligence

A not uncommon view considers a computer to be a dumb servant that will carry out any task tirelessly, but must be told every little detail of the correct procedure to follow to get the desired results. We call this the *procedural details view*, or just *procedural view* for short.

Procedural view: A *computer* is a machine that transforms information by proceeding through a sequence of steps. Unless it is programmed it does nothing.

Somewhat like an uninspired Bob Crachet, the computer inputs data, plods along step by step in a totally programmed algorithm, and eventually produces the desired output. The programmer encodes the algorithms into the computer.

The job task of a *computer programmer* is to tell the computer how to solve the problem by encoding into the

computer the detailed steps to follow to arrive at the correct answer.

A *computer program* is a detailed set of sequential steps that the computer must follow to produce any results.

Within the procedural view of computer power, various tools, programs, and computers have been developed to tackle problem types and job tasks of sector III. Figure 1.2 indicates some sector III problem types (keeping track of things, regulating movement in space, disseminating information, and projecting "what if" problems). Within each problem type I indicate some of the factors that define or relate to specific job tasks.

Insofar as any job task in any problem area has yielded to analysis that has produced a computational tool, the tool mechanizes only the most rudimentary aspects of intelligence. In particular, the computational tools are external aids to human reasoning. They do not incorporate any aspects of human reasoning and judgment capacities. An **external aid** to human reasoning is something that increases a human's *memory, speed,* or *accuracy.* A pencil and paper is an external aid in that, by using them, we can do mathematical calculations with bigger numbers than we can manipulate in our head. The invention of writing and the development of books offered an external aid to the limits of the human memory. Pencils, paper, writing, and books increase a human's capacity to do tasks requiring intelligence, but no one would claim that they are capable of reasoning or logic. They are external buffers to our limited capacities.

Under the procedural view of computer power, the computational tools that have been developed to match the problem types and job tasks of sector III are for the most part external aids to human reasoning. In the same way as a pencil and paper, but at a more sophisticated level, they are external aids to reasoning in three dimensions: They increase *memory* and enable a person to deal with vast quantities of data and information. They increase *speed* and enable a person to process large amounts of data per unit time. They increase *accuracy* and make fewer mistakes than people do.

Within the procedural view of computer power there has been little, if any, attempt to develop analyses that "automate," "mechanize," or "computerize" aspects of human *logic, reason, judgment, creativity,* or *imagination.* For the most part, computer power has been channeled into the job tasks of sector III in order to computerize the most menial aspects of human intelligence.

Productivity in sector I must have jumped with the introduction

A. Problem Type: *Keep Track of Things.*

	Job Tasks involve:
1. time	Time management schedulers
2. space	Architectural layout, landscape design
3. people	Personnel and medical records, appointments, student records
4. money	Financial Management, budget control, checking accounts, etc.
5. objects	Database management

B. Problem Type: *Regulate Movement in Space.*

	Job Tasks involve:
1. traffic	Traffic control, meter flow, schedule lights, etc.
2. people	Elevator operation, crowd control...
3. airplanes	Air traffic controller, schedules, ticket sales, etc.
4. medicine	Complex surgical and x-ray machine control
5. packages	Postal services, delivery services

C. Problem Type: *Dissemination of Information.*

	Job Tasks involve:
1. memos	Word processing, E-mail programs, etc.
2. manuals	Desktop publishing
3. graphics	Drawing and graphics design programs
4. presentations	Chart/graph overhead design
5. CAD/CAM	Graphics/Engineering Design

D. Problem Type: *"What if" Projections.*

	Job Tasks involve:
1. numbers	Spreadsheets
2. time	Construct Pert - Gantt charts

Figure 1.2. Some sector III problems and job types.

of *tools* such as the digging stick, the hoe, the spade, and the iron plow. But productivity went through the roof with the development of *machines* such as the tractor, the thresher, and the harvester. Productivity in sector III has certainly increased with the introduction of *intelligent tools*, which are external aids to human memory, speed, and accuracy. What concepts of *computer power* and *intelligence* are required to enable us to develop *intelligent machines* that can be creative and also reason about and judge their own creations? In what types of sector III problem types and job tasks could productivity be increased by the introduction of *intelligent machines*?

1.3.   A New Theory of Computer Power and Intelligence

A new view of artificial intelligence is to regard the computer as a babbling idiot, a pandora's box, or an idiot savant, somewhat like a young toddler that prattles incessantly. The computer is not a dumb servant that awaits step–by–step commands before it does anything. The computer is always on, always has everything right at its fingertips ready to print out or display at a moments notice. But, the computer has no taste. It cannot tell relevant data from irrelevant. The computer is like someone who tells the same joke over because it got a big laugh the first time.

> *Idiot–Savant View:* **A computer is a machine that has instantly available every permutation and combination of data that can be composed from the facts stored in its inventory.**

The main goal of a programmer is to tell the computer *how to recognize* the answer and differentiate it from the myriad of wrong and just plain silly answers that the computer has ready to go. It is not the function of a programmer to tell the computer *how to find* the correct answer.

Imagine an eager employee who delivers to customers any item they want from an inventory that includes every part ever made for any car ever made. The employee never even has to turn around. Any part that is desired by any customer is always right within an arm's reach. Further, every part is completely specified in all relevant details on his inventory list. If you ask for a *left–handed thread clutch thrust bearing relief pressure gasket spring oil cover seal for a 1950 Studebaker*, the employee hands it to you instantly. The same for any conceivable part.

This employee has every object in his inventory classified in elaborate detail. If you ask him for a piece using his classifications, you

11

get it instantly. But therein lies the rub: Most people do not know what to ask for as most people do not know the classifications and detailed specifications of what they want. I might have an object that I need, but not know that it is a *relief pressure gasket spring oil cover seal*. In order to interact with this employee, and to get him to deliver precisely the inventory item I need, I must describe to him what I want in *my terminology* and let him focus in on it using *his classifications*.

We might ask: *Do you have a piece for a 1950 Studebaker that comes from the clutch assembly and that is about a half inch in diameter and is held down by a pin?* The employee might answer: I have 208 pieces like that.

I might ask: Describe them to me. He responds: Part #1 was manufactured in Toledo, O. in 1949 and stored in a warehouse in Kansas for 21 years. It weighs 1 ounce and is made of an alloy that does not conduct electricity. We sold 19 of them last year. Four of them were returned and are back in stock. Part #2 was made in Taiwan last year and is a synthetic plastic that is as durable as the metal original. Blah, blah, blah.

It is entirely possible that the employee could identify your piece if you asked: I need a piece that was made in Oregon and stored in a warehouse in Newark, N.J.; further, it must have a specific gravity of 2.31 and be in stock now, but have been back ordered 3 times in the past 11 years. This may be as unique as asking for *a left–handed thread clutch thrust bearing relief pressure gasket spring oil cover seal for a 1950 Studebaker.*

To get the inventory item we want from this employee we must engage in a sort of 20–questions guessing game. From our point of view, some facts are more relevant than others. Few people looking for a part would mention its manufacture, storage, shipping weight per hundred, and cost per thousand. Most people would describe its physical properties and what they thought was its function. To the employee one fact is as relevant as the next. Think of what it would be like to interact with this person.

All the properties of every item are immediately available to him. But there is no sense in that one property is more relevant than another. If you provide enough properties so that he can locate an inventory item that may be what you want, he may ask you if it is small and round, or if it is green, but he may also ask if there are 6 dozen stored in a warehouse in Alaska. If you can imagine dealing with this person, you can imagine Prolog programming.

The job task of the *computer programmer* is to describe to the computer in *our terminology* which item is the answer and let the computer find that item in *its own classification system*.

> A *computer program* is a logically defined specification of the conditions that must be met by the item that we want.

To really get a feel for Prolog programming, I would have to expand this example. Imagine if the inventory control person had instantly available all the data about any item in the inventory and also all data relating to all possible relations among all items in the inventory, instantly available knowledge about which pieces attach to each other, which pieces were manufactured at the same plant, which pieces are the most frequently ordered, which piece can substitute for which other pieces, and so on.

1.4.   A Prolog Theory of Computer Power and Intelligence

Prolog is an abbreviation for *PROgramming* in *LOGic*. Although the earlier inventory example above illustrates one side of Prolog, there is more to the story. Prolog is ideally suited to solving problems in which there are a number of objects that have complicated relations among them. In general, we are looking for a specific permutation or combination of the objects that satisfies specific logical conditions on possible combinations. Consider some examples.

Most puzzles and brain teasers are Prolog–type problems. If you want to see complex Prolog–type problems you should look at the books by J. Fixx, *Problems for the Super Intelligent* (1972), and *More Problems for the Super Intelligent* (1976). All the problems presented by Fixx can be solved naturally in Prolog. Two excellent examples are *A Love Story* and *Batter Up!*

A Love Story

Four men and four women are shipwrecked on a desert island. Eventually each one falls in love with one other, and is himself loved by one person. John falls in love with a woman who is, unfortunately, in love with Jim. Arthur loves a woman who loves the man who loves Ellen. Mary is loved by the man who is loved by the woman who is loved by Bruce. Gloria hates Bruce and is hated by the man whom Hazel loves. Who loves Arthur? (Fixx, 1976, p. 48)

Batter up!

Andy dislikes the catcher. Ed's sister is engaged to the second baseman. The center fielder is taller than the right fielder. Harry and the third baseman live in the same building. Paul and Allen each won $20 from the pitcher at pinochle. Ed and the outfielders play poker during their free time. The pitcher's wife is the third baseman's sister. The pitcher, catcher, and infielders except Allen, Harry, and Andy, are shorter than Sam. Paul, Harry, Bill, and the catcher took a trouncing from the second baseman at pool. Sam is involved in a divorce suit. The catcher and the third baseman each have two children. Ed, Paul, Jerry, the rightfielder, and the center fielder are bachelors. The others are married. The shortstop, the third baseman, and Bill each cleaned up $100 betting on the fight. One of the outfielders is either Mike or Andy. Jerry is taller than Bill. Mike is shorter than Bill. Each of them is heavier than the third baseman.

Using these facts, determine the names of the men playing the various positions on the baseball team. (Fixx, 1972, p. 46)

J. Sowa (1987) discussed the Prolog solutions to the following examples.

A farmer has a wolf, a goat, and a cabbage (a very large one). He wants to get all three of them plus himself across a river, but his boat is only large enough to hold one item plus himself. How can he cross the river without leaving the wolf alone with the goat or the goat alone with the cabbage? (p. 50)

Four bands, each from a different side of town, marched in a parade. Each band played only one piece, and no two bands played the same piece. From the following clues, determine the order in which the bands marched and the pieces they played.

(a)   The band from the North side was at the head of the parade.
(b)   "American Patrol" was the second piece played.
(c)   The band from the East or West side played "Yankee Doodle."
(d)   The last band played "When the Saints Go Marching in," just behind the band from the West side.
(e)   The bands that played "American Patrol" and "Stars and Stripes Forever" are from opposite sides of town. (p. 103).

Many problems that arise in practical situations, such as the following, lend themselves to Prolog analysis:

A university has 3214 students enrolled in 225 different courses for the Fall term. Each course has at least 1 student. Each student is taking 5 courses. The registrar has a list of which students are in which classes, details omitted here. Each course has a 2 hour final exam offered at time scheduled by the registrar subject to these constraints: (a) All exams are scheduled over five days, Monday to Friday, at 8–10, 10–12, 12–2, 2–4, and 4–6. (b) No student shall be scheduled to take two exams at the same time. (c) No student shall be scheduled to take more than 2 exams on any given day.

How can the 225 exams be scheduled?

A company is moving into three floors of a new building. Each floor has 40 offices. Following are the office requirements for each department that is moving in: Department m43 needs 9 offices; d48, 6 offices; m77, 11 offices, m34, 13 offices; j39, 9 offices; j76, 12 offices; m20, 11 offices; j92, 11 offices; j83, 7 offices; j64, 10 offices, m06, 11 offices, and j48, 10 offices. All the offices for a given department must be on the same floor. Furthermore, the following pairs of departments that work closely together must also be on the same floor: m43 and m77; d48 and m34, and j92 and j83. (Sowa, 1987, pp. 69,103)

These problems have four characteristics:

- There appear to be a large number of possibilities, in which each possibility is a different arrangement or combination of items.
- It would appear that the only way to arrive at a correct answer is to try one possibility after another until one of them works.
- There is almost a "random" sense in the testing of alternatives in that the alternative that works may be the next one you try or may still be far away. The fact that you have already tested a lot of possibilities simply eliminates alternatives, but may not give you any sense that you are closing in on an answer.
- One often does not know where to start to solve the problem. This not uncommonly is connected with a sense that there is no clear way to diagram or symbolize the problem.

The typical Prolog–type problem is defined over a large number of facts that are intertwined in specific relations, some of which may follow rules and others of which may be completely arbitrary. We are led to these views:

> *Prolog View:* A *computer* is a machine that has instantly available all properties of all objects in its database plus all possible relations that exist among these objects.
>
> The job task of the *computer programmer* is to describe to the computer in our terminology which objects and logical relations among the objects define possible answers.
>
> A *computer program* is a filter to separate the wheat (combinations meeting our logical conditions) from the chaff.

Because the computer already has at its disposal all conceivable alternatives of all objects, the correct answer is already available. The correct answer is smothered by incorrect answers. The programmer must write a program to instruct the computer with logical conditions *to choose the correct answer*, not step–by–step procedures *to find the correct answer*.

1.5.   Why Study Linguistics and Prolog?

The increase in worker productivity that revolutionized sectors I and II cannot transform sector III until we have answered this question:

What is a well–defined idea of *worker productivity* for sector III?

In order to answer this question, we must first answer:

What is the *theory of problem types* and *job tasks* for the workers in sector III?

It is believed that many basic problem types in sector III involve making decisions about objects (items, facts, things) that are bound to each other by complex interrelations. The problems are often symbolic and not numerical. The problems often involve what is called *reason, logic,* and *judgment*. Consider this anecdote.

> **Smith applies to Jones, a service employee at the Better Business Bureau, to register his complaint against a shoestore called Feet First. Smith informs Jones that the shoestore tends toward the unscrupulous, using bait–and–switch techniques and worse. As proof, Smith says that yesterday he bought a pair of socks there, and, hoisting his trouser legs, shows one blue and one red sock. He lamented: "I picked out a nice pair of socks, but when I got home, this is what was in the bag." Jones dutifully registered the complaint. To strengthen his case, Smith added: "It is even worse. I bought two pairs there yesterday, and they gave me another pair just like this one."**

What aspects of his problem–solving skills did Jones bring to his handling of Smith's complaint? Jones based his response on the data in Smith's testimony, which would offer two counts against Feet First, plus all the data acquired in life from education, experience, and common sense. As Smith presented his data, Jones did not simply passively register the information. Jones did two things: First, Jones integrated all the data given by Smith into a database of all Jone's knowledge. Second, as new data came in, Jones actively offered new analyses to form a unified hypothesis that synthesizes all the data into a coherent picture.

There are at least three properties of the *intelligence* **required for job tasks in sector III**. First, **perspicacity**: Decisions must be based on data in the problem statement plus all of the data in the (perhaps huge) database gained from past experience. Second, **creativity**: As each new datum is entered, one must reformulate all possible combinations of data to *generate* new solutions. And third, **judgment**: One must be prepared to make *judgments* that jettison old solutions for new ones. Prolog is ideally suited for representing these three properties of intelligence in a computational model.

A computer system (including hardware, firmware, software, and operators) that exhibits perspicacity, creativity, and judgment is sometimes called an **expert system**.

How can science and technology enable us to understand, harness, shape, and transform *information* and *intelligence* into job tasks that match problem types?

Rather than discuss *intelligence* in the abstract, I offer some practical examples. What kind of intelligence is it that enables Jones, and anyone else, to integrate each piece of data into a database collected over a lifetime, and to instantaneously be able to form new combinations that integrate that item with all previously acquired items? Where do we find this intelligent capacity in a form that can be studied scientifically? I maintain that **linguistics**, the scientific study of language as defined by the ideas about generative grammar offered by Noam Chomsky, focuses precisely on this concept of *intelligence*.

Consider this deservedly little known fact. The word *absquatulate* was coined in the early 1800s and meant to forcibly remove squatters from government lands. *Ab* = a prefix meaning *from*, *squat* = the stem from *squatter*, and *ulate* = a verbalizing suffix combined to yield *ab–squat–ulate*. Except for history buffs, few people have this word in their vocabulary. Now that you have it, you know that one can say *anti–absquatulation*, as in, *There were several anti–absquatulation movements formed in Scotland aimed at keeping absquatulationism in check*. You also know that you cannot say **absquatulateness*.

In general, when a child or adult hears one form of a word, the word becomes integrated into his or her language knowledge database (grammar) and the person knows all possible forms of the word. The type of intelligent capacity that is basic to the normal acquisition, knowledge, and use of human language by a human being seems to be the type of intelligence that is crucial to developing a theory of job tasks in sector III.

1.6.   Why Study Natural Language Computing In Prolog?

The words, phrases, and sentences of any human language provide one of the most complex examples of items bound to each other by rigid interrelations. The number of sentences of English that contain 15 words or less exceeds the number of seconds in the history of the universe. But a speaker of English will understand any of these sentences instantly. Further, if a sentence contains an error, a speaker will usually recognize it instantly. How long does it take to recognize a foreign accent? A speaker of English has at virtually instantaneous disposal an unbounded number of sentences, each of which is constructed according to precise grammatical constraints. Anyone who doubts this should study Arzan (1992), who presented a Prolog–based English grammar that analyzes the errors made in essays by college students at the University of Puerto Rico learning English as a second language. As Arzan showed, a computer can readily be programmed to detect some errors: *She explained me how to go. *I hoped Mary to win. But other errors, such as the possible use of *assist* to mean *to be present* and not *to help*, are hard to detect. A Spanish student learning English might write *I assisted at the party* hoping to mean *I was present at the party*. The differences between the Spanish *assistar* and the English *assist* yields errors that can elude simple detection.

Consider the following thought experiment. Suppose you go to the library, open a book at random, and place a pencil point on a sentence on the page. Now start searching through all the books in the library until you encounter this sentence again. This example brings home three points. The number of sentences that are in general use is enormous. Second, any sentence, except for a greeting (*How are you feeling?*) or banal civility (*Your baby looks just like you.*), is rarely used twice. Third, a normal human can instantly recognize any given sentence as *grammatical*, in that it can be generated by the grammar, or as *ungrammatical*, in that it violates the laws of combination of words defined in the grammar.

Work in natural language processing has much in common with the earlier inventory control problem in which we considered asking for a *Studebaker clutch oil cover seal*. Suppose we ask for possible verbs that could fill the slots in sentences 1 and 2.

1.   Mary _____ John to behave himself.
2.   Mary _____ John to behave herself.

The slot in (1) could be filled by *expected*, yielding *Mary expected John to behave himself*. Other verbs possible are: *persuaded, wanted, told*, and so on. The slot in (2) could be filled by *promised*, yielding *Mary promised John to behave herself*. English has no other verbs that would fill the slot in 2.

If we had English programmed into Prolog, we could ask Prolog to find all the examples for us. But, as will be shown, programming questions about human language into Prolog has a rub: We want to tell the computer *in our terminology* which verbs are the answers and let the computer find those verbs in *its own classification system*. In our terminology, we ask: *Give me verbs that can fill the slot in (1)*, but the English grammar database lists these verbs as *verbs subcategorized for an NP S complement in which the S has an infinite INFL head and the verb is object control*. We ask: *Give me verbs that can fill the slot in (2)*, but in the English grammar database these are classified as *verbs subcategorized for an NP S complement in which the S has an infinite INFL head and the verb is subject control*. Although it would be getting ahead of the story, we could also ask obscure questions such as: *Give me all English verbs that are romance but borrowed from French and not Latin and that have the possibility of a "for" complementizer*. Questions of this level of obscurity might provide answers as to which verbs could fill the slot in (2) and why there are so few verbs that could occur in (2).

In attempting to encode English, French, and German into Prolog, we are tackling large and complex databases constructed by humans over hundreds, if not thousands, of generations, in which each generation added and subtracted items sometimes according to rule and sometimes willynilly. In this presentation, I differentiate between the processes that define words and idioms, that I call the **lexicon** (or **dictionary**), and the processes of sentence construction, that I call **syntax**.

This study assumes that the optimal theory of the lexicon is the **Finite Automata Model** developed by M. Gross, D. Perrin, and M. Silberztein at the University of Paris. Extensive studies by Gross and his colleagues over the past 25 years shows rather conclusively that most, if not all, the generative processes internal to the lexicon can be analyzed in terms of *finite state automata* (see Gross 1986, 1989a, 1989b; Gross & Perrin 1989; Perrin 1989; Silberztein 1989). Assuming they are correct, the internal structure and organization of a human being's knowledge of words and idioms can be analyzed and formulated into precise mathematical theories.

If our goal is to obtain a computerized representation of the structures of human language, the work of Gross, Perrin, and Silberztein represents a milestone in that it specifies the type of computational processes, pattern–recognition devices, and memory–storage capacities an *artificial intelligence* (computing machine) must have in order to process words and idioms in a fashion that parallels the *natural intelligence* of a human being. Anyone interested in the complexity of lexical structures for words and idioms would do well to examine the work of Gross et. al., which is one of the largest computerized dictionaries in existence. All the linguistic material I present concerning lexical structure could be formalized as a finite–state grammar using the computational tools of the Finite Automata Model.

This study assumes that the optimal theory of syntax is that called the **Minimalist Theory of Generative Grammar** by Chomsky's school centered at MIT (see Chomsky 1992b; Chomsky & Lasnik 1991). The linguistic material in chapters 7–9 is formulated in terms of a lexically driven bottom–up parser that constructs trees as X–bar projections of lexical heads. These representations and derivations match those discussed in Chomsky (1986b, pp. 101–105; 1988, pp. 93–100). I follow the view of Leacock (1990, 1991) and assume that (a) the distribution, type, interpretation, and reference of any empty category can be determined from its string context by the parser by using lexical information, (b) there is no motivation for any level of deep structure or any transformational movement rules, and (c) control and binding are separate modules.

Subject to refinement as the study progresses, I define a **grammar** as the database of all facts and relations about a language known by a native speaker. *Syntax* and the *lexicon* are two components of a *grammar*. Sometimes, usually when I speculate about practical uses of a computerized grammar, I use the term *grammar* a bit broader to include all facts and relations about a language known by a native speaker plus all data in the *Oxford English Dictionary*, the seven volume work by Jespersen *A Modern English Grammar on Historical Principles* (1913/1961), and *Harrap's New Collegiate French and English Dictionary* (1982). The terms used earlier (e.g., *verb, subcategorization, complement, object control*) are the coordinates (database keys) used by linguists working in Chomsky's theoretical framework to index the items in the grammatical database. In undertaking to read this book, you are committing yourself to learn as much about the grammar of human languages as you learn about Prolog.

The main reason for studying natural language computing in Prolog is to gain a scientific understanding of the problem–solving skills, pattern–matching capacities, and memory structures that underlie the particular concept of *intelligence* exemplified in the Smith–Jones story. We argue that the scientific concept of **intelligence** that must be understood if one is to understand the theory of job tasks in sector III is exactly the

20

concept of *intelligence* discussed by Noam Chomsky in his generative grammar theories aimed at answering the questions: What constitutes knowledge of a language? How is knowledge of language acquired? How is knowledge of language put to use?

The intelligence defined by Chomsky, which underlies a normal human being's knowledge of language, the acquisition of that knowledge, and the use of that knowledge, is **natural intelligence**. It is part of the genetic endowment of a human being, a part of the human's biological specification. The natural intelligence that underlies a human's acquisition and knowledge of language is part of the biological world. One main goal of this present research is to isolate and define three aspects of a human's natural intelligence (**unboundedness**: the ability to recognize a vast inventory of sentences; **rule–governed creativity**: the ability to generate vast combinations and permutations of facts instantly; and **judgment**: the ability to differentiate a "well–formed" from an "ill–formed" combination). Insofar as one can encode into Prolog these aspects of *natural intelligence*, one will have constructed an **artificial intelligence** that has the type of intelligence relevant for solving problems in sector III.

On a practical note, the scientific study of human language will eventually enable us to interact with a computer in English. At this point, much traditional procedural–type programming in languages such as Fortran, Cobol, Pascal, and Basic will become obsolete. A future user will simply write or talk to the computer using English and get a written or spoken response. It is quite possible that teaching students to program in procedural languages today – as extremely fast parallel–processing computers with large memories are on the horizon – can be likened to teaching students how to care for horses in the 1900s as automobiles began to dot the roads.

1.7.   Artificial Intelligence Machines

Prolog gives a concrete new way to think about computer power and computer programming. This has three ramifications.

First, as we shall see, Prolog enables us to encode many of the data structures of human language in a natural way. This suggests that the basic process of *unification* and the concepts underlying the management of *relational databases* may be similar to the processes underlying human grammars. These same Prolog mechanisms, which describe the processes of human language, can be used to solve sector III problems in logic, reasoning, and judgment like the ones earlier involving Smith and Jones, the farmer, the bands, the exam schedules, and the office allocations.

Through theoretical studies based on Chomsky's universal grammar, we can obtain a scientific conception of *intelligence* in terms of *unboundedness*, *rule–governed creativity*, and *judgment*. This linguistic conception of *intelligence*, based on studies of natural intelligence, can be encoded into Prolog to implement a grammar on a computing machine. This same notion of *intelligence* also has practical application for the implementation of artificial intelligence into computer analyses that attempt to automate the reasoning and decision processes that a human brings to job tasks in sector III. Thus, the current study in computational linguistics illustrates how the science of linguistics and the technology underlying Prolog computers enables us to understand and shape a concept of *intelligence* into job tasks that match sector III problem types.

Second, Prolog gives us a handle on **resource allocation** in sector III. Prolog enables us to see how best to allocate human, computational, and financial resources to incorporate artificial intelligence into computerized implementations of problem types and job tasks arising in sector III. Programming in a nonprocedural language is a hedge against obsolesence and an almost certain guarantee that any resources allocated to data processing will yield cumulative results. If a certain amount of money is allocated into solving a problem by programming in a procedural language, then there is a good chance that resources will be lost if a "better way" is found to solve the problem. When a better procedure for solving the problem arises, any computer encoding of the old procedural steps may become obsolete. On the other hand, because programming in Prolog only requires us to encode (a) the database of facts and their interrelations and (b) the logical conditions that any answer must satisfy, we do not have to change anything if anyone figures out some new way to generate alternative combinations of facts. The only time we have to change our program is if the database of facts change or if we want some different answer.

If anyone invents a "better" or "faster" way to generate permutations and combinations of facts, or a powerful new way of testing combinations against logical criteria, this will improve the Prolog machine on which we run our programs, but it will require no reprogramming on our part. To some extent the same thing can be said about object oriented programming techniques. For most students, this basic concept of the software as a monotonically increasing asset can be understood more easily by studying Prolog than by attempting to master object oriented programming techniques. If serial machines, which are current, are replaced by parallel machines at some future date, we do not have to modify our programs. We can simply enjoy the fact that they run faster. Programming efforts in nonprocedural languages yield monotonically increasing assets as long as those facts in the database and the questions being asked have value.

Third, Prolog, in particular as it is applied to yield a computational implementation of the processes underlying human language, may well leapfrog over concepts of *intelligent tools* and usher in the development of *intelligent machines* in sector III. From my understanding, the Japanese Fifth Generation Computer Project intended to develop intelligent machines. The project's difficulties seem to stem from two areas.

At the technical level, the computers were essentially serial (procedural) machines, too slow, and did not have enough memory. Further, much work on knowledge representation (expert systems) only dealt with hierarchical knowledge (which could be represented by conditional *if–then* statements) and did not consider cross–classifications of knowledge (which are represented by biconditional *iff* statements). It is only a matter of time until these problems are overcome.

At a basic conceptual level, the Fifth Generation Project appeared to lack a scientific definition of *intelligence* that related to the concept of intelligence required for the job tasks in sector III. Such a definition of *intelligence* is the North Star that gives projects in *artificial intelligence* and *expert systems* sense and direction. It is quite possible that given Chomsky's definition of *intelligence* as a part of the biological world (which is both scientific and pragmatic), we could exploit technical improvements (fast parallel machines with huge memories) to make something like the Fifth Generation Project eminently successful. At such point we could abandon today's *artificial intelligence tools* with which we hoe and rake the data. We could develop *artificial intelligence machines* to aid us in tasks that require the creation of hypotheses, reasoning about "what if" projections, and judgments about how to act on our knowledge.

chapter 2

HOW TO
READ AND WRITE
IN PROLOG

Many newcomers to Prolog find the task of writing a Prolog program is not like specifying an algorithm in the same way as in a conventional programming language. Instead, the Prolog programmer asks more what formal relationships and objects occur in his problem and what relationships are "true" about the desired solution. So, Prolog can be viewed as a descriptive language as well as a prescriptive one. The Prolog approach is rather to describe known facts and relationships about a problem, than to prescribe the sequence of steps taken by a computer to solve the problem. When a computer is programmed in Prolog, the actual way the computer carries out the computation is specified partly by the logical declarative semantics of Prolog, partly by what new facts Prolog can "infer" from the given ones, and only partly by explicit control information supplied by the Programmer.

W.F. Clocksin and C.S. Mellish, 1981
Programming in Prolog

2.1. Six Characteristics of Prolog Problems

A **Prolog-type** problem

- often involves a large number of facts
- may be defined in terms of symbols, patterns, and logical relations and may not require any numerical calculations
- is always defined by boundary conditions that define an acceptable answer. The boundary conditions present an explicit recognition procedure or formula that defines the answer
- lends itself to a nonprocedural solution mechanism that

24

searches through lots of alternatives until one meeting the boundary conditions is found
- often permits parallel computation, that is, several computers working simultaneously on the problem could yield the correct answer quicker than a single machine operating on the problem.

To find a problem defined over a large number of facts that are intertwined in specific relations, some of which follow rules and others of which may be completely arbitrary, we need look no further than the English dictionary. Suppose we ask: What is a five–letter word such that the letters are in alphabetical order? The database of facts is the dictionary. Number is peripheral in that we do not need to do any calculations. The boundary conditions are a simple relation among the letters: The letters must be in alphabetical order. An acceptable word could be almost anywhere in the dictionary. In our search we could start with any letter, although our chances would be better if we consider words starting with *a* because there are then more possibilities. If we consider words that start with *z*, we will not find any five–letter words with the letters in alphabetical order. The problem lends itself to parallel computation in that we could have one person search for words starting with *a*, another for words starting with *b*, and so on. We need not search the *a* words before we search the *b* words. Among the possible answers would be the word *almost*.

Any problem statement defined in the dictionary breaks down into simple facts and complex facts. A **simple fact** is one that cannot be further reduced. Each letter in the English alphabet is a simple fact. A **complex fact** is a combination or permutation of simple facts. Each word in English is a string of letters from the alphabet, and hence, is a complex fact.

A **word** is a string of symbols in which the symbols are taken from a fixed list of symbols called an alphabet. For writing (orthography), the alphabet is the 26 letters {a,b...z}, and a word is a sequence of the letters chosen from the alphabet. For pronunciation (phonetics), the alphabet is the International Phonetic Alphabet, which consists of about 150 symbols, one for each basic sound in English. The IPA is found in most dictionaries and is often called a pronunciation guide.

A *dictionary* is a list of all of the words in English. Dictionaries intended for use by speakers of English usually contain only root words without any predictable endings. For instance, there is an entry for *boy* but not *boys* because the plural is formed by simply adding an *s*. There would be an entry for *ox* and *oxen* because the plural of *ox* is irregular.

A dictionary that is a part of a spelling checker for a word processor would contain all possible forms of English words, both regular and irregular. By **dictionary** (or **lexicon**) we mean a list of all possible forms of all possible words in English. Our dictionary contains *boy/boys* as well as *ox/oxen*, and *look/looked/looked* as well as *take/took/taken*.

I am concerned with a word and with its spelling. Let us write a string of letters in italics when we mean it as a word, for example, *boy*, and as a string of letters separated by commas and in square brackets when we mean the spelling of that word, for example, *[b,o,y]*.

> *boy* is spelled *[b,o,y]*.
> *boy* rhymes with *toy*, *soy*, and *ploy*.
> *boy* has three letters.
> *[b,o,y]* is three letters.
> The three letters in *boy* are *[b]*,*[o]*, and *[y]*.
> The letters *[o]*, *[b]*, and *[y]* can be used to spell the word *boy*, which is spelled *[b,o,y]*.
> *almost* has five letters in alphabetical order.
> *[a,l,m,o,s,t]* is five letters in alphabetical order.
> With the letters *[t]*, *[a]*, *[l]*, *[s]*, *[m]*, and *[o]* we can spell the word *almost* by putting them in the sequence *[a,l,m,o,s,t]*.
> The word *almost* has two syllables, *al* spelled *[a,l]* and *most* spelled *[m,o,s,t]*.
> *[t,a,b]* is *[b,a,t]* spelled backwards.
> *Otto* contains two different letters: *[o]* and *[t]*.
> *Otto* contains four letters: *[o]*, *[o]*, *[t]*, and *[t]*.
> *Otto* and *toot* contain the same letters.

In playing hangman or in working crossword puzzles, sometimes we know how many letters the word has and perhaps even some of the letters. Let us represent an unknown letter in a word by a question mark (*?*), an underline (_), or a capital letter, such as *X* or *Y*. If we were playing hangman, the initial state for a three–letter word might be written like this:

> **[?,?,?]**   or   **[_,_,_]**

If we guess *s*, and the guess is correct, the representation might become:

> **[s,?,?]**   or   **[s,_,_]**

This is an abbreviation for the spellings of all three–letter words beginning in *s*: *sat*, *sad*, *sin*, *sun* and so on. If we guess *y* and the guess is correct, the form might become:

[s,?,y]   or   **[s,_,y]**

This is an abbreviation for the spellings of all words that begin in *s* and end in *y*: *say, soy, spy, sly,* and so on.

A variable symbol, such as *X* or *Y*, is useful for expressing that some letters must be the same. The following would be an abbreviation for all four–letter words in which the two middle letters are the same, but the first and last letter can be anything, for example *soon, moon, itty.*

[?,X,X,?]   or   **[_,X,X,_]**

The following abbreviates all four–letter words in which the first and last letters are the same and the two middle letters are the same: *toot, noon, otto.*

[X,Y,Y,X]

The request for a seven–letter crossword puzzle word, such as *surgeon*, in which the second and sixth letters are *u* and *o* would be:

[?,u,?,?,?,o,?]   or   **[_,u,_,_,_,o,_]**

Some of the representations do not correspond to any real English words. For instance, the following could not be completed to yield any English words:

[z,b,d,_,_,_]
[n,g,_,_]

No English word has the three–letter sequence *[z,b,d]* anywhere in the word. The sequence *[n,g]* occurs at the end of words, such as *sing*, and in the middle of words, such as *singer*, but never at the beginning of any English word.

Suppose we place 26 marbles in a jar, each inscribed with one letter of the alphabet. We can construct a string of letters by pulling out a series of marbles and writing down the letters in sequence. Assume that each time we write down the letter, we replace the marble in the jar. If we pull out five marbles at random, we might obtain these strings:

[a,d,q,r,m]
[z,p,l,i,n,t]
[w,o,m,e,n]
[p,l,a,d,q]

[s,o,u,p,s]

Some of the strings will be English words, as found in a dictionary, and other strings will be ill-formed English words. By definition, a **well-formed word** is one found in a dictionary. An **ill-formed word** is one not found in a dictionary.

One children's game has the players select a word at random from a book and try to form other words by recombining the word's letters in different orders. Let us consider a simple game in which the goal is to construct all possible three–letter words from the word *boulder.*

The database for the problem consists of simple and complex facts. *Simple facts*: We are given seven letters *[b], [o], [u], [l], [d], [e], [r].* *Complex facts:* We are given an English dictionary that lists all words, including the three–letter words. The problem is: What combinations of the given letters result in a three–letter word? This is a typical Prolog problem in that it requires a search over a large number of complex facts (the words in the dictionary) for various well-defined combinations and permutations of simple facts (the seven letters given).

There are two ways we could perform the search. Both will give the same answers, but they will do it by different procedures and may differ in efficiency.

The **generate/filter strategy** requires us (a) to produce every three–letter combination and permutation possible for the seven letters, (b) to look each of these possibilities up in the dictionary, and (c) filter out the ungrammatical words. This procedural strategy generates the three–letter strings listed in Table 2.1. and then looks up each of these words in an English dictionary to see which ones are words. Most will be clear–cut cases: *[b,e,d]* is a word and *[l,d,b]* is not. The three–letter words that can be formed from the letters in *[b,o,u,l,d,e,r]* are in Table 2.2.

The **scan/recognize strategy** requires us (a) to look up a three–letter word in the dictionary and (b) to see if we could construct that word using our given letters. This procedural strategy requires us to scan the dictionary and locate all three–letter words. The computerized dictionary on our UNIX VAX contains thousands of three–letter words from *aah* (exclaim in amazement) to *zoo* (a collection of living animals). For each word in the dictionary, we examine its letters to see if the word could be constructed using the letters in *[b,o,u,l,d,e,r]*. The dictionary scan might select the word *[a,t,e]*, but this would be filtered out because the list of seven letters contains no *[a]* or *[t]*. If the scan selects *[r,e,d]* from the dictionary, this will pass the filter because *[r], [e],* and *[d]* are acceptable letters. This strategy will produce the words in Table 2.2. Linguists have discussed the generate/filer strategy and the scan/recognize strategy when presenting topics such as filters and control.

bbb	dbl	ebu	lde	odr	red	ueo
bbd	dbo	edb	ldl	odu	ree	uer
bbe	dbr	edd	ldo	oeb	rel	ueu
bbl	dbu	ede	ldr	oed	reo	ulb
bbo	ddb	edl	ldu	oee	rer	uld
bbr	ddd	edo	leb	oel	reu	ule
bbu	dde	edr	led	oeo	rlb	ull
bdb	ddl	edu	lee	oer	rld	ulo
bdd	ddo	eeb	lel	oeu	rle	ulr
bde	ddr	eed	leo	olb	rll	ulu
bdl	ddu	eee	ler	old	rlo	uob
bdo	deb	eel	leu	ole	rlr	uod
bdr	ded	eeo	llb	oll	rlu	uoe
bdu	dee	eer	lld	olo	rob	uol
beb	del	eeu	lle	olr	rod	uoo
bed	deo	elb	lll	olu	roe	uor
bee	der	eld	llo	oob	rol	uou
bel	deu	ele	llr	ood	roo	urb
beo	dlb	ell	llu	ooe	ror	urd
ber	dld	elo	lob	ool	rou	ure
beu	dle	elr	lod	ooo	rrb	url
blb	dll	elu	loe	oor	rrd	uro
bld	dlo	eob	lol	oou	rre	urr
ble	dlr	eod	loo	orb	rrl	uru
bll	dlu	eoe	lor	ord	rro	uub
blo	dob	eol	lou	ore	rrr	uud
blr	dod	eoo	lrb	orl	rru	uue
blu	doe	eor	lrd	oro	rub	uul
bob	dol	eou	lre	orr	rud	uuo
bod	doo	erb	lrl	oru	rue	uur
boe	dor	erd	lro	oub	rul	uuu
bol	dou	ere	lrr	oud	ruo	
boo	drb	erl	lru	oue	rur	
bor	drd	ero	lub	oul	ruu	
bou	dre	err	lud	ouo	ubb	
brb	drl	eru	lue	our	ubd	
brd	dro	eub	lul	ouu	ube	
bre	drr	eud	luo	rbb	ubl	
brl	dru	eue	lur	rbd	ubo	
bro	dub	eul	luu	rbe	ubr	
brr	dud	euo	obb	rbl	ubu	
bru	due	eur	obd	rbo	udb	
bub	dul	euu	obe	rbr	udd	
bud	duo	lbb	obl	rbu	ude	
bue	dur	lbd	obo	rdb	udl	
bul	duu	lbe	obr	rdd	udo	
buo	ebb	lbl	obu	rde	udr	
bur	ebd	lbo	odb	rdl	udu	
buu	ebe	lbr	odd	rdo	ueb	
dbb	ebl	lbu	ode	rdr	ued	
dbd	ebo	ldb	odl	rdu	uee	
dbe	ebr	ldd	odo	reb	uel	

Table 2.1. Three-letter strings from the letters in *boulder.*

There are well over 1,000 three–letter words in the dictionary and only 35 possible three–letter words defined by *[b,o,u,l,d,e,r]* in Table 2.2. The *generate/filter strategy* requires us to consider only the 343 three–letter strings in Table 2.1. Most of these three–letter strings will not be English forms. They will be filtered out as not being in the dictionary. The *scan/recognize strategy* requires us to consider all of the thousands of forms in the dictionary; however, we will never have to consider any forms that are not English words.

bed	dub	leo	ore
bee	dud	lob	our
bob	due	lou	red
boo	duo	obo	rob
bub	eel	odd	rod
bud	ere	ode	roe
deb	err	old	rub
dee	led	ole	rue
doe	lee	orb	

Table 2.2. Three–letter words from the letters in *boulder*.

For the example here, the *generate/filter strategy* is more efficient and executes faster. If we consider problems with a wider range of letters, the *scan/recognize strategy* becomes more efficient. If we ask how many three–letter English words can be constructed from the first 18 letters of the alphabet *[a,b...p,q,r]*, then the number of possibilities generated as random combination is more than 10 with 25 zeros after it. Because this is larger than the number of three–letter words in the dictionary, it would require less searching to scan the dictionary and see if the entries could be constructed using the given letters than it would be to generate all possible three–letter sequences and filter out those that are not in the dictionary.

Any Prolog-type problem possesses a **logical side**, which requires us to specify the conditions that define the solution, and a **procedural side**, which requires specification of the steps to follow and alternatives to consider, in arriving at a solution. In writing a Prolog program, one must specify in meticulous detail the logical conditions that must be met by any possible answer. On the procedural side, however, one can often ignore considerations concerning how the search for alternatives will proceed. An essential part of Prolog – the **Prolog interpreter** – will in and of itself with no programming provide a strategy for considering alternatives. Only if you are dissatisfied with the procedural search strategy chosen by the Prolog interpreter must you program in considerations concerning procedural information. This leads to a sixth property:

- A Prolog-type problem must always have an answer that can be defined as a set of *logical conditions*, called **goals**, that any answer must meet. Any concerns about *procedures* (or *search strategies*) used to find the answer(s) are irrelevant to the defining of the set of possible answers and influence only the efficiency of the search and the order in which Prolog outputs the answer(s).

2.2. How to Read and Write In Prolog

A **Prolog program** consists of facts, relations among those facts, and queries about the facts and relations. In the following, each line in the left column is a fact written in grammatical Prolog notation. In all cases a Prolog fact ends with a period. The right column indicates how to read the notation in English.

For a fact of the form *x(y).*, one reads it: *y is an x.*

Prolog Statement	English Equivalent
x(y).	y is an x.
letter(a).	a is a letter.
letter(b).	b is a letter.
word(boy).	boy is a word.
word_spelling([b,o,y]).	[b,o,y] is a word_spelling.
fruit(apple).	apple is a fruit.
president(washington).	washington is a president.
girl(tracy).	tracy is a girl.
number(5).	5 is a number.
number(five).	five is a number.

The are three rules to observe in writing **a simple fact**:

- A fact cannot contain any capital letters anywhere. Hence, if we want to list a name like *Tess*, we must write it in lower case like *tess*.
- There can be no spaces anywhere. If we want to indicate a space, we will use an underline: *name(mary_louise_smith), word(eke_out)..,* but never **word(eke out), *name(mary lou smith).* We will put an asterisk (*) in front of any statement that is ungrammatical Prolog.

31

■   Every fact must end in a Period.

A **simple fact** is unanalyzable, or undecomposable, into smaller facts. It is written with no punctuation (commas, semicolons) except for the period, which must end any Prolog statement. A letter of the alphabet, being the smallest logical unit in our analysis, is a simple fact. A **complex fact** is a combination of simple facts and always contains punctuation (e.g., commas) in addition to the terminal period. A word, being analyzable into a sequence of letters, is a complex fact.

Whether a fact is simple or complex is relative to the problem being analyzed. A chemist analyzing compounds into their elements might consider the simple facts to be the atomic elements – *atom(carbon).*, *atom(oxygen).* – and the complex facts to be molecules – *molecule(carbon, oxygen).*, *molecule(carbon,oxygen,oxygen).*, *molecule(hydrogen,hydrogen,oxygen).* A physicist analyzing elements into their atomic parts might consider the simple facts to be nuclear particles – *particle(proton).*, *particle(electron).* – and the complex facts to be the atoms – *atom(proton,electron).*, *atom(proton, neutron,electron).*

In our dictionary, let us assume that all words are listed in their spelled form, that is, the dictionary contains *[g,i,r,l]* and not *girl*. Each word is listed in the dictionary as a fact: *word([g,i,r,l])*, *word([b,o,y])*, *word([s,u,e])*. We will also list parts of words in the dictionary. We will list **suffixes** such as *[t,i,o,n]* in *action, deduction* and *[l,y]* in *slowly, quickly*. We also list **prefixes** like *[p,r,e]* in *prenatal, prerevolutionary* and *[p,o,s,t]* in *postrevolutionary, postoperational.*

Prolog Statement	**English Equivalent**
word([m,a,n]).	[m,a,n] is a word.
word([o,p,t]).	[o,p,t] is a word.
word([t,e,n]).	[t,en] is a word.
suffix([t,i,o,n]).	[t,i,o,n] is a suffix.
suffix([l,y]).	[l,y] is a suffix.
prefix([p,r,e]).	[p,r,e] is a prefix.
prefix([p,o,s,t]).	[p,o,s,t] is a prefix.

One is free to select any name for any fact with a few exceptions. Prolog has some **reserved words** that it uses for its built-in functions: *write, name,* and *join* to indicate a few. You cannot define a fact of your own called *write, name,* or *join*. If you try to use a Prolog reserved word for a fact of your own, either Prolog will produce an error message or you will get an obviously incorrect response. Aside from some small restrictions on reserved names, you are free to call any fact by any name.

The following are all valid facts:

```
english_word(hello).
french_word(bonjour).
german_word(guten_tag).
names_of_first_grade_teacher(molly_alpert_jones).
word([b,o,y]).
word_spelling([b,o,y]).
spelled_out_word([b,o,y]).
pea_soup_recipe_from_the_old_country([b,u,t]).
planet_near_the_sun(peanut_butter).
```

These are all grammatical Prolog statements defining facts. It is another question as to whether they make any sense in any program.

Let us write a program to answer this question:

What are the three–letter words that can be constructed from the letters in *boulder: [b], [o], [u], [l], [d], [e], [r]*?

A Prolog program is usually broken into two parts and stored in two different files: a *database_file* and a *query_file*. The database_file is often large, and once it is programmed into Prolog, it rarely changes, for example, the dictionary of English. The query_file is usually much smaller than the database_file and varies depending on the questions we want to answer.

The **database_file** contains the simple and complex facts over which we will search for a solution. Throughout this book I will always present the database_file shaded inside of double lines. Assume our database is in a file – p0201 – called **database_letters_dictionary**. The database over which we will search for answers consists of the seven letters of *boulder* and all of the words in the English dictionary, including the words: *man, led, red, put, bed, only,* and *old.*

We can insert a **comment line** into any Prolog program. Any information typed between a slash+asterisk (/*) and an asterisk+slash (*/) on a line is ignored by Prolog. This provides a convenient way to indicate filenames, dates, and notes to ourselves about our programs.

The **query_file** – p0202 – contains one or more queries, in which a **query** states the boundary conditions that define which combinations and permutations of facts in the database constitute acceptable answers. We will always write the query_file inside of a shaded rectangle with no boundary lines. We define four queries: *possible_words_a/b/c/d.*

Prolog programs do not "execute" in the sense that programs in Basic, Pascal, Fortran, or Lisp "execute". There is no sense in which a line

```
/*      FILENAME:      p0201   database_letters_dictionary      */
/*                     Any text between these slash–asterisk symbols   */
/*                     will be ignored by the Prolog interpreter.  These   */
/*                     are called comment lines and can occur almost   */
/*                     anywhere.  Some examples are given below.   */

/*      simple facts:  A list of the letters of the word boulder.   */
letter(b).                     /*      a consonant   */
letter(o).                     /*      a vowel   */
letter(u).                                          /*      line x   */
letter(l).                                          /*      line y   */
letter(d).
letter(e).
letter(r).

/*      complex facts:  A list of the spellings of all   */
/*                      English Words, including:   */
word([m,a,n]).
word([o,l,d]).
word([p,u,t]).
word([l,e,d]).
word([r,e,d]).
word([b,e,d]).
word([o,n,l,y]).   /*      last word      */
```

of Prolog (with the exception of *write* and *print* commands, and the like) can be considered an instruction to "do this." Lines of Prolog code are *filters* to restrict possible answers, not *commands* to perform some action. A **query** is a list of goals such that when all goals are satisfied, Prolog can stop searching. A query is a list of conditions defining *when to stop* (or *where to direct*) a search rather than a set of steps indicating *how to perform* a search. Consider an analogy.

A husband and wife setting up an invitation list for their 50th anniversary party have a large database of friends, each one earmarked for numerous characteristics. The husband, having forgotten a name, asks: "What is the name of the man who plays golf and is married to the tall lawyer?" The wife offers names, "Joe Kolupke, Bob Steigler, Tom Choate." "No," says the husband, "he sells insurance and lives in New Jersey and raises tulips." The wife continues: "Herman Rickerman, Donald Duffus." "None of those. He played professional tennis and has a grandmother in Alaska." The wife continues: "Duane Ray, Bob Taris." "That"s the one,"

```
/*      FILENAME:     p0202          query_file              */

possible_words_a(A,B,C) :-           /*    the first query     */
          letter(A),letter(B),letter(C),
          word([A,B,C]).

possible_words_b(A,B,C) :-           /*    the second query    */
          word([A,B,C]),
          letter(A),letter(B),letter(C).

possible_words_c :-                  /*    the third query     */
          letter(A),letter(B),letter(C),
          word([A,B,C]),
          nl,write(A),write(B),write(C),
          fail.

possible_words_d :-                  /*    the fourth query    */
          word([A,B,C]),
          letter(A),letter(B),letter(C),
          nl,write(A),write(B),write(C),
          fail.
```

interrupts the husband. In this drama, the role of the Prolog interpreter is played by the wife. A **Prolog interpreter** will exhaustively enumerate all possible entries in the database. The husband stars as the query: He offers a set of conditions that narrow the search and eventually recognizes one of the possible names as the correct one. Let us now reverse roles. A woman working a crossword puzzle defines a query with two conditions. She asks her husband for a five–letter word meaning *bird*. He starts recalling words from memory: "*robin, eagle.*" The lady adds: "*The last letter is k.*" The husband says: "*hawk.*" His wife informs him that *hawk* has only four letters and fails the first condition. He offers *shark* and is informed that this fails the second goal. He mumbles "*hawk,*" which causes his wife to suspect he is in a loop. He continues, "*stork,*" and his wife stops him, "*That is an acceptable answer since it satisfies both goals of the query.*"

Assume that we have loaded the file **database_letters_dictionary** into Prolog. This constrains Prolog to only search over combinations of the letters *[b], [o], [u], [l], [d], [e],* and *[r].* The following English sentence defines the conditions any string of letters *[A,B,C]* must have to be an answer to our problem.

[A,B,C] is a possible_word if
    A is a letter defined in the database and
    B is a letter defined in the database and
    C is a letter defined in the database and
    [A,B,C] is a word defined in the data base.

This is almost a Prolog statement.

Prolog is an abbreviation for *Programming in Logic* because, in most cases, Prolog is trying to find if some statement is true or false or is trying to find some combination of variables that makes a statement true. A Prolog **clause** has a general head-condition-body form and always can be understood as stating: *The head is true if the conditions in the body are true.* The symbol composed of a colon and dash (:-) always means *if*. A comma (,) always means *and*. A capital letter is a **variable** that can have any value defined in the database.

Basic Prolog Clause Format

HEAD	CONDITION	BODY
x is a y	**if**	**(goal1 is true) and (goal2 is true) and...**
y(x)	**:-**	**goal1,goal2,goal3,...**

Consider this Prolog statement, the first query in the *query_file*. In our simple example, each query is a single clause. In more complex examples, a query might consist of several clauses.

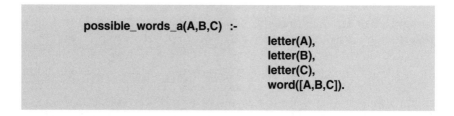

possible_words_a(A,B,C) :-
                  letter(A),
                  letter(B),
                  letter(C),
                  word([A,B,C]).

This is read:

possible_words_a is true for the values A, B, and C if
    A is a letter in the database and
    B is a letter in the database and
    C is a letter in the database and
    [A,B,C] is a word in the database.

Consider the second query in the query_file:

```
1.      possible_words_b(A,B,C) :-
2.                                  word([A,B,C],
3.                                  letter(A),
4.                                  letter(B),
5.                                  letter(C).
```

This is read:

1.   **possible_words_b is true for the values A, B, and C if**
2.   **[A,B,C] is a word in the database,**
3.   **A is a letter in the database and**
4.   **B is a letter in the database and**
5.   **C is a letter in the database.**

For illustration, assume that the only words in the dictionary are those listed in *database_letters_dictionary*: *man, led, red, put, bed, only,* and *old.* The **Prolog interpreter,** which is sometimes called the **Prolog machine** or just **Prolog,** will by itself produce all possible permutations and combinations of facts in the database. The query *possible_words_b* operates to constrain the Prolog interpreter as follows.

Suppose Prolog sets $A = b$, $B = b$, and $C = b$. In this case, lines 3–5 are satisfied (or rather we say are *true*), but line 2 is *false* because there is no entry *word([b,b,b])*. The goal in line 2 fails, hence the head, (line 1) fails, and Prolog produces another combination.

Because the Prolog interpreter tries all combinations, it will eventually set $A = m$, $B = a$, and $C = n$. Because *word([m,a,n]).* is in the database, line 2 is true. Line 3 is false because the database has no simple fact *letter(m).* Lines 3–5 are false because *m, a* and *n* are not letters in *boulder* and hence not in the database. Because lines 3–5 fail, the head – line 1 – fails and Prolog tries some new combination of letters.

Suppose the Prolog interpreter sets A = *o*, B = *l*, and C = *d*. Because all lines of code in the body of the statement – 2–5 – are true, the entire statement is true for the values Prolog assigned to the variables. At this point the Prolog interpreter will print its findings to the screen ($A = o$, $B = l$, $C = d$) and stop. As will be shown, there are various ways to tell Prolog to **backtrack,** that is, to keep searching, to go back and try to find some other combination of facts in the database that will satisfy the query. Let us assume we tell Prolog to look for more combinations.

Prolog might set *A = p, B = u,* and *C = t.* This combination satisfies line 2 because *word([p,u,t]).* is in the database. Line 4 is true because *[u]* is a letter in the database. However, lines 3 and 5 are false because neither of the letters *[p]* or *[t]* is in the database. Because some of the tests in the body of the query statement fail, the statement is false.

A test in a Prolog statement is often called a **goal**. So *letter(A)* is a *goal*, and *word([A,B,C])* is a *goal*. When *A = b, B = e,* and *C = d,* then all goals in the query *possible_words_c* are true and the query is true. Normally, at this point Prolog stops or pauses. When *A = p, B = u,* and *C = t,* some goals are true and others are false with the result that *possible_words_c* is false and Prolog must go back and try to find another set of letters.

Prolog will arrive at the settings *A = l, B = e,* and *C = d.* Line 2 is satisfied because the database contains *word([l,e,d]).* Lines 3–5 are true because *l, e,* and *d* are letters in the database. Because the body is true, the head is true, so Prolog prints out its findings (*A = l, B = e, C = d*) and pauses. If we signal Prolog to backtrack for more alternatives, it will continue to search for new combinations. If we do not wish Prolog to backtrack, the Prolog interpreter will stop.

A Prolog **statement** is anything that ends in a period. A statement can be a simple or complex fact in the database, or it can be a query. A **goal** is any fact between two commas. A statement, particularly a query, is composed of goals. The following are statements:

letter([a]).	simple fact
word([d,u,ck]).	complex fact
entry(A,B,C) :- word([A,B,C]).	clause (head–condition–body format)

One basic property of Prolog programming is the **unordered goals condition:**

> **Subject to a few restrictions, if the goals in a Prolog clause are separated by commas (i.e., *and*), then the goals can be shuffled to occur in any order with no change in the *truth value*. That is, Prolog will produce the same answers for each permutation of goals.**

A Prolog query defining possible words is composed of goals, in which each goal defines some condition that the answer must meet. The order in which the goals occur is irrelevant in determining the set of valid answers. All of the following Prolog statements will give the same answers as the statements in the file *query_file*.

```
poss_word_1(A,B,C)  :-  letter(A),word([A,B,C]),letter(B),letter(C).
poss_word_2(A,B,C)  :-  letter(C),letter(B),word([A,B,C]),letter(A).
poss_word_3(A,B,C)  :-  letter(C),letter(A), word([A,B,C]),letter(B).
poss_word_4(A,B,C)  :-  letter(B),letter(C),letter(A),word([A,B,C]).
```

Prolog has several built–in functions, including *nl, write,* and *fail.* In order to print out our results, we need *nl* and *write.* The statement *write(A)* will output to a printer (or to the computer screen) the value of *A* Prolog has selected. The statement *nl* causes the printing operation to skip to the left margin of the next line; *nl* is like hitting the carriage return. The function *fail* causes Prolog to keep searching for alternatives until none are left. (I will discuss *write, nl,* and *fail* later.)

Consider the third query in *query_file*:

1.	possible_words_c :-	/*	head	*/
2.	letter(A),letter(B),letter(C),	/*	test	*/
3.	word([A,B,C]),	/*	test	*/
4.	nl,	/*	output	*/
5.	write(A),	/*	output	*/
6.	write(B),	/*	output	*/
7.	write(C),	/*	output	*/
8	fail.	/*	loop	*/

This is read:

1.	possible_words_c is true if
2.	A is a letter in the database and
2.	B is a letter in the database and
2.	C is a letter in the database and
3.	[A,B,C] is a word in the database and
4.	Prolog moves the printer to the next line and
5.	Prolog writes the value of A and
6.	Prolog writes the value of B and
7.	Prolog writes the value of C and
8.	Prolog goes back and looks for another combination of A, B and C.

The Prolog program, consisting of the information in the file *database_letters_dictionary* and any one of the query statements given in *query_file*, defines the possible answers to the question: What are the three–letter words that can be constructed from the letters in *boulder*?

When we look at a **Prolog program** (a *database_file* and a *query_file*) consisting of several lines of code, we should not think that Prolog "runs" the program and sequentially "executes" the lines of code. Lines of Prolog code are not instructions on *how to search*, they are conditions specifying *where to search* and the conditions under which Prolog can *stop* its built–in search routines. The **Prolog interpreter**, which interprets the Prolog program, does one thing on its own with little help from your program: The Prolog interpreter will list every possible item in the database_file that might potentially satisfy the conditions defined in the query_file. Your database_file tells Prolog *where to look* for possible answers. Your query_file tells it *how to recognize an answer* and hence *when to stop*. The next section investigates the mechanical details of loading and running Prolog on a UNIX machine.

2.3. Four Steps to Running a Prolog Program

We assume that the user has one of the three computer configurations in Figure 2.1. Either there is a computer/terminal connected to a large computer that is running UNIX, or there is a version of public domain Prolog running on an IBM PC–compatible computer or a Macintosh. These possibilities are the extremes of the cost spectrum for a normal user. This discussion is valid for any Prolog on any computer, but all of these examples are taken from these three configurations.

A Prolog session on any computer involves the four steps indicated in Figure 2.2. These steps are essentially the same for any Prolog on any system. We assume that the operating system prompt is % and that the Prolog prompt is I ?-. The text in **bold** must be typed in by the user. The text not in bold is the computer response.

The **flavor_file**, loaded in line 2, is optional in any session. After you have used Prolog for a while, you will find that you are using some Prolog facts and relations all the time. In general, most of the facts and relations in a flavor_file contain special commands to operate the printers, disk drives, and devices connected to the computer. (I discuss flavor_files in appendix III.)

I will always indicate a Session on the computer by enclosing the text in a **Session box**, a single line box surrounding unshaded text. Session 2.1 indicates the steps involved in loading and using the files developed in Section 2.2 to solve the problem: What are the three–letter words one can form using the letters in the word *boulder*?

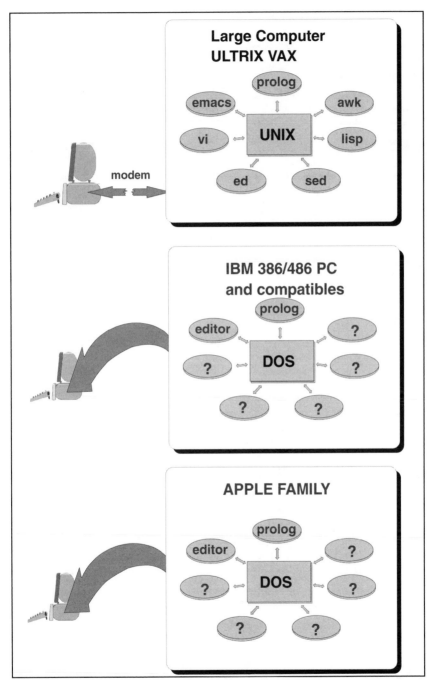

Figure 2.1. Three possible computer configurations.

```
1.    % prolog
2.    C-Prolog version 1.5

3.    | ?- [database_letters_dictionary].
4.    database_letters_dictionary consulted 784 bytes
              0.0666667 sec.
5.    yes

6.    | ?- [query_file].
7.    query_file consulted 800 bytes 0.0333334 sec.
8.    yes

9.    | ?- possible_words_c.
10.   bed
11.   old
12.   led
13.   red
14.   no

15.   | ?- possible_words_d.
16.   old
17.   led
18.   red
19.   bed
20.   no

21.   | ?- cntl-d
22.   [ Prolog execution halted ]
23.   %
```

Session 2.1. Using C–Prolog under a UNIX operating system.

Figure 2.3 indicates that the **Session_file** (in UNIX called a **script_file**) contains all of the information that appears on the screen of the computer. The arrows to the **bold** type indicate this is user input from the keyboard.

Consider Session 2.1. At line 1 in response to the UNIX system prompt %, the user types **prolog**. This causes UNIX to load the Prolog interpreter, indicated by line 2. The Prolog interpreter takes over the computer and displays the Prolog prompt I ?-, line 3. In UNIX, you must type **prolog** in lower case letters, **Prolog** or **PROLOG** are errors.

The user must load the Prolog program files which have been written to solve the problem: p0201 and p0202.

On line 3, the user types the filename of the *database_file* in square brackets, which is the instruction to Prolog to load the file named inside the square brackets: **database_letters_dictionary**. Prolog then responds –

42

LOAD PROLOG

1. % prolog   At the system prompt, type prolog to load the language.

2. |?- [flavor].   Load a file of your personal prolog information.

LOAD THE PROLOG PROGRAM FILES

3. |?-[database_file].   At the prolog prompt, type the name of the database file in square brackets to load the database file.

4. |?- [query_file].   At the prolog prompt, type the name of the query file in square brackets to load the query file.

ENTER USER QUERIES FROM TERMINAL

5. |?- query_*yes/no*.   From the terminal pose *yes/no* questions.

6. |?- query_*wh-*.   From the terminal pose *wh*-questions.

END PROLOG - RETURN TO OPERATING SYSTEM

7. |?- cntl-d   Exit prolog and return to operating system by entering control-d.

8. %   Computer responds with operating system prompt.

Figure 2.2. The four steps of any Prolog Session.

line 4 – with information about the file size and loading times, and line 5, with a *yes* indicating that the loading operation was totally successful. If Prolog could not find the file or could only load part of the file, the response would have been *no*.

On line 6, the user enters the name of the **query_file** inside of square brackets. Prolog responds with the load time and a *yes* indicating success.

The query_file contains four different queries: *possible_words_a/b/c/d*. We will run only versions *c* and *d*. To initiate a search defined by a query, the user need only type the name of the query, followed, of course, by a period.

On line 9, the user enters the name of a query, **possible_words_c.**, in response to the Prolog prompt. Lines 10–13 indicate the words Prolog finds in the database meeting the conditions defined by the query. On line 14 the Prolog interpreter responds *no*, indicating that there are no more words in the database meeting the conditions defined by the query.

On line 15, the user enters the name of another query, **possible_words_d.** Prolog responds with examples on lines 16–19 and says *no* on line 20 indicating there are no more possible answers.

The user stops the Prolog interpreter and returns to the UNIX operating system by entering a control–d. A **control–d (cntl–d)** is sent to the computer by holding down the *control key* and simultaneously pressing lower case *d*.

The two query functions – *possible_words_c* and *possible_words_d* – are **logically equivalent** and have the **same truth value**, both of which mean that they give the same set of words as the answer to the problem. Although they are the same logically, they are not the same pragmatically. They give the same words, but in different order, for instance, *bed* – line 10 – is the first response of *possible_words_c*, but the last response of *possible_words_d* – line 19.

I spend considerable time discussing why two logically equivalent Prolog programs present the data in different orders. For the present, however, I am only concerned with whether or not a program gives the desired valid response (the true set of words meeting the conditions). For present purposes, one query is as good (valid, legitimate, true) as the next.

2.4.   Running Shareware Prolog on an IBM PC

Appendix I contains information about obtaining and installing Prolog–2 on an IBM PC. We assume that you have installed Prolog–2 on

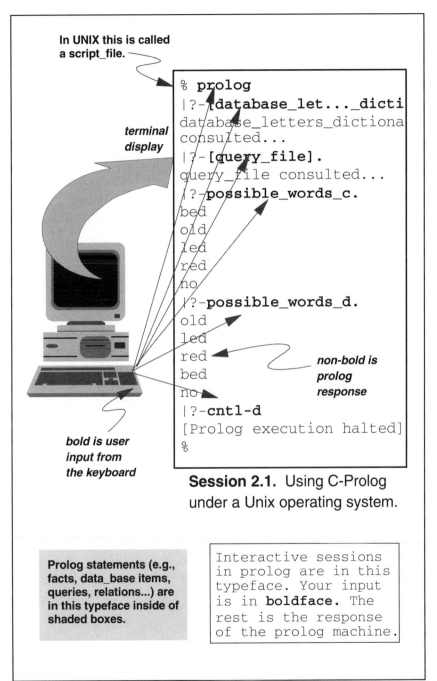

In UNIX this is called a script_file.

terminal display

```
% prolog
|?-[database_let..._dicti
database_letters_dictiona
consulted...
|?-[query_file].
query_file consulted...
|?-possible_words_c.
bed
old
led
red
no
|?-possible_words_d.
old
led
red
bed
no
|?-cntl-d
[Prolog execution halted]
%
```

non-bold is prolog response

bold is user input from the keyboard

Session 2.1. Using C-Prolog under a Unix operating system.

Prolog statements (e.g., facts, data_base items, queries, relations...) are in this typeface inside of shaded boxes.

```
Interactive sessions
in prolog are in this
typeface. Your input
is in boldface. The
rest is the response
of the prolog machine.
```

Figure 2.3. The Session (script) file is the screen contents.

45

your C drive in a directory called *Prolog2*. On your IBM PC, when you are in the Prolog2 directory, you should have the files in Session 2.2. This display is taken from the computer system at New York University which has over 330 IBM PCs on this network. The display may vary from one installation to the next.

```
C:\Prolog2> dir
 Volume in drive C has no label
 Volume Serial Number is 1947-8309
 Directory of C:\Prolog2

 .              <DIR>       11-01-92   1:55p
 ..             <DIR>       11-01-92   1:55p
 ESLPDPRO ZIP     153600 09-19-92   1:47p
 DEC10    PRM       7552 01-30-91   8:00a
 DEBUG    PRM      11520 01-30-91   8:00a
 EDIT     BAT        640 01-30-91   8:00a
 EFILE    PRM      24576 01-30-91   8:00a
 ERROR    PRM       5888 01-30-91   8:00a
 GRULES   PRM       2048 01-30-91   8:00a
 INT      PRM       1792 01-30-91   8:00a
 READ     ME        2432 01-30-91   8:00a
 PRETTY   PRM       6016 01-30-91   8:00a
 SYSMESS  PRM       5376 01-30-91   8:00a
 SYSTED   PRM      11776 01-30-91   8:00a
 TOP      PRM       5376 01-30-91   8:00a
 WINDOW   PRM      37888 01-30-91   8:00a
 Prolog2  EXE     180208 01-30-91   2:04p

      17 file(s)       458833 bytes
                     19568640 bytes free

C:\Prolog2>
```

Session 2.2. The Prolog2 directory on a PC.

To start the Prolog interpreter, type **prolog2** at the system prompt, which in DOS 6.0 under our recommended configuration is *C:\Prolog2>*. The screen should present the information in Session 2.3. On the IBM using Prolog–2 it is possible to type **prolog2**, **Prolog2**, or **PROLOG2** since the IBM operating system is not case sensitive. Once Prolog is running, however, a capital is always a variable.

In Session 2.3 we hit the **RETURN key** and the Prolog prompt appears (l ?-). On some IBM PC's, the prompt appears as (?-) without the vertical line. We follow the instructions on the screen and type **noadvert.** to eliminate the display of the advertisement in future sessions.

46

```
C:\Prolog2> prolog2

Loading from C:\Prolog2\PD.MNU   TOP.PRM

Welcome to Public Domain Prolog-2.  This is an
implementation of Clocksin and Mellish Prolog complete
with most of the standard additions, such as the
debugger and the grammar rule package.  Documentation
is available from bookshops, in two volumes:  "The
Prolog-2 User Guide" and "The Prolog-2 Encyclopedia",
published by Intellect Ltd and Ablex Publishing Corp.

There are three other versions of Prolog-2 for the PC,
Personal, Programmer, and Professional Plus, as well as
80386, VMS and UNIX versions.  These include extra
features, such as an integral editor, a fast
tokenisation system, interfaces to C, Pascal and
FORTRAN and a compiler; the complete package is
documented in the books.  The upgrade to Personal
Prolog-2 costs #110 (or #49 if you buy the books
separately).

For further details contact
        Expert Systems Ltd
        Unit 12
        7 West Way
        Oxford OX2 OJB
        Telephone: +44 865 794474
        Fax: + 44 865 250270

When you are tired of reading this screen type
'noadvert' to get rid of it.
Typing 'advert' will still display it.
Press any key to continue...
RETURN

        Prolog-2   V2.35 PDE Press F1 for help

|?- noadvert.
|?- halt.

Maximum memory usage

Local stack:              1158
Global stack:            10172
Heap:                    97890
Atoms:                     n/a
Elapsed time        1m        12.39 seconds
Garbage collection             2.17 seconds

C:\Prolog2>
```

Session 2.3. First time running Prolog2 on a PC.

```
C:\Prolog2> prolog2

        Prolog-2  V2.35   PDE
Insert          Press F1 for help

|?- F1
Full versions of Prolog-2 have context-sensitive help
on all predicates.  In this version this screen gives a
quick summary of options.

When you see the prompt ?- you may enter a query to
Prolog; a query must be a Prolog term and must end with
a full stop.  A query asks whether something is true,
but some queries, such as write('Hello World') are
actually commands that cause an action to be performed.

To add clauses to Prolog, enter the characters [user].
at the ?- prompt.  This puts you in consult mode,
indicated by a prompt C:  Once you have typed in this
clauses you type ^Z to return to query mode.
You can also consult clauses from a file by entering
the name of the file in square brackets,  [myprog].

The F3 and F4 keys allow you access to previous
commands, which you can edit.  The F1 key gives this
message.  Other function keys are not useful in this
version.  Break allows you to interrupt whatever Prolog
is doing.  If from a break or error you find yourself
in a break state (indicated by a number before the
prompt) use ^Z or abort to get out.

RETURN

|?- write('Hello World').
Hello World
yes

|?-halt.

Maximum Memory Usage

Local stack:                        1159
Global stack:                      19231
Heap:                              99466
Atoms:                               n/a

Elapsed time            1m      12.39 seconds
Garbage collection               2.32 seconds

C:\Prolog2>
```

Session 2.4. Using *help* and *write* on PC Prolog2.

To exit Prolog2 we type **halt.** Prolog2 displays some information about memory usage and elapsed times before returning to the system prompt *C:\Prolog2>*.

In Session 2.4, we type **prolog2** at the DOS prompt to invoke the interpreter. Instead of typing a Prolog statement, we press the **F1 function key**. This displays the *help screen*. We hit the **return key** to clear the help screen and get the Prolog prompt. In response to the Prolog prompt we type **write('Hello World')**. Prolog writes *Hello World* to the screen. There are two ways to exit Prolog–2. We can type **halt.** or we can send a control–Z. A **cntl–Z**, often symbolized by ^Z, is sent to the interpreter by holding down the *control key* and typing the letter Z. On many IBM PC's **cntl–Z** has no effect and you must use **halt** to exit.

Filenames for Prolog–2, see p0203 and p0204, can have at most eight letters and a three–letter extension. All programs to be loaded into Prolog–2 must end in the extension *.PRO*. The following are legitimate filenames for Prolog files: *A.PRO, BCD.PRO, SPUDS.PRO, DATABASE.PRO, QUERY.PRO*.

```
/*      FILENAME:      p0203   databse1.pro              */
/*      This file must be an ASCII DOS text file.        */
/*      Any text between these slash-asterisk symbols will be */
/*      ignored by the Prolog interpreter.  These are called */
/*      comment lines and can occur almost anywhere.     */

/*      simple facts: A list of the letters of the word boulder.  */
letter(b).
letter(o).
letter(u).
letter(l).
letter(d).
letter(e).
letter(r).

/*      complex facts: A list of the spellings of all     */
/*              English Words, including:                 */
word([m,a,n]).
word([o,l,d]).
word([p,u,t]).
word([l,e,d]).
word([r,e,d]).
word([b,e,d]).
word([o,n,l,y]).
```

All Prolog programs must be in ASCII, ANSI, or DOS text format. If you use a word processor, like Word Perfect or Word, you must save the file as an ASCII or DOS text file.

```
/*      Program:        p0204              query1.pro          */
/*              This must be an ASCII DOS text file.           */

possible_words_a(A,B,C) :-                  /*    the first query     */
                letter(A),letter(B),letter(C),
                word([A,B,C]).

possible_words_b(A,B,C) :-                  /*    the second query    */
                word([A,B,C]),
                letter(A),letter(B),letter(C).

possible_words_c :-                         /*    the third query     */
                letter(A),letter(B),letter(C),
                word([A,B,C]),
                nl,write(A),write(B),write(C),
                fail.

possible_words_d :-                         /*    the fourth query    */
                word([A,B,C]),
                letter(A),letter(B),letter(C),
                nl,write(A),write(B),write(C),
                fail.
```

The two files – *databse1.pro* (p0203) and *query1.pro* (p0204) – are the solution to the problem: *What three–letter words can be formed from the letters in "boulder"?* We run the programs in Session 2.5.

```
C:\Prolog2> dir *.pro

      Volume in drive C has no label
      Volume Serial Number is 1947-8309
      Directory of C:\Prolog2

QUERY1        PRO    561    12-02-92      10:12a
DATABSE1      PRO    206    12-02-92      10:09a
              2 file(s)           767 bytes
                          19456000 bytes free


C:Prolog2> prolog2

      Prolog-2   V2.35   PDE
Insert
Press F1 for help

?- [databse1].
databse1 consulted.
?- [query1].
query1 consulted.

?- possible_words_c.
bed
old
led
red
no

?- possible_words_d.
old
led
red
bed
no

?- halt.

Maximum memory usage

Local stack:        426
Global stack:       10172
Heap:               91062
Atoms:              n/a

Elapsed time        3m     6.30 seconds
Garbage collection         2.56 seconds

C:\Prolog2>
```

Session 2.5. Executing programs in PC Prolog2.

chapter 3

HOW TO
LOAD, RUN, AND EDIT
A PROLOG PROGRAM

A logic program is a set of axioms, or rules, defining relationships between objects. A computation of a logic program is a deduction of consequences of the program. A program defines a set of consequences, which is its meaning. The art of logic programming is constructing concise and elegant programs that have the desired meaning.

Leon Sterling and Ehud Shapiro, 1986
The Art of Prolog

3.1   The Prolog Interpreter and Work Space

Figure 3.1. dissects a Prolog session into its functional components. When you type **prolog** at the UNIX prompt, this starts the **Prolog language program**, represented as the large rectangular box. This program, called C–Prolog on the UNIX machine and Prolog–2 on the IBM PC, sets up three different areas: The *Prolog interpreter*, the *user file space*, and the *user workspace*. In some Prolog manuals *workspace* is a single word, and in others it is two words *work space*. We use the two interchangeably. The workspace is broken into various types of memory storage areas called *stacks, buffers, garbage*, and almost all of the errors that can appear on the screen complain about the state of one or more of these memory storage areas.

Rarely do any error messages occur when you type **prolog** to load the Prolog language. If you encounter any error messages it is likely that you have not installed Prolog correctly on your machine. If you are using C–Prolog over a modem connection, you may have problems with your terminal program.

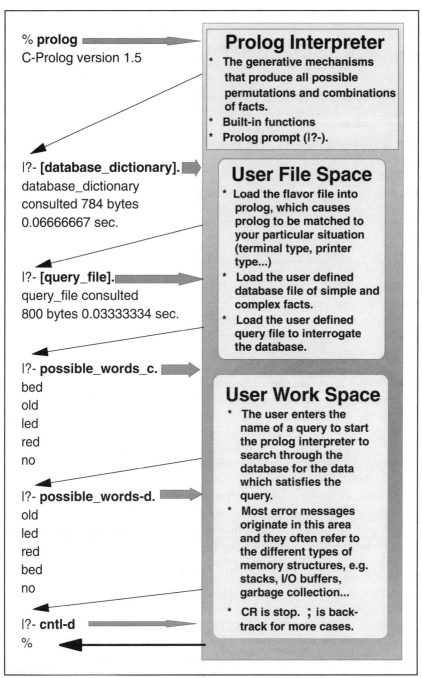

% **prolog**
C-Prolog version 1.5

Prolog Interpreter
* **The generative mechanisms that produce all possible permutations and combinations of facts.**
* **Built-in functions**
* **Prolog prompt (I?-).**

I?- **[database_dictionary].**
database_dictionary
consulted 784 bytes
0.06666667 sec.

User File Space
* **Load the flavor file into prolog, which causes prolog to be matched to your particular situation (terminal type, printer type...)**
* **Load the user defined database file of simple and complex facts.**
* **Load the user defined query file to interrogate the database.**

I?- **[query_file].**
query_file consulted
800 bytes 0.03333334 sec.

I?- **possible_words_c.**
bed
old
led
red
no

User Work Space
* **The user enters the name of a query to start the prolog interpreter to search through the database for the data which satisfies the query.**
* **Most error messages originate in this area and they often refer to the different types of memory structures, e.g. stacks, I/O buffers, garbage collection...**

I?- **possible_words-d.**
old
led
red
bed
no

* **CR is stop. ; is back-track for more cases.**

I?- **cntl-d**
%

Figure 3.1. A functional view of the Prolog machine.

One can avoid a lot of potential problems by never using any of these symbols as parts of names of variables, facts, and queries: \, /, *, ?, -. Also avoid using the comma, period, semicolon, and other punctuation symbols unless needed. If you use names like *nouns/definite, verbs\stative, adj?4, *?\verb-fin*ite* you are composing your own obituary. The underline never causes problems, so names like *nouns_definite, participle_passive, a_b_cd_c* will make your life simpler.

The **Prolog interpreter** contains: (a) the **generative mechanisms** that produce all possible permutations and combinations of facts, (b) the **built–in functions** with reserved names (*write, nl, name...*), and (c) the **Prolog conventions** such as: I ?- is the prompt, *[file].* is the loader, comma means *and*, semicolon means *or*, colon + dash (*:-*) means *if*.

The **user file space** is a section of the Prolog interpreter in which the user can store the information in the *flavor_file*, the *database_file*, and the *query_file*. After the files have been loaded, a built–in function, **listing.**, will output to the screen the Prolog representation of the loaded files. This function, although prized by experts, intimidates beginners. Because the Prolog representation of your files is rather complicated, the listing of the user file space is unilluminating and daunting for a first–time user. One can encounter a number of different error messages while loading user files. The most common are *"out of memory"* messages. Most error messages are understandable and appeal to common sense, for example *"file not found."*

The **user workspace** is the portion of the Prolog interpreter in which the combinations and permutations generated by Prolog are tested against the conditions on possible answers defined in your queries. Error messages here are usually few and far between, and when an error message appears, it is often unintelligible to the beginning user. My favorite is: *"You are thrashing in the garbage collector."*

After you gain some familiarity with Prolog, most error messages from the user workspace make perfect sense. For instance, Prolog uses various kinds of memory structures, and often the error message tells you which type of memory is currently suffering, such as *stack overflow* or *out of stack space during execution* indicates that there is not enough stack memory (see Session 3.4). Sometimes you can remedy the error message by modifying your program. Other times, you may have to go to the computer store and buy more memory chips. The main indication of error is that the computer produces no output. This strongly suggests that the Prolog interpreter is in a *loop*, that is, the program is testing the same combinations over and over (see Session 3.5.) Loops constitute a particular tragedy because Prolog can take a long time to produce any output even when all goes fine. There are several ways to see what is happening in the user workspace, mainly *breakpoints* and *trace*. I discuss these tools in Appendix IV.

USER FILE SPACE ERROR MESSAGES appear during the loading of Prolog programs. Let us consider some typical examples (see p0301).

```
/*      Program:       p0301          query.one              */
/*             Notice this program name contains a period.   */
/*             This means it must be loaded between quotes.   */


poss_word_1(A,B,C)  :-  letter(A),word([A,B,C]),letter(B),letter(C).
poss_word_2(A,B,C)  :-  letter(C),letter(B),word([A,B,C]),letter(A).
poss_word_3(A,B,C)  :-  letter(C),letter(A), word([A,B,C]),letter(B).
poss_word_4(A,B,C)  :-  letter(B),letter(C),letter(B),word([A,B,C]).
```

Assume we have a file called *query.one*, p0301, in our directory. Referring to Session 3.1, if we make a mistake in the name and try to load *query_one*, we will get the error message on line 4, *The file query_one*

```
1.     % prolog
2.     C-Prolog version 1.5

3.     | ?- [query_one].

4.     ! The file query_one does not exist.
5.     yes

6.     | ?- [query.one].

7.     ***Syntax error***
8.     [query.
9.     **here**
10.    one].

11.    | ?- ['query.one'].

12.    query.one consulted 484 bytes 0.0333334 sec.
13.    yes

14.    | ?- cntl-d
15.    [ Prolog execution halted ]
16.    %
```

Session 3.1. Errors loading programs into user file space.

55

does not exist. If we try to load *query.one* by using the command **[query.one].**, as in line 6, we will get the error on lines 7–10. The problem is that the period between *query* and *one* is understood to end the Prolog statement. In order to load any filename that contains a period (or any punctuation), we must enclose the filename in single quotes, **['query.one'].**, as in line 11.

Each of the database files, *bad_news_1/2/3*, p0302 – p0304, contains an error. The simple fact *letter([o])* is missing a period. The simple fact *Letter([o]).* illegally begins with a capital. Any capital is a variable, not a fact. In *bad_news_3*, there is a mismatch of parentheses and brackets.

```
/*      Program:       p0302            bad_news_1        */
/*               Notice the missing period on the second fact.   */

letter([b]).
letter([o])
letter([u]).
```

```
/*      Program:       p0303            bad_news_2        */
/*               Notice the capital on the second fact.          */
letter([b]).
Letter([o]).
letter([u]).
```

```
/*      Program:       p0304            bad_news_3        */
/*               Notice the mismatched parentheses               */
/*                       and brackets.                           */

word([r,a,t).
word(p,i,g]).
word[a,n,t].
word([d,o,g]).
```

Session 3.2 shows that the Prolog interpreter detects each of these errors while trying to load the file.

```
1.      % prolog
2.      C-Prolog version 1.5

3.      | ?- [p0302].

4.      ***Syntax error***
5.      letter([o]) letter
6.      **here**
7.      ([u]).
8.      bad_news_1 consulted 80 bytes 1.98682e-08 sec.
9.      yes

10.     | ?- [p0303].

11.     ***Syntax error***
12.     Letter
13.     **here**
14.     ([o]).
15.     bad_news_2 consulted 88 bytes 5.16573e-08 sec.
16.     yes

17.     | ?- [p0304].

18.     ***Syntax error***
19.     word([r,a,t
20.     **here**
21.     ).

22.     ***Syntax error***
23.     word(p,i,g
24.     **here**
25.     ]).

26.     ***Syntax error***
27.     word
28.     **here**
29.     [a,n,t]).

30.     ***Syntax error***
31.     word([d,o,g
32.     **here**
33.     )].
34.     bad_news_3 consulted 80 bytes 7.94729e-09 sec.
35.     yes

36.     | ?- cntl-d
37.     [ Prolog execution halted ]
38.     %
```

Session 3.2. Punctuation errors loading files into user file space.

The error messages are usually interpretable. Line 4 indicates an error has been detected. Line 5 is the line Prolog found indigestible. Line 6, **here**, indicates the point at which Prolog choked on the line. The **here** does not mean that the error is at this point, and, in general, the error is usually somewhere just before the **here**. In this case, the error is that there is no period after the first fact, and hence, is quite before the **here**. It is worth studying the error messages in Session 3.2 to help you recognize errors in your own programs.

The truly insidious errors are those that the Prolog interpreter cannot detect (see p0305). These are cases in which the statements are grammatical Prolog and all punctuation is correct.

```
/*       Program:        p0305           worst_news          */
/*               These will all load normally, but some are not     */
/*               formatted correctly to be dictionary entries.      */
/*               We require a dictionary entry to have each letter   */
/*               separated by commas.                               */

word([do,g]).
word([C,a,t]).
word([p_i_g]).
word([bug]).
word(fly).
word([r,a,t]).
word([a,n,t]).
word([p,u,p]).
```

The problems arise because the statements do not match the requirements of the program. In our program, all words are in the dictionary according to their spelling. Our entry for *antidisestablishmentarianism* would be:

word([a,n,t,i,d,i,s,e,s,t,a,b,l,i,s,h,m,e,n,t,a,r,i,a,n,i,s,m]).

For other programs, one might enter words broken into syllables:

word([anti,dis,est,ab,lish,ment,arian,ism]).

For complex words, one might indicate how the word is broken into prefixes (*anti, dis*), suffixes (*ment, ari,an, ism*), and a stem (*establish*):

58

word([anti,dis,establish,ment,ari,an,ism]).

For compound words, the lexical entry might indicate how the word is broken into components:

word([black,board]).

Some words that consist of two parts (*look up, eke out, fritter away...*) might be indicated in the database with an underline:

word([fritter_away]).

Each of these forms is a valid grammatical Prolog fact.

The program we have written to find all the three–letter words that can be formed from the letters in *boulder* requires all words to be spelled out with each letter separated by commas and all the letters between square brackets. In the file *worst_news*, p0305, only the words *rat, ant*, and *pup* have acceptable entries. The worst type of error often involves entries like those in *worst_news*, which load properly but which are not formatted correctly for the program. Session 3.3 indicates no errors during loading.

```
1.      % prolog
2.      C-Prolog version 1.5

3.      | ?- [p0305].
4.      worst_news consulted 484 bytes 0.0333333 sec.
5.      yes

6.      | ?- cntl-d
7.      [ Prolog execution halted ]
8.      %
```

Session 3.3. No errors loading incorrectly formatted data.

There are other errors given by the Prolog interpreter while loading the user file space, but these cover the ones most likely to be encountered.

USER WORKSPACE ERROR MESSAGES appear while Prolog is searching for answers to a query. The main error is looping. The Prolog interpreter is in a **loop** if in order to find the answer to query A it must answer query B, and in order to answer query B it must answer query A.

The file *origin_query_1*, p0306, presents a fine example of a loop.

```
/*      Program:      p0306            origin_query1       */
/*                    Query to resolve issue of which came first  */

chicken(X)      :-      egg(Y).
egg(Y)          :-      chicken(X).
```

The first statement says:

> chicken(X) :- egg(Y).   (1)
> X is a chicken if Y is an egg.

The second statement says:

> egg(Y) :- chicken(X).   (2)
> Y is an egg if X is a chicken.

When we query, **chicken(X).**, *Is X a chicken?*, as in Session 3.4, the Prolog interpreter tests to find the conditions under which *X is a chicken* is true. Statement 1 says to first check if Y is an egg. In checking statement 2 to verify if Y is an egg, Prolog again tries to find if X is a chicken and returns to statement 1. This is a loop.

Line 7 indicates that the query has exhausted the memory of the Prolog workspace: *Out of local stack during execution*. The precise interpretation of this message is less important than the spirit it conveys:

```
1.      % prolog
2.      C-Prolog version 1.5

3.      | ?- [p0306].
4.      origin_query1 consulted 152 bytes 0.0166667 sec.
5.      yes

6.      | ?- chicken(X).

7.      ! Out of local stack during execution
8.      [ execution aborted ]

9.      | ?- cntl-d
10.     [ Prolog execution halted ]
11.     %
```

Session 3.4. Program in a loop in user workspace.

60

This program will not work and must be rethought. Line 8 indicates that the query is abandoned by the Prolog interpreter. Prolog returns the prompt, line 9. We enter **control–d** to exit Prolog and return to UNIX, line 9.

The query *origin_query2*, p0307, is logically identical to *origin_query1* except that it includes **write** statements to output the steps of the search.

```
/*      Program:       p0307          origin_query2        */
/*              Query to resolve issue of which came first  */
/*              and print out the results.                  */

chicken(X)   :-   nl,write('X is a chicken if Y is an egg. '),egg(Y).
egg(Y)       :-   write('Y is an egg if X is a chicken.'),chicken(X).
```

The first line is read:

X is a chicken if
Prolog prints a new line and
Prolog writes 'X is a chicken if Y is an egg.' and
Y is an egg.

The second line is read:

Y is an egg if
Prolog writes 'Y is an egg if X is a chicken.' and
X is a chicken.

Session 3.5 indicates the Prolog output to the query in line 6, that is:

chicken(X).
Is X a chicken?

Immediately the screen comes alive with Prolog reporting the state of the search. If we leave it alone, eventually we will obtain the same error message as in Session 3.4: *Out of local stack space during execution*. However, this will take a long time. The printing operation greatly slows down the program, so it may take several minutes to run out of memory.

```
1.    % prolog
2.    C-Prolog version 1.5

3.    | ?- [p0307].
4.    origin_query2 consulted 204 bytes 0.0166667 sec.
5.    yes

6.    | ?- chicken(X).

7.    X is a chicken if Y is an egg.
8.    Y is an egg if X is a chicken.
9.    X is a chicken if Y is an egg.
10.   Y is an egg if X is a chicken.
11.   cntl-c
12.   X is a chicken if Y is an egg.
13.   Y is an egg if X is a chicken.
14.   ...
15.   X is a chicken if Y is an egg.
16.   Y is an egg if X is a chicken.
17.   ^Caction (h for help): h
18.   a       abort
19.   c       continue
20.   d       debug
21.   t       trace
22.
23.   Action (h for help): a
24.   [ execution aborted ]

25.   | ?- cntl-d
26.   [ Prolog execution halted ]
27.   %
```

Session 3.5. Program in a loop while printing.

While Prolog is filling the screen with information about the chicken–egg search, you can type **control–c** (**cntl–c**) by holding down the *control key* and typing *c*. We did this at about line 11. We say "about" because we typed it in while Prolog was madly writing to the screen.

The **control–c** we typed in has a delayed effect in that Prolog continues to print out about seven more printed pages (another 380 lines) of XY chicken–egg information. These seven pages are indicated by the ... at line 14.

Eventually the Prolog interpreter presents the message in line 17. The ^C is the **control–c** we entered seven pages of information ago, line 11. We have caused the Prolog interpreter to INTERRUPT, that is, to interrupt (halt, pause) the search and ask us what we want to do. The key combination **control–c** is often called an interrupt. We enter **h**

62

because we need help.

```
^CAction        (h for help): h
      a               abort
      c               continue
      d               debug
      t               trace
Action (h for help):
```

We enter **a**, which causes the Prolog interpreter to abandon the search and return the Prolog prompt. If we had typed **c**, Prolog would have resumed the search where it left off and eventually have delivered an *out of memory* message. If we had entered **d**, we could have used the *debugger* to examine all of the memory storage of Prolog to see how things were going. Most of the information that debug makes available in great quantity is useless to anyone who has not devoted their lives to the study of computer languages. Presumably, for those in the know, it is a gold mine. If we enter **t** for *trace*, we obtain a step–by–step output of the Prolog interpreter's actions as it looks for answers. Trace can be very useful, even to beginners. In most cases, trace produces an enormous amount of output to the screen (see Appendix IV).

The chicken–egg loop occurs frequently in carelessly written programs. Consider a linguistic example.

English contains noun phrases, and every sentence has a noun phrase as a subject. Some verbs have noun phrases as objects. *The fact* and *a scandal* are noun phrases, abbreviated *NP*. *The fact* is the subject NP of the sentence, S1, *the fact caused an uproar*. *A scandal* is the object of the sentence, S2, *it was a scandal*.

(S1 (NP the fact) caused an uproar)
(S2 it was (NP a scandal))

This notation indicates that an NP can be a constituent part of an S. But the following shows that an S can be a constituent part of an NP. The sentence *it was a scandal* is a part of the NP, *the fact it was a scandal*.

(S1 (NP the fact (S2 it was a scandal)) caused an uproar))

If we fully specify the constituent embeddings, then the NPb *a scandal* is a part of sentence S2 *it was a scandal*, which is part of NPa *the fact it was a scandal*, which is part of S1, *the fact it was a scandal caused an uproar*.

(S1 (NPa the fact (S2 it was (NPb a scandal))) caused an uproar))

If we write a program to identify sentences, then part of the test for *sentence* will be to see if some part of the sentence is a *noun phrase*. But part of the identification of *noun phrase* is a test to see if some part of the noun phrase is a *sentence*. If we are not careful in our queries that define *sentence* and *noun phrase*, we can easily send Prolog into a loop.

The following error, in p0308, can cause considerable difficulty (see Session 3.6) because, if the program contains the error, Prolog will report the error during the loading of the program, but will misload the program and keep running.

```
/*      Program:        p0308          test_file              */
/*              This file attempts to redefine a system predicate  */

        number(a).
```

The word *number* is a system predicate, a reserved word that is a built-in Prolog function. This program attempts to define a simple fact

```
1.      % prolog
2.      C-Prolog version 1.5

3.      | ?- number(a).
4.      no

5.      | ?- number(1).
6.      yes

7.      | ?- [p0308].

8.      ! Attempt to redefine a system predicate
9.      ! clause: number(a)
10.           test_file consulted 0 bytes
                   1.98682e-08 sec.
11.     yes

12.     | ?- cnt1-d
13.     [ Prolog execution halted ]
14.     %
```

Session 3.6. The anatomy of a pernicious error.

64

number(a).

Referring to Session 3.6, on line 1 we start Prolog. The term **number** is *reserved word* already used by Prolog to define a built in test. The test **number(X)** is false if X is not a number, like in lines 3–4, and true if X is a number, as in lines 5–6.

On line 7 we try to load the file *test_file*, p0308. Lines 8–11 indicate that the load operation failed because **number**, defined in *test_file*, is already a reserved word or system predicate. Line 10 indicates that 0 bytes were loaded.

This is the definition of a LOAD FAILURE: 0 bytes loaded.

This error can go undetected if you do not stare at the screen while the program loads. Some machines have an option that causes the terminal or computer to beep for every error. This can be a useful option.

3.2. How to Load and Run a Prolog Program

A **word square** is an arrangement of letters in a square such that each row and each column is a word in the dictionary. The following are valid 3X3 word squares (see Figure 3.2).

```
m a n     t a b     t a b     n e t     j a b
a p e     e p a     a p e     e p a     a p e
n e t     n e t     n e t     t a b     b e d
```

The following are invalid word squares. In each case, one or more rows or columns is not an English three–letter word.

```
m a n     t a b     t u b     s o n     x o x
x y z     a e t     o 3 b     j o b     o x o
p d m     z o o     p u t     r e d     o x o
```

Let us represent the general 3X3 word square as a square of symbols (A, B, C, D, E, F, G, H, I), in which each of these capital letters can be any of the twenty six letters of the alphabet.

In deciding what is a three–letter word, most cases will be clear cut: *man* is a word and *xdb* is not. Some will require this decision: *eke* is a word in the sentence: *The poor eke out a living*. However, *eke* never occurs alone: **The poor always eke. Eke* is a word that must occur with *out*. We define a **word** following the *white–space rule* as anything that occurs in a sentence with a space on either side of it and is also in the dictionary. By this definition, *eke* is a word. We must also decide if a name like *Jan*, or abbreviations like *IBM*, *ATT*, and *EPA* will be words in the dictionary. We will assume they are English words, hence, the earlier squares are acceptable.

The problem of constructing word squares fits the Prolog ideal: There is a well–defined database – the dictionary – over which we must perform a search for a combination of items. There exists a well–defined set of conditions that any acceptable solution must meet. The problem we wish to solve is simply stated:

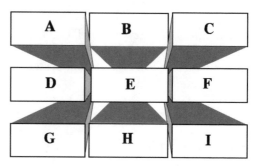

Figure 3.2. A word square.

Find a set of values for the variables (A,B,C,D,E,F,G,H,I) such that
                [A,B,C] is a word and
                [D,E,F] is a word and
                [G,H,I] is a word and
                [A,D,G] is a word and
                [B,E,H] is a word and
                [C,F,I] is a word.

The **database** is the set of facts over which we will search for a solution. The problem of constructing word squares has as its database the English dictionary. Following our convention, we present the database shaded inside of double lines. Assume our database is in a file called *database_dict*. To make the problem and its Prolog solution easier to follow, we will only consider the small dictionary listed in the file *database_dict*, p0309. The queries are in the file *query_word_sq*, p0310 (see Figure 3.3).

The query **wordsq(A,B,C,D,E,F,G,H,I)** is read like this:

1.   The query wordsq is true for the values of the
                        variables A, B, C, D, E, F, G, H, and I if
2.   [A,B,C] is a word and
3.   [D,E,F] is a word and
4.   [G,H,I] is a word and
5.   [A,D,G] is a word and

```
/*      Program:      p0309          database_dict        */

word([t,a,b]).
word([e,p,a]).
word([b,a,t]).
word([t,e,n]).
word([t,a,n]).
word([r,a,t]).
word([r,a,n]).
word([a,t,e]).
word([j,a,b]).
word([j,o,e]).
word([b,e,t]).
word([a,p,e]).
word([n,e,t]).
word([a,p,t]).
word([o,f,t]).
word([o,p,t]).
```

| 6. | [B,E,H] is a word and |
| 7. | [C,F,I] is a word. |

The query **sqword** is read like this:

1.	The query sqword is true if
2.	[A,B,C] is a word and
3.	[D,E,F] is a word and
4.	[G,H,I] is a word and
5.	[A,D,G] is a word and
6.	[B,E,H] is a word and
7.	[C,F,I] is a word and
8.	Prolog writes A, B and C and starts a new line and
9.	Prolog writes D, E and F and starts a new line and
10.	Prolog writes G, H and I and jumps two lines and
11.	Prolog fails, that is, backtracks to find more alternatives.

Figures 3.3 gives an overview of the general form of the Prolog solution to the word square problem. Figure 3.4 shows how Prolog seeks values that make *sqword* true. Figure 3.5 illustrates how Prolog seeks values which make *wordsq(...)* true.

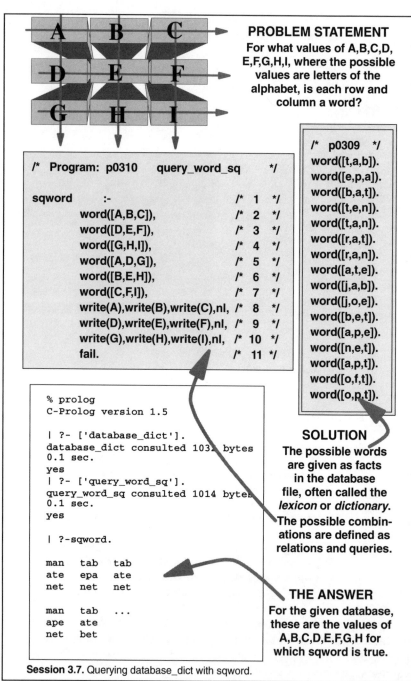

PROBLEM STATEMENT
For what values of A,B,C,D, E,F,G,H,I, where the possible values are letters of the alphabet, is each row and column a word?

```
/*  p0309  */
word([t,a,b]).
word([e,p,a]).
word([b,a,t]).
word([t,e,n]).
word([t,a,n]).
word([r,a,t]).
word([r,a,n]).
word([a,t,e]).
word([j,a,b]).
word([j,o,e]).
word([b,e,t]).
word([a,p,e]).
word([n,e,t]).
word([a,p,t]).
word([o,f,t]).
word([o,p,t]).
```

```
/*  Program: p0310    query_word_sq    */

sqword          :-                      /*  1  */
        word([A,B,C]),                  /*  2  */
        word([D,E,F]),                  /*  3  */
        word([G,H,I]),                  /*  4  */
        word([A,D,G]),                  /*  5  */
        word([B,E,H]),                  /*  6  */
        word([C,F,I]),                  /*  7  */
        write(A),write(B),write(C),nl,  /*  8  */
        write(D),write(E),write(F),nl,  /*  9  */
        write(G),write(H),write(I),nl,  /* 10  */
        fail.                           /* 11  */
```

SOLUTION
The possible words are given as facts in the database file, often called the *lexicon* or *dictionary*. The possible combinations are defined as relations and queries.

```
% prolog
C-Prolog version 1.5

| ?- ['database_dict'].
database_dict consulted 103  bytes
0.1 sec.
yes
| ?- ['query_word_sq'].
query_word_sq consulted 1014 bytes
0.1 sec.
yes

| ?-sqword.

man     tab     tab
ate     epa     ate
net     net     net

man     tab     ...
ape     ate
net     bet
```

THE ANSWER
For the given database, these are the values of A,B,C,D,E,F,G,H for which sqword is true.

Session 3.7. Querying database_dict with sqword.

Figure 3.3. The form of Prolog problems, solutions, and answers.

```
/*      Program:        p0310           query_word_sq    */

wordsq(A,B,C,D,E,F,G,H,I) :-                      /*      1*/
                        word([A,B,C]),           /*      2*/
                        word([D,E,F]),           /*      3*/
                        word([G,H,I]),           /*      4*/
                        word([A,D,G]),           /*      5*/
                        word([B,E,H]),           /*      6*/
                        word([C,F,I]).           /*      7*/


sqword :-                                        /*      1*/
                word([A,B,C]),                   /*      2*/
                word([D,E,F]),                   /*      3*/
                word([G,H,I]),                   /*      4*/
                word([A,D,G]),                   /*      5*/
                word([B,E,H]),                   /*      6*/
                word([C,F,I]),                   /*      7*/
                write(A),write(B),write(C),nl,   /*      8*/
                write(D),write(E),write(F),nl,   /*      9*/
                write(G),write(H),write(I),nl,nl,/*     10*/
                fail.                            /*     11*/
```

If we consider the problem statement and compare it with the two query statements, we see that they are almost the same. In general, a clear statement of the problem often defines the conditions that define the possible answers. Because the Prolog query is a statement of the conditions on answers, a clear statement of the problem is often only slightly different than a query.

Session 3.7 indicates the results of querying the database with *sqword.*

Figure 3.3 indicates the various components of a Prolog solution to any problem statement that involves searching for particular permutations and combinations of elements, in which the elements are selected from a given database. The forms over which the search is defined can be placed into a file – a database. In this example the database is p0309, the English lexicon. The query basically states the conditions that must be true for Prolog to accept an answer. In this case, the query is *sqword* in the query_file p0310. The solution to the problem is defined by the database_file and the query_file.

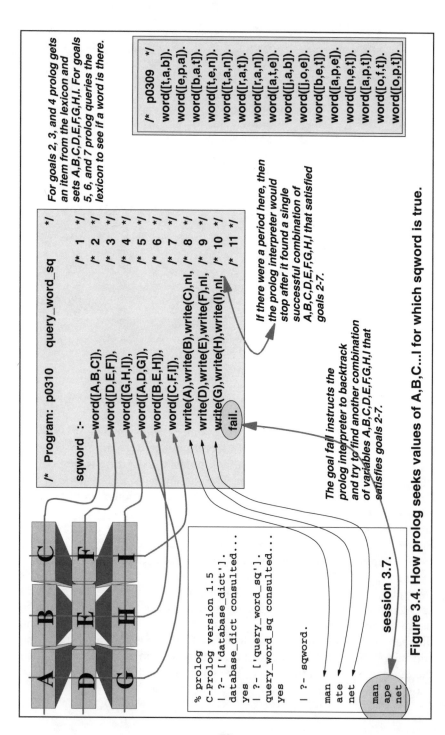

Figure 3.4. How prolog seeks values of A,B,C...I for which sqword is true.

```
% prolog
C-Prolog version 1.5

| ?- ['database_dict'].
database_dict consulted 1032 bytes 0.1 sec.
yes
| ?- ['query_word_sq'].
query_word_sq consulted 1014 bytes 0.1 sec.
yes

|
?-sqword.

man             bat             tan             bet
ate             epa             ape             epa
net             ten             net             tab

man             bat             rat             bet
ape             ate             ate             epa
net             ten             ten             tan

tab             bat             rat             bet
epa             ape             ape             ape
net             ten             ten             tan

tab             ten             ran             net
ate             ape             ate             epa
bet             bat             net             tab

tab             tan             ran             net
ate             ate             ape             epa
net             bet             net             tan

tab             tan             jab             no
ape             ate             ate             | ?-cntl-d
bet             net             bet             [ Prolog
                                                execution
tab             tan             jab             halted ]
ape             ape             ape             %
net             bet             bet
```

Session 3.7. Querying *database_dict* with *sqword.*

The Prolog interpreter will test all possible combinations in order to arrive at any answer(s).

Figure 3.4 indicates how Prolog seeks values of *A,B,C...I* for which *sqword* is true. The upper left of Figure 3.4 indicates that the condition that the rows and columns of the word square define words corresponds to individual goals in the Prolog statement, *sqword.*

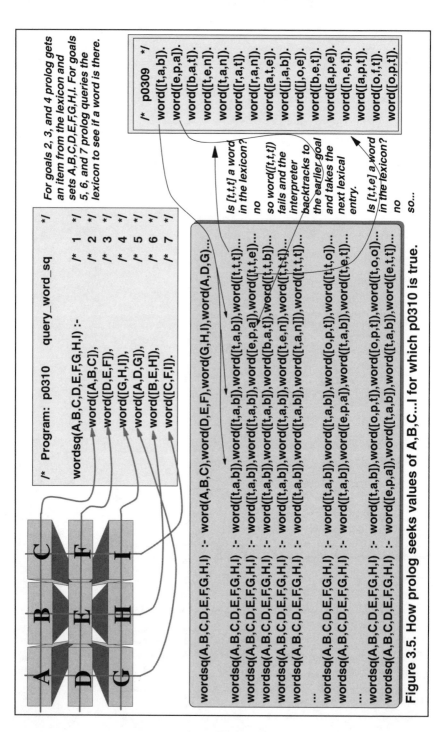

Figure 3.5. How prolog seeks values of A,B,C...I for which p0310 is true.

/* Program: p0310   query_word_sq   */

wordsq(A,B,C,D,E,F,G,H,I) :-
    word([A,B,C]),   /* 1 */
    word([D,E,F]),   /* 2 */
    word([G,H,I]),   /* 3 */
    word([A,D,G]),   /* 4 */
    word([B,E,H]),   /* 5 */
    word([C,F,I]).   /* 6 */
                         /* 7 */

For goals 2, 3, and 4 prolog gets an item from the lexicon and sets A,B,C,D,E,F,G,H,I. For goals 5, 6, and 7 prolog queries the lexicon to see if a word is there.

/* p0309 */
word([t,a,b]).
word([e,p,a]).
word([b,a,t]).
word([t,e,n]).
word([t,a,n]).
word([r,a,t]).
word([r,a,n]).
word([a,t,e]).
word([i,a,b]).
word([i,o,e]).
word([b,e,t]).
word([a,p,e]).
word([n,e,t]).
word([a,p,t]).
word([o,f,t]).
word([o,p,t]).

Is [t,t,t] a word in the lexicon?

no

so word([t,t,t]) fails and the interpreter backtracks to the earlier goal and takes the next lexical entry.

Is [t,t,e] a word in the lexicon?

no

so...

wordsq(A,B,C,D,E,F,G,H,I) :- word(A,B,C),word(D,E,F),word(G,H,I),word(A,D,G)...

wordsq(A,B,C,D,E,F,G,H,I) :- word([t,a,b]),word([t,a,b]),word([t,t,t])...
wordsq(A,B,C,D,E,F,G,H,I) :- word([t,a,b]),word([t,a,b]),word([e,p,a]),word([t,t,e])...
wordsq(A,B,C,D,E,F,G,H,I) :- word([t,a,b]),word([t,a,b]),word([b,a,t]),word([t,t,b])...
wordsq(A,B,C,D,E,F,G,H,I) :- word([t,a,b]),word([t,a,b]),word([t,e,n]),word([t,t,t])...
wordsq(A,B,C,D,E,F,G,H,I) :- word([t,a,b]),word([t,a,b]),word([t,a,n]),word([t,t,t])...

...

wordsq(A,B,C,D,E,F,G,H,I) :- word([t,a,b]),word([t,a,b]),word([o,p,t]),word([t,t,o])...
wordsq(A,B,C,D,E,F,G,H,I) :- word([t,a,b]),word([e,p,a]),word([t,a,b]),word([t,e,t])...

...

wordsq(A,B,C,D,E,F,G,H,I) :- word([t,a,b]),word([o,p,t]),word([o,p,t]),word([t,o,o])...
wordsq(A,B,C,D,E,F,G,H,I) :- word([e,p,a]),word([t,a,b]),word([t,a,b]),word([e,t,t])...

72

The last goal of sqword – line 11 – is *fail*, which causes the Prolog interpreter to backtrack for another solution. After the Prolog interpreter finds the first word square (*man, ate, net*), it backtracks to find the next (*man, ape, net*). If there were a period after line 11 of *sqword*, the interpreter would stop after it found the first successful combination.

Session 3.8 shows the output for *wordsq(A,B,C,D,E,F,G,H,I)*.

```
% prolog
Prolog loaded
|?- [database_dict].
database_dict loaded.
.0333 sec
yes
|?- [query_word_sq].
query_word_sq loaded
.0060 sec
|?- wordsq(A,B,C,D,E,F,G,H,I).
A = m
B = a
C = n
D = a
E = p
F = e
G = n
H = e
I = t
yes
|?- cntl-d
%
```

Session 3.8. Querying *database_dict* with *wordsq(A,B,...,I)*.

Figure 3.5 illustrates how Prolog seeks values of *A,B,C...I* for which *wordsq(..)* is true. For goals 2–4, Prolog gets an item from the lexicon and sets *A,B,C,D,E,F,G,H,I*. This is indicated in Figure 3.5 by arrows which point from the lexicon to the *wordsq(...)* statement. For goals 5–7 Prolog queries the lexicon to see if a word is there. This is indicated by arrows which point from the *wordsq(...)* statement to the lexicon. When one of the goals 5–7 fails, Prolog backtracks to goals 2–4 to select a new word.

3.3.   Running Prolog on an IBM PC

Program p0311, *databse2.pro*, is the database for the word squares

73

problem. Prolog–2 has the requirement that every program file that is loaded must end in the extension *.PRO*. So it would be impossible to load either program p*0311 or databse2*. The files must have the names: *p0311.pro* and *databse2.pro*. This must be their names in the directory.

```
/*      Program:       p0311            databse2.pro        */
/*                                                          */
/*                 This is the database_file to load into   */
/*                 Prolog2.  Notice the filename is eight    */
/*                 characters and ends in the extension .PRO. */
word([t,a,b]).
word([e,p,a]).
word([b,a,t]).
word([t,e,n]).
word([t,a,n]).
word([r,a,t]).
word([r,a,n]).
word([a,t,e]).
word([j,a,b]).
word([j,o,e]).
word([b,e,t]).
word([a,p,e]).
word([n,e,t]).
word([a,p,t]).
word([o,f,t]).
word([o,p,t]).
```

When the files are loaded by the command *[...].*, it is possible to leave off the extension. So Prolog–2 will load either of these files without the extension mentioned, as long as they have the extension in their directory names. In Prolog–2, these are valid: *[p0311].* and *[databse2].*

UNIX permits us to have long descriptive filenames. The IBM operating systems require us to have filenames of at most eight characters followed by a maximum of three–letters as the file extension. So *database2.pro* is invalid, but *databse2.pro* is acceptable.

Session 3.9 queries *databse2.pro*, p0311, for wordsquares using p0312. In C–Prolog, one terminates the query by entering a carriage return, and continues the query by entering a semicolon. Prolog–2 dispenses with this and asks *More (y/n)?* If you enter *no*, this is equivalent to the carriage return in C–Prolog. If you enter *yes*, Prolog–2 backtracks to look for more cases, just as it would if you entered a semicolon in C–Prolog.

In Session 3.9, lines 1–8 indicate how the Prolog program files are listed in the directory with the extension .PRO. Lines 9–15 call up Prolog–2 and load the database and query files. Notice in lines 12 and 14, the files are named without the extension .PRO.

Line 16 is our query, entered from the terminal. Lines 17–26 comprise the Prolog response. Line 26 asks if we want more. We enter *y*, and Prolog–2 searches for another combination of letters to make statement 16 true.

```
/*      Program:       p0312           query2.pro          */
/*                                                          */
/*      This file contains the queries to be loaded into    */
/*      Prolog2.  Notice the filename ends in               */
/*      the extension .PRO                                   */

wordsq(A,B,C,D,E,F,G,H,I) :-                    /*  1   */
                    word([A,B,C]),              /*  2   */
                    word([D,E,F]),              /*  3   */
                    word([G,H,I]),              /*  4   */
                    word([A,D,G]),              /*  5   */
                    word([B,E,H]),              /*  6   */
                    word([C,F,I]).              /*  7   */

sqword :-                                       /*  1   */
            word([A,B,C]),                      /*  2   */
            word([D,E,F]),                      /*  3   */
            word([G,H,I]),                      /*  4   */
            word([A,D,G]),                      /*  5   */
            word([B,E,H]),                      /*  6   */
            word([C,F,I]),                      /*  7   */
            write(A),write(B),write(C),nl,      /*  8   */
            write(D),write(E),write(F),nl,      /*  9   */
            write(G),write(H),write(I),nl,nl,   /*  10  */
            fail.                               /*  11  */
```

In line 36, we type *no*, and the query ceases. In line 38 we type *halt* to terminate the Prolog Session. Prolog types out several lines of information about usage. By line 46, we are back at the IBM operating system prompt.

```
1.       C:\Prolog2>  DIR *.PRO
2.        Volume in drive C has no label
3.        Volume Serial Number is 1947-8309
4.        Directory of C:\P\Prolog
5.       DATABSE2 PRO          274 12-02-92   11:42a
6.       QUERY2    PRO          638 12-02-92   11:52a
7.                 2 file(s)              912 bytes
8.                                   19445760 bytes free

9.       C:\Prolog2> Prolog2
10.              Prolog-2  V2.35    PDE        Insert
11.      Press F1 for help

12.      ?- [databse2].
13.      databse2 consulted.
14.      ?- [query2].
15.      query2 consulted.

16.      ?- wordsq(A,B,C,D,E,F,G,H,I).

17.      A = t
18.      B = a
19.      C = b
20.      D = e
21.      E = p
22.      F = a
23.      G = n
24.      H = e
25.      I = t
26.      More (y/n)?  y

27.      A = t
28.      B = a
29.      C = b
30.      D = a
31.      E = t
32.      F = e
33.      G = b
34.      H = e
35.      I = t
36.      More (y/n)? n
37.      yes

38.      ?- halt.
39.-43. concern memory usage and are omitted

44.      Elapsed time          4m      17.22 seconds
45.      Garbage collection            1.85 seconds

46.      C:\Prolog2>
```

Session 3.9. Querying *databas2* for word squares on an IBM PC.

76

The bulletin board at New York University contains the most recent versions of the Prolog programs we discuss and gives information about problems users have had (and have overcome) in implementing various versions of Prolog on IBM and Apple computers.

3.4.   Modifying the Word Squares Program

Suppose we crave a 3X3 word square in which the diagonals are also words, that is, [A,E,I] and [C,E,G] are words. We simply have to add two conditions to the query: *word([A,E,I])* and *word([C,E,G])*. We can add these conditions anywhere in the query (see p0313). The queries *wordsq1* and *wordsq2* will produce exactly the same set of word squares. They will, however, be printed out in different orders.

```
/*      Program:      p0313           query_diagonals     */
/*      In order to load this file into Prolog-2 the filename    */
/*      will have to be changed to have only eight letters    */
/*      and end in .PRO                                         */
/*      The two queries are logically equivalent.             */


wordsq1(A,B,C,D,E,F,G,H,I) :-
                word([A,B,C]),
                word([D,E,F]),
                word([G,H,I]),
                word([A,D,G]),
                word([B,E,H]),
                word([C,F,I]),
                word([A,E,I]),          /*    diag test    */
                word([C,E,G]).          /*    diag test    */


wordsq2(A,B,C,D,E,F,G,H,I) :-
                word([C,E,G]),          /*    diag test    */
                word([A,B,C]),
                word([D,E,F]),
                word([G,H,I]),
                word([A,D,G]),
                word([A,E,I]),          /*    diag test    */
                word([B,E,H]),
                word([C,F,I]).
```

English contains many three–letter sequences, [X,Y,Z], that spell a word in both directions, that is, [X,Y,Z] is a word and [Z,Y,X] is a word: *but/tub, ten/net, pip/pip...* The query *wordsq3* defines those wordsquares in which all horizontal and vertical words can be spelled in both directions (see p0314).

```
/*      Program:        p0314           query_both_ways    */
/*              This query outputs word squares in which   */
/*              each horizontal (left-right) and vertical (up-down) */
/*              sequence of letters is a valid three–letter word.  */
/*              The word definitions, which are separated by    */
/*              commas, can occur in any order.              */

wordsq3(A,B,C,D,E,F,G,H)  :-
                    word([A,B,C]),
                    word([C,B,A]),
                    word([D,E,F]),
                    word([F,E,D]),
                    word([G,H,I]),
                    word([I,H,G]),
                    word([A,D,G]),
                    word([G,D,A]),
                    word([B,E,H]),
                    word([H,E,B]),
                    word([C,F,I]),
                    word([I,F,C]).
```

As a person's taste in word squares becomes more sophisticated, they might only be satisfied by word squares in which all sequences of letters define valid words: foreword and backward, horizontal and vertical, and diagonal. Any desire can be gratified by adding more conditions to the query. However, the small database in *database_file* does not contain enough words to define very specialized word squares. We would have to add more words to our database, perhaps even include all the words there are in English.

A common strategy in writing a Prolog program is to write a simple program that gives you almost what you want and then to modify it by adding more goals to narrow the answers to precisely what you want. If our true desire is for all the omnidirectional both–ways word squares, we would be wise to write a simple program that gives us word squares in which each unidirectional sequence of letters was a valid word. We could then use our text editor (or word processor) to modify our simple program by adding goals. The versions of the word square program, *wordsq1–5*, are modified versions of the basic program *wordsq*.

Producing and editing the database poses another type of problem. If we decided to add more words to our dictionary, the optimal route is not to type in several thousand more words using a word processor. We should think of using some dictionary that is already on a computer to provide us with the words to fill our database.

```
/*      Program:      p0315          query_e            */
/*            These queries will only find word squares    */
/*            in which the center letter, E, is a "t".      */
/*            The two queries are logically equivalent, but */
/*            differ radically in efficiency.               */

wordsq4(A,B,C,D,E,F,G,H,I) :-
                word([A,B,C]),
                word([D,E,F]),
                word([G,H,I]),
                word([A,D,G]),
                word([B,E,H]),
                word([C,F,I]),
                E == "t".

wordsq5(A,B,C,D,E,F,G,H,I) :-
                word([A,B,C]),
                word([D,E,F]),
                E == "t",
                word([G,H,I]),
                word([A,D,G]),
                word([B,E,H]),
                word([C,F,I]).
```

In most cases, the order in which the goals are given influences the order in which the answers are output. Sometimes the order will greatly affect the efficiency of the search. In looking for possible answers, Prolog applies the tests in the order in which they are listed in the query. In the earlier examples, the efficiency is not affected much by the order of goals.

We can give a hint of what lies ahead in our study by

programming to fill a demand for word squares in which the center letter is "*t*". We need merely add a goal that limits the possible word squares to those in which the center letter, *E*, is the letter "*t*". The test for equality uses two equal signs: ...,*E*=="*t*",... is read ...*and E is equal to "t", and* . The double equal sign is a *test for equality*; it is true if *E* is equal to "*t*" and false otherwise. The double equal sign is not a command to set *E* equal to "*t*".

Both *wordsq4* and *wordsq5* contain the goal, *E*=="*t*", to test if Prolog has set the center square to "*t*" (see p0315). They will give exactly the same set of word squares. However, *wordsq5* will produce output more rapidly than will *wordsq4*. *Wordsq4* will find a completely specified valid word square with all words tested before it tests to see if the center letter is "*t*". *Wordsq5* will test to see if the center letter is "*t*" immediately after it has found a valid *word([D,E,F])* and before it has found words for *[G,H,I]*, *[A,D,G]*, *[B,E,H]*, and *[C,F,I]*. If the center letter is not "*t*", Prolog will backtrack and look for another *word([D,E,F])* in which the *E* is a "*t*". I will go over these issues in later sections. For the present, you are encouraged to run these two programs and time them.

3.5.   The Edit–Prolog–Edit Loop.

After you have used a text editor to create a *database_file* and a *query_file*, and you have loaded this program into Prolog, you face several possibilities (see Figure 3.6). First, everything may work perfectly. The program loads with no errors, and Prolog provides correct answers to your queries. More plausibly, however, something will go awry. Perhaps the program will not load into Prolog. Maybe the answers to queries are incorrect. The system may be very slow to respond, or perhaps it gives "out of memory" messages. In these cases, you will have to leave Prolog and modify your program in the text editor. This movement from the text editor to Prolog, back to the text editor, then to Prolog, back to the text editor is called the **edit–Prolog–edit loop**. The loop ends only when you are perfectly content with the execution and output of your program. A **Prolog hacker**, that is, someone never content with any program, remains forever in the edit–Prolog–edit loop endlessly tweaking the program to shave off microseconds of response time and to save a few bytes of memory.

Before you approach the computer, you must **define your problem**, that is, organize your database and formulate the logical constraints on answers that define the queries. There is no reason to try to program anything until you have a firm idea of what the basic facts are and what combination(s) of facts will satisfy your desires.

80

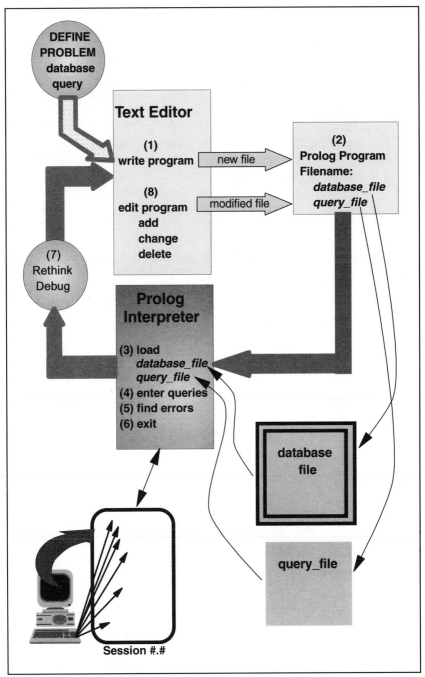

Figure 3.6. The Edit–Prolog–Edit loop.

One avoids the fate of the Prolog hacker by not starting until you have a well–defined problem and a firm idea of what constitutes an acceptable solution.

Referring to Figure 3.6, with a well–defined problem, step (1) is to use the text editor to **write the program**. The **Prolog program** (2) is in one or more files. In this study we will always have a *database_file* and a *query_file*. In some cases, one might have only one file – *program.file* – which contains the database and the queries.

After Prolog is running, **the program is loaded** (3), **the queries are entered** (4), any error messages or **errors are encountered** (5), and **Prolog is exited** (6) for the operating system.

Step (7) requires you to **debug the program files**. Perhaps the errors are simple and involve only changing capital to small letters or adding a forgotten period. On the other hand, one might have to rethink the entire approach.

When the required program modifications are known, you reenter the program into the text editor and **edit the Prolog statements** (8). The results of the editing session will be a modified **Prolog program** (2). One continues the **edit–Prolog–edit loop** through steps 3, 4–8, 2–8, 2–8, until the program works.

chapter **4**

TABLES OF DATA AS PROLOG FACTS AND RELATIONS

It was originally my plan after the first volume of this work, which deals with sounds and spellings, to go on to Morphology, and finally to Syntax – these two terms taken in the sense explained in my *Progress in Language*, 1894, p. 141, and again below, p. 1. My reasons for now deviating from this order and bringing out the syntactical before the morphological part, are partly of a purely personal character. When I took up work again after a rest necessitated by overstrain during a nine months' stay in America, I wanted something pleasurable to do and thought Syntax more attractive than Morphology; consequently I let my extensive preparatory work on endings, etc., lie undisturbed in my drawers....

The arrangement of grammatical matter is sometimes extremely difficult on account of the numerous cross–associations which determine the structure of a language. I have spent many weary hours arranging and rearranging my thousands of paragraphs and my tens of thousands of slips; and though in some particulars I might now wish that I had followed a different order, I venture to think that I have here and there succeeded in finding the arrangement best suited to lay bare the inner connexion of the phenomena concerned. Numerous cross–references and the index will enable the reader to find what he is looking for, even if it has been put in an unexpected place.

Otto Jespersen, 1913/1961
A Modern English Grammar on Historical Principles

4.1.   Converting Tables into Prolog Facts and Relations

Prolog defines a logical way of thinking about data and about the organization of data. In learning Prolog, we are learning to think about how to organize, classify, and cross–classify data in order to respond promptly and accurately to questions that can be answered by appealing to: (a) the data, (b) general grammatical constraints on the data, and (c) specific idiomatic constraints on the data. Situations in which one tries to manage data that are in thousands of paragraphs and on tens of thousands of slips are eminently suited to Prolog formulations. What at one time would be organized and classified through cross–referencing and indexing can be programmed into Prolog facts and relations. In Prolog programming, the basic question is: What arrangement of data, what Prolog information structure, is best suited to lay bare the inner connection of the phenomena concerned?

If at some point we wish that in some particulars we had followed a different order, we need only to define the appropriate query to express the desired relation among the simple and complex facts.

Data that exist in tabular form convert readily into Prolog facts and relations. One can enter queries to find specific data in the tables or inquire about how information in one table relates to information in another. Figure 4.1 may help understand the following.

When we learn Prolog, we are disciplining our mind to organize data in terms of the questions we might ask. Programming in Prolog consists of identifying the simple facts and of formulating interdependencies among the simple facts into more complex facts and relations. In converting a table, like Table 4.1 in Figure 4.1, into Prolog, the simple facts are the table name, the row and column labels, and the entries. In later sections I consider tables for the irregular verbs *cost, see, go,* and *dive.* Each **root** verb has a table of forms for each tense (see Tables 4.1, 4.2, and 4.3):

Table 4.1 root(be). tense(present)		
	numero	
person	**sing**	**plu**
1	am	are
2	are	are
3	is	are

root(be).	/*	name of table
root(cost).	/*	name of table
root(see).	/*	name of table

Here three **tenses** are considered: *past, present,* and *future:*

In general, any information that can be represented in tables can be easily represented in prolog as a set of simple and complex facts. The table name and row and column labels become simple facts. Each entry is represented as a complex fact.

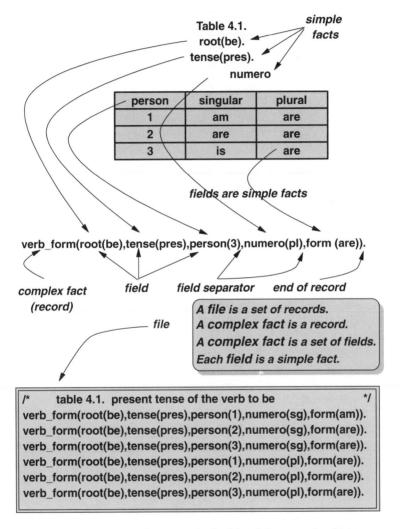

The simple facts can be in any order inside of the complex fact. Normally we arrange them with the most general simple fact on the left and the most specific simple fact (the form of the word) on the right. The fields in the middle range from less to more specific.

Figure 4.1. Representing a table in Prolog.

Table 4.2 root(be). tense(past)		
	numero	
person	**sing**	**plu**
1	was	were
2	were	were
3	was	were

tense(past).
tense(pres).
tense(fut).

In English there are three **persons**: first person is the speaker (*I*, *we*), second person is the person spoken to (*you*), and the third person is the person spoken about (*he, she, it, they*). Some languages may have more than three persons, others may have more than three numbers, for instance, Arabic has a singular, dual, and plural. There are also languages that have more tenses than English.

In Table 4.1, **person** is the row label:

```
person(1).      /*    i, we                    */
person(2).      /*    you, you all             */
person(3).      /*    he, she, it, they        */
```

English verbs can be marked for number: *singular* (one individual) or *plural* (more than one individual). As was shown in Session 3.6, the word **number** is a basic Prolog primitive built in function, so let us use the word **numero** for what is traditionally called *number* by grammarians. In Table 4.1, **number** is a column heading:

```
numero(sg).
numero(pl).
```

Each **form** of a verb, that is, each entry in a table, is a simple fact. Linguists say that a root can be *inflected* for *tense, person, number,* and several other properties I do not discuss here (*mood, aspect,* etc.). What we call *forms* would at a more technical level be called *inflected forms*. *Inflectional morphology* is the study of inflected forms. Some **forms** for the root *to be* are:

```
form(am).
form(are).
form(is).
```

Table 4.3 root(be). tense(future).		
	numero	
person	**both**	
all	**will_be**	

form(was).
form(were).

The information in the tables can be represented as complex facts, in which a **complex fact** expresses relations about the simple facts listed earlier. Let us define a complex fact, called **verb_form**, which gives each tabular datum in the form of a Prolog statement. Consider this statement:

verb_form(root(be),tense(pres),person(1),numero(sg),form(am)).

This can be understood as a logical formula to define one cell of Table 4.1, (see p0401). There are many equivalent ways to read the statement in English using the words *when, for, if* and *and*. The best way to read the statement in English is this:

verb_form is *true* when *be* is a root and *pres* is a tense and *first* is a person and *sg* is a number and *am* is a form.

We could also read the statement as:

verb_form is *true* if *be* is a root and *pres* is a tense and *first* is a person and *sg* is a number and *am* is a form.

We can avoid confusion in complex programs by always reading a complex fact using *when* and using the term *if* for explicit mention of the Prolog *if* (*colon + dash, :-*).

We can avoid more confusion by realizing that English *if* is used in two quite different cases:

Two uses/interpretations of *If X then Y.*

CASE I.   iff: X is true if Y is true and Y is true if X is true.

The volume of the cube is 1 if the side has length 1.
If the side had length 1, the volume of a cube is 1.

If John is married, then he is a husband.
If John is a husband, then he is married.

```
/*      Program:        p0401           tobe_ppf.prg            */

/*                  row and column labels and names of tables       */
root(be).
tense(pres).
tense(past).
tense(fut).
person(1).
person(2).
person(3).
numero(sg).
numero(pl).
/*                  entries in the tables                         */
form(am).
form(are).
form(is).
form(was).
form(were).
form(will_be).


/*      table 4.1 information:  present tense of  verb to be */
verb_form(root(be),tense(pres),person(1),numero(sg),form(am)).
verb_form(root(be),tense(pres),person(2),numero(sg),form(are)).
verb_form(root(be),tense(pres),person(3),numero(sg),form(is)).
verb_form(root(be),tense(pres),person(1),numero(pl),form(are)).
verb_form(root(be),tense(pres),person(2),numero(pl),form(are)).
verb_form(root(be),tense(pres),person(3),numero(pl),form(are)).


/*      table 4.2 information: past tense of verb to be      */
verb_form(root(be),tense(past),person(1),numero(sg),form(was)).
verb_form(root(be),tense(past),person(2),numero(sg),form(were)).
verb_form(root(be),tense(past),person(3),numero(sg),form(was)).
verb_form(root(be),tense(past),person(1),numero(pl),form(were)).
verb_form(root(be),tense(past),person(2),numero(pl),form(were)).
verb_form(root(be),tense(past),person(3),numero(pl),form(were)).


/*      table 4.3 information:  future tense of the verb to be*/
verb_form(root(be),tense(fut),person(1),numero(sg),form(will_be)).
verb_form(root(be),tense(fut),person(2),numero(sg),form(will_be)).
verb_form(root(be),tense(fut),person(3),numero(sg),form(will_be)).
verb_form(root(be),tense(fut),person(1),numero(pl),form(will_be)).
verb_form(root(be),tense(fut),person(2),numero(pl),form(will_be)).
verb_form(root(be),tense(fut),person(3),numero(pl),form(will_be)).
```

CASE II.   if: X is true if Y is true, but Y may not be true if X
is true.

The volume of the rectangle is 6 if the length is 3, the side
is 2, and the height is 1.
The length is 3, the side is 2, and the height is 1 if the
volume of the rectangle is 6.

If John is a father, then he is a male over six.
If John is a male over six, then he is a father.

Prolog relations using the *colon+dash* can be either Case I or Case II. Programs would be easier to read and understand if :- always were Case I. Unfortunately, many programs incorporate Case II conditionals. The term PURE PROLOG refers to a complex of properties, but in a nutshell, if all of our Prolog programs incorporate only Case I conditionals, we are programming in pure Prolog.

If a Prolog program always used :- such that all relations were Case I, then all programs would be "reversible." In an example to be discussed later, suppose we had a program *sing_plural(SING,PLU)* that relates the singular with the plural form of a noun. In a Case I relation, we could enter *sing_plu(girl,X)* and get *X=girls*, or *sing_plu(X,girls)* and get *X=girl*. In a Case II relation, which might be thought of as forming the plural from the singular by adding an ending (or as extracting the singular from the plural by removing an ending), we might be able to enter *sing_plu(girl,X)* and get *X=girls,* but not be able to enter *sing_plu(X,girls)* and get any answer. This point, although perhaps obscure now, will play a major role in later program design. For the moment, acquire the habit of thinking about which sense of *if* is involved when you read a Prolog statement.

Another good habit to acquire requires abstention: Always read **root(be)** as *be is a root*, and never as *root equals be* or *root = be*. Never use the word *equals* when reading a simple or complex fact. Although the point may be subtle now, it will facilitate understanding complex cases. One might think of **root, tense,** and the simple facts as containers (memory addresses) that hold or point to variables. If I have a cup of coffee and a cup of tea, I might point and say, *this cup is tea* and *that cup is coffee*. What I mean is that this cup contains tea and the other contains coffee. Usually it does not pay to think of the Prolog interpreter as setting one thing equal to another. The optimal way to think is this: Prolog has a set of memory locations that are labels of simple facts and Prolog puts into the memory location an address that points to the simple fact(s). When the label points to a fact, as **root** points to *b* in **root(b)**, we say **root** is bound to *b* (or sometimes *b* is bound to **root**).

In general, a variable can be considered to be a memory location in the computer. The memory location can contain a datum or the address of a datum. We will say that the variable – a memory location – is BOUND to the datum in the memory location or the datum to which the address in the memory location points. In very complicated sentences (e.g., *Who was John persuaded to visit*), a memory location (variable) may contain an address that points to another memory location that contains an address, that contains an address, that points to a datum.

Consider an example that is easier to understand in terms of binding facts to labels than in terms of setting a label equal to a variable. How many words can one build using the letters in the word *Mississippi*? This query is ambiguous. Do we mean using the 4 letters {*m,i,s,p*} or the 11 letters {*m,i,i,i,i,s,s,s,p,p*}? In the first case, we get a small number of words (*is, sip*), but in the second case a large number of words (*miss, pip*, etc.). If we think of 4 letter words formed from the letters in *Mississippi*, we might form *miss*. Suppose in our program we represented the 4 letter word as *letter(A),letter(B),letter(C),letter(D)*, where *A, B, C, D* range over the database of 11 letters. In the word *miss* we do not say that *C equals D* or that *C* equal **letter**. Rather we speak of pointers and bindings:

```
head   :-    goal1,  goal2,  goal3,  goal4.
word   :-    letter(A),letter(B),letter(C),letter(D).
```

The values over which the variables *A, B,* and so on, can range is the 11 member set {m,i,i,i,i,s,s,s,p,p}. The binding of the variables ranges over these 11 items. *A* can point to (or be bound to) *m*, or to *i*, or to *i*, or to *i*, or to *i*, or to *s*, or to *s*, and so on. Discussion of the difference between *equals* and *binding* (or *pointers*) can only lead to confusion unless we discuss how information is stored and represented internal to the computer. Just as we once learned to drive a car, here we are learning to maneuver Prolog, and our goal is to start, stop, and stay on the road. For our purposes it suffices to realize that Prolog never sets one thing equal to another. The interpreter always makes one thing, *X*, point to another thing, *Y*, which may point to another thing, *Z*, which can go on and on. For anyone interested in looking under the hood, see Bratko (1990) and Dodd (1990).

This discussion boils down to three healthy habits:

- read a complex fact using *when*, and use *if* only for relations.

- in relations, be clear whether :- is Case I or Case II.

- always read **fact(datum)** as *datum is a fact* or *datum is bound to fact*. Shun and abhor: *fact equals datum*.

The six cells of Table 4.1 correspond to these complex facts:

verb_form(root(be),tense(pres),person(1),numero(sg),form(am)).
verb_form(root(be),tense(pres),person(2),numero(sg),form(are)).
verb_form(root(be),tense(pres),person(3),numero(sg),form(is)).

verb_form(root(be),tense(pres),person(1),numero(plu),form(are))
verb_form(root(be),tense(pres),person(2),numero(plu),form(are)).
verb_form(root(be),tense(pres),person(3),numero(plu),form(are)).

A complex fact indicates there is a necessary (iff) interrelation among the simple facts, that is, a complex fact is always equivalent to a Case I *if*. An entry in the table – a **verb_form** – is a specific interrelation among the simple facts: table label, row and column labels, and forms. The order of elements in the complex fact is irrelevant. The following are logically equivalent:

verb_form(root(be),tense(pres),person(1),numero(sg),form(am)).
verb_form1(form(am),numero(sg),person(1),tense(pres),root(be)).
verb_form2(tense(pres),person(1),form(am),root(be),numero(sg)).

Program *p0401, tobe_ppf.prg*, incorporates the simple and complex facts of Tables 4.1, 4.2, and 4.3 into a Prolog program. Let us define a relation called **data**, p0402, which will enable us to query the database of verb forms in English.

In passing, we should note that in Prolog, computer science, and information processing textbooks, what we call a *complex fact* is often called a *record*. What we call a *simple fact* is often called a *field*. The *comma* is the *field separator*.

Let us approach this relation by first considering how it can be used to pose queries to the database. The relation, *data*, will be our window into the database.

```
/*      Program:      p0402          search.prg          */
/*                Date:          November 17, 1989        */

data(R,T,P,N,F)   :-    root(R),tense(T),person(P),numero(N),
                        form(F),verb_form(root(R),tense(T),
                        person(P),numero(N), form(F)).
```

91

4.2. How to Extract Information from Tables: Querying the Database of Facts and Relations.

Session 4.1 is the scriptfile for a Prolog session in which we query the database. Let us examine the steps of the query session.

Lines 1–2 call up Prolog. Lines 3–5 load program p0401, the database. Lines 6–8 load the query, program p0402.

Query 1:   Is *am* the first–person present singular of the verb *to be*?

> | ?-**data(be,pres,1,sg,am).**   line 9

Is data *true* when *be* is a root and *pres* is a tense and *1* is a person and *sg* is a numero and *am* is a form?

Prolog answers *yes* to this query because we say: *I am*, line 10.

Query 2:   Is *are* the third–person present singular of the verb *to be*?

> | ?-**data(be,pres,3,sg,are).**   line 11

Is data *true* when *be* is a root and *pres* is a tense and *3* is a person and *sg* is a numero and *are* is a form?

Prolog answers *no* to this query because we do not say: *he/she/it are*, line 12.

Query 3:   What is the third–person present singular of the verb *to be*?

> | ?-**data(be,pres,3,sg,X).**   line 13

For what value of X is data *true* when *be* is a root and *pres* is a tense and *3* is a person and *sg* is a numero.

Prolog answers X = *is* to this query because we say *he/she/it is*, line 14. The user types **;** to see if there is any other value of X that meets the conditions, line 13. Prolog answers *no*, line 15.

Query 4: What is the root verb, the tense, the person, and the number that yields the form *is*?

For what values of *R, T, P,* and *N* is the relation data *true* when *R* is a root and *T* is a tense and *P* is a person and *N* is a number and *is* is a form?

```
                                        LOAD PROLOG
1.      % prolog
2.      C-Prolog version 1.5
                                        LOAD DATABASE
3.      | ?- ['tobe_ppf.prg'].
4.      tobe_ppf.prg consulted 2320 bytes 0.166667 sec.
5.      yes
                                        LOAD QUERIES
6.      | ?- ['search.prg'].
7.      search.prg consulted 2120 bytes 0.166667 sec.
8.      yes
                                        QUERY 1
9.      | ?- data(be,pres,1,sg,am).
10.     yes
                                        QUERY 2
11.     | ?- data(be,pres,3,sg,are).
12.     no
                                        QUERY 3
13.     | ?- data(be,pres,3,sg,X).
14.     X = is ;
15.     no
                                        QUERY 4
16.     | ?- data(R,T,P,N,is).
17.     R = be
18.     T = pres
19.     P = 3
20.     N = sg ;
21.     no
                                        QUERY 5
22.     | ?- data(be,past,P,N,was).
23.     P = 1
24.     N = sg ;
                                        LOOK AGAIN
25.     P = 3
26.     N = sg ;
27.     no
                                        EXIT PROLOG
28.     | ?- cntl-d
29.     [ Prolog execution halted ]
30.     %
```

Session 4.1. Querying a database.

Prolog answers: *R* is *be*, *T* is *pres*, *P* is *3*, *N* is *sg* because *is* is the third–person singular present of the verb *to be*, lines 17–20. The user enters **;** to search for another value of *R,T,P,N* that meets the conditions, line 20. Prolog answers *no* indicating that the values are unique, line 21.

Query 5: For the root verb *to be* in the past tense, what is the person and number of the form *was*?

| ?-**data(be,past,P,N,was).** line 22

For what values of *P* and *N* is the search function data *true* such that *be* is a root and *past* is a tense and *P* is a person and *N* is a number and *was* is a form?

Prolog should answer: *P* is *1*, *N* is *sg*, and also *P* is *3* and *N* is *sg* because we say *I was* and *he/she/it was*, lines 23–24, Prolog answers for *I was*. The user enters **;** to look for more possible answers. Lines 25–26 give Prolog answers for *he/she/it was*. The user enters **;** to keep searching. Prolog answers *no*, line 27.

On line 28 the user enters **control–d** to exit Prolog.

4.3. Variables in a Query

There are two main types of Prolog query: *yes/no* and *wh–*. In Session 4.1 queries 1 and 2 are *yes/no*; queries 3, 4 and 5 are *wh–*. Sessions 4.2 and 4.3 contain only *wh–* queries.

A **yes/no query** has no variables (capital letters) in the statement. It asks: Is the statement true for the values selected? The answer can only be *yes* or *no*. These are yes/no queries:

data(be,pres,1,sg,am).
data(be,pres,3,sg,are).

A **wh–query** has variables in the statement. It asks: For which values of the variables is the statement true? If there are values that make the statement true, Prolog returns those values and the answer *yes* indicating the statement is true. If there are no such values, Prolog returns a *no*. These are *wh–*queries:

data(be,pres,3,sg,X).
data(R,T,P,N,is).
data(be,past,P,N,was).

```
1.    % prolog
2.    C-Prolog version 1.5
3.    | ?- ['tobe_ppf.prg'].
4.    tobe_ppf.prg consulted 2320 bytes 0.166667 sec.
5.    yes
6.    | ?- ['search.prg'].
7.    search.prg consulted 2130 bytes 0.166667 sec.
8.    yes

9.    | ?- data(R,T,P,N,F).
10.   R = be
11.   T = pres
12.   P = 1
13.   N = sg
14.   F = am ;

15.   R = be
16.   T = pres
17.   P = 1
18.   N = pl
19.   F = are ;

20.   R = be
21.   T = pres
22.   P = 2
23.   N = sg
24.   F = are
25.   yes

26.   | ?- data(A,B,C,D,is).
27.   A = be
28.   B = pres
29.   C = 3
30.   D = sg ;
31.   no

32.   | ?- data(Oranges,Apples,Grapefruit,
              Ducksoup,is).
33.   Oranges = be
34.   Apples = pres
35.   Grapefruit = 3
36.   Ducksoup = sg ;
37.   no

38.   | ?- cntl-d
39.   [ Prolog execution halted ]
40.   %
```

**This session file indicates how the information will appear on the
computer screen. Session 4.3, which contains the same information,
is flattened to take less space.**

Session 4.2. Querying a database using variables.

Consider this query:

data(R,T,P,N,F).   Session 4.2: line 9.

What is the form of each root for every tense person and number? This query will cause Prolog to list every form of every root verb for every tense and every person and every number. It essentially causes a search over every value of every variable in order to extract every possible **verb_form.** In Session 4.2, Prolog responds to this query by listing all values of *R*, *T*, *P*, *N*, and *F* that are contained as facts in **verb_form.** Session 4.2, lines 10–24, give the first three values returned by Prolog to this query. The query was stopped by entering a carriage return with no semicolon.

```
1.   % prolog
2.   C-Prolog version 1.5
3.   | ?- ['tobe_ppf.prg'].
4.   tobe_ppf.prg consulted 2320 bytes 0.166667 sec.
5.   yes
6.   | ?- ['search.prg'].
7.   search.prg consulted 2130 bytes 0.166667 sec.
8.   yes

9.   | ?- data(R,T,P,N,F).
10-  R = be    T = pres    P = 1    N = sg    F = am ;
14.
15-  R = be    T = pres    P = 1    N = pl    F = are ;
19.
20-  R = be    T = pres    P = 2    N = sg    F = are ;
24
25.  yes

26.  | ?- data(A,B,C,D,is).
27-  A = be    B = pres    C = 3    D = sg ;
30.
31.  no

32.  | ?- data(Oranges,Apples,Grapefruit,
                Ducksoup,is).
33-  Oranges = be    Apples = pres    Grapefruit = 3
36.  Ducksoup = sg ;
37.  no

38.  | ?- cntl-d
39.  [ Prolog execution halted ]
40.  %
```

Session 4.3. Querying a database. Prolog output "flattened".

Session 4.3 contains exactly the same information as Session 4.2, but in a "flattened" form. The actual screen response of Prolog is given in 4.2, but this requires one line per variable (R, T,,,). Session 4.2 indicates the Prolog input and output by giving one line per query response not per variable. I present the Prolog output in flattened form because it requires less space.

This query is more modest:

data(A,B,C,D,is).   Session 4.2: line 26.

What is the root, tense, person, and number of the form *is*? Lines 27–30 indicate the values for which the relation **data** is true. In response to the semicolon and carriage return, Prolog responds *no* indicating there is no other set of values for which the search function **data** is true, line 31.

This query is identical to the last, except the variable names are changed:

data(Oranges,Apples,Grapefruit,Ducksoup,is). Session 4.2.: line 32.

Lines 33–36 indicate the values for which the statement **data** is true. A variable can have any name. *Oranges* is as good as *R*. In writing programs, it is always best to pick names that will help you and others understand the problem.

4.4.   Variables in The Database

A variable in a database entry indicates information you know to be redundant among the facts. If we incorporate variables into the facts stored in the database and order the facts in the database judiciously, we will find Prolog is very efficient for representing tables in which most of the entries are the same.

In Table 4.1, for the plural of the verb *to be*, the **form** is *are* in all persons: *we are, you are, they are*. Program p0403 is an excerpt from p0401. These are the uncondensed complex facts that contain no variables.

We can abbreviate the three statements for the plural to one by placing a variable as the argument of **person**, for example, **person(X)** or **person (_)**. This gives us program p0404, Version 2 of Table 4.1.
This statement:

verb_form(root(be),tense(pres),person(X),numero(pl),form(are)).

is equivalent to this one:

verb_form(root(be),tense(pres),person(_),numero(pl),form(are)).

These facts are read: verb_form is *true* when *be* is a root and *pres* is a tense and anything is a person and *pl* is a numero and *are* is a form.

Because **person** has three values (*1, 2, 3*), X will range over these three values.

```
/*      Program:      p0403  Extract of: tobe_ppf.prg    */
/*             table  4.1 information:  present tense of    */
/*             the verb to be                              */

verb_form(root(be),tense(pres),person(1),numero(sg),form(am)).
verb_form(root(be),tense(pres),person(2),numero(sg),form(are)).
verb_form(root(be),tense(pres),person(3),numero(sg),form(is)).
verb_form(root(be),tense(pres),person(1),numero(pl),form(are)).
verb_form(root(be),tense(pres),person(2),numero(pl),form(are)).
verb_form(root(be),tense(pres),person(3),numero(pl),form(are)).
```

```
/*      Program:      p0404            Version 2           */
/*             table  4.1 information:  present tense of    */
/*             the  verb to be                             */

verb_form(root(be),tense(pres),person(1),numero(sg),form(am)).
verb_form(root(be),tense(pres),person(2),numero(sg),form(are)).
verb_form(root(be),tense(pres),person(3),numero(sg),form(is)).
verb_form(root(be),tense(pres),person(X),numero(pl),form(are)).
```

If we substitute Version 2 into program p0401 for Table 4.1, there would be no change in the output of the program for any query. Before considering the next examples, one should understand why p0403 and p0404 are logically equivalent.

Suppose we reorder the statements so that the facts about plural occur first, yielding Version 3, p0405. If we substitute Version 3 into program 4.1, there would be no change in the output of the program for any query.

We can squeeze more redundancy out of these facts because the form *are* occurs twice. Suppose we have one fact for *are*. The following are equivalent:

```
verb_form(root(be),tense(pres),person(X),numero(Y),form(are)).
verb_form(root(be),tense(pres),person(_),numero(Y),form(are)).
verb_form(root(be),tense(pres),person(X),numero(_),form(are)).
verb_form(root(be),tense(pres),person(_),numero(_),form(are)).
```

These facts are read: verb_form is *true* when *be* is a root and *pres* is a tense and anything is a person and anything is a numero and *are* is a form. Unfortunately, this fact makes the incorrect claim that for any person and any number *are* is a form. Ignoring the erroneous claims we can incorporate this fact into the very compressed program p0406, Version 4.

```
/*      Program:        p0405           Version 3        */
/*              table 4.1 information:  present tense of  */
/*              the verb to be                            */

verb_form(root(be),tense(pres),person(X),numero(pl),form(are)).
verb_form(root(be),tense(pres),person(1),numero(sg),form(am)).
verb_form(root(be),tense(pres),person(2),numero(sg),form(are)).
verb_form(root(be),tense(pres),person(3),numero(sg),form(is)).
```

```
/*      Program:        p0406           Version 4        */
/*              table 4.1 information:  present tense of  */
/*              the verb to be                            */

verb_form(root(be),tense(pres),person(1),numero(sg),form(am)).
verb_form(root(be),tense(pres),person(3),numero(sg),form(is)).
verb_form(root(be),tense(pres),person(_),numero(_),form(are)).
```

Suppose we query the modified versions of program p0401 with the following:

data(be,pres,1,pl,F). What is/are the **form(s)** when root is *be* and tense is *pres* and person is *1* and numero is *pl*?

data(be,pres,1,sg,F). What is/are the **form(s)** when root is *be* and tense is *pres* and person is *1* and numero is *sg*?

Session 4.4 is the script for program p0406, that is, p0401 with Version 4 of Table 4.1. For the plural, the answer is correct. For the singular, there are two answers: first, the correct answer; then, in response to the semicolon, a second incorrect answer.

```
% prolog
C-Prolog version 1.5
| ?- [p0402].
p0402 consulted 4096 bytes 0.166667 sec.
yes
| ?- [p0406].
p0406 consulted 2320 bytes 0.166667 sec.
yes

|?-data(be,pres,1,sg,F).
F = am;
F = are:
no
|?-data(be,pres,1,pl,F).
F = are;
no

| ?- cntl-d
[ Prolog execution halted ]
%
```

Session 4.4. Version 4, p0406, gives the right answer first.

Program p0407, Version 5, is identical to Version 4 except that the fact with variables occurs first.

Session 4.5 is the script for program p0407, that is, p0401 with Version 5 of Table 4.1. The answer to the query for plural forms is correct. In response to the query for singular forms, Prolog gives first the incorrect answer and then, in response to the semicolon, the correct answer.

Let us analyze our results by asking three questions:

- **Does the Prolog program give all the correct answers to a query?**
- **Does the Prolog program give only correct answers to a query?**
- **Does the Prolog program give the correct or incorrect answer(s) first?**

Program p0401, with Table 4.1 unabbreviated, gives all and only

100

correct answers to any query.

Programs p0404 and p0405, Versions 2 and 3, with the plurals abbreviated, gives all and only correct answers to any query.

```
/*      Program:      p0407        Version 5            */
/*      table  4.1 information:  present tense of       */
/*              the verb to be                          */

verb_form(root(be),tense(pres),person(X),numero(Y),form(are)).
verb_form(root(be),tense(pres),person(1),numero(sg),form(am)).
verb_form(root(be),tense(pres),person(3),numero(sg),form(is)).
```

```
% prolog
C-Prolog version 1.5
| ?- [p0402].
p0402 consulted 2320 bytes 0.166667 sec.
yes
| ?- [p0407].
p0407 consulted 2320 bytes 0.166667 sec.
yes

|?-data(be,pres,1,pl,F).
F = are;
no
|?-data(be,pres,1,sg,F).
F = are;
F = am;
no

| ?- cntl-d
[ Prolog execution haltled ]
%
```

Session 4.5. Version 5, p0407, gives the wrong answer first.

Versions 4 and 5, with only one entry for the form *are*, gives all the correct answers, but not only the correct answers. These versions claim that in English one can say: *I am* and *I are* in the first–person singular. They differ in that p0406, Version 4, gives the correct answer *I am* before it gives the incorrect answer *I are*, whereas p0407, Version 5, gives the incorrect answer first.

Which version of program 4.1 is the best? The answer depends on your needs and resources. If you want a bulletproof database, then structure all facts so that any query will get all and only correct answers. But you must pay the price in having redundancy among the entries. If you want the most compressed database possible and can live with the fact that some queries will receive all but not only correct answers, then factor all redundancy from the entries.

Planning a Prolog database means organizing and structuring redundancy. Developing search functions means exploiting the redundancy structure of the problem and the database to keep the search pointed in the correct direction.

If we know that verbs have only one form for any given tense, person, and number, then we could live comfortably with Version 4 because it gives the correct answer before it gives the incorrect answer.

Unfortunately, there are some verbs that have two forms in some cases, for example, *dive* has two past–tense forms: *Tess dove into the water and Tracy dived in after her.* If we restrict the query system to returning only one form, then we will get only correct forms, but not all the forms. I discuss verbs such as *dive* in Chapter 6.

The problems of *all* and *only* and *in which order* are general problems of all database management systems. Suppose you were looking in the library for some books about bread–making techniques used by the Roman legions during the Egyptian campaign. How did the Romans grind their flour and keep it from going rancid? What did they use to make their bread rise? Yeast, sourdough, baking powder? If you used a library search routine, you would probably be happy to know that you got *all* the relevant books even if there might be some incorrect (irrelevant) books in the list. If you knew that you had a list of *only* books dealing with Roman baking techniques, but had no assurance that your list contained *all* the relevant books, you would probably have a gnawing dissatisfaction that would impel you back into the library.

4.5. Tables with holes: *Cut, Fail,* and the *Empty Category*

English contains a rule of negative contraction that takes a *verb* + *not* and converts it to *verbn't* as in:

root	verb + not	contraction
be	was not	wasn't
do	does not	doesn't
can	can not	can't
will	will not	won't

Because English has negative contractions for certain verb roots, if there is a well–formed sentence containing *verb + not*, like those on the left, then there is a well–formed sentence containing *verbn't*, like those on the right:

(1)   We have not eaten anything.   We haven't eaten anything.
(2)   We should not forget John.   We shouldn't forget John.

For simple technical reasons, it is difficult to have Prolog programs that manipulate the contraction symbol, ', so we will not place this symbol in any words. We will discuss *isnt* and not *isn't*, *dont* and not *don't*. Basically, the quotation and apostrophe have a specific meaning to the Prolog interpreter. They are not treated as simple symbols, but as instructions.

The contractions can be formulated into Prolog statements like this one:

neg_cont(root(R),tense(T),person(P),numero(N),form(F)).

The contracted form can vary according to root, tense, person, and number. The forms of root(*have*) would be these:

neg_cont(root(have),tense(pres),person(3),numero(sg),form(hasnt)).
neg_cont(root(have),tense(pres),person(X),numero(X),form(havent)).
neg_cont(root(have),tense(past),person(X),numero(X),form(hadnt)).

There are two types of irregularities. First, the root verb *will* does not yield **willn't*. The stem changes to yield the form *won't*. This poses no problems and can simply be programmed into this Prolog statement:

neg_cont(root(will),tense(fut),person(X),numero(Y),form(wont)).

A more formidable irregularity arises when a form, such as **amn't*, does not exist:

(3)   We are not hungry.   We aren't hungry.
(4)   You are not hungry.   You aren't hungry.
(5)   They are not hungry.   They aren't hungry.
(6)   I am not hungry.   *I amn't hungry.
(7)   You are not hungry.   You aren't hungry.
(8)   She is not hungry.   She isn't hungry.

The first–person singular of the verb *to be* – *am* – does not have

103

a negative contracted form: *am not* does not form **amn't*. This is a **hole** in the table.

Alert students of English grammar recognize that the form *ain't* arose originally as the contraction of *am+not*. This form – *ain't* – gradually spread across the set of forms for *be* and *have*. We could add these entries to account for *aint*, as in: *We ain't got any. She ain't here. We ain't eaten since breakfast. Ain't* is a variant of *have* only for the auxiliary *haven't* – *I haven't/ain't got any* – not for the main verb *have* – *I haven't any time, *I ain't any time:*

neg_cont(root(be),tense(pres),person(X),numero(Y),form(aint)).
neg_cont(root(have),tense(pres),person(X),numero(Y),form(aint)).

We must differentiate a *hole* from a *null*. We will consider two examples: negative contraction and the English determiner system. The English determiner system contains a null form, but the French system does not (see Tables 4.4 and 4.5).

A **NULL FORM** exists as an entry in a table if there is a value for the form, but the value happens to be nothing. We will often call a null form an *empty category* and represent it as a lower case *e* or as two quotation marks with nothing between them, *"* or *""*.

A **HOLE** exists in a table if there is no actual form at all for the entry. To say that the value of the contraction of *am+not* is null is to say that the contracted form of *I am not hungry* is *I hungry*. But this is false. The correct

Table 4.4. English Determiners

	def	indef
sing	the man	a man
plu	the men	men

response of Prolog to the query – *What is the negative contracted form of the first person present singular of the verb to be?* – must be: *Such a form does not exist*. One might program the Prolog interpreter to return *aint* as the form, but then the question arises: Why does Prolog return only one form, *aint*, for the first person singular, and two forms, *aint* plus the contraction, for all other forms?

Let us consider some empty categories in English and see how to program *null forms* into Prolog statements as simple facts, *"* or *""*. We will then examine how to encode *holes* into the Prolog statements *fail* and *cut*. We will call the Prolog expression *""*, (or *"*), that is, two quotation marks with nothing between them, a null form. Sadly, these notations,

Table 4.5. French Determiners		
	def	indef
sing	le/la	un/une
plu	les	des

the single quote and the double quote, are understood differently by different versions of Prolog.

English has a definite determiner (*the*) and an indefinite determiner (*a*) in the singular. In the plural, English has a definite determiner with the form *the*. The plural indefinite determiner exists, but has a null form.

Table 4.4 would be encoded into Prolog by the statements in p0408, *articles.prg*.

```
/*      Program:       p0408        articles.prg          */

type(definite).
type(indefinite).
numero(plural).
numero(sing).
form(the).
form(a).
form(").

determiner(type(definite),numero(sing),form(the)).
determiner(type(definite),numero(pl),form(the)).
determiner(type(indefinite),numero(sing),form(a)).
determiner(type(indefinite),numero(pl),form(")).
```

When the value of a null form is returned from the database to the Prolog program, the value returned is: (a) the string (null string) between the quotation marks, which happens to be nothing, and (b) the quotation marks. When Prolog presents the value on the screen or in a write command, it does not present the quotation marks. The value presented is only the value between the quotation marks, which is nothing. This is true in C–Prolog and in Prolog–2.

In Session 4.6, we query program p0408 about the forms of the definite and indefinite determiner. Notice that the value returned for the plural indefinite is a blank.

```
% prolog
C-Prolog version 1.5
| ?- [p0408].
p0408 consulted 4096 bytes 0.166667 sec.
yes

|?-determiner(type(indefinite),numero(sing),form(X)).
X = a
yes

|?-determiner(type(indefinite),numero(pl),form(X)).
X =                      null form
yes

| ?- cntl-d
[ Prolog execution halted ]
%
```

Session 4.6. Where is the plural indefinite determiner, ''.?

Suppose we load the determiner database, program p0408, along with the search relation, p0409, as in Session 4.7.

```
/*       Program:        p0409          detlook.prg          */

det(X)   :-      type(T),numero(N),
                 determiner(type(T),numero(N),form(X)),
                 write('The '),
                 write(T),
                 write(' '),
                 write(N),
                 write(' determiner is: '),
                 write(X),
                 write('.'),
                 nl.
```

In Session 4.7, for the indefinite sing determiner, the statement *write(X)* outputs nothing, not even a space.

Basically, a **null form** means that the entry is phonologically and orthographically empty, although it has syntactic and semantic properties. We often call a null form an EMPTY CATEGORY. It exists, and is logically well defined, but has no phonological (sound) or orthographic (written) properties. Because it has no orthographic properties, you cannot see it in print or on the terminal screen. The location of null entries is language particular. Contrary to English, French has nonnull forms for both the plural and singular definite and indefinite determiners (see Table 4.5).

```
% prolog
C-Prolog version 1.5
| ?- [p0408].
p0408 consulted 4096 bytes 0.166667 sec.
yes
| ?- [p0409].
p0409 consulted 4096 bytes 0.166667 sec.
yes

|?-    det(X).
The definite plural determiner is: the. ;
The definite sing determiner is: a. ;
The indefinite plural determiner is: the. ;
The indefinite sing determiner is: . ;   null form
no

| ?- cntl-d
[ Prolog execution halted ]
%
```

Session 4.7. The plural indefinite det is an empty category.

The facts describing negative contractions are summarized in p0410, *form_nt.prg*, and p0411, *negcont.prg*.

The relation *nc*, defined in p0412, can be used to query the database.

A HOLE in the cell of a table must cause the Prolog interpreter to return with the news that there is no possible thing at the coordinates specified by the row and column labels. A hole must not be returned as a null form.

When Prolog wants to indicate there is a *hole* in the database and to say *Such a form does not exist*, or *The query has no possible answer*, then Prolog responds with a *fail*. This is not accomplished by having Prolog store some "hole" value in a fact. This is accomplished by having Prolog execute the two goals: !, *fail*. When the two goals *!,fail* are executed, Prolog abandons the search, returns no response to the query, and evaluates to *no*.

```
/*        Program:    p0410              form_nt.prg          */

/*  row and column labels   */
tense(pres).
tense(past).
tense(fut).
person(1).
person(2).
person(3).
numero(sg).
numero(pl).

/*  forms in tables          */
form(hasnt).
form(havent).
form(doesnt).
form(dont).
form(wont).
form(cant).
form(couldnt).
form(wasnt).
form(werent).
form(arent).
form(isnt).
```

The two goals, *!,fail*, send the message to the Prolog interpreter: *stop dead.* I discuss these goals later, but basically the exclamation point, called a CUT, is a door with the doorknob on one side so that Prolog can pass through one way, but never go back to try alternative combinations before the **cut**. FAIL is a simple goal saying: *go back and try alternatives.* The Prolog interpreter that passes a **cut** and immediately attempts to execute a **fail** is like someone who enters a closet with no doorknob on the inside. With no place to go, the interpreter quits.

A query_file normally will contain relations that incorporate the *if* (:-). A database_file normally contains only simple facts and complex facts. Sometimes, however, one must encode some program control into the database. The statement in the database_file, p0411, that includes the :- *!,fail* encodes program control into the database. There are other cases in which one can encode instructions in the entries for lexical items, but few are more complex than the entry for **amn't*, which requires us to encode instructions to the parser for a lexical item not in the lexicon.

```
/*        Program:        p0411            negcont.prg            */

root(have).            /*        root forms of verbs            */
root(be).
root(do).
root(will).
root(can).

/*        tables of negative contraction forms for root verbs        */
neg_cont(root(have),tense(pres),person(3),numero(sg),form(hasnt)).
neg_cont(root(have),tense(pres),person(X),numero(Y),form(havent)).
neg_cont(root(have),tense(past),person(X),numero(Y),form(hadnt)).

neg_cont(root(do),tense(pres),person(3),numero(sg),form(doesnt)).
neg_cont(root(do),tense(past),person(X),numero(Y),form(didnt)).

neg_cont(root(will),tense(fut),person(X),numero(Y),form(wont)).

neg_cont(root(can),tense(pres),person(X),numero(Y),form(cant)).
neg_cont(root(can),tense(past),person(X),numero(Y),form(couldnt)).

neg_cont(root(be),tense(past),person(3),numero(sg),form(wasnt)).
neg_cont(root(be),tense(past),person(1),numero(sg),form(wasnt)).
neg_cont(root(be),tense(past),person(X),numero(Y),form(werent)).
neg_cont(root(be),tense(pres),person(1),numero(sg),form(X)) :- !,fail.
neg_cont(root(be),tense(pres),person(3),numero(sg),form(isnt)).
neg_cont(root(be),tense(pres),person(X),numero(Y),form(arent)).
```

In the following, the first–person singular form is defined in a relation; the second and third person forms are defined as facts. Under each statement is the way to read the line of code:

neg_cont(root(be),tense(pres),person(1),numero(sg),form(X)) :- !,fail.

neg_cont is *true* when root is *be*, tense is *present*, person is 1, numero is sg, and form is anything if Prolog stops dead in its tracks and returns no value for X. Notice this is a *relation* with an :- separating the two parts.

neg_cont(root(be),tense(pres),person(2),numero(sg),form(arent)) .

neg_cont is *true* when root is *be*, tense is *present*, person is 2, numero is *sg*, and form is *arent*. This is a complex fact.

neg_cont(root(be),tense(pres),person(3),numero(sg),form(isnt)).

neg_cont is *true* when root is *be*, tense is *present*, person is *3*, numero is *sg*, and form is *isnt*. This is a complex fact.

```
/*        Program:        p0412        nc_look.prg        */

nc(R,T,P,N,F)    :-      root(R),tense(T),person(P),numero(N),
                        neg_cont(root(R),tense(T),
                        person(P),numero(N),form(F)).
```

Session 4.8 indicates the results of the search.

```
% prolog
C-Prolog version 1.5
| ?- [p0410].
p0410 consulted 2040 bytes 0.166667 sec.
| ?- [p0411].
p0411 consulted 8096 bytes 0.166667 sec.
| ?- [p0412].
p0412 consulted 2040 bytes 0.166667 sec.
yes

| ?- nc(be,pres,1,pl,F).
F = arent ;
no

| ?- nc(be,pres,1,sg,F).
no                                          hole

| ?- nc(be,pres,2,sg,F).
F = arent
no

| ?- nc(be,pres,3,sg,F).
F = isnt
no

| ?- cntl-D
%
```

Session 4.8. Searching database for contraction information.

chapter 5

HOW PROLOG
EXHAUSTIVELY BACKTRACKS
IN SEARCHES

However, it is not enough to have some sound and complete set of rules of inference and some procedure to apply them systematically to have a logic programming system. To be satisfactory as a computation device, a proof procedure should not leave proof possibilities unchecked (*search completeness*), that is, the procedure should terminate without a proof only if no proof exists. We do not want our programs to terminate with no answer if there is one (except possibly for running out of computational resources such as computer memory). Furthermore, a set of premises has many consequences that are definitely irrelevant to the proof of a given consequence. The proof procedure should be *goal directed* in that derivations of irrelevant consequences are avoided. We do not want the computations of a program to include subcomputations that do not at least potentially contribute in some way to the program's output.

Fernando C.N. Pereira and Stuart M. Shieber, 1987
Prolog and Natural Language Analysis

5.1.   Information Retrieval: Bibliographic Searches

A bibliography, such as Bibliography 1, can readily be programmed into simple facts, complex facts, and relations in a Prolog program.

Bibliography 1

Aoun, J. (1982). "The Formal Nature of Anaphoric

111

Relations." Ph.D. dissertation, MIT.

aker, C.L. (1970). "Notes on the Description of English
Questions," *Foundations of Language* 6.
Chomsky, N. (1965). *Aspects of the Theory of Syntax*
(Cambridge: MIT Press).
Hockney, D. (1975). "The Bifurcation of Scientific Theories
and Indeterminacy of Translation." *Philosophy of
Science*, 42.4.
Wittgenstein, L. (1953). *Philosophical Investigations*
(Oxford: Blackwell).
Zubizarreta, M.–L. (1982). "On the Relationship of the
Lexicon to Syntax." Ph.D. dissertation, MIT.

Let us program a simplified bibliography, Bibliography 2, of
fictitious authors and titles in order to illustrate how Prolog performs its
searches and to show how to modify a query to govern the order in
which Prolog presents the results of its searches. Bibliography 2 contains
books listed in order of publication, earliest first.

Bibliography 2

Franklin, Ben. 1789. Autobiography.
Durber, Tess, 1895. He Done Her Wrong.
Benton, Tess. 1933. Accounting Primer.
Morton, Ann. 1943. Introduction to Geometry.
Adler, Ben. 1944. Democracy in Action.
Morton, Zeke. 1974. Plants of the Carolinas.
Zabrisky, Albert. 1982. Space Reentry Vehicles.
Talbot, Ann. 1984. Spanish for Travelers.
Douglas, Ben. 1989. Bread Baking in France.
Durber, Tracy. 1991. Advanced Calculus.

The simple facts in the bibliography are **last** (= author's last
name), **first** (= author's first name), **date** (= date of publication), and **title**.
Program p0501, *books1.prg*, lists the facts **last** and **first** in alphabetical
order. There are no simple facts **date(...)** and **title(...)** in the database.

Notice there are no capital letters anywhere in p0501. All first and
last names must be in lower case letters. Any capital letter would be
interpreted as a variable.

Each entry is a complex fact. An entry consists of a quadruple of
simple facts: **last, first, date**, and **title**. Each entry is a record. Each simple

112

fact is a field in the entry (see Figure 5.1). The set of records for Bibliography 2 is given in p0501.

The complex facts in the bibliography program are entered in a simpler structure than were the complex facts in the *tobe_ppf.prg*, p0401. (Compare how the simple facts are incorporated into the complex facts in Figures 4.1 and 5.1.)

```
/*      Program:       p0501           books1.prg      */
/*              contains the information in bibliography 2     */

/*      entries for author and title ordered by date      */
entry(franklin,ben,1789,autobiography).
entry(durber,tess,1885,he_done_her_wrong).
entry(benton,tess,1933,accounting_primer).
entry(morton,ann,1943,introduction_to_geometry).
entry(adler,ben,1944,democracy_in_action).
entry(morton,zeke,1974,plants_of_the_carolinas).
entry(zabrisky,albert,1982,space_reentry_vehicles).
entry(talbot,ann,1984,spanish_for_travelers).
entry(douglas,ben,1989,bread_baking_in_france).
entry(durber,tracy,1991,advanced_calculus).

/*      alphabetically ordered list of last names      */

last(adler).
last(benton).
last(douglas).
last(durber).
last(franklin).
last(morton).
last(talbot).
last(zabrisky).

/*      alphabetically ordered list of first names      */

first(albert).
first(ann).
first(ben).
first(tess).
first(tracy).
first(zeke).
```

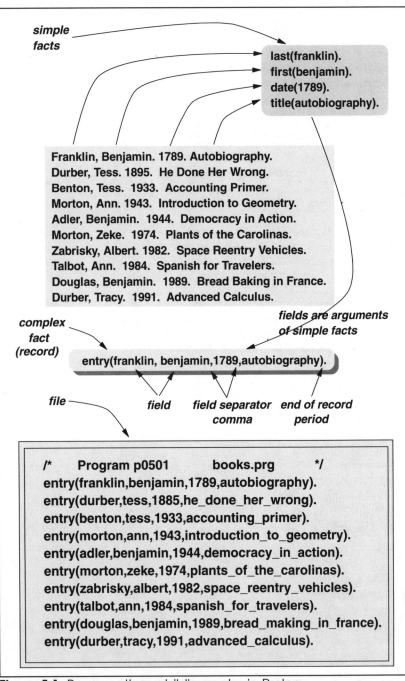

simple facts

last(franklin).
first(benjamin).
date(1789).
title(autobiography).

Franklin, Benjamin. 1789. Autobiography.
Durber, Tess. 1895. He Done Her Wrong.
Benton, Tess. 1933. Accounting Primer.
Morton, Ann. 1943. Introduction to Geometry.
Adler, Benjamin. 1944. Democracy in Action.
Morton, Zeke. 1974. Plants of the Carolinas.
Zabrisky, Albert. 1982. Space Reentry Vehicles.
Talbot, Ann. 1984. Spanish for Travelers.
Douglas, Benjamin. 1989. Bread Baking in France.
Durber, Tracy. 1991. Advanced Calculus.

complex fact (record)

fields are arguments of simple facts

entry(franklin, benjamin,1789,autobiography).

file   **field**   **field separator comma**   **end of record period**

```
/*      Program p0501        books.prg       */
entry(franklin,benjamin,1789,autobiography).
entry(durber,tess,1885,he_done_her_wrong).
entry(benton,tess,1933,accounting_primer).
entry(morton,ann,1943,introduction_to_geometry).
entry(adler,benjamin,1944,democracy_in_action).
entry(morton,zeke,1974,plants_of_the_carolinas).
entry(zabrisky,albert,1982,space_reentry_vehicles).
entry(talbot,ann,1984,spanish_for_travelers).
entry(douglas,benjamin,1989,bread_making_in_france).
entry(durber,tracy,1991,advanced_calculus).
```

Figure 5.1. Representing a bibliography in Prolog.

114

We could have made each complex fact (record) look like this:

entry(last(franklin),first(ben),date(1789),title(autobiography)).

If we did this, however, we would have to list all the possibilities for **date** and **title** as simple facts in the database. It is much simpler and less redundant to give an entry simply as:

entry(franklin,ben,1789,autobiography).

P0502 defines two search functions as relations among the facts.

```
/*      Program:      p0502        search1_2.pr        */
/*         Date:                   9/2/76              */

search1(L,F,T)  :-  last(L),first(F),entry(L,F,D,T).
search2(L,F,T)  :-  first(F),last(L),entry(L,F,D,T).
```

These functions differ only in the order of the simple facts. Although date and title are not listed in the database as simple facts, they are defined as simple facts by being presented between commas in the complex facts in the database. Each field in a complex fact is de facto a simple fact.

search1(L,F,T) :- last(L),first(F),entry(L,F,D,T).

Search1 is *true* for the values *L*, *F*, and *T* if *L* is a **last**, *F* is a **first**, and **entry** is *true* for the values *L*, *F*, *D*, and *T*.

search2(L,F,T) :- first(F),last(L),entry(L,F,D,T).

Search2 is *true* for the values *L*, *F*, and *T* if *F* is a **first**, *L* is a **last**, and **entry** is *true* for the values *L*, *F*, *D*, and *T*.

Semantically, these two functions are identical. They have exactly the same truth conditions. **Search 1** is true if and only if **search 2** is true. They will find exactly the same values for *L*, *F*, and *T*. Pragmatically, the functions differ in how they will search the database for values and in the order they will present the results of their queries.

The two searches will list every entry in the database. In the database, the entries are ordered according to date of publication. The last names and first names of authors are in alphabetical order.

115

Referring to Session 5.1, **search1**, with the order *last(L),first(F)*, lists the entries in alphabetical order according to the author's last name. If two authors have the same last name, the program lists these entries in alphabetical order according to the author's first name. Figure 5.2 indicates the flow of program control during the execution of search1 in Session 5.1.

Search2, with the order *first(F),last(L)*, lists the entries in alphabetical order according to the author's first name. If two authors have the same first name, these entries are listed in alphabetical order

```
% Prolog
C-Prolog version 1.5
| ?- ['g0501'].
g0501 consulted 2020 bytes 0.166667 sec.
yes
|?-['g0502'].
g0502 consulted 867 bytes 0.166667 sec.
yes

| ?- search1(A,B,C).
A = adler     B = ben      C = democracy_in_action ;
A = benton    B = tess     C = accounting_primer ;
A = douglas   B = ben      C = bread_baking_in_france ;
A = durber    B = tracy    C = advanced_calculus ;
A = durber    B = tess     C = he_done_her_wrong ;
A = franklin  B = ben      C = autobiography ;
A = morton    B = ann      C = introduction_to_geometry ;
A = morton    B = zeke     C = plants_of_the_carolinas ;
A = talbot    B = ann      C = spanish_for_travelers ;
A = zabrisky  B = albert   C = space_reentry_vehicles ;
no

| ?- search2(A,B,C).
A = zabrisky  B = albert   C = space_reentry_vehicles ;
A = morton    B = ann      C = introduction_to_geometry ;
A = talbot    B = ann      C = spanish_for_travelers ;
A = adler     B = ben      C = democracy_in_action ;
A = douglas   B = ben      C = bread_baking_in_france ;
A = franklin  B = ben      C = autobiography ;
A = durber    B = tracy    C = advanced_calculus ;
A = benton    B = tess     C = accounting_primer ;
A = durber    B = tess     C = he_done_her_wrong ;
A = morton    B = zeke     C = plants_of_the_carolinas ;
no

|?-cntl-d
[ Prolog execution halted ]
%
```

Session 5.1. Two search functions querying p0501, *books1.lst.*

according to the author's last name.

5.2.   Searches with and without Backtracking

In a bibliography encoded into Prolog, an entry containing one or more variables often has an unusual interpretation. Consider this entry:

entry(smith,john,D,how_to_deal_with_backache).

This states that for any given year over which D can vary, a person with the last name *Smith* and the first name *John* published a book titled: *How to deal with backache*. Depending on how many entries are listed for **date**, this could claim that *John Smith* is very prolific. It could be that one person, *John Smith*, publishes a book with the same title each year or that several different *John Smiths* each publish a book with the same title. This next entry claims that in *1932*, for all the first names over which X can vary, everyone with the last name *Murphy* wrote a book called *Latin for everyone*.

entry(murphy,X,1932,latin_for_everyone).

We will examine a database, program *books2.prg*, with this entry:

entry(X,Y,2000,real_world_semantics).

For every **last** name X and every **first** name Y in the database, in the year *2000*, each possible combination of **last** and **first** names will publish a book called *Real World Semantics*.

Program p0503, *books2.prg*, has four last names and four first names as alphabetically ordered simple facts.

When we query p0503, *books2.prg*, with **search1** and **search2**, we get the results in Session 5.2. The numbers are added to aid in discussion. Both queries list every possible combination of last and first names. **Search1** selects a last name and then selects each possible first name and therefore lists the output alphabetically according to last names. **Search2** selects a first name and then selects each possible last name and hence lists the output alphabetically by first names.

In an **exhaustive search** every possible combination of values for simple facts is generated and tested against the complex facts. Because **entry** claims that every possible combination of first and last names is an author, the responses to **search1/2** exhaust every possible combination of first and last names in the database. Both lists begin with *ann adler* and

```
/*      Program:      p0503             books2.prg             */

/*      entries for author and title ordered by date          */

entry(X,Y,2000,real_world_semantics).

/*      alphabetically ordered list of last names             */

last(adler).
last(douglas).
last(durber).
last(zabrisky).

/*      alphabetically ordered list of first names            */

first(ann).
first(ben).
first(tess).
first(zeke).
```

end with *zeke zabrisky*. Other names, such as *ann zabrisky*, are the 13th entry found by **search1** and the 4th entry found by **search2**.

Let us consider how Prolog responds to the following query posed to program *books1.prg*, in which every possible combination of first and last names is not a possible answer.

What is the first and last name of the author of *Space Reentry Vehicles*?

> **search1(A,B,space_reentry_vehicles).**
> **search2(A,B,space_reentry_vehicles).**

These queries result in Session 5.3.

In each case we obtain the correct answer, but at what cost? In **search1**, Prolog fixed the last name in goal1 as *adler* and then tried all first names, but was unable to find any entries to match. After trying each last name with every possible first name, **search1** eventually came to *A = zabrisky, B = albert* and found the entry. In **search2**, Prolog fixed the first name as *albert* and tried all the last names. On the eighth try (*adler, benton, douglas...zabrisky*), Prolog set *A = zabrisky, B = albert* and found the entry.

Consider Session 5.4. which queries p0503, *books2.prg*, for the first and last name of the (or an) author of *Real World Semantics*.

118

```
% prolog
C-Prolog version 1.5
| ?- [p0502].
p0502 consulted 1368 bytes 0.0833333 sec.
yes
| ?- [p0503].
p0503 consulted 1368 bytes 0.0833333 sec.
yes

| ?- search1(A,B,C).
A = adler     B = ann    C = real_world_semantics ;   1
A = adler     B = ben    C = real_world_semantics ;   2
A = adler     B = tess   C = real_world_semantics ;   3
A = adler     B = zeke   C = real_world_semantics ;   4
A = douglas   B = ann    C = real_world_semantics ;   5
A = douglas   B = ben    C = real_world_semantics ;   6
A = douglas   B = tess   C = real_world_semantics ;   7
A = douglas   B = zeke   C = real_world_semantics ;   8
A = durber    B = ann    C = real_world_semantics ;   9
A = durber    B = ben    C = real_world_semantics ;  10
A = durber    B = tess   C = real_world_semantics ;  11
A = durber    B = zeke   C = real_world_semantics ;  12
A = zabrisky  B = ann    C = real_world_semantics ;  13
A = zabrisky  B = ben    C = real_world_semantics ;  14
A = zabrisky  B = tess   C = real_world_semantics ;  15
A = zabrisky  B = zeke   C = real_world_semantics ;  16
no

| ?- search2(A,B,C).
A = adler     B = ann    C = real_world_semantics ;   1
A = douglas   B = ann    C = real_world_semantics ;   2
A = durber    B = ann    C = real_world_semantics ;   3
A = zabrisky  B = ann    C = real_world_semantics ;   4
A = adler     B = ben    C = real_world_semantics ;   5
A = douglas   B = ben    C = real_world_semantics ;   6
A = durber    B = ben    C = real_world_semantics ;   7
A = zabrisky  B = ben    C = real_world_semantics ;   8
A = adler     B = tess   C = real_world_semantics ;   9
A = douglas   B = tess   C = real_world_semantics ;  10
A = durber    B = tess   C = real_world_semantics ;  11
A = zabrisky  B = tess   C = real_world_semantics ;  12
A = adler     B = zeke   C = real_world_semantics ;  13
A = douglas   B = zeke   C = real_world_semantics ;  14
A = durber    B = zeke   C = real_world_semantics ;  15
A = zabrisky  B = zeke   C = real_world_semantics ;  16
no

| ?- cnt1-d
[ Prolog execution halted ]
%
```

Session 5.2. Exhaustive query for author's first and last names.

```
% prolog
C-Prolog version 1.5
|?- [p0501].
p0501 consulted 2020 bytes 0.166667 sec.
yes
|?-[p0502].
p0502 consulted 867 bytes 0.166667 sec.
yes

|?-search1(A,B,space_reentry_vehicles).
A = zabrisky  B = albert
yes

|?-search2(A,B,space_reentry_vehicles).
A = zabrisky  B = albert
yes

|?-cntl-d
[ Prolog execution halted ]
%
```

Session 5.3. Query for first and last names.

In **search1**, the last name is fixed as *adler* and the first name starts as *ann*. Because this is a possible author, it is listed. Entering a colon sends Prolog back to seek another possible answer. The Prolog interpreter keeps the last name constant and tries the next name listed in the database (*ben*). This is also acceptable, and the entry is listed. In **search2**, the first name is fixed at *ann*, and Prolog outputs the possibilities by searching the alphabetically ordered last names in the database (*adler*, *douglas*, etc.). Because every pairing of a first and last name is true, every combination is output.

Prolog searches are *exhaustive* in that they try every possible combination of simple facts in order to find all the possibilities for satisfying the query. Some searches, Session 5.1, involve *backtracking* to obtain a "correct" combination of variables, whereas others, Session 5.2, do not because every combination of variables is "correct".

The Prolog interpreter **backtracks**, that is, returns to the database to seek alternative combinations and permutations of the facts in three cases:

- when the combination of simple facts it has selected does not satisfy the query and there are still other possible alternatives that have not been tried

120

```
C-Prolog version 1.5
|?- [p0502].
p0502 consulted 2020 bytes 0.166667 sec.
yes
|?-[p0503].
p0503 consulted 1368 bytes 0.166667 sec.
yes

|?-search1(A,B,real_world_semantics).
A = adler B = ann ;
A = adler B = ben
yes

|?-search2(A,B,real_world_semantics).
A = adler B = ann ;
A = douglas        B = ann
yes

|?-cntl-d
[ Prolog execution halted ]
%
```

Session 5.4. Query for first and last names.

- when the interpreter encounters the goal **fail**
- when the user inputs a semicolon (;) when Prolog is paused.
  A carriage return terminates the search.

Both Sessions 5.1 and 5.2 illustrate backtracking. In Session 5.2, the query is satisfied by every possible combination of first and last names tried by Prolog and the interpreter only backtracks in response to the user input of a semicolon. But in session 5.1, the interpreter backtracks both during the search (because Prolog does not succeed in satisfying the query with every possible combination) and in response to the semicolon entered when Prolog pauses.

5.3.   Backtracking caused by Filters

Prolog will initiate backtracking at any point when the combination of simple facts selected cannot result in a successful query and there are still simple facts left to try. This can happen if there is no entry (complex fact) in the database to satisfy the combination selected, but it can also happen in other ways. Here I consider two factors that can initiate backtracking.

121

Let us search the database in *books1.prg* for female authors. First names can be classified according to **male** and **female** and entered as simple facts, as in p0504, *gensort.prg*.

```
/*      Program:      p0504        gensort.prg         */
/*         Date:                   3/28/85             */
/*         load:                   books1.prg          */

/*      Basic search relations for first and last names.   */

search1(L,F,T) :- first(F),last(L),entry(L,F,D,T).
search2(L,F,T) :- last(L),first(F),entry(L,F,D,T).

/*      Unordered facts about the gender associated     */
/*              with first names                        */

male(albert).
male(zeke).
female(tracy).
female(ann).
male(ben).
female(tess).

/*      These relations enable searches for female authors   */

search3(L,F,T) :- first(F),last(L),female(F),entry(L,F,D,T).
search4(L,F,T) :- last(L),first(F),female(F),entry(L,F,D,T).
```

We define two new search functions:.

search3(L,F,T) :- first(F),last(L),female(F),entry(L,F,D,T).

Search3 is true for the variables L, F, and T, if F is a first, and L is a last, and F is a female; and entry is true when L is a last, and F is a first, and D is a date, and T is a title.

search4(L,F,T) :- last(L),first(F),female(F),entry(L,F,D,T).

Search4 is true for the variables *L, F,* and *T,* if *L* is a last, and *F* is a first, and *F* is a female; and entry is *true* when *L* is a last, and *F* is a first, and D is a date, and T is a title.

These are the same as **search1/2** except that the new fact,

female(*F*), has been added.

Session 5.5 indicates the results of **search3/4** on the database in *books1.prg*. One must load both programs *books1.prg* and *gensort.prg*. **Search3** yields female authors listed alphabetically by last name. **Search4** yields the female authors alphabetically by first name.

```
% prolog
C-Prolog version 1.5
| ?- [p0501].
p0501 consulted 2020 bytes 0.166667 sec.
yes
| ?- [p0504].
p0504 consulted 2318 bytes 0.166667 sec.
yes

| ?- search3(A,B,C).
A = morton    B = ann     C = introduction_to_geometry ;
A = talbot    B = ann     C = spanish_for_travelers ;
A = durber    B = tess    C = he_done_her_wrong ;
A = benton    B = tess    C = accounting_primer ;
A = durber    B = tracy   C = advanced_calculus ;
no

| ?- search4(A,B,C).
A = benton    B = tess    C = accounting_primer ;
A = durber    B = tess    C = he_done_her_wrong ;
A = durber    B = tracy   C = advanced_calculus ;
A = morton    B = ann     C = introduction_to_geometry ;
A = talbot    B = ann     C = spanish_for_travelers ;
no

| ?- cntl-d
[ Prolog execution halted ]
%
```

Session 5.5. Querying the database for female authors.

Backtracking is always initiated by a failure at some point in the search procedure. A *failure* occurs when Prolog looks for some element in the database, but it is not there. A *success* occurs when the element is present in the database. Referring to Figure 5.2, backtracking occurs in search1 only if there is no **entry(L,F,D,T)** for the selected values of *L* and *F*. When querying p0501, **search1** initially selects *L* = *adler*, then *F* = *albert*, which results in a failure because there is no entry for an author *Albert Adler*. This failure causes Prolog to backtrack to the last variable selected, **first(F)**, and to choose the next available value in the database *F* = *ann*.

Because there is no entry for *Ann Adler*, the search fails and Prolog backtracks to the last variable selected, **first(F)**, and chooses *F = ben*. Because there is an entry for *Ben Adler*, the search succeeds and the results are printed.

Search4 on *books1.prg* can fail for two reasons. Either there is no entry for the *L* and *F* selected, or the *F* selected may not be **female**.

Referring to Figure 5.3, Prolog selects L = *adler* and F = *albert*. This fails because there is no simple fact *female(albert)*. Prolog backtracks and selects F = *ann*, but this fails because there is no entry for such an author. Prolog backtracks and selects *F = ben*. This fails because there is no entry *female(ben)*. Backtracking upon each failure, Prolog will exhaust the possible first names. When this happens, Prolog backtracks to the next higher variable that is last(L) and selects a new value, L = *benton*. The variable first(F) starts again at F = *albert*. Figure 5.3 shows the backtracking involved in locating the entry for *Tess Benton*.

Figure 5.4 attempts to represent that at any point that the search fails, Prolog always backtracks to the closest variable – the one it just set – and selects the next value in the database and tries again. If Prolog has exhausted the range of values of the closest variable, it backtracks to the next closest variable, selects the next value in the database, and tries again. If all values of all variables have been tried in all combinations and the search does not succeed, Prolog returns a *no* indicating failure. As will be shown, much of Prolog programming is coping with failure.

Search5 in p0505, *samelast.prg*, is a query that searches a database for authors with the same last name but different first names (see Session 5.6).

```
/*     Program:       p0505          samelast.prg        */
/*            Date:                   11/17/90            */
/*            load:                   books1.prg          */
/*     Relation to search for same last name, but        */
/*            different first names                       */

search5(L1,F1,T1,L2,F2,T2) :-
                 first(F1),last(L1),entry(L1,F1,XD,T1),
                 last(L2),L2==L1,
                 first(F2),not(F1==F2),
                 entry(L2,F2,YD,T2).
```

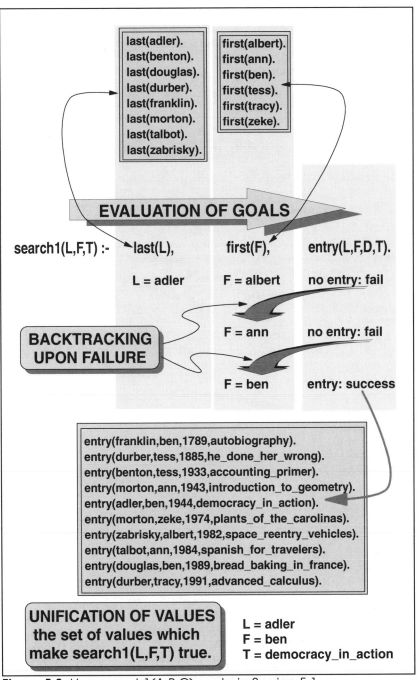

Figure 5.2. How search1(A,B,C) works in Session 5.1.

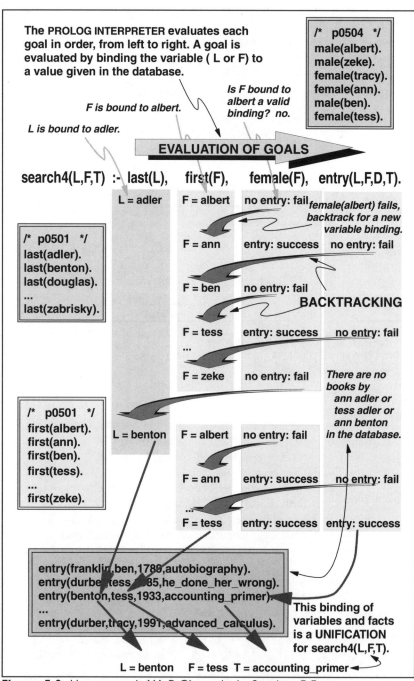

The PROLOG INTERPRETER evaluates each goal in order, from left to right. A goal is evaluated by binding the variable (L or F) to a value given in the database.

/* p0504 */
male(albert).
male(zeke).
female(tracy).
female(ann).
male(ben).
female(tess).

Is F bound to albert a valid binding? no.

F is bound to albert.

L is bound to adler.

EVALUATION OF GOALS

search4(L,F,T) :- last(L), first(F), female(F), entry(L,F,D,T).

L = adler   F = albert   no entry: fail *female(albert) fails, backtrack for a new variable binding.*

/* p0501 */
last(adler).
last(benton).
last(douglas).
...
last(zabrisky).

F = ann   entry: success   no entry: fail

F = ben   no entry: fail

BACKTRACKING

F = tess   entry: success   no entry: fail
...
F = zeke   no entry: fail

There are no books by ann adler or tess adler or ann benton in the database.

/* p0501 */
first(albert).
first(ann).
first(ben).
first(tess).
...
first(zeke).

L = benton   F = albert   no entry: fail

F = ann   entry: success   no entry: fail
...
F = tess   entry: success   entry: success

entry(franklin,ben,1789,autobiography).
entry(durber,tess,1985,he_done_her_wrong).
entry(benton,tess,1933,accounting_primer).
...
entry(durber,tracy,1991,advanced_calculus).

This binding of variables and facts is a UNIFICATION for search4(L,F,T).

L = benton   F = tess   T = accounting_primer

Figure 5.3. How search4(A,B,C) works in Session 5.5.

126

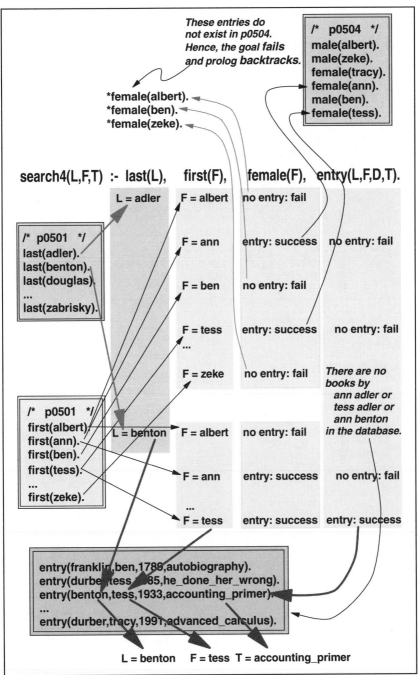

Figure 5.4. How search4(A,B,C) works in Session 5.5.

127

This query uses two built–in Prolog functions: == and *not*. Some Prologs have no way of expressing *not*. Other Prologs may express *not* by a symbol such as \= or =\=. The double equal sign (==) means "equals" and is a test for equality. The following segments are read as indicated:

last(L1),last(L2),L2==L1,

and L1 is a **last**, and L2 is a **last**, and L1 is equal to L2, and

,first(F1),first(F2),not(F1==F2),

and F1 is a first, and F2 is a first, and F1 and F2 are not equal, and

== and *not* are Prolog test functions. The statement L2==L1 is true and succeeds if L1 and L2 are equal. It is false and fails if they are not equal. The statement not(X) is true and succeeds if X is false, and it

```
% prolog
C-Prolog version 1.5
| ?- [p0501].
p0501 consulted 744 bytes 0.0333333 sec.
yes
| ?- [p0505].
p0505 consulted 1900 bytes 0.183333 sec.
yes

| ?- search5(A,B,C,D,E,F).
A = morton    B = ann      C = introduction_to_geometry
D = morton    E = zeke     F = plants_of_the_carolinas

A = durber    B = tess     C = he_done_her_wrong
D = durber    E = tracy    F = advanced_calculus

A = durber    B = tracy    C = advanced_calculus
D = durber    E = tess     F = he_done_her_wrong

A = morton    B = zeke     C = plants_of_the_carolinas
D = morton    E = ann      F = introduction_to_geometry

no

| ?-cntl-d
[ Prolog execution halted ]
%
```

Session 5.6. Querying for authors with the same last name.

128

is false and fails if X is true. So *not(F1==F2)* fails if F1 and F2 are equal, and it succeeds if F1 and F2 are different. Prolog initiates backtracking if a test function fails.

Session 5.6 indicates the results of search5 on the database in books1.prg.

Notice that search5 finds all pairs two times. This follows from the way Prolog performs exhaustive searches and backtracks. F1 and F2 can range over all possible first names, for example, F1 can be *ann* or *zeke*, and F2 can be *ann* or *zeke*. And F1 can be *ann*, when F2 is *zeke*, and vice versa. Hence, each pair is found two times. Notice that the first time the pair is listed, the first names are in alphabetical order. The second time, they are in reverse alphabetical order. As Prolog searches, it sets F1 = *ann* and F2 = *zeke*. As it continues, it eventually sets F1 = *zeke* and F2 = *ann*. Hence, owing to its exhaustive searching of all possible combinations, it finds each pair twice.

5.4.   Bound and Unbound Variables

A variable is represented by a capital letter or by any word that begins with a capital letter. A variable is *bound* when it has been assigned a particular value from the range of possible values and is *unbound* otherwise.

Consider a simple session, Session 5.7. The query *last(L)* contains a variable L. The response *L = adler* indicates that L is bound to *adler*. Entering a colon causes Prolog to backtrack to see if there is another value to which L can be bound. *L = benton* indicates the second binding for L. Each simple fact **last(...)** in the database defines one possible binding for L. There are no simple facts **date** and **title** entered in the database, so there is no way for Prolog to bind D and T in the queries *date(D)* or *title(T)* to any values. Prolog answers *no* indicating that there is no successful binding possible. In the following, however, Prolog can bind D and T to values in one query, but not in the other.

P0506 includes search6, 7, and 8.

search6(L,F,D,T) :- last(L),first(F),entry(L,F,D,T).

Search6 is true for the values L, F, D, and T if L is a last, F is a first; and entry is true for the values L, F, D, and T.

search7(L,F,D,T) :- last(L),first(F),title(T),entry(L,F,D,T).

Search7 is true if L is a last, F is a first, and T is a title; and entry is true for the values L, F, D, and T.

```
% prolog
C-Prolog version 1.5
| ?- [p0501].
p0501 consulted 1744 bytes 0.0333333 sec.
yes

|?-last(L).
L = adler ;
L = benton ;
L  = douglas
yes

|?-date(D).
no

|?-title(T).
no

| ?-cntl-d
[ Prolog execution halted ]
%
```

Session 5.7. Testing for binding to simple facts.

```
/*      Program:       p0506        search68.prg       */
/*                Date:                       Jan 5, 1992   */

search6(L,F,D,T) :- last(L),first(F),entry(L,F,D,T).
search7(L,F,D,T) :- last(L),first(F),title(T),entry(L,F,D,T).
search8(L,F,D,T) :- first(F),entry(L,F,D,T).
```

Consider Session 5.8. In **search7**, Prolog starts by binding L to *adler*, F to *ann*. But *title* is not a simple fact in the database, hence, *title(T)* fails, and the search fails. **Search6** succeeds, and T is bound to its possible values by *entry(L,F,D,T)*. Any complex fact in the database consists of a set of simple facts strung together by commas. Any item that is between commas is, by definition, a simple fact and can bind a variable. **Search6** never looks for *title(T)* as an entry in the database.

```
%  prolog
C-Prolog version 1.5
| ?- [p0501].
p0501 consulted 1744 bytes 0.0333333 sec.
yes
| ?- [p0506].
p0506 consulted 874 bytes 0.0333333 sec.
yes

|?-search6(L,F,D,T).
L = adler      F = ben            D = 1944
        T = democracy_in_action ;
L = benton     F = tess           D = 1933
        T = accounting_primer
yes

|?-search7(L,F,D,T).
no

| ?- cntl-d
[ Prolog execution halted ]
%
```

Session 5.8. Testing for unbounded variables.

Suppose we add another book to the bibliography and another entry to *books1.prg* (see p0507).

Abbot, Albert. 1985. History of the Erie Canal.

```
/*      Program:       p0507          newitem.prg        */
/*      Add this to the database  books1.prg.            */

entry(abbot,albert,1985,history_of_the_erie_canal).
```

Consider Session 5.9 with **search6** versus **search8**:

search8(L,F,D,T) :- first(F),entry(L,F,D,T).

Search8 is true for the values L, F, D, and T if F is a first, and entry is true for the values L, F, D, and T.

In Session 5.9, load p0501 – *books1.prg* – and p0507, the entry for *Albert Abbot*. We have not added a simple fact **last**(*abbot*).

131

```
%  prolog
C-Prolog version 1.5
|  ?-  [p0501].
p0501 consulted 1744 bytes 0.0333333 sec.
yes
|  ?-  [p0506].
p0506 consulted 874 bytes 0.0333333 sec.
yes
|  ?-  [p0507].
p0507 consulted 165 bytes 0.0333333 sec.
yes

|?-search6(L,F,D,T).
L = adler      F = ben          D = 1944
       T = democracy_in_action
yes

|?-search8(L,F,D,T).
L = abbot      F = albert          D = 1985
       T = history_of_the_erie_canal ;
L = adler      F = ben          D = 1944
       T = democracy_in_action
yes

 ?- cntl-d
[ Prolog execution halted ]
%
```

Session 5.9. Search6 overlooks entries.

Search6 overlooks *Albert Abbot* because there is no simple fact **last**(*abbot*), hence, *abbot* cannot be bound to *L*. **Search8** succeeds in finding the entry for *abbot* because at no point is there ever a test to see if *abbot* is a **last** in the database. **Search8** binds *abbot* to *L* by the item **entry** in the database.

5.5.   Bounded and Unbounded Variables

As discussed in Section 5.4, a variable is *bound* if it has been assigned a value by the Prolog interpreter, and it is *unbound* if it has not been assigned a value. This is the *bound/unbound distinction*.

Now let us focus on the *bounded/unbounded distinction*. Suppose we have two Prolog relations, each of which contains variables. How can we instruct the Prolog interpreter to set the variable in one relation to the same value as the variable in another relation? Usually the value of a

132

variable is *bounded*, that is, if there is a variable X in a relation, then any value to which that variable is bound in that relation does not carry over to any other occurrence of X in any other relations. The issues can be clarified by considering an example.

Often some part of a query might involve a search strategy that can be factored out of the main query and made a *subfunction* (or subquery). Some authors use the term *auxiliary function*. Later I present a case in which the print–out functions can be modularized into a subfunction. By isolating all the relations controlling the printer, one can output the results on different printers, or in different formats, simply by changing one module. In some cases, such a division into subfunctions enables the work of developing a complex Prolog program to be apportioned to different groups. In other cases the program might be modularized in order to keep some parts of the program "secret" or only in the hands of those who are privy to particular information. For instance, in a company, general employee facts such as name and address might be available to anyone. But other facts such as payroll data or age, race, and gender statistics might be kept private.

Let us develop queries, **search9** p0508 and **search10** p0509 that will examine a database, *books1.prg*, for all and only those authors that the judges have deemed "acceptable".

```
/*      Program:      p0508                                    */

search9(L,F,T)   :-      last(L),first(F),censorship_record(F,L,R),
                         acceptable(R),entry(L,F,D,T).
```

```
/*      Program:      p0509          search10.prg            */

test(F,L,R)        :-    censorship_record(F,L,R),acceptable(R).
search10(L,F,T)  :-      last(L),first(F),test(F,L,R),entry(L,F,D,T).
```

The judges rate authors and assign each one a rating: *r* = restricted to over 14, *pg* = parental guidance required, *x* = appeals to prurient interests, and *f* = foreign. The only acceptable ratings, *r* and *pg*, are listed in p0510, *censorship.prg*.

```
/*        Program Name:        p0510  censor.prg          */
/*                Date:               September 18, 1992   */
/*                load:               books1.prg           */

acceptable(r).
acceptable(pg).

censorship_record(ben,franklin,pg).
censorship_record(tess,durberville,r).
censorship_record(tess,benton,pg).
censorship_record(ann,morton,x).
censorship_record(adler,ben,x).
censorship_record(zeke,morton,r).
censorship_record(albert,zabrisky,pg).
censorship_record(ann,talbot,f).
censorship_record(ben,douglas,f).
censorship_record(tracy,durberville,r).

search9(L,F,T)   :-        last(L),first(F),censorship_record(F,L,R),
                           acceptable(R),entry(L,F,D,T).

test(F,L,R)      :-        censorship_record(F,L,R),acceptable(R).

search10(L,F,T) :-         last(L),first(F),test(F,L,R),entry(L,F,D,T).
```

Consider these program steps:

,last(L),first(F),censorship_record(F,L,R),acceptable(R),

L is a **last**, and *F* is a **first**, and **censorship_record** is *true* when *F* is a **first**, and *L* is a **last**, and *R* is a **rating**, and *R* is an **acceptable**, and

The **censorship_record** statement can *fail* if there is no complex fact in the database for the values bound to *L* and *F*. If there is an entry, then *R* is bound to the value of the rating in the entry: *r, pg, x,* or *f*. The **acceptable**(R) statement can fail if there is no simple fact in the database for the value *R*. Because there are no database entries for *x* or *f*, the statement **acceptable**(R) will fail for R bound to *x* or *f*. One could liberalize the censorship by adding **acceptable**(*x*) and perhaps even **acceptable**(*f*). Censors can tighten the screws by removing *pg* or *r* from the database.

In **search10**, the two steps of the censorship test are factored out of the general search and placed into a subprogram (subquery, subrelation) called **test(F,L,R)**. In **search9**, the censorship test is part of the main query.

Session 5.10 shows how Prolog responds to the censored searches.

```
%  prolog
C-Prolog version 1.5
| ?- [p0501].
p0501 consulted 1744 bytes 0.0333333 sec.
yes

| ?- [p0510].
p0510 consulted 4048 bytes 0.0333333 sec.
yes

| ?- search10(A,B,C).
A = benton    B = tess   C = accounting_primer ;
A = durber    B = tracy  C = advanced_calculus ;
A = durber    B = tess   C = he_done_her_wrong ;
A = franklin  B = ben    C = autobiography ;
A = morton    B = ann    C = introduction_to_geometry ;
A = zabrisky  B = albert C= space_reentry_vehicles ;
no

 ?- cntl-d
[ Prolog execution halted ]
%
```

Session 5.10. Censored searches for acceptable authors.

Search9 and **search10** produce identical outputs. Prolog binds L to *adler*, F to *albert*, and fails to find any appropriate censorship_record. Backtracking, Prolog binds F to *ben* and succeeds in finding a censorship_record. Censorship_record, according to the data_base, binds R to *x*. The next goal searches for a simple fact **acceptable(r)** and fails. Prolog continues backtracking and trying alternatives until it binds L to *benton* and F to *tess*. In the database, censorship_record for *Tess Benton* binds R to *pg*. Prolog succeeds in finding **acceptable(pg)**. Prolog succeeds in finding an entry for *Tess Benton*, and so the query can be answered. Prolog continues and produces a list of uncensored authors.

When we break off a test and make it into a subfunction, the names of the variables in the subfunction do not have to be the same as those in the main query. P0511 produces the same results as p0512.

A variable is only defined within one statement. If we have a

```
/*      Program:        p0511   censorship example 1           */

test(A,B,C)      :-         censorship_record(A,B,C),acceptable(C).
search10(L,F,T) :-          last(L),first(F),test(F,L,R),entry(L,F,D,T).
```

```
/*      Program:        p0512   censorship example 2           */

test(F,L,R)      :-         censorship_record(F,L,R),acceptable(R).
search10(L,F,T) :-          last(L),first(F),test(F,L,R),entry(L,F,D,T).
```

variable R in a statement, such as **search10**, and a variable R in another statement, such as **test**, these two variables are unrelated. The variables in one statement, and the values bound to those variables, have no bearing on the variables and the values bound to them in any other statement. In Prolog, the definition of a variable, and any values bound to that variable, are **bounded**: They are valid only internal to one statement. An **unbounded variable** would be defined over more than one statement. These are best avoided because any change in an unbounded variable in one statement will have implications for all other statements in the program.

Internal to any given statement, the variables must be consistently used. The two searches in p0513 will not produce the same output.

```
/*      Program:        p0513                                  */

/*      censorship example 3                                   */
search9(L,F,T)   :-         last(L),first(F),censorship_record(A,B,C),
                            acceptable(C),entry(L,F,D,T).

/*      censorship example 4                                   */
search9(L,F,T)   :-         last(L),first(F),censorship_record(F,L,R),
                            acceptable(R),entry(L,F,D,T).
```

5.6.   A Blunder Popular with Beginning Programmers

In discussing *bound/unbound* and *bounded/unbounded*, we indicated various logical properties of the Prolog interpreter. Now let us focus on a type of error made by almost all beginning programmers. Call it the DASH PROBLEM, because it is often encountered when the program prints dashes, underlines, or numbers instead of the anticipated values.

```
/*      illustration of the dash_problem */
letter(a).
letter(b).
lettter(c).
dash_problem   :-      write(X),letter(X),fail.
no_problem     :-      letter(X),write(X),fail.
```

In this illustration, no_problem binds X to *a* and writes *a* and fails; backtracking, it binds X to *b* and writes *b* and fails; backtracking, it returns to bind X to *c* and writes *c* and fails. Dash_problem tries to write(X) before it has bound X to anything. What does Prolog do when it has to print a variable, X, when X is not bound to anything? It depends on the Prolog version. Usually it prints an underline, sometimes an underline or a dash, or sometimes a number. From a *logical point of view*, dash_problem and no_problem are equivalent. But from a *procedural point of view* – remember that Prolog evaluates the goals from left to right – these are very different.

Prevention is the best cure for the dash problem. If you have a case, then when you read your program use the procedural phrase *has been* instead of *is* when you think about variable bindings. Do not say, X *is bound to a*, say rather X **has been** *bound to a*, as you read your program from left to right. The dash problem usually arises from procedural considerations not from logical inconsistency. In the earlier example, X is logically bound to a variable in both dash_problem and no_problem. But at the point the Prolog interpreter is evaluating the truth of the write(X) goal, the X has not been bound in dash_problem, but it has been bound in no_problem.

Consider next a case in which the dash problem is less obvious.

P0514 defines two relations: search11 and search12. The dash problem rears its ugly head in search11.

```
/*      Program:        p0514   gensort.lst             */
/*              sort by gender                           */
/*              load   books1.lst                        */

/*      unordered facts about the gender associated      */
/*              with first names                          */

male(albert).
male(zeke).
female(tracy).
female(ann).
male(ben).
female(tess).

/*      relations which enable a search for woman authors    */

man(X)          :-      first(X),male(X).
woman(X)        :-      first(X),female(X).

search11(L,F,T) :-      woman(F),entry(L,F,D,T).
search12(L,F,T) :-      last(L),woman(F),entry(L,F,D,T).
```

Session 5.11 indicates why this is called the dash problem. Notice that variable A in the query, which should be a last name, is printed as _0. Search12 produces acceptable output but search 11 has a problem.

To measure your understanding, answer this question: What would be the output of the search11 and search12 in this session:

```
% prolog
| ?- [p0501].
| ?- [p0514].
| ?- search11(A,B,C).
        results-11
| ?- search12(A,B,C).
        results-12
|?- cntl-d
%
```

In learning to program in Prolog you should be able to answer two questions before you run a program: (a) What will the output of the program be? (b) Why will this be the output? Of the two questions, the latter is the more important. Answer these two questions for the earlier session with p0501. Notice that in one case the dash problem appears on the first query and then disappears on subsequent queries.

```
% prolog
C-Prolog version 1.5
| ?- [p0503].
p0503 consulted 2048 bytes 0.0833333 sec.
yes
| ?- [p0514].
p0514 consulted 1368 bytes 0.0833333 sec.
yes

| ?- search11(A,B,C).
A = _0          B = ann       C = real_world_semantics
A = _0          B = tess      C = real_world_semantics
no

| ?- search12(A,B,C).
A = adler      B = ann       C = real_world_semantics
A = adler      B = tess      C = real_world_semantics
A = douglas    B = ann       C = real_world_semantics
A = douglas    B = tess      C = real_world_semantics
A = durber     B = ann       C = real_world_semantics
A = durber     B = tess      C = real_world_semantics
A = zabrisky   B = ann       C = real_world_semantics
A = zabrisky   B = tess      C = real_world_semantics
no

| ?- cntl-d
[ Prolog execution halted ]
%
```

Session 5.11. A search with unbound variables.

5.7. Report Generation: Formatting Output and Write

When we present Chomsky's grammar and show how to encode the dictionaries and rules of grammar, we will often use square brackets [ ] and parentheses ( ). This opens a formidable host of problems. Prolog treats square brackets and parentheses as instructions to the interpreter. Prolog statements use ( ) to enclose argument lists, for example, *write('hello').*, and [ ] to indicate a list structure (see Session 5.12). But we want to treat (,), [, and] as part of the data. To get ahead of the story, we will want to have a Prolog program analyze a string, such as, *the girl*, into its parts, *(np (det the) (n girl))*.

The best way to learn to manipulate (,), [, and] in Prolog programs is to study the types of data structures that exist in

139

```
% prolog
C-Prolog version 1.5

|?-write('This is a message.').
This is a message.
yes

|?-write('abcd'),write('efgh').
abcdefgh
yes

|?-write('abcd'),nl,write('e,f,g,h').
abcd
efgh
yes

|?-write('abcd'),write(' '),write('efgh'),nl.
abcd efgh

yes

|?-write('').

yes

| ?- cntl-d
[ Prolog execution halted ]
%
```

Session 5.12. Examples of the *write* goal.

bibliographies. Real bibliographies found in scholarly journals use many punctuation characters (that Prolog treats as instructions to the interpreter) as data. I give more complicated examples in Chapter 7. Here, let us begin to scratch the surface. First I discuss the properties of Prolog output goals, then turn to bibliographic formats.

A Prolog *output goal* is a statement that writes data to the screen, to a disk, or to some other output medium. A Prolog *input goal* accepts data from some source, such as, a keyboard, a mouse, a disk, or a touch screen. Prolog input and output goals, although easy to understand, behave differently on various computers (VAX, IBM, Apple). Also, each version of Prolog seems to have its own idiosyncratic way of handling input and output functions. In this work, we will write everything to the computer screen.

If you want to use information on a disk, usually the instructions for disk operation include: *open, close, tell, told, say, said, read, see, seen, put,* and *get*. If you have a manual, read it, because information about disk usage is subject to many constraints specific to your machine and your version of Prolog. The materials in this text were developed using UNIX script files on an ULTRIX VAX. For information about how to output information to disk using *script*, type *man script* at the % UNIX prompt.

The Prolog instruction *write(X)* is *true* and succeeds if Prolog can write the information X to the screen (printer, disk, tape), and it is *false* and fails if it cannot (if perhaps the screen is turned off, printer out of paper, etc.). The instruction *nl* (newline) is *true* and succeeds if Prolog can send a carriage return and start printing on a new line, and it is *false* and fails otherwise (see session 5.12).

It is odd to think of *write(X)* and *nl* as "logical" statements that have an incidental property in that they cause output to appear somewhere. Normally one would think that the *write* and *nl* statements are "action" statements that cause some output to appear and, only incidentally, they have the "logical" property of reporting back *yes*, the print was successful, or *no*, the operation failed. In any event, Prolog considers all statements to be primarily "logical" statements, some of which may secondarily have "side effects" that cause actions.

The statement *write(', ')* is *true* if Prolog outputs to the screen a comma and a space, and false otherwise. If the printers, screen, and so on, are plugged in, have paper and disks, and are not jammed, *write* and *nl* statements are always true.

Bibliographies have specific formats that vary from publication to publication. The following bibliographies contain the same information, but in different formats.

Bibliography Format I

Chomsky, Noam. 1955. Syntactic Structures. The Hague: Mouton.
Jespersen, Otto. 1964. Essentials of English Grammar. Forge Valley,
    Mass.: Murray Company.
Chomsky, Noam. 1965. Aspects of the Theory of Syntax. Cambridge,
    Mass.: MIT Press.
Chomsky, Carol 1969. The Acquisition of Syntax in Children from 5 to 10.
    Cambridge, Mass.: MIT Press.
Lorenz, Konrad. 1973. Behind the Mirror. New York: Harcourt Brace Co.

Bibliography Format II

Chomsky, Noam. (1957) Syntactic Structures. (Mouton) The Hague.
Jespersen, Otto. (1964) Essentials of English Grammar. (Murray Company)
    Forge Valley, Mass.

Chomsky, Noam. (1965) Aspects of the Theory of Syntax. (MIT Press) Cambridge, Mass.
Chomsky, Carol. (1969) The Acquisition of Syntax in Children from 5 to 10. (MIT Press) Cambridge, Mass.
Lorenz, Konrad. (1973) Behind the Mirror. (Harcourt Brace Co) New York.

These two bibliographies differ in punctuation and the order of information. Bibliography II contains parentheses, whereas I does not, and Bibliography II presents the publisher before the address, whereas I has the reverse order. The database in p0515, *realthng.pgr*, has the information in Bibliographies I and II encoded into Prolog statements.

```
/*  Program:   p0515              realthng.prg          */
/*             Date:              November 17, 1990      */

/*  alphabetical list of last names                     */
last(chomsky).
last(jespersen).
last(lorenz).

/*  alphabetical list of first names                    */
first(carol).
first(konrad).
first(noam).
first(otto).

entry(chomsky, noam, 1957,syntactic_structures,the_hague,
          mouton).
entry(jespersen,otto,1964,essentials_of_english_grammar,
          forge_valley_mass,murray_co).
entry(chomsky,noam,1965,aspects_of_the_theory_of_syntax,
          cambridge_mass,mit_press).
entry(chomsky,carol,1969,the_acquisition_of_syntax_in_
          children_from_5_to_10,cambridge_mass,mit_press).
entry(lorenz,konrad,1973,behind_the_mirror,new_york,
          harcourt_brace_co).
```

The entries are not in alphabetical order in our examples. In order to alphabetize the entries, we would have to introduce new data structures (some sort of array or matrix) and delve into Prolog relations for greater_than and less_than. Because these data structures and relations seem to play no role in defining the properties of human

142

memory and computation that underly human language, we have no interest in presenting them. Hence, we will not worry about alphabetizing the entries.

Search13 and search14, in p0516, differ only in the format statement: *format1* outputs the information in the database in the format of Bibliography I and *format2* in the style of Bibliography II. These statements input information and output the information to the screen.

```
/*      Program:      p0516   bibliog.prg                    */
/*            Date:           November 18, 1990              */

format1(L,F,D,T,W,P)    :-    write(L),write(', '),write(F),write('. '),
                              write(D),write('. '),write(T),write('. '),
                              write(W),write(': '),write(P),write('.'),nl.


format2(L,F,D,T,W,P)    :-    write(L),write(', '),write(F),write('. '),
                              write('('),write(D),write(') '),
                              write(T),write(' '),
                              write('('),write(P),write(') '),
                              write(W),write('.'),nl.


search13(L,F)           :-    last(L),first(F),entry(L,F,D,T,W,P),
                              format1(L,F,D,T,W,P).

search14(L,F)           :-    last(L),first(F),entry(L,F,D,T,W,P),
                              format2(L,F,D,T,W,P).
```

Consider the Prolog relation, *format1*, which formats the database according to the structure of bibliography I.

```
format1(L,F,D,T,W,P)    :-    write(L),write(', '),write(F),write('. '),
                              write(D),write('. '),write(T),write('. '),
                              write(W),write(': '),write(P),write('. '),nl.
```

This is read:

Format is true for the variables L, F, D, T, W, and P if
L is written, and ', ' is written, and F is written, and '. ' is written, and
D is written, and '. ' is written, and T is written, and '. ' is written, and
W is written, and ': ' is written, and P is written, and '. ' is written, and

143

newline is true.

Session 5.13 indicates how search13 and search14 produce formatted output from the bibliography in p0515, *realthng.prg*. There are three problems with the program as it exists.

```
% prolog
C-Prolog version 1.5
| ?- ['p0515'].
p0515 consulted 1716 bytes 0.1 sec.
yes

| ?- [p0516].
p0516 consulted 1716 bytes 0.1 sec.
yes

| ?- search13(L,F).

chomsky, carol. 1969.
the_acquisition_of_syntax_in_children_from_5_to_10.
cambridge_mass: mit_press.
L = chomsky
F = carol ;

chomsky, noam. 1957. syntactic_structures. the_hague:
mouton.
L = chomsky
F = noam

yes

| ?- search14(L,F).

chomsky, carol. (1969)
the_acquisition_of_syntax_in_children_from_5_to_10
(mit_press) cambridge_mass.
L = chomsky
F = carol ;

chomsky, noam. (1957) syntactic_structures (mouton)
the_hague.
L = chomsky
F = noam

yes

| ?- cntl-d
[ Prolog execution halted ]
%
```

Session 5.13. Two formatted bibliographies.

First, the bibliographies have no capital letters and have a dash instead of a space. These curious features could be rectified by elaboration of the technical details of the programs. The simplest way to adorn the bibliography with capitals, spaces, and colons is to use the *name* relation (discussed in Chapter 7, see Figures 7.21 and 7.22).

Second, the bibliographies output the values of L and F each time they locate an entry. This is readily cured by changing the *wh*-query to a *yes/no* query. These statements will produce formatted bibliographies with no extraneous information.

search15 :- last(L),first(F),entry(L,F,D,T,W,P),format1(L,F,D,T,W,P).
search16 :- last(L),first(F),entry(L,F,D,T,W,P),format2(L,F,D,T,W,P).

Third, the searches will not output the full bibliography unless the user inputs a semicolon and carriage return after each entry. The remedy for this is an instruction, *fail*, which has the same effect as hitting a semicolon and a carriage return. The instruction **fail**, by definition, always fails and causes the program to backtrack.

search17 :- last(L),first(F),entry(L,F,D,T,W,P),format1(L,F,D,T,W,P),fail.
search18 :- last(L),first(F),entry(L,F,D,T,W,P),format2(L,F,D,T,W,P),fail.

Session 5.14 indicates the results of querying the database in p0515 with search17 and search18 defined in p0517.

```
/*      Program:      p0517   bibliog1.prg                */
/*                    Date:            March 28, 1986      */

search15        :-      last(L),first(F),entry(L,F,D,T,W,P),
                        format1(L,F,D,T,W,P).

search16        :-      last(L),first(F),entry(L,F,D,T,W,P),
                        format2(L,F,D,T,W,P).

search17        :-      last(L),first(F),entry(L,F,D,T,W,P),
                        format1(L,F,D,T,W,P),fail.

search18        :-      last(L),first(F),entry(L,F,D,T,W,P),
                        format2(L,F,D,T,W,P),fail.
```

145

```
% prolog
C-Prolog version 1.5
| ?- [p0515].
p0515 consulted 1636 bytes 0.1 sec.
yes

| ?- [p0516].
p0516 consulted 1636 bytes 0.1 sec.
yes

| ?- [p0517].
p0517 consulted 1636 bytes 0.1 sec.
yes

| ?- search17.
chomsky, carol. 1969.
the_acquisition_of_syntax_in_children_from_5_to_10.
cambridge_mass: mit_press.
chomsky, noam. 1955. syntactic_structures. the_hague:
mouton.
chomsky, noam. 1965. aspects_of_the_theory_of_syntax.
cambridge_mass: mit_press.
jespersen, otto. 1964. essentials_of_english_grammar.
forge_valley_mass: murray_co.
lorenz, konrad. 1973. behind_the_mirror. new_york:
harcourt_brace_co.
no

| ?- search18.
chomsky, carol. (1969)
the_acquisition_of_syntax_in_children_from_5_to_10
(mit_press) cambridge_mass.
chomsky, noam. (1957) syntactic_structures (mouton)
the_hague.
chomsky, noam. (1965) aspects_of_the_theory_of_syntax
(mit_press) cambridge_mass.
jespersen, otto. (1964) essentials_of_english_grammar
(murray_co) forge_valley_mass.
lorenz, konrad. (1973) behind_the_mirror
(harcourt_brace_co) new_york.
no

| ?- cntl-d
[ Prolog execution halted ]
%
```

Session 5.14. Two formatted bibliographies.

chapter **6**

THE CANONICAL FORM
OF A
PROLOG RELATION

Meno. And how will you enquire, Socrates, into that which you do not know? What will you put forth as the subject of enquiry? And if you find what you want, how will you ever know that this is the thing that you did not know?

Socrates. I know, Meno, what you mean; but just see what a tiresome dispute you are introducing. You argue that a person cannot enquire either about that which he knows, or about that which he does not know; for if he knows, he has no need to enquire; and if not, he cannot; for he does not know the very subject about which he is to enquire.

Meno. Well, Socrates, and is not the argument sound?

Socrates. I think not.

Meno. Why not?

Socrates. I will tell you why: I have heard from certain wise men and women who spoke of things divine that –

Meno. What did they say?

Socrates. They spoke of a glorious truth, as I conceive.

Plato
Meno

6.1.   Some Irregular Verbs in English

Most verbs in English have three different forms that occur in the present and past tenses. The root *look*, a typical regular verb, has the present–tense forms *look* and *looks*: *I look, you look, we look, you guys look, they look*. For the third–person singular, one adds an *s* to the root: *he/she/it looks*. The past–tense form is *looked* in all cases.

```
root(look).
form(looks).
form(look).
form(looked).
```

P0601, *irreg.prg*, gives a Prolog database for some irregular verbs in English.

Some verbs (*cost, hit...*) have only two forms. The form *cost* is both present and past: *They cost a dollar today. They cost (*costed) two dollars yesterday.* The third–person singular present is *costs*: *It costs a dollar today, but it cost two dollars yesterday.* The verb *read* has the same form in the present and past, but only at the orthographic level.

```
root(cost).
form(costs).
form(cost).
```

Some verbs (*awake, bless, dive, dream, burn, hung, grind, shine...*) have four forms. They have two different past tense forms. The third–person present adds an *s* on the root: *he/she/it dives into the water.* The remaining present forms are identical to the root: *I, you, we, you guys, they dive into the water.* In the past tense we can say: *She dived into the water.* And also: *She dove into the water.* More examples are: *I never dreamed/dreamt... The fire burnt/burned...*

```
root(dive).
form(dive).
form(dives).
form(dived).
form(dove).
```

A verb like *lay* has two past–tense forms (*lay and laid*), and one of the past–tense forms (*lay*) is identical to the present–tense form (*lay*). Present tense: *Now I lay me down to sleep.* Past tense: *Jesus lay in the manger, while the more affluent slept in the hotel. Jesus laid in the manger waiting for the wise men.*

```
root(lay).
form(lays).
form(laid).
form(lay).
```

In this chapter, we will assume that *lay* is a verb with two past tenses. An alternative analysis is to assume that there are two different verbs: *lie* with the past tense *lay*, and *lay* with the past tense *laid*. There

```
/*  Program:          p0601          irreg.prg          */

    root(cost).                    form(lay).
    root(look).                    form(laid).
    root(dive).                    form(will_lay).
    root(hit).
    root(lay).
    root(shine).                   vf(shine,pres,3,sg,shines).
                                   vf(shine,pres,X,Y,shine).
    tense(past).                   vf(shine,past,X,Y,shined).
    tense(pres).                   vf(shine,past,X,Y,shone).
    tense(fut).                    vf(shine,fut,X,Y,will_shine).
    person(1).
    person(2).                     vf(cost,pres,3,sg,costs).
    person(3).                     vf(cost,pres,X,Y,cost).
    numero(sg).                    vf(cost,past,X,Y,cost).
    numero(plu).                   vf(cost,fut,X,Y,will_cost).

                                   vf(dive,pres,3,sg,dives).
    form(shines).                  vf(dive,pres,X,Y,dive).
    form(shine).                   vf(dive,past,X,Y,dove).
    form(shined).                  vf(dive,past,X,Y,dived).
    form(will_shine).              vf(dive,fut,X,Y,will_dive).
    form(costs).
    form(cost).                    vf(look,pres,3,sg,looks).
    form(will_cost).               vf(look,pres,X,Y,look).
    form(dives).                   vf(look,past,X,Y,looked).
    form(dive).                    vf(look,fut,X,Y,will_look).
    form(dove).
    form(dived).                   vf(hit,pres,3,sg,hits).
    form(will_dive).               vf(hit,pres,X,Y,hit).
    form(looks).                   vf(hit,past,X,Y,hit).
    form(look).                    vf(hit,fut,X,Y,will_hit).
    form(looked).
    form(will_look).               vf(lay,pres,3,sg,lays).
    form(hits).                    vf(lay,pres,X,Y,lay).
    form(hit).                     vf(lay,past,X,Y,lay).
    form(will_hit).                vf(lay,past,X,Y,laid).
    form(lays).                    vf(lay,fut,X,Y,will_lay).
```

149

are several verbs with two past–tense forms such that one of them is the same as the present form, for instance: *spit, spat/spit*; and *outbid, outbade/outbid*. *Outbid/outbade* sounds archaic and *spit/spat* sounds vulgar. Concessions to modernity and our concern with propriety suggest we use *lay/laid* in examples. The mechanisms extend readily to other verbs. In some computer manuals, one encounters *output* and *outputted* as past tense forms of *to output*. I have not seen **putted* as the past–tense of *put*.

We will design Prolog queries to answer the question Which verb(s) have the same form in two tenses? Answers should include: *cost* and *hit*.

6.2.   Head, Generator, Filter, Database, Output, Backtrack.

There are two types of Prolog queries. A *wh–query* contains variables in the head and returns either a *yes* along with the values of the variables that make the head *true* or *no*. A **yes/no query** does not contain variables in the head and returns either *yes* or *no*.

A query can be directed at simple facts, complex facts, or it can be a relation that questions logical interactions among the simple and complex facts.

yes/no query on simple fact.
    last(durber).
wh–query on simple fact.
    last(X).
yes/no query on complex fact.
    entry(benton,tess,1933,accounting_primer).
wh–query on a complex fact.
    entry(X,Y,1933,accounting_primer).

The most interesting cases are queries defined by relations.

yes/no query defined by a relation
    search :- last(L),first(F),entry(L,F,D,T),fail.
wh–query defined by a relation
    search(L,T) :- last(L),first(F),entry(L,F,D,T).

Any relation can be cast into a *canonical form*, as in Figure 6.1. We can think of any relation as being composed of six modules. A *module* is a set of Prolog statements that are related in that they all interact to perform some single function. The first module, required in any Prolog relation, is the *head*. The other five modules comprise the *body*.

BODY of the Prolog relation

HEAD :-	GENERATOR	FILTER	DATABASE	OUTPUT	BACKTRACK
Fixes order of responses for interactive *wh-* query. Types: *wh-* and *yes/no*. Names the relation.	Fixes order of search combinations over simple facts.	Eliminate fruitless searches. Restrict searches.	Test prolog's generated combination of facts against the complex facts that exist.	Generate a report formatted for the screen, printer, disk... Add comments to the report.	Look again: fail. Look again: ; Stop: ! = cut
search2 :-	last(L),first(F),		entry(L,F,D,T).		
search4 :-	last(L),first(F),	female(F),	entry(L,F,D,T).		
search10 :-	last(L),firstF),	test(F,L,R),	entry(L,F,D,T).		
search## :-	last(L),first(F),		entry(L,F,D,T,W,P),	format1(L,F,D,T,W,P),	fail.

Figure 6.1. The canonical form of a prolog relation. Any prolog relation can be logically divided into six different modules. Each module could be factored out and made into a sub-program. The most common modules factored out are *filter* and *output*.

If we are writing a program, it is useful to conceptualize our problem in terms of these six modules. As we shall see, however, once we have written a program in this format, we often can make it more efficient by rewriting the program to combine some of the modules.

Referring to p0601 and p0602 (see Session 6.1), *irreg.prg* defines two queries to ask: *Which verb roots have the same form in two tenses?* **Searcha** is a *wh*–query and **searchb** a *yes/no* query. Very often a *yes/no* query contains an output module to generate a report.

```
/*      Program:      p0602           irreg.prg               */

/*      wh-:  Which verb roots have the same form in          */
/*              two tenses?                                    */
searcha(R) :-                                 HEAD, wh-
        root(R),tense(T1),tense(T2),form(F1),  GENERATOR
                form(F2),person(P),numero(N),
        not(T1==T2),F1==F2,                    TEST
        vf(R,T1,P,N,F1),                       DATABASE
        vf(R,T2,P,N,F2),                       DATABASE
        fail.                                  +BACKTRACK

/*      yes/no  Which verb roots have the same form           */
/*              in two tenses?                                 */
searchb :-                                    HEAD, yes/no
        root(R),tense(T1),tense(T2),form(F1),  GENERATOR
                form(F2),person(P),numero(N),
        not(T1==T2),F1==F2,                    TEST
        vf(R,T1,P,N,F1),                       DATABASE
        vf(R,T2,P,N,F2),                       DATABASE
        write('Root verb = '),write(R),nl,     OUTPUT
        fail.                                  +BACKTRACK
```

Any *wh*– relation can be made into a *yes/no* query by giving the variable a value in the query. *Searcha(R)* is a *wh*–query that will return the values of *R* for which the relation is true. *Searcha(cost)* is a *yes/no* question that will respond *yes* if *cost* has the same form in two tenses and *no* if it does not. *Searcha(hit)* responds *yes*. *Searcha(dive)* responds *no*.

Searcha/b are quite inefficient in that the generator modules produce an enormous number of possible combinations of simple facts and then the filter module eliminates most of them. In general, in Prolog programming we can make the searches more efficient in two ways.

First, we can draw upon our knowledge of the problem. In all cases, one tense will be *present* and the other *past*. Rather than set T1 and T2 to all possibilities (nine combinations of past, present, and future) and then eliminate most of them, we can simply include in the DATABASE module the information that we are looking for – one *past*–tense entry and one *present*–tense entry.

Second, we can use simple logic to eliminate redundancy. We can eliminate the statements *form(F1),form(F2),F1==F2*, and replace them with a single statement *form(F12)*. If we use the item *F12* in every place we used *F1* and *F2*, then *F1* will always equal *F2* because they are the same variable.

When we do not follow the standard format for a Prolog program, it is usually because we are exploiting our knowledge of the problem or because we are using logic to simplify redundant statements. In these cases, it is best to include a few lines of comment to serve as documentation for future reference. In p0603, **Searchc/d** are efficient versions of **searcha/b** and include the information in the comment that they look for a single form (*F12*) in only the *past* and the *present* tenses.

```
/*      Program:      p0603          irreg1.prg          */

/*      wh-:    Which verb root has the same form (F12)  in    */
/*      the past tense and the present tense?            */
searchc(R) :-
        root(R),form(F12),person(P),numero(N),
        vf(R,past,P,N,F12),
        vf(R,pres,P,N,F12),
        fail.

/*      yes/no: Which verb root has the same form (F12)       */
/*      in the past tense and the present tense?              */
searchd :-
        root(R),form(F12),person(P),numero(N),
        vf(R,past,P,N,F12),
        vf(R,pres,P,N,F12),nl,
        write('Root verb = '),write(R),write('.'),
        fail.
```

Session 6.1 indicates the results of querying p0601, *irreg.prg*, with **searchb** and **searchd**. Although we get all and only the correct answers – *cost*, *hit*, and *lay* – we get the correct answers too many times.

Searchb takes a lot longer (eight times on our machine) than searchd. When searchb runs, there is a long wait while Prolog executes

```
% prolog
C-Prolog version 1.5
| ?- [p0601].
p0601 consulted 3896 bytes 0.3 sec.
yes
| ?- [p0602].
p0602 consulted 3896 bytes 0.3 sec.
yes
| ?- [p0603].
p0603 consulted 3896 bytes 0.3 sec.
yes

| ?- searchb.                       Root verb = lay
        long wait                   Root verb = lay
Root verb = cost                         short wait
Root verb = cost                    Root verb = lay
Root verb = cost                    Root verb = lay
Root verb = cost                    Root verb = lay
Root verb = cost                    Root verb = lay
Root verb = cost                    Root verb = lay
        short wait                  Root verb = lay
Root verb = cost                    yes
Root verb = cost
Root verb = cost                    | ?- searchd.
Root verb = cost                    Root verb = cost.
Root verb = cost                    Root verb = cost.
        long wait                   Root verb = cost.
Root verb = hit                     Root verb = cost.
Root verb = hit                     Root verb = cost.
Root verb = hit                     Root verb = hit.
Root verb = hit                     Root verb = hit.
Root verb = hit                     Root verb = hit.
Root verb = hit                     Root verb = hit.
                                    Root verb = hit.
        short wait                  Root verb = hit.
Root verb = hit                     Root verb = lay.
Root verb = hit                     Root verb = lay.
Root verb = hit                     Root verb = lay.
Root verb = hit                     Root verb = lay.
Root verb = hit                     Root verb = lay.
Root verb = hit                     Root verb = lay.
        long wait                   no
Root verb = lay
Root verb = lay                     |?-cnt1-d
Root verb = lay                     %
```

Session 6.1. Querying the lexicon for irregular verbs.

154

the generator and test parts of the program. The generator hits a winning combination with R = *cost*, T1 = *pres*, T2 = *past*, P = *1*, and N = *sg*, so it types out Root verb = *cost*. It quickly backtracks to run P and N through five more combinations, and succeeds on each. After a short pause during which **searchb** backtracks to reset T1 = *past* and T2 = *pres*, it again outputs the six responses for *cost*.

The long pause indicates that Prolog has backtracked in **searchb** to reset the root(R). One can vary how long the long pauses will be by reordering the simple facts root in the database. The short pause indicates that Prolog has backtracked to reset T1, T2, F1, and F2.

Searchd proceeds very quickly. It gives the correct answers, but too many times. Because it never resets any tense variables, it outputs the information for each verb only for the six variations of *P* and *N*.

There are two errors indicated in the scriptfile for **searchb**. First, it would be best if *cost* were listed only once, and I discuss this in the next section. Second, the program should have listed *cost* only five times because the third–person singular present is *costs* and the past is *cost*. However, our database gives *all, but not only*, the correct forms for the present of *cost*. On the first try, the third–person singular is *costs*, but on the second try, the erroneous *cost* is offered.

Prolog programs are often difficult to read and understand because they do not follow the standard form. In virtually every case, however, a program can be rewritten in the standard form to make it more comprehensible, albeit less efficient. Consider **search5** in program p0604, *samelast.prg*. This could be rewritten as **search5a**, p0605.

```
/*      Program:      p0604          samelast.prg          */
/*                    load:    books1.lst                  */
/*      relation to search for same last name, but         */
/*                 different first names                   */

search5(L1,F1,T1,L2,F2,T2) :-
                      first(F1),last(L1),entry(L1,F1,XD,T1),
                      last(L2),L2==L1,
                      first(F2),not(F1==F2),
                      entry(L2,F2,YD,T2).
```

Search5 tests to see if there is an entry for the values L1 and F1 before it selects an L2 and F2 and runs the tests. If there is no entry for L1 and F1, then it backtracks until it hits a successful combination.

Search5a selects a combination of L1, F1, L2, and F2. Next it tests for same *last* and different *first*. Then it checks the database for an entry for L1 and F1. If there is no entry, time was wasted in selecting an L2 and F2 and running the tests.

```
/*      Program:        p0605         samelst1.prg        */

search5a(L1,F1,T1,L2,F2,T2) :-                    HEAD
            first(F1),last(L1),first(F2),last(L2), GENERATOR
            L2==L1,not(F1==F2),                   FILTER
            entry(L1,F1,XD,T1),                   DATABASE
            entry(L2,F2,YD,T2).                   DATABASE
```

A query searches more quickly if it can identify dead ends, fruitless alternatives, and low profit regions as quickly as possible. Often it pays to refer immediately to the entries in the database in the first few goals so that the interpreter restricts searches over combinations of actually existing possibilities.

6.3.   The Bracketing of Logical Constituents: Flow Control.

All and only correct answers to a query is a good thing, but **searchd** gives too much of a good thing. Once we have a verb root in which one person and number have the same form, we do not want Prolog to repeat the answer for another person and number. In **searchd** we would like Prolog to bind *R* to a root verb and then try the three person and two number possibilities until it finds past and present forms that are the same. When it finds a correct answer, we would like to it stop backtracking to the *P* and *N* variables and move all the way back to the *root(R)*. We want to exert **flow control** in the program: We want to be able to specify how far back Prolog will backtrack when it hits a correct answer, but we are quite content to let Prolog backtrack to the closest variable if it has failed to find a solution.

We need some mechanism to place brackets around the italicized portion of **searchd**, lines 3–6 in p0606. If these statements fail, then Prolog should backtrack to the closest (most recently set) variable. If the statements internal to the italicized portion succeed once, then the *fail* should cause Prolog to skip over the italicized portion and reset *R*. The best way to factor out the relevant statements is to use them as the body of an auxiliary subfunction, **dbtest**, as in **searche** in p0607.

```
/*      Program:      p0606          prespas1.prg      */
/*      Which verbs have the same form in the present  */
/*                and the past?                        */

searchd :-                                    /*  1   */
        root(R),                              /*  2   */
        form(F12),person(P),numero(N),        /*  3   */
        vf(R,past,P,N,F12),                   /*  4   */
        vf(R,pres,P,N,F12),                   /*  5   */
        write('Root verb = '),write(R),write('.'),nl,   /*  6   */
        fail.                                 /*  7   */
```

```
/*      Program:      p0607          prespas2.prg      */
/*      Which verbs have the same form in the          */
/*                present and the past?                */

searche         :-      root(R),dbtest(R),fail.

dbtest(R)       :-
                        form(F12),person(P),numero(N),
                        vf(R,past,P,N,F12),
                        vf(R,pres,P,N,F12),
                        write('Root verb = '),write(R),write('.'),nl,!.
```

The relation **dbtest** ends in a *cut*, written by an exclamation point: *!*. The *cut* has two properties. First, it is always true and always succeeds, hence, it never causes backtracking. Second, it is like a door with a doorknob on only one side. Prolog will find cut succeeds and will pass that step and go on to the next; however, Prolog can never backtrack beyond a cut. In **dbtest**, if all the statements succeed, the **write** statements will output the relevant root *R* and a *newline* and then pass through the cut. After the cut, there is no going back, and the only way forward is a period that ends the statement. So **dbtest**, if it succeeds, returns only one value. If any one of the statements internal to **dbtest** fails, Prolog will backtrack internal to **dbtest** and even backtrack into **searche** to select another value for *R* when all possibilities internal to **dbtest** are exhausted (see Session 6.2).

Prolog executes **searche** as follows: *R* is bound to a root value.

Prolog tries alternatives to see if **dbtest** is *true* for the value selected of R. If **dbtest** is not true for all the possibilities (*F12, P, N*) defined internal to **dbtest**, then Prolog backtracks and another value of *R* is selected. If **dbtest** succeeds, Prolog cannot backtrack through **dbtest** because Prolog shuts the door behind it when it goes through a cut. The next statement, *fail* in **searche**, causes Prolog to select the closest variable, which is *R* in **searche**. As a value, **searche** returns *no* because it ends on the *fail*.

```
% prolog
C-Prolog version 1.5
| ?- [p0601].
p0601 consulted 3896 bytes 0.3 sec.
yes
| ?- [p0607].
p0602 consulted 3108 bytes 0.3 sec.
yes

| ?- searche.
Root verb = cost.
Root verb = hit.
Root verb = lay.
no

| ?- cntl-d
[ Prolog execution hallted ]
%
```

Session 6.2. Searching with a subfunction that has a cut.

The *cut* functions solely to prevent backtracking over alternatives that you do not want to try after it has found a successful combination. *Successful* means that all of the statements before the cut are *true* with the combination of variables selected. *Success* does not always carry with it a sense of joy. For instance, a chess–playing program may try all sorts of alternatives to find a best move, but if the result of one combination of variables shows that you must move a specific piece to a specific place or suffer checkmate on your opponent's next move, then you might not want to consider alternatives. If a tic–tac–toe program finds two *X*s with a blank spot between them, it must place an *O* in that spot, and it can forget possible alternatives.

If we are searching a family tree with a *wh*–query looking for possible brothers and sisters for Tess Durber, we might perform an exhaustive search because there might be none, one, two, or more. If we are looking for the father or mother of Ms. Durber, then once we have a successful candidate, it would be useless to look for alternatives. A cut is useful if you know that there is only one possibility and want to stop the program when it is found.

Searchf, in p0608, is a *wh*–query similar in structure to **searche** (see Session 6.3).

```
/*      Program:      p0608         prespas3.prg      */
/*      wh-  Which verbs have the same form in the    */
/*                present and past?                    */

searchf(R)      :-      root(R),dbtest(R).
```

```
% prolog
C-Prolog version 1.5
| ?- [p0601].
p0601 consulted 3896 bytes 0.3 sec.
yes
| ?- [p0608].
p0608 consulted 3896 bytes 0.3 sec.
yes

|?-searchf(R).
Root verb = cost.
R = cost ;
Root verb = hit
R = hit ;
Root verb = lay
R = lay ;
no

|?-searchf(cost).
Root verb = cost.
yes
|?-searchf(look).
no
|?-searchf(read).
no

| ?- cntl-d
[ Prolog execution halted ]
%
```

Sesssion 6.3. A *wh*–query examining p0601 for verbs.

159

Session 6.3 shows the results of querying the database p0601, *irreg.prg*, with **searchf**. The first query asks: *What is a root that has the same form in the past and present tenses?* The next queries ask: *Is cost/look/read a verb with the same form in the past and present tenses?*

Session 6.3 indicates that **searchf** gives the correct answers for *cost, hit, lay,* and *look,* but the wrong answer for *read. Read* does have the same form in two tenses: *I read the book yesterday. I read aloud at noon today.* More specifically, the root *read* has the same **orthographic** form (sequence of letters) in the past and present, but has different **phonetic** forms (pronunciations) in the two tenses. Because all of our interaction with the Prolog interpreter is via the keyboard and screen, we consider only the orthographic forms.

Session 6.3 shows that Prolog will answer *no* for two reasons: Either the verb is in the database but does not satisfy the criteria specified by the body of the relation, such as *look;* or the verb is not in the database and hence the search fails. We need some mechanism to differentiate between a real *no,* when the verb is in the database but does not satisfy the goals of the search, and an *'I don't know,'* when the root is not present. In short, we need a search that incorporates a logical *or* in order to be able to express alternatives: **Either** *R* is in the database and satisfies the test criteria (*cost*), **or** *R* is in the database and does not satisfy the test criteria (*look*), **or** *R* is not in the database and we cannot apply the test criteria (*read*).

By using a complex logical statement involving the Prolog comma (*and*) and semicolon (*or*) the correct statement could be written. We could go on but the words of G. Stein (1935) come to guide us:

> So now to come to the real question of punctuation, periods, commas, colons, semicolons and capitals and small letters.
>
> I have had a long and complicated life with all these.
>
> Let us begin with these I use the least first and these are colons and semicolons, one might add to these commas. (p. 86)

We have learned enough about periods, commas, colons, semicolons, capitals, and small letters – not to mention the dash and exclamation point – in order to encode much of Chomsky's generative grammar into Prolog. Prolog enthusiasts might refer to Dodd (1990) to learn how to punctuate to get the ideal query function. We follow the insights of G. Stein and turn our attention next to the problems posed by human language structures.

chapter **7**

COMPUTATIONAL TOOLS FOR LANGUAGE PROCESSING

The central notion in linguistic theory is that of "linguistic level." A linguistic level, such as phonemics, morphology, phrase structure, is essentially a set of descriptive devices that are made available for the construction of grammars; it constitutes a certain method for representing utterances. We can determine the adequacy of a linguistic theory by developing rigorously and precisely the form of grammar corresponding to the set of levels contained within this theory, and then investigating the possibility of constructing simple and revealing grammars of this form for natural languages. We shall study several different conceptions of linguistic structure in this manner, considering a succession of linguistic levels of increasing complexity which correspond to more and more powerful modes of grammatical description; and we shall attempt to show that linguistic theory must contain at least these levels if it is to provide, in particular, a satisfactory grammar of English. Finally, we shall suggest that this purely formal investigation of the structure of language has certain interesting implications for semantic studies.

Noam Chomsky, 1957
Syntactic Structures

7.1. The Levels of Human Language Structure

The term **grammar** is systematically ambiguous between two ideas, as illustrated in Figure 7.1.

An **internalized grammar** is the internalized knowledge of a native speaker of English that enables him or her to make judgments about language data. In particular, a native speaker, henceforth called an **informant**, can:

- make **grammaticality judgments**: The informant can differentiate a grammatical sentence (*The girl depends on her computer*) from an ungrammatical sentence (**The girl depend her computer*).
- recognize **ambiguous** utterances and identify the degree of ambiguity. *Mary decided on the boat* is two ways ambiguous: Either *Mary decided while located on the boat*, or *Mary opted for the boat*.
- recognize sentences that are **synonymous** or **partial paraphrases**. *John and Bill are identical* is synonymous with *John is identical to Bill*. If one sentence is true, the other must be true; and if either sentence is false, the other must be false. The sentence *John knows all the irregular past–tense forms of all French verbs* is a partial paraphrase of *John knows all the forms of all French verbs*. If the latter is true, the former must be true. But if the former is true, the latter may or may not be true.

A linguist's grammar, called a **generative grammar**, is the logical/computational model constructed by a linguist using computers, programs, logical notations, and other descriptive tools. The programs we formulate in Prolog offer representations of human language structures and grammatical processes.

Linguistics is an **empirical science** in that any proposed linguist's model can be supported or refuted by comparing the consequences deduced from the model against empirical data collected from native speakers. If the computational model asserts that a particular sentence, Sx, is ambiguous, we must test this against observational data: Does an informant think that the sentence is ambiguous? When a linguist proposes a particular grammatical model to characterize some range of the informant's judgments, it is an **empirical question** to decide whether or not the linguist's model matches the informant's judgments: Are the consequences deduced from the linguist's computational model in accord with the judgments of the informant?

For the most part, linguistic research does not involve experiments such as one finds in physics, chemistry, or psychology. The place where astronomers have their telescope is called an *observatory*, not a *laboratory*. Linguistics, like astronomy, is an **observational science.** The **observable data** that can support or refute a linguistic grammar consist of the informant's judgments.

GRAMMAR

The LINGUIST'S REPRESENTATION of the human's knowledge in the form of a computer program that defines the elements and combinations at each level of structure.

GENERATIVE GRAMMAR

DATABASE OF THE ELEMENTS WHICH FUNCTION IN THE LANGUAGE

simple facts
complex facts

COMBINATORIAL PRINCIPLES OF GRAMMAR

relations
queries

The INTERNALIZED KNOWLEDGE of a human. The linguistic competence which underlies the performance of the informant, i.e. the use of language in thinking, talking, teaching...

OBSERVATIONAL DATA

The EMPIRICAL ADEQUACY of the linguist's representation is judged by how well it describes, and in some cases explains, the patterns of data and the sound, meaning, and syntactic phenomena that constitute the informant's knowledge of their language.

These terms are synonyms.

grammaticality
ambiguity
paraphrase
synonymy
pronunciation
rhyme
(These are the data discussed in the text. For more examples, see the references.)

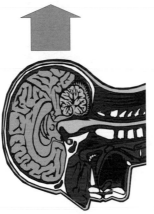

The informant's KNOWLEDGE underlies all judgements about linguistic utterances, and in particular, enables judgements about these data.

The LINGUIST'S GOAL is to characterize the content, form, organization, and structure of a human's knowledge of language.

Figure 7.1. The term *grammar* is ambiguous.

The informant's knowledge of the language underlies his or her judgments about grammaticality, ambiguity, paraphrase, synonymy, pronunciation, rhyme, and so on. Other **primary data**, that is, data used by a linguist to construct and justify a generative grammar, derive from dialect studies, child language research, animal communication studies, historical reconstructions of past languages, studies of language problems following brain damage, and research into language disorders such as deafness, speech impediments, and autism. There are certainly experiments that one could design to provide relevant data for constructing a theory of human language structures. Unfortunately, most of them would violate moral constraints.

LINGUISTICS abstracts for separate and independent study a cognitive system, a system of knowledge and belief, that develops in early childhood and that interacts with many other factors to determine the kinds of behavior that we observe. To introduce a technical term, we must isolate and study the system of *linguistic competence* (*grammar*) that underlies behavior but that is not realized in any direct or simple way in behavior. Linguistics is part of **cognitive psychology**, which begins with the problem of characterizing various systems of human knowledge and belief, the concepts in terms of which they are organized and the principles that underlie them, and examines how these systems develop through a combination of innate structure and organism–environment interaction (for discussion, see Chomsky, 1968, pp. 1–7).

Suppose an electronics engineer specifies the logical diagram that characterizes the design of a computer. This logical diagram can be implemented using vacuum tubes, individual transistors, computer chips, or gears and pulleys as in the early machines of Pascal and Babbage. The logical function diagram is at a level of abstraction above any particular hardware/software implementation. One can think of **linguistics** as providing logical function diagrams of the human linguistic capacity. We assume that the informant's grammar is somehow represented in his or her brain and nervous system. Insofar as our research succeeds, we will duplicate the grammar represented in the brain in our Prolog computer programs. The **goal of linguistic research** is to explicate the informant's intuitive judgments about grammaticality, ambiguity, synonymy, and other observable properties of the informant's knowledge.

Just as the problem of describing human anatomy can be broken down into *systems* (the skeletal system, the nervous system, the muscle system), the grammar can be segmented into parts, called **levels** (see Figure 7.2). We will modify the definition several times as we develop our grammar, but essentially:

DISCOURSE LEVEL

A *discourse* is sentences or utterances exchanged between two persons (e.g. question/answer pairs) or directed by one soul to another (as in prayer). Studies include: adult-adult, female-male, adult-child, human-God, and human-animal interactions.

FACTOR: Simple elements at the higher level factor into the complex elements at the lower level.

PARAGRAPH LEVEL

A *paragraph* is sentences joined in a sequence with sentence separators (period, question, or exclamation marks) between them. Adverbs (*therefore, hence, thus, nevertheless*...) can occur to show the logical connectedness among the sentences.

SENTENCE LEVEL

A *simple sentence* is a full proposition consisting of a subject and a predicate. A *complex sentence* consists of two or more simple sentences joined by a coordinating conjunction (*and, but*...) or a subordinating conjunction (*although, after, that*...).

PHRASE LEVEL

A *phrase* consists of a lexical item (*noun, verb, adjective*...) and its associated modifiers, e.g. *the, a*... precede nouns; *very, too*... precede adjectives; *will, can*... precede verbs. A phrase is always defined by the type of lexical head: noun, verb, adverb...

WORD (LEXICAL AND GRAMMATICAL FORMATIVE) LEVEL

A *word*, in our study, is anything in a sentence that has white spaces on either side. So *eke* is a word. The *lexical entry* would be *eke out*. An *orthographic string* is a written series of words. The grammar contains each possible word in its lexicon.

Figure 7.2. Levels of linguistic structure.

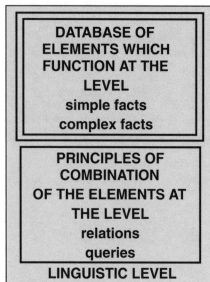

A LEVEL is defined by specifying the basic elements that function at that level and by defining the principles of combination of those elements.

Figure 7.3. A Prolog program defines each level.

The human informant's knowledge of language, the internalized grammar, can be factored into a hierarchy of levels, as in Figure 7.2. As indicated in Figure 7.3, Prolog is ideally suited to express the properties of any level because the basic elements that function at the level fit nicely into the database of simple and complex facts, and we can formulate the principles that regulate the combinations into Prolog relations and queries defined on the database. In this presentation, I try to distinguish the lexicon, Prolog statements in a shaded box surrounded with double lines, from the computational system, Prolog statements in a shaded box with no border. Insofar as possible, we try to embody the division expressed in Chomsky's statement (I have emphasized keywords, RCD.):

> Another standard assumption is that a language consists of two components: a lexicon and a computational system. The **lexicon** specifies the items that enter into the computational system, with their idiosyncratic properties. The **computational system** uses these elements to generate derivations and Structural Descriptions, SD's. The **derivation** of a particular linguistic expression, then, involves a choice of items from the lexicon and a computation that constructs the pair of interface representations. (Chomsky, 1992b, p. 3)

A main goal of linguistic research is to find out how many levels there are in a human language structure, to isolate and define all of the significant properties of each level, and to show how the levels interact. Chomsky (1992b) said:

166

A standard assumption is that universal grammar specifies certain *linguistic levels,* each a symbolic system, often called a "representational system." Each linguistic level provides the means for presenting certain systematic information about linguistic expressions. Each linguistic expression (SC) is a sequence of representations, one at each linguistic level. (p. 2)

In a **hierarchy of levels**, like in Figure 7.2, the basic notational elements at any level are the complex notational elements of the level immediately below. The arrows in Figure 7.2 imply that the elements at the discourse level, a *discourse,* can be factored into *paragraphs.* A *paragraph* can be factored into *sentences.* A *sentence* can be factored into *phrases.* And a *phrase* can be factored into *words.* This process of factoring the technical terms used at a higher level of integration into technical elements at a lower level of integration is called, obviously, FACTORING. Factoring is sometimes confused with parsing.

Universal grammar defines the structure of levels, the number of levels, and the interrelations among levels. **Factoring**, a part of *universal grammar*, plays a role in defining the technical terminology used to represent information at each level and in relating the technical terminology used at one level to that used at another, for example, to get ahead of our story, X–bar theory of phrase structure defines the primitive elements at the phrase level in terms of the complex items – fully specified lexical heads – at the word/lexical level. **Parsing**, a derivational mechanism of a grammar, relates to the processes by which a particular sequence of orthographic symbols (or words) in English is assigned a specific structure at each level. A question in universal grammar (factoring) is: What is a noun phrase? The answer would be to define *noun phrase* in terms of the types of words that compose it: *determiners* (the, a), *nouns* (*girl, thought, adjectives* (*tall, red*). A question in English grammar (parsing) is: What is *the tall grass*? The parser might answer that *the tall grass* is a *noun phrase* with the structure *determiner + adjective + noun.* Let us return to this after injecting some substance into the discussion.

A text sample that is to be analyzed is called a CORPUS. A corpus could be a discourse, a paragraph, or a collection of sentences, phrases, or words. Consider the following corpus extracted from Samuel Johnson's introduction to his dictionary.

Preface to the English Dictionary
By Samuel Johnson (1755)

It is the fate of those who toil at the lower

employments of life, to be rather driven by the fear of evil, than attracted by the prospect of good; to be exposed to censure, without hope of praise; to be disgraced by miscarriage, or punished for neglect, where success would have been without applause, and diligence without reward.

Among these unhappy mortals is the writer of dictionaries; whom mankind have considered, not as the pupil, but the slave of science, the pioneer of literature, doomed only to remove rubbish and clear obstructions from the paths through which Learning and Genius press forward to conquest and glory, without bestowing a smile on the humble drudge that facilitates their progress. Every other author may aspire to praise; the lexicographer can only hope to escape reproach, and even this negative recompense has been yet granted to a very few.

I have, notwithstanding this discouragement, attempted a Dictionary of the English Language, which, while it was employed in the cultivation of every species of literature, has itself been hitherto neglected, suffered to spread, under the direction of chance, in wild exuberance; resigned to the tyranny of time and fashion, and exposed to the corruptions of ignorance, and caprices of innovation.

When I took the first survey of my undertaking, I found our speech copious without order, and energetic without rule; wherever I turned my view, there was perplexity to be disentangled and confusion to be regulated; choice was to be made out of boundless variety, without any established principle of selection; adulterations were to be detected, without a settled sense of purity; and modes of expression to be rejected or received, without the suffrages of any writers of classical reputation or acknowledged authority. (Johnson, 1755/1938, pp. 182–183)

This is a discourse, albeit one sided. Mr. Johnson is addressing the reader. The discourse consists of four paragraphs. The second paragraph contains two long complex sentences, the others only one. The second complex sentence is composed of three simple sentences: *Every other author may aspire to praise. The lexicographer can only hope to escape reproach. Even this negative recompense has been yet granted to a very few.*

At the phrase level, the simple sentence, *Every other author may aspire to praise*, can be broken into a subject **noun phrase**, *every other author*, and a **verb phrase**, *may aspire to praise*. These phrases are themselves analyzable into smaller phrases. The verb phrase can be decomposed into the **auxiliary**, *may*, the main **verb** *aspire*, and the **prepositional phrase**, *to praise*. This latter phrase consists of the

preposition *to* and the **noun** *praise*. The subject **noun phrase** decomposes into the **quantifier** *every*, the **adjective** *other*, and the **noun** *author*.

At the center, or **head**, of each phrase is a word (**lexical item**). The **head** of the noun phrase, *every other author*, is the **noun** *author*. The **head** of the verb phrase, *may aspire to praise*, is the **verb** *aspire*. The **head** of the prepositional phrase, *to praise*, is the **preposition**, *to*.

We can eliminate potential misunderstandings by distinguishing these two questions:

- The FACTORING Question: How do we know that the levels in Figure 7.2 are the "real" levels? What evidence is there that a human language, like English, contains some linguistic object that one can call a *sentence*, or a *phrase*, or a *word*? How is a *noun phrase* (*verb phrase*) related to a lexical *noun* (*verb*)? What evidence is there for differentiating a *noun phrase* from a *verb phrase*? How are the grammatical primitives at each level defined? In general, how is a sentence defined in terms of phrases? How is a phrase defined in terms of lexical items, words, and heads? How is a lexical item defined? In brief, the factoring question is: What is the organization and structure of a *universal grammar*, and what are the primitive terms of the *universal grammar*?
- The PARSING Question: The parsing question only arises after the factoring question has been resolved (however tentatively). Once we have agreed that the levels in Figure 7.2 exist, and that the linguistic objects (*sentence, phrase, noun phrase*) exist, then we can ask: How is a specific structure at each level assigned to a given string of words or typewritten symbols? For a given string of words in a given corpus, how can we assign a particular structure at each level to that string? In short, if we accept the hierarchy of levels in Figure 7.2, and assume that each level can be represented by a Prolog program, as in Figure 7.3, what is in fact the optimal Prolog program for each level?

At the level of sentence, phrase, and word, this book assumes Chomsky's (1975b, 1986b, 1992b) answers to the factoring problem as developed in recent work by linguists working in the framework of N. Chomsky, called the *minimalist theory, universal grammar*, and *generative grammar*. The bulk of this book focuses on the parsing problem, under the assumption that the primitives of the linguistic theory are given by the minimalist version of generative grammar (Chomsky, 1992b).

The MINIMALIST THEORY, discussed in section 7.5, claims that there is a specific organization to the levels of a human language (see Figure

7.23). More about the organization and structure of levels after I discuss what qualifies as a level. For now, it is assumed that the minimalist theory is mainly a set of logical constraints on sentence, phrase, and word structure. I include some discussion of discourse and paragraphs because they are the focus of much recent work in computational linguistics and underlay the discussion of appropriateness in analyzing a human's creativity in the generative grammar perspective.

The theory of UNIVERSAL GRAMMAR claims that the **factoring question** (What are the basic levels of human language structure? What are the possible items and principles of combination at each level? How do the levels interact?) has one answer that is valid for all human languages because (see Figure 7.1) the organization and structure – and to some extent the content – of a grammar must directly reflect genetically specified human cognitive capacities.

A GENERATIVE GRAMMAR contains mechanisms (a **parser**) that assign the (or justify the assigned) structure at each level to a string of words or orthographic symbols. If the parser is a computer program that assigns the structures at each level automatically with no human input, then the program is a *generative grammar*. If the program requires human input as it functions, then it may be a useful linguistic tool for some purpose, but it is not an explication of the human informant's capacity to link sounds and meanings, and hence, it is not a generative grammar. Some authors use *generative* as a synonym for *explicit*.

In our computational model the definition of any level is given by the Prolog simple and complex facts that comprise the lexicon of elements that function at that level and by the Prolog relations and queries that define the principles of combination of the lexical elements. These explicit proposals all match the organization given in Figure 7.3. The following heuristic discussion attempts to define the levels through illustration via examples. Our main focus is on the level of phrase, (see Figure 7.4).

The highest level is the **discourse level**. A **discourse** is a sequence of utterances or sentences in which perhaps some come from one speaker and some come from another. There is a vast linguistic literature on the analysis of discourse ranging from the study of prayer (for discourse between a human and God, see Job, Matthew, St. Augustine), to the discourse habits of mothers talking to infants (repair sentences), to the study of human–animal communication.

At the discourse level, we will only be interested in adult–adult interactions and consider only question–answer pairs. Typically, in an adult discourse, one person asks the question and another person answers it. Discourse analysis is one of the most complicated areas of linguistics because so many factors interact. Consider this simple fact. Normally, when one asks a *wh*–question, the answer sentence has the stress on the information requested. For instance, suppose we ask: *Who hurt John?* Because the subject is the focus of the question (*who*), the answer will have the subject stressed (assume capitals indicates stress):

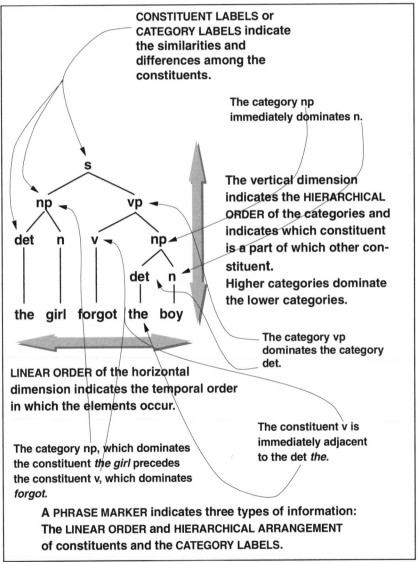

Figure 7.4. A phrase marker is a linguistic data structure.

MARY hurt John, BILL hurt John. The response – *Mary hurt JOHN* – answers the question – *Who did Mary hurt?* However, if the hurt arose from a self–inflicted injury, the subject is not stressed: *Who hurt John? John hurt HIMSELF.* The sentence *JOHN hurt himself* does not answer the question *Who hurt John?* It answers: *Who hurt himself?* See Katz and Levin (1988) for some interesting examples and discussion.

The objects of study at the **paragraph level** are sentences and the interactions between them. Words such as *therefore, however, thus,* and *hence* in a sentence usually imply that there is some previous sentence. Imagine if you were introduced to a total stranger who started his conversation with you: *'Therefore, I just bought a new car.'* It would not be odd for him to say, *'I just bought a new car.'* The sentences in a paragraph have an overriding logical connection and, usually, a sentence with a *therefore* comes after a few other sentences.

The **sentence level** is the focal point of Chapter 8. One of the main goals of linguistic research on English is to define the concept *sentence* in English. A main goal of linguistic research on universal grammar is to define the concept *sentence in a human language.*

We will represent the information at the sentence, phrase, and word levels in a phrase marker. A **phrase marker**, also called a **tree**, indicates that the elements of the sentence occur in a linear order, they have a hierarchical structure, and that there are similarities and differences among the constituents. Each of the nodes of the phrase marker bears a constituent label (see Table 7.1). We will sometimes refer to the phrase marker of a

Table 7.1. Abbreviations.

CATEGORY LABEL	AB
sentence	s
noun phrase	np
verb phrase	vp
prepositional phrase	pp
adjective phrase	ap
inflection phrase	ip
noun	n
preposition	p
verb	v
adjective	adj
inflection	i
auxiliary	aux
determiner	det
article	art

sentence as the **syntactic structure** of the sentence. For many examples this will suffice, but, in general, the syntactic structure of a sentence is significantly more complex than a simple phrase marker. Chapter 8 provides an investigation of phrase markers.

A sentence containing only one verb is a **simple sentence**, for example, *Mary sees John, Susan promised Albert an ice cream cone.* (I discuss simple sentences in this chapter and the next.) For illustration, and subject to later discussion, Figure 7.5 presents the phrase markers of the following simple sentences.

(1)	**The girl forgot the boy.**	active declarative
(2)	**Did the girl forget the boy?**	active question
(3)	**The boy was forgotten by the girl.**	passive declarative
(4)	**Was the boy forgotten by the girl?**	passive question

A sentence containing two verbs is a **compound sentence**, for example, *Alice thinks that Mary sees John, Greta hoped for Mary to win the prize.*

Among the variety of sentence types that exist (*question, declarative, indicative, imperative, subjunctive*), I focus on only two: declarative and question. A **declarative sentence** is a simple statement of fact: *John thinks that Mary knows the answer.* A **question** requests a response. A **yes/no question** requests a yes/no response: *Does Mary know the answer?* A **wh–question** requests a fact for an answer: *Who knows the answer?*

The linguistic objects at the **phrase level** consist of words strung together according to the rules of English. A **phrase** is a string of words (and morphemes) that has internal structure. Table 7.1 gives the names and abbreviations for commonly used phrase labels. The string *American history teacher* is a phrase (a noun phrase), and it has two possible internal structures: teacher of American history, *(American history) teacher*; and a history teacher who is American, *American (history teacher)*. The internal structure of a phrase can be indicated by parentheses that indicate the conceptual groupings of words.

I discuss the phrase level at length and indicate how Prolog programs can both recognize grammatical phrases and identify the conceptual groupings of words. These are noun phrases: *the girl, some very green apples, a spotted dog.* The following are not English phrases: **girl then, *green very the apples, *dog a spotted.* I focus on noun phrases, verb phrases (*will see Bill, has been seen by Mary*), prepositional phrases (*on the house, between you and me*), and some other types of phrases that are the subject of current research.

The **word level** is familiar to most people. Structuralists often defined a **word** as the smallest meaningful unit that can occur on its own. The words – *girl, girls, singing, slow,* and *slowly* – can occur in isolation. But the morphemes – *–s* (the plural ending), *–ing* (the verb ending), and *–ly* (the adverb ending) – cannot occur in isolation and are not words. It is difficult to define word precisely because of items like *eke* which requires the second word *out*: *The matchgirl eked a living out selling matches.* **The matchgirl eked a living selling matches.* In computational linguistics, following the "white space rule," **word** is often defined as any string of letters between blank (white) spaces. From this point of view, the sentences *Mary will look up John* and *Mary will look John up* each have five words: *John, Mary, up, look,* and *will*. We will assume that *look, eke, up,* and *out* are all words, and that the linguist's grammar will indicate restrictions on their cooccurrence. We will call *look up* and *eke out* **lexical items** that consist of two words.

The **lexicon** expresses the idiosyncratic properties of items at each level of description. The morphemes *–ly, –tion, –ness, –ing, –ed, –s* are lexical items. The words *eke, out, look, but, fritter* are lexical items. At the phrase level, some lexical items consist of two or more words: *eke out, fritter away, look up.* Idioms are present in the lexicon as frozen forms of word strings: *kick the bucket, take it easy, don't rock the boat,* and so on.

Structuralist research at the word level produces compilations of words for special interests. Most people have used a **dictionary** in which the words are ordered alphabetically in order to determine the meaning of a word or to check on spelling or pronunciation. A **thesaurus** lists words grouped according to similarity of meaning and is useful for finding synonyms. Whitfield's **Rhyming Dictionary**, which lists words in alphabetical order according to the pronunciation of the last syllable, places words that end on the same sound next to each other and is a boon to amateur poets and jingle writers. A **word frequency dictionary** lists words in the order of their frequency of occurrence in English text. If a student wants to learn English sufficiently to read the newspapers, it would pay to learn the words that most frequently occur first.

Computational linguists assume that the morphemes and words of a language are listed in a **lexicon** that is in computer–readable form. One main focus of the following chapters is the content, organization, structure, and internal and external views of the lexicon. Anything listed in the lexicon is a **lexical item**, also called a **lexical entry**.

The **word level** includes the study of compound nouns, that is, combinations of nouns (or words) to yield a new large noun. If a school graduates both males and females, we can ask about *women graduates* and *men graduates*, but not about **girls graduates* or **boys graduates*.

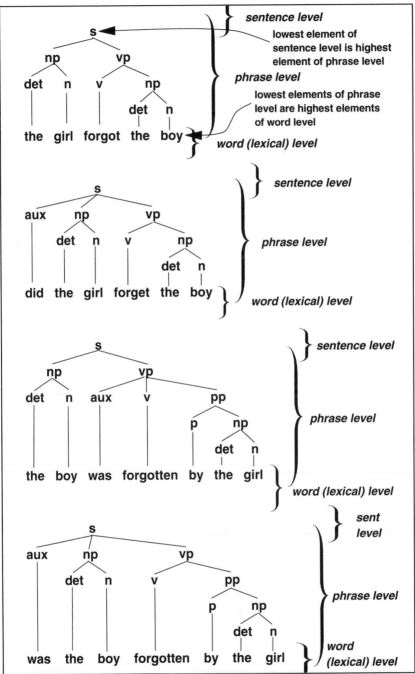

Figure 7.5. Four phrase markers for simple sentences.

We can say *girl graduate* and *boy graduate*, but in the plural we cannot say **girls graduates*, only *girl graduates*. At the level of compound nouns, the elements are the nouns of the dictionary. One of the observational constraints on combination says: *Pluralize both nouns if the first is irregular and only the last if the first is regular.* Thus, assuming animals join the space program, we have: *oxen astronauts, geese astronauts,* and *mice astronauts,* but not **cows astronauts, *ducks astronauts,* or **rats astronauts.* A computational model describes the facts by assuming that all irregular plurals are in the computer's lexicon, but regular plurals are not. Compounds are formed by combining only lexical items but not regular forms that are calculated from lexical items.

Figure 7.6 gives a perspective of our research in the framework of generative grammar research. A grammar is neutral between production (speaking and the production of sentences) and perception (understanding of heard or read sentences). An informant has a single grammar that relates a sound to a meaning, and this grammar is used to convert meanings to sounds (production) and to convert sounds to meanings (perception). A **grammar** can be considered to represent an informant's **knowledge** of their language or to represent the informant's **competence**. The actual production or perception of any individual sentence is a **performance** phenomenon (see L. Susman 1990). Languages have a specific modality that can involve production by the mouth and reception by the ears as in English, production by the hand and reception by the eye as in Sign Language, or hand–hand communication as in the language of the deaf–blind. We will be concerned with language in its written (orthographic) form. We will develop a grammar that correlates a written sequence of letters, such as *the girl forgot the boy,* with a phrase marker, as in Figure 7.4.

A person who knows a language knows a way of pairing an unbounded number of signals (typewritten sequences of symbols) with an unbounded number of meanings. This knowledge of the pairing of signals with meanings is similar to the knowledge of a code. A code is a device to pair signals and messages. A grammar, like a code, is neutral. A code can be used for production – to encode a message into a signal – or for reception – to decode a signal into its message. Much of what is presented will become clearer if we think of the Prolog parser that models English grammar as a code.

In recent work, Chomsky used the term *I–language* instead of *grammar.* Chomsky states (my emphasis, RCD):

> It should be noted that familiar characterization of 'language' as a *code* or *game* point correctly toward I–language, not the artificial construct E–language.

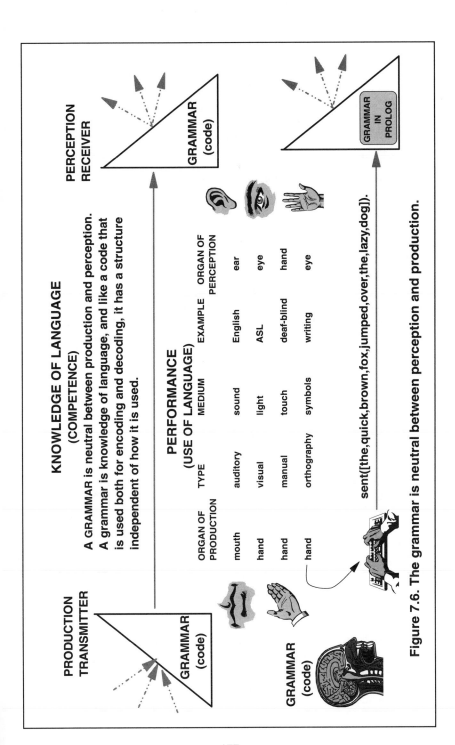

Figure 7.6. The grammar is neutral between perception and production.

A **code** is not a set of representations but rather a specific system of rules that assigns coded representations to message–representations. Two codes may be different, although extensionally identical in the message–code pairings that they provide. Similarly, a game is not a set of moves but rather the rule system that underlies them. The Saussurean concept of *langue*, although far too narrow in conception, might be interpreted as appropriate in this respect.... Perhaps the clearest account is Jespersen's in terms of the 'notion of structure' that guides the speaker 'in framing sentences of his own...,' this being 'free expressions.' (Chomsky, 1986a, pp. 31–32)

Although a grammar (code) is neutral between perception and production (see Figure 7.6), it is easier to understand the operation of the grammatical devices and the types of data structures involved in natural language processing if we approach the problem of grammar design by attempting to construct a decoder.

Figure 7.7, a detailed view of the grammars that are represented as triangles in the right half of Figure 7.6, indicates how a grammar used as a decoder expands (parses) an orthographic string into representations at each level. We will develop a grammar in Prolog that can analyze sentences into their component parts and indicate the constituent structures of those sentences. Chapter 7 focuses on the morphological level and word level. Chapter 8 presents grammars for the phrase level and sentence level.

Figure 7.7 indicates that a **parser** is a Prolog program that relates an ordered sequence of symbols typed on the computer keyboard to a phrase marker, like those in Figures 7.4 and 7.5 (see also Figures 8.21 and 8.22). I assume that if the grammatical parser is formulated in pure Prolog – using purely logical relations and devoid of any procedural considerations – then the grammar will be neutral between production (assigning a sound to a meaning) and perception (assigning a meaning to a sound). The Prolog grammar (decoder) for the triangle on the right of Figure 7.6 will – without modification – function in the triangle on the left (encoder). The arrows in Figures 7.6 and 7.7 reflect our misleading procedural thinking about use of language. Knowledge of language is one triangle with bidirectional arrows (see Figure 8.5).

We will consider the lexical level to be the level of words. **Morphology** and **orthography** comprise the study of the rules of combination of elements the size of words or smaller. The next three sections focus on problems in morphology. **Syntax**, the study of the rules of combination of elements the size of a word or larger, forms the main focus of Chapter 8.

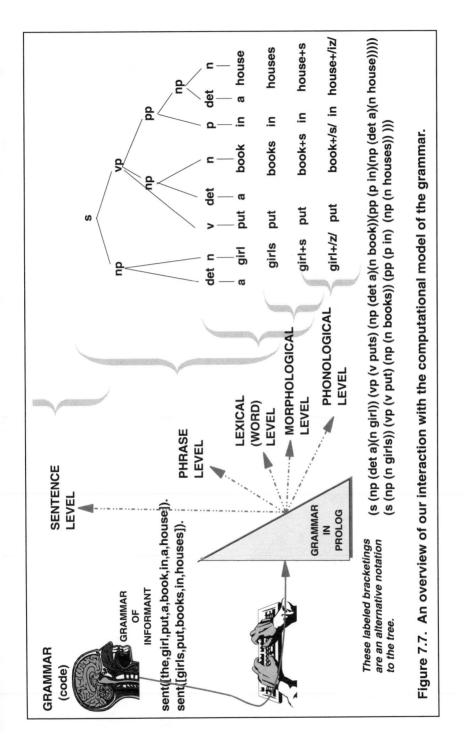

Figure 7.7. An overview of our interaction with the computational model of the grammar.

GRAMMAR
(code)

GRAMMAR OF INFORMANT

sent([the,girl,put,a,book,in,a,house]).
sent([girls,put,books,in,houses]).

SENTENCE LEVEL

PHRASE LEVEL

LEXICAL (WORD) LEVEL

MORPHOLOGICAL LEVEL

PHONOLOGICAL LEVEL

GRAMMAR IN PROLOG

These labeled bracketings are an alternative notation to the tree.

(s (np (det a)(n girl)) (vp (v puts)) (np (det a)(n book))(pp (p in)(np (det a)(n house)))))
(s (np (n girls)) (vp (v put)) (np (n books)) (pp (p in)) (np (n houses)))))

s

np   vp

det n   v   det   n   pp
a   girl   put a   book   p   np
                            in det   n
                                 a house

girls put books in houses

girl+s put book+s in house+s

girl+/z/ put book+/s/ in house+/iz/

179

7.2. Morphological Parsers

For this discussion, we can consider a **morpheme** to be the smallest meaning–bearing element of a language. It can be a word (*old, but*) or a part of a word (*anti–, de–, –ly, –s*). Some elements are considered morphemes although they correlate with no particular meaning, for example, the *a* in *perspir+a+tion*. Traditionally, linguists have discussed three types of morphology (see Figure 7.8).

These definitions follow from the goal of constructing a parser that can assign structure to an ordered string of elements. We assume that the lexicon specifies the items that enter into the computational system with their idiosyncratic properties. The main goal of *derivational* and *word formation morphology* is to define the items that enter into the computational system. The computational system uses these elements to generate derivations and structural descriptions. The main goal of *inflectional morphology* is to specify this computational system. From a linguistic point of view, we define inflectional morphology narrowly. From a computational point of view, we define inflectional morphology as a computational system using pure Prolog (unification and subsumption) and the definition *append*. In my notation, viewed from the syntactic level, derivational and word–formation morphology are Prolog expressions in a shaded box enclosed in double lines. Inflectional morphology is in a shaded box with no edges.

Derivational morphology studies the variation of forms according to syntactic or semantic properties for person (*I/you/she*), number (*I/we*), case (*he/his/him*), gender (*he/she/it*), tense (*be/is/was*). The information represented in the tables found in the back of dictionaries and grammar books about the variation in verb forms for tense, number, person, as well as the variation of determiners, nouns, and adjectives in German are studies in derivational morphology. Questions in derivational morphology would include: What is the past third–person singular of *be*? What is the person, number, and tense of *am*? Which verbs have the same form in the past and present tense? What is the plural of *girl*? What is the plural of *woman*? What are the irregular plurals of English?

Word–formation morphology is the study of permutations and combinations of prefixes, roots, and suffixes (*prefix+root+suffix: un+avail+able*), as well as compound constructions with two or more roots, such as *any+thing, black+berry, rasp+berry*. Among the many concerns are **order of morphemes** – *revol+u+tion+ary*, but not **revol+u+ary+tion* – and **cooccurrence restrictions** – *super+struct+ure* and *con+struct+tion*, but not **super+struct+ion* or **con+struct+ure*.

WORD LEVEL
(LEXICAL AND GRAMMATICAL FORMATIVE) LEVEL

A LEXICAL FORMATIVE is an element from an open class of lexical items: noun, verb, adjective.

A GRAMMATICAL FORMATIVE is an element from a closed class of lexical items: preposition, conjunction, determiner...

MORPHEME LEVEL

A MORPHEME is often defined as the smallest meaningful element of a language. This definition has its limits in that the *a* in *perspiration* (*per+spir+a+tion*), which is not in *perspire*, is a morpheme, but has no meaning. We assume a MORPHEME is the smallest functional unit in the lexicon. There are three types of morphology:

DERIVATIONAL MORPHOLOGY

The study of form variation according to syntactic or semantic properties for person (*I/you/she*), number (*I/we*), case (*he/his/him*), gender (*he/she/it*), tense (*be/am/was*)...

WORD FORMATION MORPHOLOGY

The study of permutations and combinations of prefixes, roots, and suffixes (prefix+root+suffix: *un+avail+able*); and also compound constructions with two or more roots, e.g. *any+thing*, *black+berry*,

INFLECTIONAL MORPHOLOGY

The study of agreement (concord) between

subject and verbs:	*I am/*are*
prepositions and nouns:	*among them/*they*
pronouns and antecedents:	*she behaved herself/*himself*
determiners and nouns:	*these girls/*girl*

ORTHOGRAPHY/PHONETIC LEVEL

The elements are the symbols on a typewriter or the sounds of a language. The sound elements have specific rules of combination which form the basis of *phonology* and *phonetics*. The written elements, comprising the ORTHOGRAPHY, have specific properties which are studied by optical character recognition research, spelling reformers, and dictionary writers.

Figure 7.8. Linguistic levels below the word level.

181

Word formation morphology includes the study of **compound elements**, i.e. words composed of two or more words or morphemes (*blackboard, keynote, hand–me–down*...); and affixed elements. An **affix** is either a **prefix**, which occurs on the front of words, an **infix**, which occurs internal to a word, or a **suffix**, which occurs at the end of a word. Questions in word formation morphology usually involve the order and cooccurrence restrictions on elements (called **distributional properties**). For instance, if we are discussing people who have completed a university program, we might ask: *How many girl graduates do you have? Or how many boy graduates?* We could also ask: *How many women graduates (or men graduates) do you have?* But we cannot ask: **How many girls graduates do you have?* or **How many boys graduates are there?*

Inflectional Morphology is the study of **agreement** (often called **concord** by grammarians) between elements in a sentence or phrase and includes the cases of determiner–adjective–noun agreement in German; subject–verb agreement; pronoun–antecedent agreement for person, number, and gender; preposition–noun agreement; and so on.

These definitions of morphology, and the tripartite division, reflect traditional thinking. These are the terms used by grammarians such as Jespersen, Curme, and so on, whose main concern was to classify constructions in languages in order to clarify problems in the historical evolution of language, translation, language learning, and language typology. When we study any particular constituent in any particular sentence, often it is impossible to distinguish derivational from word formation morphology. I use these terms so that this discussion matches the presentations in traditional grammars. This facilitates reference to primary sources for more examples.

Figure 7.9 illustrates the three types of morphology in the sentence: *The boys don't smoke anything, but one inhales with perspiration.* This sentence was selected less for its literary flavor than for its morphological richness. When a word is a compound composed of other words (*any+thing, black+board, choke+cherry*) most agree that word–formation morphology provides the analysis. When the word is a root plus affixes (*boy+s, look+ed, un+do*) most agree derivational morphology is the key. When the word includes both words and affixes (*do+n't, blackberryish, over+turn+s*) various types of morphology are less distinct.

In a computational model, like the one sketched later, these definitions and classifications might have to be modified or replaced. I am less interested in the "correct" or "traditional" terminology than with illustrating the basic Prolog computational tools that underlie morphology.

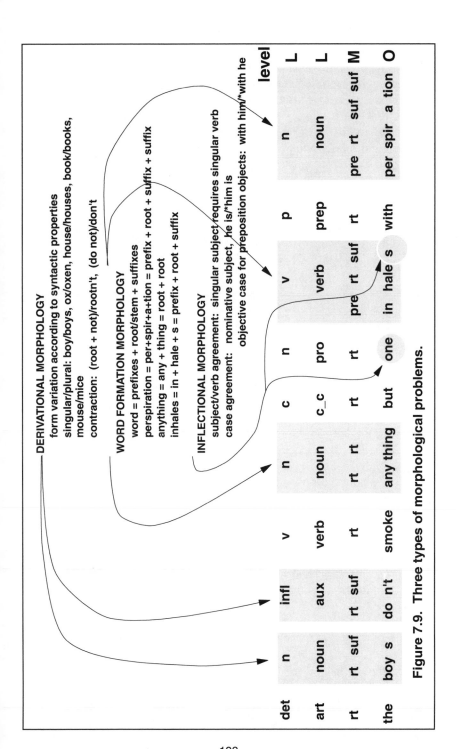

Figure 7.9. Three types of morphological problems.

DERIVATIONAL MORPHOLOGY
form variation according to syntactic properties
singular/plural: boy/boys, ox/oxen, house/houses, book/books,
mouse/mice
contraction: (root + not)/rootn't, (do not)/don't

WORD FORMATION MORPHOLOGY
word = prefixes + root/stem + suffixes
perspiration = per+spir+a+tion = prefix + root + suffix + suffix
anything = any + thing = root + root
inhales = in + hale + s = prefix + root + suffix

INFLECTIONAL MORPHOLOGY
subject/verb agreement: singular subject requires singular verb
case agreement: nominative subject, he is/*him is
objective case for preposition objects: with him/*with he

det	infl	v	n	c	n	v	p	n	level
art	aux	verb	noun	c_c	pro	verb	prep	noun	L
									L
									M
rt	rt suf	rt	rt rt	rt	rt	pre rt suf	rt	pre rt suf suf	O
the	do n't	smoke	any thing	but	one	in hale s	with	per spir a tion	

183

If the computational mechanisms were understood that formed the basis for morphological analysis, the terminology and classifications defining any morphological construction would presumably stem from the mechanisms and configurations of the computational tools used to describe that construction (see Figures 7.10–7.12). The basic computational tool we will use is the Prolog relation **append** (see g0701). In some Prolog versions (Quintus), append is a built-in statement. In other versions (C-Prolog and Prolog-2), append must be user–defined and loaded.

```
/*      Program:       g0701          PROFUNCT.a        */
/*             append is a basic combinatorial tool for      */
/*             analyzing large constituents into smaller      */
/*             ones or synthesizing large constituents from   */
/*             smaller ones.                                   */

append([],X,X).
append([A|B],C,[A|D]) :- append(B,C,D).
```

Figure 7.9 indicates the Prolog representation of a word at the lexical (L), orthographic (O), and morpheme (M) level. There are two representations at the lexical level because there exist some constituents that might be one category type in syntax, at the level above the word, and a different category type at the level below the word. For instance, a gerund might be syntactically a noun, but morphologically a verb: *singing* is a noun composed of the verb *sing* and the suffix *–ing*. At the orthographic level, we represent any word as a string of letters separated by commas placed inside of square brackets:

> word([a,n,y,t,h,i,n,g]).
> word([b,l,a,c,k,b,o,a,r,d]).
> word([i,n,h,a,l,e,s]).
> word([u,n,d,o,a,b,l,e]).

At the morphological level, we represent each morpheme as a string of letters separated by commas placed inside of square brackets:

> morpheme([a,n,y]).
> morpheme([t,h,i,n,g]).
> morpheme([b,l,a,c,k]).
> morpheme([b,o,a,r,d]).

184

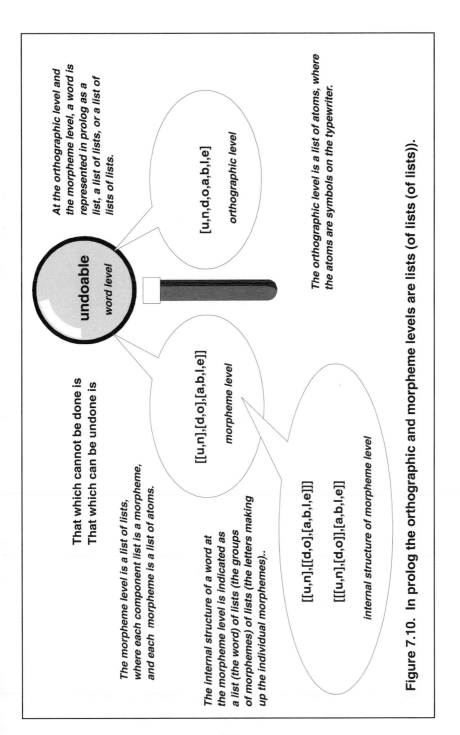

Figure 7.10. In prolog the orthographic and morpheme levels are lists (of lists (of lists)).

```
morpheme([i,n]).
morpheme([a,b,l,e]).
morpheme([s]).
```

The morpheme structure of the word *undo* could be indicated like this:

```
word(morpheme([u,n]),morpheme([d,o])).
```

or like this:

```
word([u,n],[d,o]).
```

We will represent the morpheme analysis of a word in the latter form because it is less redundant.

A word with a complex morphological structure can be ambiguous. For instance, the word *humanitarian* has the morphological structure that follows and is ambiguous. It means either a lover of humanity or a cannibal with a strict diet who eats only humans:

```
word([h,u,m,a,n],[i],[t,a,r,i,a,n]).    human + i + tarian
```

In some cases there is internal structure to the morpheme analysis, and ambiguity can be correlated with the structure of the word. The bracketing can reflect the semantic compositionality of the word. *This is undoable* can mean that this cannot be accomplished, it is not *doable*:

```
word([u,n],[[d,o],[a,b,l,e]]).        un + (do+able)
```

or it can mean that it can be undone, it is able to be *undone*:

```
word([[u,n],[d,o]],[a,b,l,e]).        (un+do) + able
```

Figure 7.10 indicates the types of Prolog data structure we will have at each level. At the sentence and word level, we represent the elements as *atoms*, that is, they are not in square brackets. At almost all other levels, the elements are represented as *lists of atoms* or *lists of lists*, that is, the elements are in square brackets. From a pragmatic point of view, this means you should pay close attention to whether an element is or is not surrounded by square brackets:

That which can be undone is undoable.

```
sentence_level([that,which,can,be,undone,is,undoable]).
```

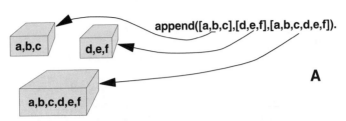

A

If [a,b,c] and [e,f,g] are appended, the result is [a,b,c,d,e,f].

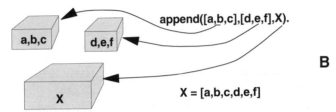

B

X = [a,b,c,d,e,f]

What is the result of appending [a,b,c] and [d,e,f]?

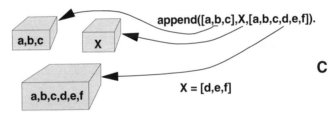

C

X = [d,e,f]

What must be appended to [a,b,c] to yield [a,b,c,d,e,f]?

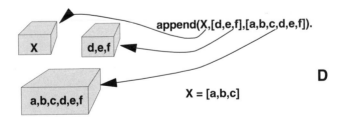

D

X = [a,b,c]

What must be appended with [d,e,f] to yield [a,b,c,d,e,f]?

Figure 7.11. Prolog *append* is a three place predicate.

word_level_representation(undoable).

lexical_level_representation([undoable]).

orthographic_level_representation([u,n,d,o,a,b,l,e]).

morpheme_level_representation([un],[do],[able]).

morpheme_structure_representation([[u,n],[d,o]],[a,b,l,e]).

There are two Prolog relations for converting from one level to another: name(A,B) and append(A,B,C).

Name(A,B) converts from an atom to a list, for example, *name(girl,[g,i,r,l])* is true; *name(girl,X)* yields *X = [g,i,r,l]*; and *name(X,[g,i,r,l])* yields *girl*. Name is the computational tool to convert from the word level to the orthographic level and back. (I discuss name(A,B) in section 7.4).

The basic Prolog tool for combining morphemes into words is **append**, given in program g0701 (see Figures 7.11 and 7.12). Assume A, B, and C are lists of the form [x,x,x,x]. Append(A,B,C) is a three–place Prolog relation that is true if C is the list formed by adding the elements of the list B to the end of the elements of the list A. Append defines a relation among the three lists.

```
1.      % prolog
2.      C-Prolog version 1.5
3.      | ?- [g0701].
4.      g0701 consulted 164 bytes
              0.0166667 sec.
5.      yes
6.      | ?- append([a,b,c],[d,e,f],[a,b,c,d,e,f]).
7.      yes
8.      | ?- append([a,b,c],[d,e,f],X).
9.      X = [a,b,c,d,e,f]
10.     yes
11.     | ?- append([a,b,c],X,[a,b,c,d,e,f]).
12.     X = [d,e,f]
13.     yes
14.     | ?- append(X,[d,e,f],[a,b,c,d,e,f]).
15.     X = [a,b,c]
16.     yes
17.     | ?- cntl-d
18.     [ Prolog execution halted ]
19.     %
```

Session 7.1. *Append* defines a relation among three lists.

188

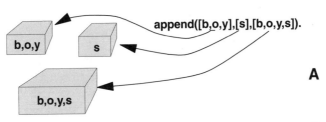

If [b,o,y] and [s] are appended, the result is [b,o,y,s].

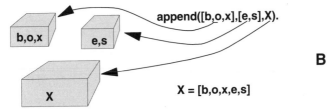

What is the result of appending [b,o,x] and [e,s]?

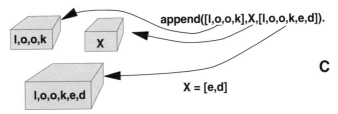

What must be appended to [l,o,o,k] to yield [l,o,o,k,e,d]?

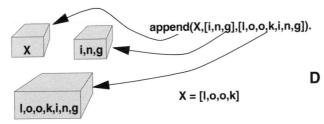

What must be appended with [i,n,g] to yield [l,o,o,k,i,n,g]?

Figure 7.12 The relation among word, root, and suffix.

Session 7.1 indicates how append can combine lists of letters, for example, [a,b,c] and [d,e,f] to make bigger lists [a,b,c,d,e,f].

Referring to Session 7.1 and Figure 7.11, the statement in line 6 is true because [a,b,c,d,e,f] is [a,b,c] with [d,e,f] added to the end of it. In line 8, append is used to synthesize a long list from two short ones. In lines 11 and 14, append is used analytically to decompose (or analyze) a long list into its component parts. The append relation with three lists and no variables, like A in Figure 7.11, asks: Is this append relation true? The relations containing the variable X ask: For what value of X is the append statement true?

Append can be thought of as a relation that combines building blocks (see Figures 7.13 and 7.14).

Line 6 of Session 7.2 corresponds to A of Figure 7.12. Line 6, equivalent to A, says: There is a list [b,o,y,s] that is composed of two smaller lists [b,o,y] and [s]. It could be understood **synthetically**, as a building process: [b,o,y,s] is built by joining [b,o,y] and [s]. And it can be understood **analytically**: [b,o,y,s] can be decomposed into two smaller lists, [b,o,y] and [s].

```
1.      % prolog
2.      C-Prolog version 1.5
3.      | ?- ['g0701'].
4.      g0701 consulted 164 bytes
            0.0166667 sec.
5.      yes
6.      | ?- append([b,o,y],[s],[b,o,y,s]).
7.      yes
8.      | ?- append([b,o,x],[e,s],X).
9.      X = [b,o,x,e,s]
10.     yes
11.     | ?- append([l,o,o,k],X,[l,o,o,k,e,d]).
12.     X = [e,d]
13.     yes
14.     | ?- append(X,[i,n,g],[l,o,o,k,i,n,g]).
15.     X = [l,o,o,k]
16.     yes
17.     | ?- cntl-d
18.     [ Prolog execution halted ]
19.     %
```

Session 7.2. *Append relates a root, an affix, and a word.*

Line 8 , and B in Figure 7.12, is a building operation: What is the result of appending [b,o,x] and [e,s]?

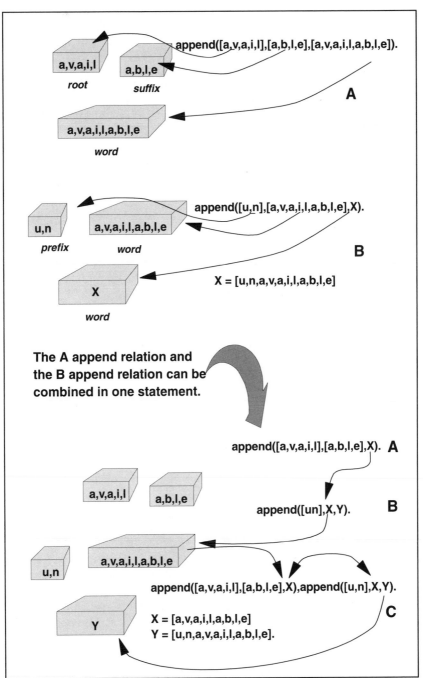

Figure 7.13. Two *append* statements linked by *and*.

191

Line 9 returns the result, which is the combined list.

Line 11, and C (Figure 7.12), is an analysis, a decomposition. It removes the list [l,o,o,k] from [l,o,o,k,e,d] and asks, What is left? What ending must be appended to *look* to get *looked*?

Line 14, and D (Figure 7.12), is an analysis. It removes the list [i,n,g] from [l,o,o,k,i,n,g] to find the remainder: [l,o,o,k].

The append relation can be combined by an *and* (*comma*) as in Session 7.3 and Figure 7.13. Line 6, and A in Figure 7.13, synthesizes the word *available* from *avail* and *able*. Line 9, and B (Figure 7.13), synthesize the word *unavailable* from *un* and *available*.

```
1.     % prolog
2.     C-Prolog version 1.5
3.     | ?- [g0701].
4.     g0701 consulted 164 bytes
              0.0166667 sec.
5.     yes
6.     | ?- append([a,v,a,i,l],[a,b,l,e],X).
7.     X = [a,v,a,i,l,a,b,l,e]
8.     yes
9.     | ?- append([u,n],[a,v,a,i,l,a,b,l,e],X).
10.    X = [u,n,a,v,a,i,l,a,b,l,e]
11.    yes
12.    | ?- append([a,v,a,i,l],[a,b,l,e],X),
                    append([u,n],X,Y).
13.    X = [a,v,a,i,l,a,b,l,e]
14.    Y = [u,n,a,v,a,i,l,a,b,l,e]
15.    yes
16.    | ?- cntl-d
17.    [ Prolog execution halted ]
18.    %
```

Session 7.3. The *append* relation can be combined.

The A and B operations can be combined (line 12 and C) in order to synthesize the word *unavailable* from the elements *avail*, *able*, and *un*. By having a variable in common (X) to store intermediate values – X = the list [a,v,a,i,l,a,b,l,e] – the two append statements can function as a unit. Line 12 is read: For what values of X and Y is it true that X is the result of adding the list [a,b,l,e] to the end of list [a,v,a,i,l], and Y is the result of adding [u,n] to the front of the list X?

Figure 7.14 attempts to clarify Session 7.4, the analysis of the ambiguous phrase *American history teacher*.

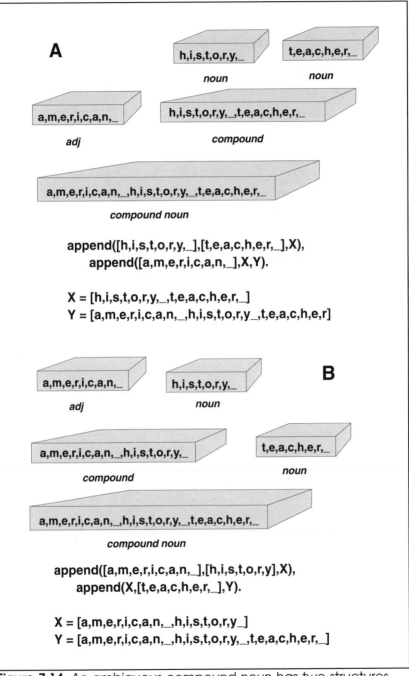

Figure 7.14. An ambiguous compound noun has two structures.

Figure 7.14 shows append can combine the lists [a,m,e,r,i,c,a,n], [h,i,s,t,o,r,y], and [t,e,a,c,h,e,r] in two different ways. Line 12 (see A of Figure 7.14) combines *history* and *teacher* and adds *american* to the front yielding *american history teacher*. Line 16 (see B of Figure 7.14) combines *american* and *history* and adds *teacher* to the end of the combination.

```
1.      % prolog
2.      C-Prolog version 1.5
3.      | ?- [g0701].
4.      g0701 consulted 164 bytes
             0.0166667 sec.
5.      yes
6.      | ?- append([h,i,s,t,o,r,y,_],
                     [t,e,a,c,h,e,r,_],X).
7.      X = [h,i,s,t,o,r,y,_,t,e,a,c,h,e,r,_]
8.      yes
9.      | ?- append([a,m,e,r,i,c,a,n,_],
                     [h,i,s,t,o,r,y,_],X).
10.     X = [a,m,e,r,i,c,a,n,_,h,i,s,t,o,r,y,_]
11.     yes
12.     | ?- append([h,i,s,t,o,r,y,_],
                  [t,e,a,c,h,e,r,_],X),append([a,m,e,r,
                  i,c,a,n,_],X,Y).
13.     X = [h,i,s,t,o,r,y,_,t,e,a,c,h,e,r,_]
14.     Y = [a,m,e,r,i,c,a,n,_h,i,s,t,o,r,y_,
                  t,e,a,c,h,e,r,_]
15.     yes
16.     | ?- append([a,m,e,r,i,c,a,n,_],
                  [h,i,s,t,o,r,y,_],X),append(X,[t,e,a,
                  c,h,e,r,_],Y).
17.     X = [a,m,e,r,i,c,a,n,_,h,i,s,t,o,r,y,_]
        Y = [a,m,e,r,i,c,a,n,_,h,i,s,t,o,r,y,_,
                  t,e,a,c,h,e,r,_]
18.     yes
19.     | ?- cntl-d
20.     [ Prolog execution halted ]
21.     %
```

Session 7.4. The *append* relation can apply ambiguously.

The list Y produced by queries 12 and 16 is [a,m,e,r,i,c,a,n,_, h,i,s,t,o,r,y,_,t,e,a,c,h,,e,r,_]. The list Y produced by query 12 is identical to the list Y produced by query 16. These queries differ in the intermediate lists X they define.

If you have any difficulty loading and executing any of the programs, be certain that the append relation has been defined only once.

7.3. Recursion: Affixes on the affixes

E. Sapir (1921) discussed morphology in his classic study of language. We follow his terminology and formulations rather closely. We use the Prolog *append* command to express what Sapir represents by the + sign in this passage. Sapir stated:

> The true, significant elements of language are generally sequences of sounds that are either words, significant parts of words, or word groupings. What distinguishes each of these elements is that it is the outward sign of a specific idea, whether of a single concept or image or of a number of such concepts or images definitely connected into a whole. The single word may or may not be the simplest significant element we have to deal with. The English words *sing, sings, singing, singer* each conveys a perfectly definite and intelligible idea, though the idea is disconnected and is therefore functionally of no practical value. We recognize immediately that these words are of two sorts. The first word, *sing*, is an indivisible phonetic entity conveying the notion of a certain specific activity. The other words all involve the same fundamental notion but, owing to the addition of other phonetic elements, this notion is given a particular twist that modifies or more closely defines it. They represent, in a sense, compounded concepts that have flowered from the fundamental one. We may, therefore, analyze the words *sings, singing*, and *singer* as binary expressions involving a fundamental concept, a concept of subject matter (*sing*), and a further concept of more abstract order – one of person, number, time, condition, function, or of several of these combined.
>
> If we symbolize such a term as *sing* by the algebraic formula A, we shall have to symbolize such terms as *sings* and *singer* by the formula A + b. We shall reserve capitals for radical elements. The element A may be either a complete and independent word (*sing*) or the fundamental substance, the so-called **root** or **stem** or "radical element" (*sing–*) of a word. The element b (*–s, –ing, –er*) is the indicator of a subsidiary and, as a rule, a more abstract concept; in the widest sense of the word "form," it puts upon the fundamental concept a formal, limitation. We may term it a **grammatical element** or **affix**. (pp. 25–26)

Among the constructions included under *root + affix* would be *know+able, hunt+er, hospital+ize, act+ive, govern+ment, sulphur+ic, sulphur+ous, mercur+ial, home+less, good+ness*, and *love+ly*. Affixes at the beginning of a root are **prefixes**, at the end are **suffixes**, and in the middle are **infixes**. Sapir discussed the variety of affixes in this passage.

> The **grammatical element** or the grammatical increment, as we had better put it, need not be suffixed to the radical element. It may be a prefixed element (like the *un–* of *unsingable*), it may be inserted into the very body of the stem (like the *n* of the Latin *vinco*, "I conquer" as contrasted with its absence in *vici* "I have conquered"), it may be the complete or partial repetition of the stem, or it may consist of some modification of the inner form of the stem (change of vowel, as *sing, sung* and *song*; change of consonant as in *dead* and *death*; change of accent; actual abbreviation). Each and every one of these types of grammatical element or modification has this peculiarity, that it may not, in the vast majority of cases, be used independently but needs to be somehow attached to or welded with a radical element in order to convey an intelligible notion. We had better, therefore, modify our formula, A + b, to A + (b), the round bracket symbolizing the incapacity of an element to stand alone. (p. 26)

Some affixes can stand alone as words, and the meanings of the affix and word are related, for example, *able* and *like*: *It is* able *to be done; it is do+*able. *He is* like *a child; he is child+*like. As Sapir pointed out, however, most affixes cannot stand alone. Sapir stated:

> The **grammatical element**, moreover, is not only nonexistent except as associated with a radical one, it does not even, as a rule, obtain its measure of significance unless it is associated with a particular class of radical elements. Thus, the *–s* of English *he hits* symbolizes an utterly different notion from the *–s* of *books*, merely because *hit* and *book* are differently classified as to function. We must hasten to observe, however, that while the radical element may, on occasion, be identical with the word, it does not follow that it may always, or even customarily, be used as a word. Thus, the *hort–* 'garden' of such Latin forms as *hortus, horti,* and *horto* is as much of an abstraction, though one yielding a more easily apprehended significance, than the *-ing* of *singing*. Neither exists as an independently intelligible and satisfying element of speech. Both the radical element, as such, and the grammatical element, therefore, are reached only by a process of abstraction. It seemed proper to symbolize *sing–er* as A + (*b*); *hort–us* must be symbolized as (A) + (b). (pp. 26–27)

196

Program g0702, lexicon_7a, contains the following information as simple facts, suf(X), and pre(X); **suffixes:** *–able, –ation, –er, –ing, ,–ion, –ive, –ment, –al, –ial, – ian, – ic, – ize, – less, –ous, –ity, –ize, – ly, –ness, –ish, –ure,* and so on; **prefixes**: *pre–, post–, ex–, de–, con–, super–, sub–, self–,* and so on.

```
/*   Program:    g0702                    lexicon_7a           */
/*      This is a database of prefixes and suffixes.           */

   suf([a,b,l,e]).        suf([l,i,k,e]).        pre([h,y,p,e,r]).
   suf([a,t,i,o,n]).      suf([l,y]).            pre([a,n,t,i]).
   suf([e,r]).            suf([u,r,e]).          pre([u,n]).
   suf([i,d,e]).          suf([i,c]).            pre([r,e]).
   suf([i,n,g]).          suf([l,e,s,s]).        pre([i,l]).
   suf([i,v,e]).          suf([a,t,e]).          pre([d,i,s]).
   suf([m,e,n,t]).        suf([o,u,s]).          pre([s,u,p,e,r]).
   suf([a,r,y]).          suf([a,t,e]).          pre([s,u,b]).
   suf([a,b,i,l]).        suf([i,t,y]).
   suf([a,l]).            suf([i,z,e]).          root([b,o,y]).
   suf([i,s,h]).          suf([i,z]).            root([h,u,m,a,n]).
   suf([i,a,l]).          suf([n,e,s,s]).        root([d,e,c,i,d,e]).
   suf([i,s,m]).          suf([u,r,e]).          root([g,e,n,t,l,e]).
   suf([i,a,n]).                                 root([m,a,n]).
   suf([m,e,n,t]).                               root([h,u,n,t]).
   suf([a,r]).            pre([e,x]).            root([c,h,a,n,g,e]).
   suf([l,i]).            pre([i,n]).            root([h,o,m,e]).
   suf([e,d]).            pre([d,e]).            root([h,o,s,p,i,t,a,l]).
                         pre([i,n,t,e,r]).
```

Some words have no affixes (*human*), some have one (*human+ize*), some have two (*human+iz+ation, de+human+ize*), some have three (*de+human+iz+ation*), and some have lots more (*anti+dis+establ+ish+ment+ ar+ian+ism*). Table 7.2 gives some examples of multiple affix constructions. Fromkin and Rodman (1993) and O'Grady et al. (1993) contain excellent discussions of the morphology of affixation.

There are at least five types of data structures that might be represented in the grammar of English morphology:

■ Affixes can be **compounded**, that is, affixes can be added to affixes. Table 7.2 presents examples of root+suffix, root+suffix+suffix, and prefix+root+suffix. Examples can be considerably more complex than indicated, for example, *anti+dis+establ+ish+ment+arian+ism*, or *un+(black+berry)+like*, *anti+white+wash*. This is the problem we will focus on because it illustrates recursive mechanisms in Prolog.

- Affixes can have **cooccurrence restrictions** with each other and with the root: *super+struct+ure, con+struct+ion, *super+struct+ion, *con+struct+ure.*

- The affixes are **ordered** with respect to each other: *revol+u+tion+ary, *revol+u+ary+tion; hunt+er+s, *hunt+s+er.*

- An affix can **change form** depending on whether it is the final affix or an intermediate affix, for example *ly/li: homely, homeliness.* When a lexical item changes

Table 7.2. Affixes can be compounded.			
1	2	3	4
ox			
oxen			
see			
saw			
boy	boy+s		
look	look+ed		
hunt	hunt+er	hunt+er+s	
home	home+less	home+less+ness	
boy	boy+ish	boy+ish+ness	
human	human+ize	human+iz+ation	de+human+iz+ation
decide	decide+able	un+decide+able	un+decide+abil+ity
gentle	gentle+man	gentle+man+ly	gentle+man+li+ness

depending on its position in a string, linguists say the form of the lexical item is *context sensitive*.

■ A word can have internal structure. The root and morphemes can be grouped to correlate with the **factorization** of meaning: *un+(do+able), (un+do)+able*.

The examples in g0702 represent a small fraction of common English affixes. They suffice to illustrate the five properties described earlier. Some special–interest groups have sublanguages with idiosyncratic sets of affixes. Chemistry prefixes include: *poly–, tri–, di–, chloro–*; suffixes include: *–ic, –ate, –ide, –ene* as in *trinitrotoluene, polyglicerides*. Medical affixes include *cardio–, hyper–, psycho–, –ology*.

Program g0703, *suffix.prg*, contains two Prolog relations. Suffixation(SHORT,LONG) is true if lexicon_7a contains a suffix SUF, that is, an entry suf(SUF), and LONG is SHORT+SUF. These conditions are spelled out in lines 1–2. Lines 3–5 print the results. In a word such as *establishmentarianism*, which contains several suffixes, suffixation will find only the outermost suffix. If we want to find all the suffixes, we must apply suffixation repeatedly (see Session 7.5).

```
/*      Program:      g0703          suffix.prg              */

suffixation(SHORT,LONG) :-    suf(SUF),                      1
                              append(SHORT,SUF,LONG),        2
                              nl,nl,write(LONG),             3
                              nl,write(SHORT),               4
                              write(' + '),write(SUF).       5

suf_all(BIG)            :-     suffixation(SMALL,BIG),        6
                              suf_all(SMALL).                7

append([],X,X).
append([A|B],C,[A|D])   :-     append(B,C,D).
```

Suf_all(BIG) is true if suffixation(SMALL,BIG) is true, that is, if BIG is SMALL+SUF and if suf_all(SMALL) is true. Suf_all(SMALL), line 7, is the recursive part of the definition of suf_all. To determine if suf_all(BIG) is true, Prolog must determine if suf_all(SMALL) is true.

A Prolog relation is RECURSIVELY DEFINED if, in order for Prolog to determine if it is true for some variable BIG, Prolog must determine if it is true for a variable SMALL,

199

where SMALL is a part of BIG.

In the following discussion I muddle two contrasting ideas for the ease of presentation. Prolog, as a nonprocedural language, offers program g0703 as a **logical definition** of a root+suffix (lines 1–2) and of a complex word consisting of a root+suffix+suffix...+suffix (lines 6–7). But, owing to the fact that this Prolog interpreter is implemented on a computer that carries out sequential operations one at a time, the program is a de facto **procedural statement** about how, and in what order, to "peel off" suffixes from the outside in.

I first present the analysis of this program in terms of procedural statements and then turn to the program as a logical definition of a construction type.

Figure 7.15 indicates five programs that must be loaded to find all prefixes and suffixes of a word. Some of these programs use the relation append.

```
% prolog
C-Prolog 1.5
| ?- [g0702].
yes
| ?- [g0703].
yes

| ?- suf_all([e,s,t,a,b,l,i,s,h,m,e,n,t,
                 a,r,i,a,n,i,s,m]).

[e,s,t,a,b,l,i,s,h,m,e,n,t,a,r,i,a,n,i,s,m]
[e,s,t,a,b,l,i,s,h,m,e,n,t,a,r,i,a,n] + [i,s,m]

[e,s,t,a,b,l,i,s,h,m,e,n,t,a,r,i,a,n]
[e,s,t,a,b,l,i,s,h,m,e,n,t,a,r] + [i,a,n]

[e,s,t,a,b,l,i,s,h,m,e,n,t,a,r,i,a,n]
[e,s,t,a,b,l,i,s,h,m,e,n,t] + [a,r]

[e,s,t,a,b,l,i,s,h,m,e,n,t]
[e,s,t,a,b,l,i,s,h] + [m,e,n,t]

[e,s,t,a,b,l,i,s,h]
[e,s,t,a,b,l] + [i,s,h]

no

| ?- ^D
%
```

Session 7.5. Recursively remove suffixes from a complex word.

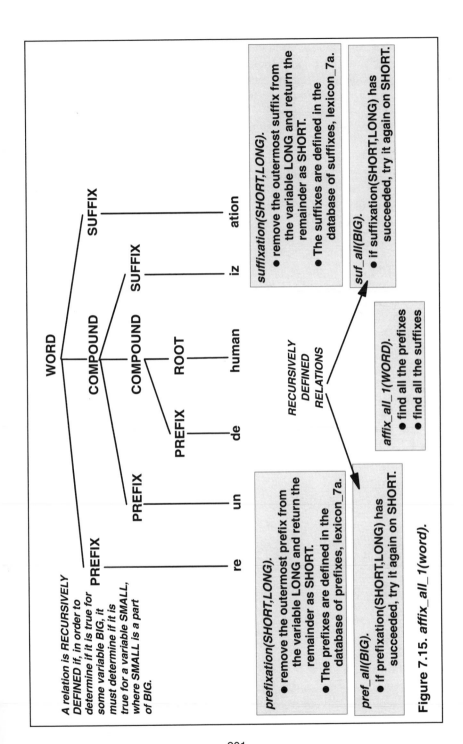

A relation is RECURSIVELY DEFINED if, in order to determine if it is true for some variable BIG, it must determine if it is true for a variable SMALL, where SMALL is a part of BIG.

prefixation(SHORT,LONG).
● remove the outermost prefix from the variable LONG and return the remainder as SHORT.
● The prefixes are defined in the database of prefixes, lexicon_7a.

pref_all(BIG).
● if prefixation(SHORT,LONG) has succeeded, try it again on SHORT.

RECURSIVELY DEFINED RELATIONS

affix_all_1(WORD).
● find all the prefixes
● find all the suffixes

suffixation(SHORT,LONG).
● remove the outermost suffix from the variable LONG and return the remainder as SHORT.
● The suffixes are defined in the database of suffixes, lexicon_7a.

suf_all(BIG).
● if suffixation(SHORT,LONG) has succeeded, try it again on SHORT.

Figure 7.15. *affix_all_1(word).*

201

Program g0703 contains a definition of append. If g0703 is loaded, one must be certain that no other program offers a definition of append. If append is loaded two times, all words will be analyzed at least twice for the same properties. This will yield extremely confusing results. Once append is loaded into the workspace, it will define all of the append relations in any programs in the workspace.

Session 7.5 indicates how g0703 finds all of the suffixes in the word *establishmentarianism*. Line 3 of g0703 writes the LONG variable with the root and suffix joined. Lines 4 and 5 write the SHORT variable, which may be a root+suffix, or a root, and the suffix found. Suffixation(LONG,SHORT) can only find a suffix if it is in lexicon_7a. Suf_all terminates when suffixation(LONG,SHORT) fails. In this case, the list [e,s,t,a,b,l] does not terminate in any list that is defined as an affix in lexicon_7a.

The boxes in Figure 7.16 correlate with the operation of the append statement in suffixation(LONG,SHORT), g0703, line 2. The arrows that loop to the left indicate how append decomposes the LONG variable into a SHORT+SUF. The arrows that loop to the right indicate how suf_all takes the remainder (SHORT), which is either a root with a suffix or a root, and calls on suffixation(LONG,SHORT) to find a suffix.

Figure 7.16 should have one more set of boxes on the bottom to indicate the failure of the statement: append(SHORT,SUF,[e,s,t,a,b,l]). This failure in the suffixation definition follows because there is no SUF in lexicon_7a corresponding to the final letters in [e,s,t,a,b,l].

Program g0704 offers a definition of prefixation. Lines 1–2 find if the list LONG begins with any list of letters defined as a PREFIX in lexicon_7a. If so, the definition succeeds and lines 3–5 print the analysis of the word. Pref_all(BIG), like suf_all(BIG), is a recursively defined statement that is only true if all prefixes have been found. Let us now consider nonprocedural versus procedural aspects of our analysis.

Affix_all(WORD), line 8, is true if pref_all(WORD) is true or if suf_all(WORD) is true. Affix_all_1(WORD) is the same and differs only in lines 9 and 11, which print headings. These are useful in tracking the operation of the program in Session 7.6 and Figure 7.17.

Figure 7.15 indicates the relation of the five programs that find all the prefixes and suffixes of the variable WORD. There are two recursively defined functions.

Session 7.6 indicates that affix_all_1 searches in a temporal sequence. First it finds all of the prefixes one after the next, starting with the outermost, and then it finds all of the suffixes, starting with the outermost. Figure 7.17 indicates the state of the append statements in the prefixation and suffixation relations in producing Session 7.6.

202

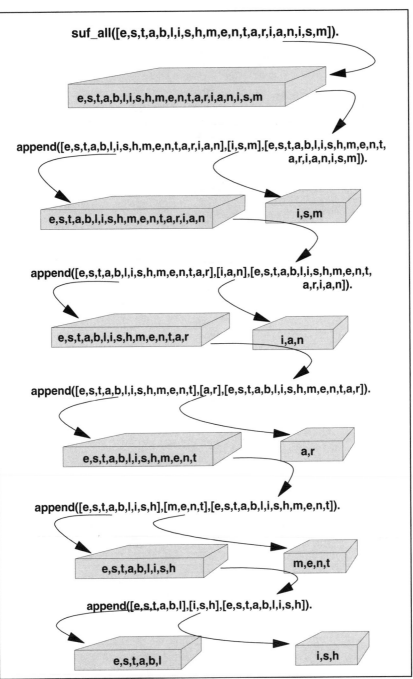

Figure 7.16. *Append* can recursively remove affixes.

203

```
/*      Program:        g0704   prefix.prg                              */

prefixation(SHORT,LONG) :-      pre(PRE),                              1
                                append(PRE,SHORT,LONG),                2
                                nl,nl,write(LONG),                     3
                                nl,write(PRE),write(' + '),            4
                                write(SHORT).                          5
pref_all(BIG)           :-      prefixation(SMALL,BIG),                6
                                pref_all(SMALL).                       7

affix_all(WORD)         :-      pref_all(WORD);nl,suf_all(WORD).       8

affix_all_1(WORD)       :-      nl,nl,write('Find all prefixes.'),     9
                                pref_all(WORD);                       10
                                nl,nl,write('Find all suffixes.'),    11
                                suf_all(WORD).                        12
```

The left looping arrows indicate the operation of the append statement in prefixation and suffixation. The right looping arrows indicate the operation in prefix_all and suffix_all to keep looking for affixes.

Program g0705 defines root(R,WORD) that is true if R is the root that is left from WORD after all of the prefixes and suffixes have been removed. Figure 7.18 indicates on a tree diagram how we might think of root(R,[r,e,u,n,d,e,h,u,m,a,n,i,z,a,t,i,o,n]) operating (see Session 7.7).

The relation starts with the whole list, and the leftmost gray arrow terminates on [r,e], indicating that prefixation located this prefix. The gray arrow departing from [r,e,] and terminating on [u,n] indicates that pref_alle(R,BIG) is only true if prefixation(SHORT,[u,n,d,e,h,u,m,a,n, i,z,a, t,i,o,n]) is true.

Eventually prefix_alle calls prefixation(SHORT,[h,u,m,a,n,i,z,a, t,i,o,n]) and fails, as indicated by the gray arrow from [d,e] to [h,u,m,a,n] stopping. The gray arrow that departs from [h,u,m,a,n] goes to the outermost suffix [a,t,i,o,n], and suf_alle calls suffixation(SHORT, [h,u,m,a,n, i,z,a,t,i,o,n]).

Finally, suf_all has the structure suf_alle(R,[h,u,m,a,n]), a BIG variable that contains no suffix. Line 10 of g0705 fails, and Prolog tries line 11. Line 11 succeeds and is true if suf_alle(R,[h,u,m,a,n]) is suff_alle([h,u,m,a,n],[h,u,m,a,n]). That is, [h,u,m,a,n] is bound to R. This value is passed back to root(R,WORD), line 1, and the program finds that the value for R that makes root(R,[r,e,u,n,d,e,h,u,m,a,n,i,z,a,t,i,o,n]) true is [h,u,m,a,n].

Figure 7.18 corresponds to the output of g0705 (see Session 7.6).

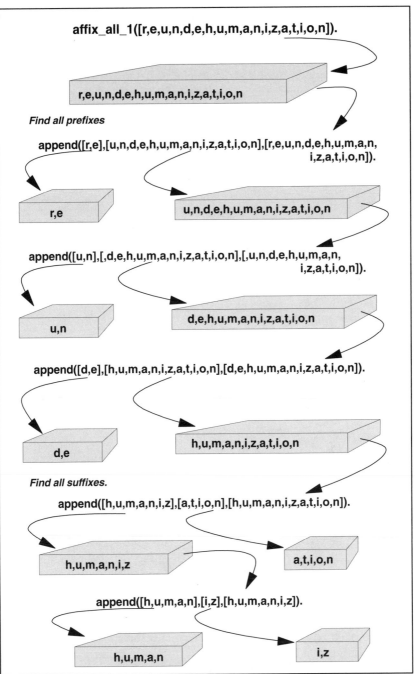

Figure 7.17. *Append* recursively removes prefixes and suffixes.

```
% prolog
C-Prolog 1.5
| ?- [g0702].
yes
| ?- [g0703].
yes
| ?- [g0704].
yes

| ?- affix_all_1([r,e,u,n,d,e,h,u,m,a,n,i,z,
            a,t,i,o,n]).

Find all prefixes.

[r,e,u,n,d,e,h,u,m,a,n,i,z,a,t,i,o,n]
[r,e] + [u,n,d,e,h,u,m,a,n,i,z,a,t,i,o,n]

[u,n,d,e,h,u,m,a,n,i,z,a,t,i,o,n]
[u,n] + [d,e,h,u,m,a,n,i,z,a,t,i,o,n]

[d,e,h,u,m,a,n,i,z,a,t,i,o,n]
[d,e] + [h,u,m,a,n,i,z,a,t,i,o,n]

Find all suffixes.

[r,e,u,n,d,e,h,u,m,a,n,i,z,a,t,i,o,n]
[r,e,u,n,d,e,h,u,m,a,n,i,z] + [a,t,i,o,n]

[r,e,u,n,d,e,h,u,m,a,n,i,z]
[r,e,u,n,d,e,h,u,m,a,n] + [i,z]
no

| ?- ^D
%
```

Session 7.6. Append recursively removes prefixes and suffixes.

In g0705, root(R,WORD) defines a recursive search for prefixes and suffixes and returns the value of the **root**, that is, the list that is the remainder after all of the prefixes and suffixes defined in lexicon_7a have been removed (see Session 7.7). As a side–effect, the write statement in the relations print to the screen the prefixes and suffixes that are located, plus information about what the program is doing: *List all prefixes* or *List all suffixes*.

Some affixes are also free–standing words: *able, like*. In these cases root(R,[u,n,a,b,l,e]) will find the prefix *un* and the suffix *able* and bind R to [] indicating that the word *unable* has no root. Similarly, root(R,X) will find no root for *inability, unlikely, likelihood*.

206

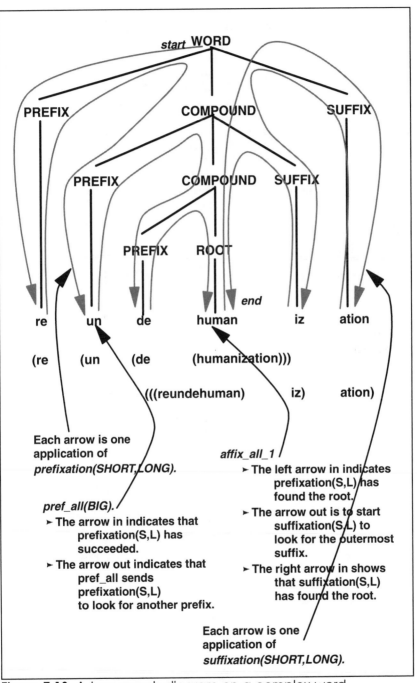

Figure 7.18. A tree search diagram on a complex word.

207

```
/*      Program:        g0705           RootFinder              */

root(R,WORD)  :-                    nl,write('List of all prefixes: '),    1
                                    pref_alle(NO_PREF,WORD),               2
                                    nl,write('List of all suffixes: '),    3
                                    suf_alle(R,NO_PREF).                   4

pref_alle(R,BIG)    :-  prefixation(SM,BIG),pref_alle(R,SM).              5
pref_alle(R,R).                                                          6

prefixation(SHORT,LONG) :-          pre(PRE),                            7
                                    append(PRE,SHORT,LONG),              8
                                    nl,write(PRE).                       9

suf_alle(R,BIG)    :-  suffixation(SM,BIG),suf_alle(R,SM).               10
suf_alle(R,R).                                                          11

suffixation(SHORT,LONG) :-          suf(SUF),                           12
                                    append(SHORT,SUF,LONG),             13
                                    nl,write(SUF).                      14

append([],X,X).                                                         15
append([A|B],C,[A|D])    :-         append(B,C,D).                      16
```

If we consider the root as being the "primary" part of the word, and assume that the root selects its possible prefixes and suffixes, then this is odd. If, however, we consider the prefixes and suffixes to be "primary," and assume that they select a possible root, then the situation with no root corresponds to an "intransitive" prefix and suffix. These programs are a first stab at a solution. Examples such as *unity*, which this program would analyze as *un+ity*, require complex lexical entries and relations.

The fact that this program first finds all prefixes and then finds all suffixes is an accidental consequence of the fact that this Prolog is operating on a serial computing machine that has one memory and one central processor. Basically, the computer can only do one thing at a time. We have written the program using the logical elements *and* and *or*, but the Prolog implementation understands them as having a temporal aspect. *And* means *and then*, or *next*.

There is no reason to find all the prefixes and then find all the suffixes, or vice versa. If we understand the *and* to be a logical *and*, then we could imagine Prolog operating as in Figure 7.19.

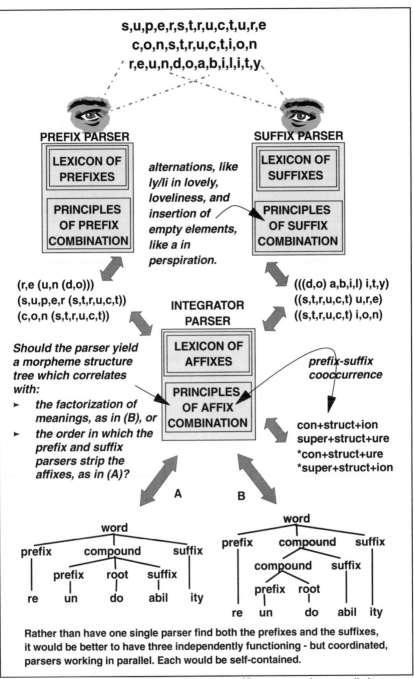

Figure 7.19. Independent prefix and suffix parsers in parallel.

```
% prolog
| ?- [g0702].
yes
| ?- [g0705].
yes

| ?- root(R,[u,n,a,n,t,i,d,i,s,e,s,t,a,b,l,i,s,h,
                    m,e,n,t,a,r,i,a,n,i,s,m]).
List of all prefixes:
[u,n]
[a,n,t,i]
[d,i,s]
List of all suffixes:
[i,s,m]
[i,a,n]
[a,r]
[m,e,n,t]
[i,s,h]
R = [e,s,t,a,b,l] ;
no

| ?- root(R,[r,e,u,n,d,o,a,b,i,l,i,t,y]).
List of all prefixes:
[r,e]
[u,n]
List of all suffixes:
[i,t,y]
[a,b,i,l]
R = [d,o] ;
no

| ?- root(R,[u,n,a,b,l,e]).
List of all prefixes:
[u,n]
List of all suffixes:
[a,b,l,e]
R = []
yes

| ?- root(R,[u,n,l,i,k,e,a,b,i,l,i,t,y]).
List of all prefixes:
[u,n]
List of all suffixes:
[i,t,y]
[a,b,i,l]
[l,i,k,e]
R = []
| ?- ^D
%
```

Session 7.7. Recursive searches for affixes.

Here we have (a) a **prefix parser** consisting of a lexicon of all prefixes and rules governing their combination, and (b) a **suffix parser** consisting of a suffix lexicon and combinatorial rules. We could implement these independent parsers on a parallel computer, a computer with several processors and shared memories, in such a way that Prolog could simultaneously search for prefixes and suffixes. In Figure 7.19, the eyes symbolize that the prefix parser would only look at the beginnings of lists and the suffix parser would only look at the list's terminal elements. On a parallel computer with shared memory, the Prolog *and* remains a logical *and* that is not understood to mean *and then*. A **parallel machine** would enable us to achieve an implementation of **pure Prolog** without the complications of precedural strategy.

A third Prolog interpreter, an **integrator parser**, could coordinate the information about prefixes, suffixes, and roots to achieve two goals. First, there are cooccurrence restrictions among prefixes and suffixes: *superstructure/*constructure*. Second, the simple parsers I have offered here for affixation would assign the structure A in Figure 7.19 to the word *reundoability*. If morphological analysis aims to assign a factorization to the affixes in order to correlate with meaning (and stress, intonation, etc.), then the integrator parser might assign a structure like B. I will not pursue these questions in morphology, but will examine such questions in detail when the syntactic structure assigned to sentences by the syntax parser is discussed.

If the general **goal of parser construction** is to construct a nonprocedural logical program to link a sound (or orthographic string) with a meaning, then computational morphology would be an excellent data domain to formulate the basic problem–solving skills, pattern–recognition devices, and memory structures required in parser research. The various factorizations discussed here for *American history teacher, undoable*, and so on, each can be correlated with a specific interpretation (*history teacher who is American* versus *teacher of American history*) and with specific sound properties (the former is stressed on *American*, the later on *history*). For *reundoability*, which parse tree (A or B or something else) provides the most natural understanding of the relation between the meaning and the stress/intonation patterns of this word?

Much of the material presented here to illustrate Prolog has been discussed widely in linguistic literature. Because the focus is on the assignment of structure to lists, let us examine some structural definitions offered by Chomsky. Chomsky (1965) discussed various types of branching constructions in the following passage:

The most obvious formal property of utterances is their bracketing into constituents of various types, that is, the 'tree structure' associated with them. Among such structures we can distinguish various kinds – for example, those to which we give the following conventional technical names, for the purposes of this discussion....

A **left–branching structure** is of the form [[[...] ...] ...] – for example, in English, such indefinitely iterable structures as *[[[[John]'s brother]'s father]'s uncle]* or *[[[the man who you met] from Boston] who was on the train]*....

Right–branching structures are those with the opposite property – for example, ...*[this is [the cat that caught [the rat that stole the cheese]]]*. (pp. 12–13)

Figure 7.14 illustrates right– and left–branching structures in compound noun constructions. *(American (history teacher))* is right branching. *((American history) teacher)* is left branching.

Figure 7.20 illustrates right– and left–branching structures in morphology and syntax. This suffixation relation defines a left–branching structure. Prefixation defines a right–branching structure. In both cases, the Prolog relation append is the computational mechanism that factors the orthographic representation into its components. In morphology, there appears to be little difference in the acceptability (or intelligibility) of left– versus right–branching structures. A word with a lot of prefixes is no more or less intelligible than a word with numerous suffixes. In syntax, however, right–branching constructions (1) are more acceptable than the left–branching equivalents (2):

(1)   [It surprised Mary [that it amused Sue [that Alice left early]]]
(2)   [[That [that Alice left early] amused Sue] surprised Mary]

From a Prolog point of view, this means that in morphology, both (3) and (4) occur regularly and productively with no degradation of intelligibility. But in syntax, the study of the relations among objects the size of a word or larger (3) is much more natural and productive than (4):

(3)   **append(A,B,C),append(X,Y,B).**   **Prolog definition of right–branching**
(4)   **append(A,B,C),append(X,Y,A).**   **Prolog definition of left–branching**

Sentences, such as (5), which mix left– and right–branching are less acceptable than pure right–branching constructions:

(5)   [It surprised Mary [that [that Alice left early] amused Sue]]

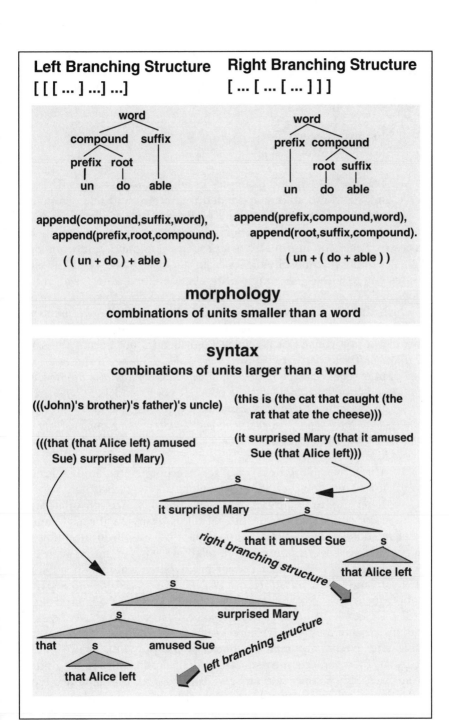

Figure 7.20. Left-branching versus right-branching structures.

But, if we assume that *unconstructable* means *not able to be constructed*, and *deconstructable* means *able to be deconstructed*, then mixed left and right bracketings seem to occur in morphology with no reduction of understanding:

(6)   [un [[con+struct] able]]
(7)   [[de [con+struct]] able]

It is possible to find examples in which a root is appended to a suffix, and this compound is appended to a prefix, and this compound is appended to a suffix, and this to a prefix, and so on. Hence, in many words, prefixation and suffixation alternate in the word formation processes. Recursion in syntax has a property not found in morphology.

Although in morphology one can stack up prefixes and affixes in various combinations, seemingly with abandon, one cannot put on the same prefix or suffix two or more times. It is possible to say *not unkind*, in which the *not* negates the *unkind*. It is impossible to say *ununkind*, *un+(un+kind)* and mean *not unkind*. There is nothing wrong with the meaning, it is a constraint in which English does not permit the same prefix or suffix to occur two times. *Doableable* does not mean *able to be doable*, but maybe *doableability* does. *Inhuman* and *not inhuman* are fine, but *ininhuman* is not, and *uninhuman* is odd but not as odd as *ininhuman*.

In syntax it would be normal to say: *I believe that you believe that triangles have three sides. I wonder why you wonder why he wonders why she wonders. I know a lady who knows a lady who knows a lady who knows where Elvis is hiding.*

There are numerous ways to incorporate this into a Prolog formulation. The simplest and most obvious are suggested here.

Referring to Figure 7.15, in morphology, we postulate two functions for parsing suffixes. One, suf_all, is recursive: it calls a "suffix finder relation," called suffixation, and then calls itself. In morphology, we could have a set of nonrecursive relations, one per suffix, such that once the relation is called, it cannot be invoked again. Rather than a general relation suffixation(SHORT,LONG), we would have a separate relation for each suffix, for example, ation(SHORT,LONG) finds *ation*, ity(SHORT,LONG) finds *ity*. Morphological parsers have two types of relations: a set of nonrecursive single–shot suffix finder relations, one per suffix, and a recursive relation that calls the individual suffix–finder programs. By separating recursion from identification, Prolog can find all the suffixes, but can only find any given suffix once. The same two types of relations exist for prefixes: a set of nonrecursive prefix identification relations, one per prefix, and, a recursive prefix_all relation which uses the individual prefix finders to find a prefix, and if successful, calls prefix_all with the remainder.

In syntax a single relation that (a) is recursive and calls itself, and (b) defines "sentence" is proposed.

In brief: A Prolog description of morphology: (a) requires a separation of suffix definitions from the recursive property, and (b) permits both (3) and (4) append constructions. A Prolog description of syntax: (a) requires a single definition of *sentence* incorporating recursion, and (b) permits – or favors – (3) append constructions over (4).

It is beyond the scope of this study to prove, but it is the separation of **recursion** from **identification** that permits both (3) and (4) append constructions in morphology. Empirically speaking, if we could say things like *unundoable* and *doableable*, then morphology would favor (3) over (4). If in syntax we could say: *I think that you wonder why he left*, but not *I think that you think that he left* or *I wonder why you wonder why he left*, then both right– and left–branching constructions would be acceptable at the syntactic level.

This analysis is concerned with the difference between morphological and syntactic processes, and with the optimal formulation of Prolog devices in order to represent these processes on a computer. At a broader level, independent of the application of Prolog to any data domain, Prolog itself has an asymmetry between left– and right–branching constructions. It would be interesting to see how many of the properties of the data structures in syntax and morphology follow from three computational processes:

- the inherent asymmetry of Prolog toward left– and right–branching structures,
- the assumption that in morphology *identification* is independent of *recursion*
- the assumption that in syntax *identification* and *recursion* are combined in a single relation that defines *sentence*.

Although I do not pursue these questions, the structure and organization of this material is arranged to focus on the issues that help sharpen them. It is always asked: What distributions of data follow from specific assumptions about the computational mechanisms underlying grammatical processes?

In Chapter 8, we ask: What aspects of syntax, the principles of combination of elements at the word level and above, can be described by using three basic computational mechanisms:

215

- the relational Prolog mechanisms discussed in Chapters 1–6
- the append relation used alone
- the two append relations, combined as in (3) and (4), to define left– and right–branching?

7.4. Regular and Irregular Morphology

English has several ways of indicating the singular/plural distinction. Before focusing on one narrow area of the problem, let us examine some of the general problems.

If we consider the phonology and phonetics of plural formation, that is, if we consider the sound combinations, we see regular plurals fall into three classes: /s/ is the final sound in the word *hiss*, and the initial sound in the word *say*, /z/ is the final sound in the word *jazz*, and the initial sound in *zoo*, and /iz/ is the sound of the word *is* (see Table 7.3).

Table 7.3 Phonologic/Phonetic level					
sing + /s/ =plu		sing + /z/ = plu		sing + /iz/ =plu	
hip	hips	girl	girls	box	boxes
hit	hits	tool	tools	house	houses
hick	hicks	bee	bees	hiss	hiss′
book	books	rib	ribs	buzz	buzz′

At the orthographic level, there are three endings: *–s* as in *girl+s* and *tool+s*, *–es* as in *box+es*, and *–′* as in *hiss′*. If a word ends in certain letters, including *x*, then the ending is *–es*. If the word ends in *s*, the ending is *–′*. In other cases, the ending is simply *–s* (see Table 7.4).

Exceptions abound. The following singular/plural pairs are not related by these rules: *woman/women, mouse/mice, ox/oxen, deer/deer, scissors/scissors* or *scissors/pairs of scissors*. Some words, such as *police* and *faculty*, have no singular form: *The police are/*is here*. Some words have the plural morphology in both singular and plural form: *scissors, pants, eye–glasses*. Some words have the singular morphology in both the singular and plural: *shrimp, sheep, deer*.

Table 7.4
Orthographic Level (plural/possessive)

sing + /s/ =plu		sing + /es/ = plu		sing + /'/ =plu	
hip	hips	box	boxes	hiss	hiss'
house	houses	tax	taxes	buzz	buzz'
girl	girls	wax	waxes	miss	miss'
axe	axes	fax	faxes	fizz	fizz'

The possessive forms (*girl's, girls'; tool's, tools'*) are related to the form of the plural in many cases. For a singular word like *girl*, the possessive singular is formed by adding *'s* and the possessive plural is formed by adding *s'*. In some cases, the possessive differs from the plural: *two wives* versus *my wife's book; two houses* versus *the house's roof.*

Program g0706 defines the relation *plural(Sing,Plural)*, which uses the append command to state that the *Singular* appended to "*s*" is the *plural*. The name relation is discussed next.

```
/*     Program:      g0706        plural.prg           */

plural(Sing,Plural)      :-     name(Sing,Sexpl),          1
                                append(Sexpl,"s",Pexpl),   2
                                name(Plural,Pexpl).        3

append([],X,X).                                            4
append([A|B],C,[A|D])    :-     append(B,C,D).             5
```

name(Sing,Sexpl) is read: *name is true if Sexpl is the exploded list of the atom Sing.*

Basically, name is a bookkeeping relation (see Session 7.8 and 7.9) that converts from atoms such as *girl* to the list [*g,i,r,l*]. In the last sections we laboriously typed in list structures such as [*r,e,u,n,d,o,a,b,i,l,i,t,y*] when we might have simply typed *redundoability*.

The relation **name(reundoability,[r,e,u,n,d,o,a,b,i,l,i,t,y])** is true.

In short, **name** is a Prolog tool that enables us to use atoms *girl, undoable*, and lets Prolog do the work of converting these atoms to the comma–drenched Prolog list notation in which all appending is done.

Line 2 of g0706, *append(Sexpl,"s",Pexpl)*, is read: *append is true if the exploded singular, Sexpl, added to [s], is the exploded plural, Pexpl.*

The two expressions *"s"* and *[s]* are identical for all practical purposes. Some impractical purposes are discussed next in which the differences are between *'s', "s"*, and *[s]* are indicated. In most of the work in the previous sections, we could replace lists in brackets, for example, *[u,n,d,o,a,b,l,e]* with *"undoable"*:

append("abc","def","abcdef") is true.

In general, if possible, always use the list notation, like *[s]*, with brackets and commas because this remains the same on any Prolog machine. In some cases the notations using double quotes (*"s"*) and single quotes (*'s'*) will behave differently from one Prolog machine to the next.

Session 7.8 indicates that *plural(Sing,Plural)* defined in g0706 gives

```
% prolog
C-Prolog version 1.5
| ?- ['g0706'].
g0706 consulted 316 bytes 1.98682e-08 sec.
yes

| ?- plural(girl,X).              If this program
X = girls                        does not work
yes                              on an IBM PC,
| ?- plural([girl],X).           see Appendix III.
! Illegal arguments name
      (atomic,list)
no
| ?- plural(box,X).
X = boxs
yes
| ?- plural(man,X).
X = mans
yes
| ?- plural(child,X).
X = childs
yes

| ?- cntl-d
%
```

Session 7.8. The first try at a plural relation.

218

the correct plural for *girl* if we query *plural(girl,X)*, where *girl* is an atom. If we blunder and make *girl* a list, as in *plural([girl],X)*, we get an error. Our relation incorrectly gives the plural form of *box* as *boxs* and also fails on all irregulars, such as, *man* and *child*.

Append can be used to relate the singular and the plural, but it can also be used to "test" a word to determine if the final letter is *x*, as in *box*. If the final letter is *x*, then we can define a relation to add *"es"*:

test_for_final_x(A)   :-   append(JUNK,"x",A).

```
| ?- test_for_final_x([b,o,x]).
yes
| ?- test_for_final_x([g,i,r,l]).
no
```

If we use name, then we could test on the atom and not the list representation of the word:

test_for_x_final(A)   :-   name(A,Alist),append(JUNK,"x",Alist).

```
| ?- test_for_x_final(box).
yes
| ?- test_for_x_final(girl).
no
```

The variable JUNK is used simply as a placeholder for the remainder of the list if in fact A terminates in an [x]. The append statements in these tests do dismantle the structure of the word A, but not for any purpose other than simply to test if the last letter in the list form of the word is [x].

Session 7.9 illustrates the operations of the name relation. The name relation is represented by a lens in Figure 7.21. Viewed through the lens, an atom such as *boy* is expanded into the list [98,111,121]. Why not into the list [b,o,y]? (If this program does not run, see Appendix III).

In the workspace, Prolog uses only numbers and no letters. Every symbol on the typewriter keyboard and on the computer screen corresponds to a number in the Prolog workspace. When you type a symbol, although you may not be aware of it, Prolog converts this into a number. After Prolog has finished all of its calculations, it converts the numbers back into symbols so that you can read them. In most cases this is done automatically and the conversion is transparent to the user.

The conversion performed by name is similar to the conversions in the telephone system. The switching circuits at the central office use only numbers and make all connections between telephone numbers. But style, fashion, and pressures of the marketplace enabled the phone

```
% prolog
C-Prolog version 1.5
                                    See Appendix III.
| ?- name(boy,X).
X = [98,111,121] .
yes

| ?- name(X,[b,o,y]).
! Type error in argument 2 of name/2
! integer expected, but b found
! goal: name(_9076,[b,o,y])
no

| ?- name(X,[98,111,121]).
X = boy
yes

| ?- name('()[],',X).
X = [40,41,91,93,44]
yes

| ?- name(X,[40,41,91,93,44]).
X = '()[],'
yes

| ?- ^D
%
```

Session 7.9. Name relates typewriter symbols to numbers.

company to market telephones with numbers corresponding to catchy words or phrases. *Name* is like the telephone pushbutton system that has numbers that correspond to letters.

For Prolog, each symbol has a number and each number has a symbol. For the phone, 0 and 1 correspond to no letters so that a person with the phone number 997–0101 must remain a telephone illiterate with no catchy phrase to replace the number. Choice numbers might be those corresponding to phrases such as *get_cash* (436–2374) or *love_bug* (568–3284). Numbers conveying no pride of ownership would include: *im_a_jerk* (462–5375) and *big_slob* (244–7562). Numbers that convert to phrases that would make a pirate blush are presumably passed on to unsuspecting customers as simple number combinations: 547–7277. Some bilingual phone subscribers code switch, that is, they have combined letters and numbers to get *i_love_u2*, *vote_4_me*, and so on. The phrase *2QT–2BGD, too cute to be good,* cannot be a telephone address because *Q* corresponds to no number.

220

Unlike the phone system, Prolog is intolerant of any mixing of the numbers in the databases and letters on the keyboard. There is one level, the user terminal keyboard level, at which Prolog uses symbols *boy* or [*b,o,y*], and the Prolog workspace level at which everything is numbers. Each keyboard symbol is replaced by its ASCII decimal equivalent. To the Prolog interpreter a typewriter symbol can be either data or an instruction, but a number is always data. The number symbols on the keyboard each have a number equivalent in the Prolog database:

```
| ?- name('0,1,2,3,4,5,6,7,8,9,0',X).
X =    [48,44,49,44,50,44,51,44,52,44,53,44,
             54,44,55,44,56,44,57,44,48]

| ?- name('01234567890',X).
X =    [48,49,50,51,52,53,54,55,56,57,48]
```

One can learn to drive a car without ever knowing whether the motor is gas, diesel, or electric. One can use a car intelligently and wisely without ever looking under the hood. Leave that to the mechanics. It is similar with Prolog. Usually it is of no concern to the Prolog programmer how the data are represented in the memory. For those interested, however, we will continue a bit. Our interests are specific. We will want to have our parser input a string such as: *undoable* and output a labeled bracketing such as *((un do) able)* and *(un (do able))*. At the level of syntax we will want the parser to link the phrase *the boy* with the bracketing *(np (det the)(n boy))*. In order to have the parser manipulate brackets and spaces as data, they must be represented as numbers.

The reason for this conversion becomes obvious when we realize that the Prolog interpreter does not treat all keyboard symbols equally. Consider the statement *append([a,b,c],[d,e],X)*. The **Prolog interpreter** is looking for:

- specific words, like *append*, that are the names of instructions
- square brackets , […], that enclose a list
- round braces, ( ), that enclose the arguments of the relation
- commas that separate the elements of a list
- a period that ends the statement
- a capital letter is always a variable.

These assumptions of the Prolog interpreter can only be overridden by using numbers, single quotes, or double quotes. Left to itself, Prolog assumes every square bracket, round bracket, comma, and so on is an instruction to the interpreter. Normally Prolog is correct. But if you want Prolog to consider a square bracket to be data, you must tell Prolog. There are three ways to do this. First, use numbers and not typewriter symbols. Second, enclose the typewriter symbols in single quotes (apostrophes), – '[(],,'. Third, enclose the typewriter symbols in double quotes, – "[(],,,]". There are differences between these representations, (see session 7.13).

Because the Prolog interpreter regards [,], (,), ,, and .. as instructions to organize the data or to do something, it would be difficult to have an append statement ever append a series of left brackets or commas. If we try to append three commas to two commas to get five commas, we cannot write append([,,,,],[,,,],X). The Prolog interpreter does not see this as including a list of three commas and a list of two commas. If we try to append square and round brackets, we cannot write append([[,(],[),]],X) and expect to get X = [[,(),]]. The Prolog interpreter would not understand what all of the brackets mean.

Prolog can append any typewriter symbol to any other typewriter symbol and indicate the results. But in order to avoid any problems with the Prolog interpreter on some special symbols, usually punctuation and bracketing, Prolog uses only numbers in the workspace and in some input/output functions.

Figure 7.21 indicates that name('()[]',',X) returns X = [40,41,91,93,44]. If you ever read a Prolog program and see numbers being manipulated, usually the numbers for the brackets and parentheses are involved. If numbers are not used, it would be difficult to have Prolog input and output expressions such as *[un + [do + able]]*, which contains not only brackets but spaces. Although the problems are not discussed here, consider the issues involved in appending an apostrophe, i.e., ', to *s* and *girl* to relate *girl* and the possessive *girl's*, or *do n't* and *don't*. The apostrophe is an instruction to Prolog, as discussed later. Apostrophe's can only be operated on – appended – as numbers.

Program g0707 contains several write statements to output the intermediate values calculated by the name and append functions. In particular, g0707 prints out the values of the variables *Sing*, Singular exploded *Sexpl*, Plural exploded *Pexpl*, and *Plural*.

Session 7.10 indicates the results of the query *plural(box,X)*. The variables printed out correspond to the stages of the relation sketched in Figure 7.22. The plural function does not operate on letters as common sense would suggest. Rather, everything is converted to numbers and converted back to letters.

Program g0708 relates the plural (–*s* and –*es* forms) to the singular forms (see Session 7.11). Irregular nouns are also included. If we

```
/*      Program:        g0707           pluralc.prg            */

plural(Sing,Plural)      :-      write('Sing = '),write(Sing),nl,
                                 name(Sing,Sexpl),
                                 write('Sexpl = '),write(Sexpl),nl,
                                 append(Sexpl,[e,s],Pexpl),
                                 write('Pexpl = '),write(Pexpl),nl,
                                 name(Plural,Pexpl),
                                 write('Plural = '),write(Plural),nl.


append([],X,X).
append([A|B],C,[A|D])    :-      append(B,C,D).
```

were consistent, we would place the irregular nouns in a database and represent it by a shaded box with double square brackets.

Lines 1–3 of g0708 correspond to nouns for which the plural and singular forms are not related by a rule. One could easily add to the list: *scissors, ox/oxen,* and so on. Each relation terminates in a cut, !, to insure that if the form is irregular, no other definition of plural will apply.

Lines 4–7 add *es* to the end of the singular to form the plural if the singular ends in *x*. Line 5 is a test to see if Sing ends in *x*. If line 5 succeeds, then line 6 adds *es* to Sing, and the cut in line 7 stops any further plural formations.

```
% prolog
C-Prolog version 1.5
| ?- ['g0707'].
g0707 consulted 524 bytes 0.0333333 sec.
yes

| ?- plural(box,X).
Sing = box
Sexpl = [98,111,120]
Pexpl = [98,111,120,101,115]
Plural = boxes
X = boxes
yes

| ?- cntl-d
[ Prolog execution halted ]
%
```

Session 7.10. The intermediate states relating singular and plural.

223

```
/*        Program:      g0708            plural1.prg                  */

plural(man,men)           :- !.                                       1
plural(woman,women)       :- !.                                       2
plural(child,children)    :- !.                                       3

plural(Sing,Plural)       :-        name(Sing,Sexpl),                 4
                                    append(JUNK,"x",Sexpl),           5
                                    append(Sexpl,"es",Pexpl),         6
                                    name(Plural,Pexpl),!.             7

plural(Sing,Plural)       :-        name(Sing,Sexpl),                 8
                                    append(Sexpl,"s",Pexpl),          9
                                    name(Plural,Pexpl).              10

append([],X,X).                                                      11
append([A|B],C,[A|D])     :-        append(B,C,D).                   12
```

```
% prolog
C-Prolog version 1.5
| ?- [g0708].
g0708 consulted 424 bytes  0.0333333 sec.
yes
| ?- plural(girl,X).
X = girls
yes
| ?- plural(box,X).
X = boxes
yes
| ?- plural(book,X).
X = books
yes
| ?- plural(man,X).
X = men
yes
| ?- plural(woman,X).
X = women
yes
| ?- plural(child,X).
X = children
yes
| ?- cntl-d
[ Prolog execution halted ]
%
```

Session 7.11. The operation of program g0708.

At the *user level*, prolog uses typewriter symbols.

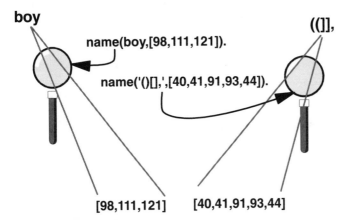

boy

name(boy,[98,111,121]).

name('()[],',[40,41,91,93,44]).

(([],

[98,111,121]   [40,41,91,93,44]

In the *prolog workspace*, prolog uses only numbers.

 The *name* relation, symbolized by a lens, is essentially a table in which each symbol on the user's typewriter corresponds to a number in the prolog workspace.

At the *user level*, the phone address can be numbers or *a,b,c,d,e,f,g,h,i,j,k,l,m,n,o,p,r,s,t,u,v,w,x,y*, but not *q,z*.

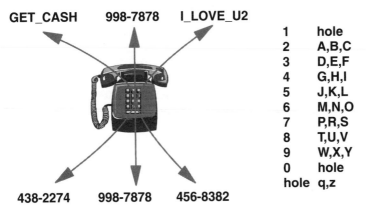

GET_CASH   998-7878   I_LOVE_U2

1	hole
2	A,B,C
3	D,E,F
4	G,H,I
5	J,K,L
6	M,N,O
7	P,R,S
8	T,U,V
9	W,X,Y
0	hole
hole	q,z

438-2274   998-7878   456-8382

At the *switching circuit level*, a phone's address is a number.

Figure 7.21. In the workspace, prolog uses only numbers.

If line 5 fails, lines 8–10 appends an *s* to Sing to form the Plural. Session 7.11 indicates that g0708 gives the correct answers.

G0709 defines a function *past(Present,Past)*, which relates the present tense of a verb with the past tense.

```
/*      Program:        g0709          past_tense          */

past(go,went) :- !.
past(take,took) :- !.
past(see, saw) :- !.
past(have,had) :- !.

past(dive,dove).
past(dream,dreamt).

past(Present,Past)              :-      name(Present,A),
                                        append(A,"ed",B),
                                        name(Past,B).

append([],X,X).
append([A|B],C,[A|D])          :-      append(B,C,D).
```

Irregular verbs such as *go*, which have only one past tense, have a database entry that ends in a cut. This cut prohibits any further searching for past–tense forms. Verbs such as *dive*, which have two past–tense forms, have an entry such as past(*dive,dove*) for the irregular form. This database entry contains no cut. In interpreting the query past(dive,X), Prolog will find the irregular form, X = dove, and then continue to form the past by adding *ed* by the general rule. This gives the "almost correct" answer: X = diveed. This function must be modified to examine the last letter of the verb. If the verb terminates in *e*, the past formation rule should add *d*. In all other cases, the rule should add *ed*. Session 7.12 indicates the results of querying g0709.

The function for past tenses would have to be modified to add *ed* in some cases (*look/looked*) and *d* in others (*dive/dived*). In some cases, spelling manuals call for duplication of the final consonant.

More complex constructions, such as the English comparative, require the Prolog program to allow for irregulars (*good/better/best*), the ending *–er* (*tall/taller*), and the word *more* (*interesting/more interesting*). A general rule is that if the adjective (or adverb) is three syllables or more, the comparative uses the word *more*.

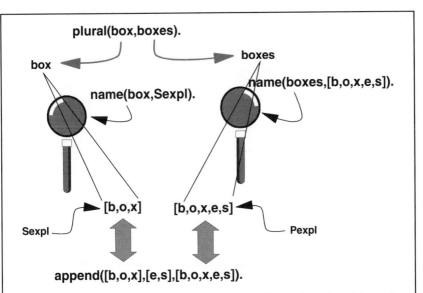

A common sense view of how the plural function should work.

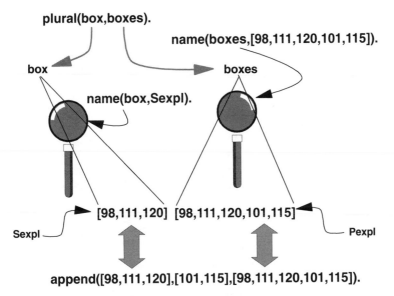

How the plural function actually works. The relation name relates the atom box to the list of numbers indicated. Each typewriter symbol corresponds to a unique number.

Figure 7.22. The prolog data structures of the *plural* relation.

```
% prolog
C-Prolog version 1.5
| ?- ['g0709'].
g0709 consulted 508 bytes          0.0333333 sec.
yes

| ?- past(look,X).
X = looked
yes

| ?- past(want,X).
X = wanted ;
no

| ?- past(see,X).
X = saw ;
no

| ?- past(dream,X).
X = dreamt ;
X = dreamed ;
no

| ?- past(dive,X).
X = dove ;
X = diveed ;
no

| ?- cntl-d
[ Prolog execution halted ]
%
```

Session 7.12. Some verbs have two past tense forms.

For two syllables or less, the ending –er is added to the form. If this is a true condition, then it is one of the few places in human language in which numbers seem to play a role. As reference to any grammar book will indicate, exceptions abound. Interesting exceptions include words such as *curious* which, as Lewis Caroll pointed out, sound strange either way: *more curious* and *curiouser* both seem odd. Words such as *superlative* have no comparative, **more superlative*. And either form can occur given the appropriate context: *This door is taller (*more tall) than that door. This door is more tall (*taller) than wide.*

There are several relations, besides name, that can display the numbers internal to the Prolog workspace. One of them is write, as shown in Session 7.13.

```
% prolog
C-Prolog version 1.5
| ?- write('hello, how are you?').
hello, how are you?
yes
| ?- write('abcdefghijklmnopqrstuvwxyz').
abcdefghijklmnopqrstuvwxyz
yes
| ?- write("hello, how are you?").
[104,101,108,108,111,44,32,104,111,119,
      32,97,114,101,32,121,111,117,63]
yes
| ?- write('girl').
girl
yes
| ?- write("girl").
[103,105,114,108]
yes
| ?- write("balloon").
[98,97,108,108,111,111,110]
yes
| ?- cntl-d
[ Prolog execution halted ]
%
```

Session 7.13. An illustration of the single and double quotes.

7.5. The Minimalist Framework

The purpose of this rather technical section is to place this study in perspective. The following discussion is aimed at readers who are familiar with current developments in linguistic theory and with research aimed at developing constraints on derivations and forms as nonprocedural logical conditions. The main function of the section is to define the framework and terminology and relate them to current terms used in the literature.

This discussion follows Chomsky (1975b, 1992b) closely; however, I cast all of his conditions and constraints as nonprocedural logical conditions. More specifically, referring to Figure 7.23:

We assume all of the conditions in the minimalist theory can be represented by statements in the first–order predicate calculus and expressed as Prolog programs

229

consisting of a database and a set of relations defined on that database.

This defines the **main goal of linguistic research**:

In the nonprocedural minimalist theory, the problem facing the grammarian is to find the contents, organization, and structure of the database and express all constraints as nonprocedural logical conditions defined on that database and its projections.

Let us summarize the components of the minimalist framework sketched in Figures 7.23-7.25.

Figure 7.23 sketches the technical and formatting assumptions we make in presenting our Prolog version of the minimalist theory. The double–headed arrows in Figure 7.23 reflect the fact that in a nonprocedural language there is no precedence of any element in a conditional. We assume that any of the three programs in g0710 summarizes the information in Figure 7.23.

At the level of technical implementation on a specific computer, we assume that optimally each of the Prolog programs that defines a condition on representation, and each of the programs that functions in the overt syntax, might best be implemented as an independent processor. All of the independent Prolog parsers operate in parallel on a shared memory space defining the data structures X and Y.

Each language will determine a set of **structural descriptions** (X,Y) (X drawn from Phonetic Form, PF, and Y from Logical Form, LF) as its formal representations of sound and meaning, insofar as these are determined by the language itself. A **language**, in turn, determines an infinite set of linguistic expressions (SDs), each a pair (X,Y) drawn from the interface levels (PF,LF), respectively.

Conditions on representations hold only at the interface and are motivated by properties of the interface, perhaps properly understood as modes of interpretation by performance systems. The linguistic expressions are the optimal realizations of the interface conditions, where "optimality" is determined by the economy conditions of UG. Let us take these assumptions also to be part of the minimalist program. The conditions on representations at LF include: control theory, binding theory, quantifier theory, theta theory, and so on. The conditions on representation at the orthographic level would include conventions on spelling, punctuation, hyphenation, and, in general, those aspects of orthography discussed in programs such as spelling checkers, the writer's workbench, and diction.

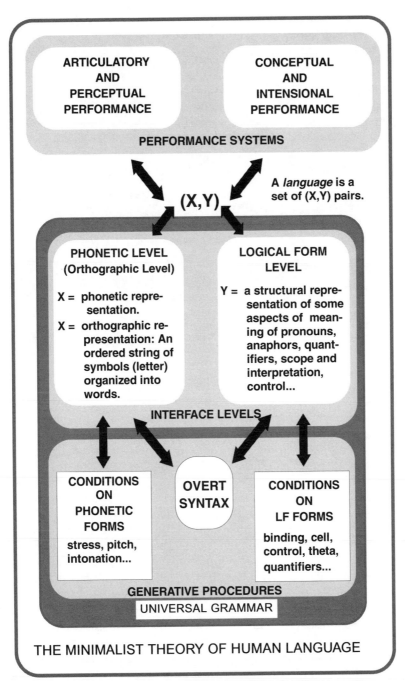

Figure 7.23. The non-procedural logic minimalist theory.

```
/*      Program:        g0710   Universal_Grammar               */

/*      Program Name:           Universal_Grammar_1             */

sd(X,Y)         :-      pf(X),lf(Y).
pf(X)           :-      overt_syntax(X,Y),cond_on_pf(X).
lf(Y)           :-      overt_syntax(X,Y),cond_on_lf(Y).
cond_on_lf(Y)   :-      binding(Y),theta(Y),control(Y),case(Y).


/*      Program Name:           Universal_Grammar_2             */

sd(X,Y)    :-   overt_syntax(X,Y),cond_on_pf(X),cond_on_lf(Y).
cond_on_lf(Y)   :-      binding(Y),theta(Y),control(Y),case(Y).


/*      Program Name:           Universal_Grammar_3             */

sd(X,Y)         :-      overt_syntax(X,Y),cond_on_pf(X),
                        binding(Y),theta(Y),control(Y),case(Y).
```

The conditions on representation at the phonetic level include constraints on stress, intonation, pitch, and pronunciation.

A **linguistic expression** is nothing other than a formal object that satisfies the interface conditions in the optimal way. A still further step would be to show that the basic principles of language are formulated in terms of notions drawn from the domain of (virtual) conceptual necessity.

Another standard assumption is that a language consists of two components: a lexicon and a computational system. The **lexicon** specifies the items that enter into the computational system, with their idiosyncratic properties. The **computational system** uses these elements to generate derivations and SDs. The derivation of a particular linguistic expression, then, involves a choice of items from the lexicon and a computation that constructs the pair of interface representations. I continue to present a *lexicon* inside a shaded double box and the *computational system* inside a shaded box. The notation for both the lexicon and the computational system is Prolog and the basic mechanisms of derivation are unification and subsumption.

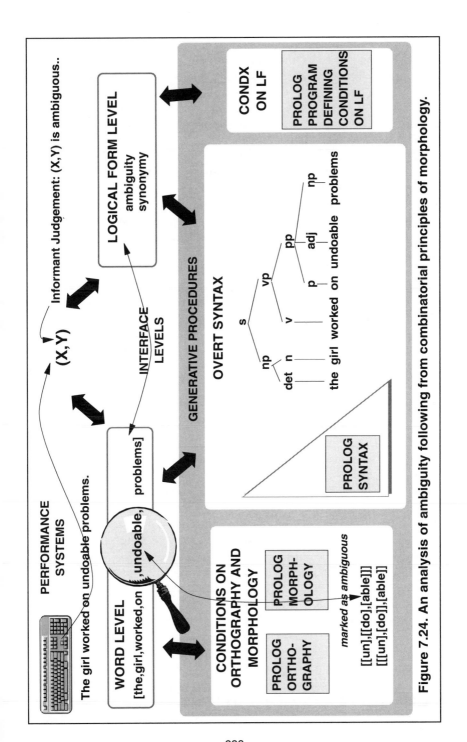

Figure 7.24. An analysis of ambiguity following from combinatorial principles of morphology.

233

Parts of the computational system are relevant only to X, not to Y: the **PF component**. Other parts are relevant only to Y, not X: the **LF component**. The parts of the computational system that are relevant to both are the **overt syntax** – a term that is a bit misleading, in that it may involve empty categories assigned no phonetic shape. The nature of these systems is an empirical matter; one should not be misled by unintended connotations of terms such as "logical form" and "represent" adopted from technical usage in different kinds of inquiry.

In the minimalist theory, the PF and LF levels define representations that constitute **primary linguistic data**. That is, an informant can make judgments about them, in particular, an informant can decide if a particular pairing of an (X,Y) is legitimate; if a particular X is ambiguous and is part of two structural descriptions (X,Y') and (X,Y''), as in *the girl works on boats*; or if two different Xs have some aspect of logical form in common, for example, X' = *he turned on the radio* and X'' = *he turned the radio on,* yield (X',Y) and (X'',Y), resulting in synonymy.

Invariant principles, defined by Universal Grammar (UG), determine what counts as a possible derivation and a possible derived object (linguistic expression, SD). Given a language, these principles determine a specific set of derivations and generated SDs, each a pair (X, Y). Let us say that a derivation D **converges** if it yields a legitimate SD, otherwise it **crashes**; D **converges at PF** if X is legitimate and **crashes at PF** if it is not; D **converges at LF** if Y is legitimate and **crashes at LF** if it is not. Thus, we assume that a derivation converges if it converges at PF and at LF; convergence is determined by independent inspection of the interface levels.

To be consistent with our Prolog first–order predicate calculus view, we will say *unifies* or *succeeds* rather than *converges*, and *fails* rather than *crashes*. Some linguists use *converge* where we will say *unifies/succeeds* and *crash* where we say *fail*.

So far, we are within the domain of virtual conceptual necessity, at least if the general outlook is adopted. UG must determine the class of possible languages. It must specify the properties of the SDs and of the symbolic representations that enter into them. In particular, it must specify the interface levels (*Articulatory–Perceptual, A–P,* and *Conceptual–Intensional, C–I*), the elements that constitute these levels, and the computations by which they are constructed. A particularly simple design for language would take the conceptually necessary interface levels to be the only levels. That assumption will be part of the "minimalist" program explored here.

Let us consider a simpler version of program g0710. G0711 is more in accord with the material in later chapters.

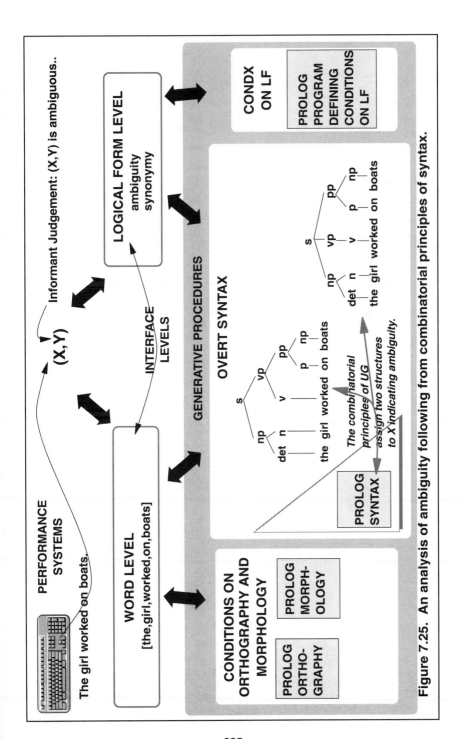

Figure 7.25. An analysis of ambiguity following from combinatorial principles of syntax.

235

```
/*      Program:        g0711   Universal_Grammar_4   */

sd(X,Y)             :-      orth_rep(X),log_form(Y).
orth_rep(X)         :-      overt_syntax(X,Y),condx_orth_rep(X).
condx_on_orth_rep(X) :-     orthography(X),morphology(X).
log_form(Y)         :-      control(Y),binding(Y).
```

We can illustrate the basic approach by examining how the grammar analyzes two sentences, each of which is ambiguous. The ambiguity must be indicated in the representation at the level of logical form. We will assume that X is a representation at the orthographic level. Sometimes we will assume X consists of a list of symbols, [t,h,e,_,g,i,r...], other times a list of words, [the,girl,worked,on,undoable,problems]. Simple Prolog programs can convert between these forms. Here, we are not concerned with the form of a logical form, LF, but with its information content. If a sentence is ambiguous, this ambiguity must be represented at the LF. Here, we simply indicate the ambiguity by indicating the information that must be given at LF. We discuss the form of LF representations when we discuss control in subjectless infinitive constructions, for example, *I want to go*:

(1) (a) X: The girl worked on undoable problems.
     (b) LF: the girl worked on not doable problems
     (c) LF: the girl worked on undoing problems

(2) (a) X: The girl worked on boats.
     (b) LF: The girl fixed/repaired/built boats.
     (c) LF: The girl was on boats when she worked.

The bulk of the material in Chapter 8 focuses on the one line of program g0711:

orth_rep(X)   :-   overt_syntax(X,Y),condx_orth_rep(X).

We assume that the condx_orth_rep(X) are defined as Prolog programs. One condition on orthographic representations is a Prolog morphological parser. Referring to Figure 7.24, the sentence *The girl worked on undoable problems* is assigned two morphological representations by the morphological parser. More specifically, *undoable* is assigned two morphological representations by the universal grammar principles that define the combinatorial mechanisms of prefixes and suffixes in English. The morphological structure assigned to the list X = *[the,girl,worked,on, undoable,problems]* indicates that X contains a morphological ambiguity. The conditions_on_morphology indicate the source of the ambiguity.

The overt_syntax(X,Y) can be formulated as a Prolog program. Referring to Figure 7.25, the sentence *The girl worked on boats* is assigned two phrase markers by the universal grammar principles that define the combinatorial mechanisms of prepositional phrase adjunction and complements in the overt_syntax parser. The syntactic structure assigned to the list X = *[the,girl,worked,on,boats]* indicates that X contains a syntactic ambiguity.

For a more thorough analysis relating the basic data structures and processes of generative syntax to the basic mechanisms of unification, see Dougherty (in preparation) and Meyers (1994).

In a nutshell, referring to Figure 7.23, the majority of the work in the Chapter 8 aims to present a specific Prolog implementation of the relations between X and Y. The focus is on the Prolog relations required to define overt_syntax(X,Y). In pure Prolog, this relation is a nondirectional biconditional. In other words, if we actually had an explicit Prolog representation for this relation, it would associate a logical form with a phonetic string or a phonetic string with a logical form. In fact, it would simply define the pairs (X,Y) for the language.

In the grammars presented in Chapter 8, there is no deep structure (D-str) level and no transformational movement rule. There is no motivation for either D-str or movement in the minimalist theory.

Chomsky (1975b), the published version of his dissertation, *The Logical Structure of Linguistic Theory* (*LSLT*), indicated that deep and surface structures were not part of the early theory. Referring to the *Aspects of the Theory of Syntax*, Chomsky (1965), theory as *ATS*, he stated:

> The terms *deep structure* and *surface structure*, familiar in later discussion (c.f. *ATS*), do not appear in *LSLT*. In the *LSLT* version of syntactic theory, a phrase–structure grammar generates terminal strings and assigns them P–markers, representation on the level **P** of phrase structure.[21] A **P**–marker is a set of strings, representable as a labeled bracketing or a tree diagram, which assigns a phrase–structure interpretation to the terminal string, determining its phrases and the categories to which they belong. More generally, the notion of phrase structure interpretation is defined in such a way that a set of strings of a particular type on the level **P**, containing a single terminal string, assigns a phrase–structure interpretation to this terminal string whether or not it is generated by the phrase–structure grammar... **P**–markers are a special case,

generated by the phrase–structure grammar,[22] and assigned by a mapping Φ to a restricted class of sentences called the *kernel sentences*...

...The nearest analogue to the notion deep structure in the LSLT theory is the T–marker of the generated sentence. (Chomsky, 1975b, pp. 14–16)

Chomsky (1992b), in presenting his minimalist position, indicated that D–structure, the most recent mutation of deep structure, plays no role in describing or explaining any phenomena of human language. He states:

> ...If so, the special assumptions underlying the postulation of *D–structure* lose credibility. Since these assumptions lacked independent conceptual support, we are led to dispense with the level of *D–structure* and the 'all–at–once' property of SATISFY, relying in its place on a theory of generalized transformations for lexical access – though the empirical consequences of the D–structure conditions remain to be faced.[24]
>
> ...We now adopt (more or less) the assumptions of LSLT, with a single generalized transformation GT that takes a phrase marker K^1 and inserts it in a designated empty position δ in a phrase marker K, forming the new phrase marker K^*, which satisfies X–bar theory. Computation proceeds in parallel, selecting from the lexicon freely at any point. At each point in the derivation, then, we have a structure Σ, which we may think of as a set of phrase markers. At any point, we may apply the operation SPELL–OUT, which switches to the PF component. If Σ is not a single phrase marker, the derivation crashes at PF, since PF rules cannot apply to a set of phrase markers and no legitimate PF representation π is generated. If sigma is a single phrase marker, the PF rules apply to it yielding π, which is either legitimate (so the derivation converges at PF) or not (the derivation again crashes at PF).
>
> After SPELL–OUT, the computational process continues, with the sole constraint that it has no further access to the lexicon (we must ensure, for example, that John left does not mean *They wondered whether John left before finishing his work*). The PF and LF outputs must satisfy the (external) interface conditions. D–structure disappears, along with the problems it raised. (pp. 28–31)

The grammars presented in Chapter 8 follow closely the views presented in Chomsky (1975b, 1992b), Gross (1991, 1992, 1993), Harris (1951, 1957, 1965), and Leacock (1990,1991).

chapter 8

COMPUTATIONAL TOOLS FOR SENTENCE PROCESSING

One fundamental contribution of what we have been calling "Cartesian Linguistics" is the observation that human language, in its normal use, is free from the control of independently identifiable external stimuli or internal states and is not restricted to any practical communicative function, in contrast, for example, to the pseudo language of animals. It is thus free to serve as an instrument of free thought and self–expression. The limitless possibilities of thought and imagination are reflected in the creative aspect of language use. The language provides finite means but infinite possibilities of expression constrained only by rules of concept formation and sentence formation, these being in part particular and idiosyncratic but in part universal, a common human endowment. The finitely specifiable form of each language – in modern terms, its generative grammar – provides an "organic unity" interrelating its basic elements and underlying each of its individual manifestations, which are potentially infinite in number.

Noam Chomsky, 1966
Cartesian Linguistics

8.1. Syntax: Representations and Parsers

Early work in generative grammar was based on these definitions:

- A **sentence** is a string of symbols (elements) in which the symbols are selected from a fixed list of symbols.
- A **language, L**, is a set (finite or infinite) of sentences, each finite in length.

239

As Chomsky (1957) pointed out:

> All natural languages in their spoken or written form are languages in this sense, since each natural language has a finite number of phonemes (or letters in its alphabet) and each sentence is representable as a finite sequence of these phonemes (or letters), though there are infinitely many sentences. Similarly, the set of 'sentences' of some formalized system of mathematics can be considered a language. (p. 13)

Let us clarify the terminology being used here.

The following are *sentences* or *strings*; these two terms are used interchangeably.

The cow jumped over the moon.
Mary likes books about horses.
The girl forgot that the boy read the story.

The data structures used to represent what linguists call *strings* are called *lists* in Prolog. A **Prolog list** is a set of atoms (or lists) separated by commas and enclosed in square brackets (see Figure 7.10). A **Prolog string** is a data structure that does not concern us. The following are Prolog lists:

[the,cow,jumped,over,the,moon]
[mary,likes,books,about,horses]
[the,girl,forgot,that,the,boy,read,the,story]

Usually the Prolog list will be part of a relation. A variable, such as X, can represent a list. Sometimes, in technical discussions, one says X *evaluates to a list*, X *is bound to a list*, or X *is a list*. In the expression *sentence(X)*, the X is not in square brackets, but X will evaluate to something in brackets:

sentence([the,cow,jumped,over,the,moon]).
sentence([mary,likes,books,about,horses]).
sentence([the,X,forgot,that,Y,Z,read,the,story]).
sentence(X).

Early generative work offered these definitions:

■ The **fundamental aim** in the linguistic analysis of a language L is to separate the grammatical sequences, which are the sentences of L, from the ungrammatical sequences, which are not sentences of L, and to study the nature of the grammatical sequences.

- The **grammar** of L will thus be a device that defines the grammatical sequences of L and no ungrammatical ones.

Much confusion can be avoided by remembering that *sentence, language, grammar,* and *grammatical* are technical terms that apply to all sorts of formal systems, and not just to what are popularly called *sentences* in adult human languages.

At the orthographic level, a *word* is a *sentence* by these definitions. A **word** is a sequence of elements (letters), in which the letters are selected from the typewriter keyboard. The set of words is a *language.* The system that defines the well–formed words is a *grammar* and is essentially a dictionary or a lexicon. The goal of defining "grammatical sentence," if we think of a word as a "sentence" according to the technical definitions, is to construct a dictionary.

At the morpheme level, *word* is a *sentence* by these definitions. A **word** is a sequence of elements (morphemes), in which the morphemes are given in the lexicon (suffixes, roots, prefixes, infixes). The set of words is a *language.* The morphological system that defines the morphemes and their rules of combination is a *grammar.* The goal of defining "grammatical sentence," if we think of the word as a string of morphemes, is to construct a morphological parser.

There is a significant potential for confusion and misunderstanding if we use *sentence* in its technical term to mean *word.* The potential increases when we realize that a *level* is defined as a set of elements that obey rules of combination. According to this, each level defines a set of sentences. Unless we sharpen our definitions, our discussion will start to sound like Abbot and Costello discussing who is on first.

A word is, technically speaking, a sentence – a string of symbols obeying rules of combination – at two levels: orthographic and morphemic. Rather than saying there are two grammars – an orthographic grammar and a morphological grammar – let us use the term **parser**. Also, to avoid confusion, we will use the word **string** instead of the technical word **sentence**.

> When we say SENTENCE, we will mean what is conventionally called a *sentence*, that is, a string of words containing a subject and predicate that is understood as a free–standing proposition.

> We will use the term STRING to mean a linearly ordered sequence of elements with no internal structure, in which

241

the elements are selected from a list.

What linguists call a string, for example, *Tess helps Tracy*, we will represent as a PROLOG LIST STRUCTURE, [tess,helps,tracy]. A string is a list of atoms, not a list of lists.

A PARSER at a level links a string, which has linear but no hierarchical order, with a phrase marker that has both linear and hierarchical order plus labels on the constituents.

Using these distinctions, we can say that a *word* of an adult language is a *string* at several levels. A *word* is a string of orthographic symbols and also a string of morphemes. This sounds better than saying the technically correct: A *word* is a sentence of orthographic symbols and a sentence of morphemes.

In Chapter 7 we discussed the strings at the morphology level and indicated how a parser can assign the morphological strings, that is, Prolog lists like [un,do,able], internal structure represented by phrase markers.

In this chapter I show how to construct a syntactic parser that will assign one or more phrase markers to a string at the sentence level. That is, I develop a parser that will assign the phrase marker in Figure 7.4 to the string *The girl forgot the boy*, represented as the Prolog list, [the,girl,forgot,the,boy].

I discuss how to construct parsers which will assign phrase markers to *simple sentences* and *compound sentences*. A **compound sentence** is composed of two or more simple sentences (see Figures 8.1 and 8.2). A **simple sentence** can be thought of as a sentence containing only one main verb.

Figure 8.3 aims to clarify one crucial difference between E–language and I–language research (see Chomsky, 1986b). Almost all early work in generative grammar was in the E–language paradigm, where E stands for *External*. The model presented in this book is in the I–language paradigm, where I represents *Internal*.

From a practical point of view, the difference is basic, but not always obvious. I present the I–language parser of English as a lot of little parsers, each of which can be considered to operate independently of the rest. Each parser module relates some aspect of the string to some aspect of the structure that underlies meaning. There is no clear cut notion of grammatical versus ungrammatical sentence in this view. From a theoretical point of view, the differences follow from the goals of research.

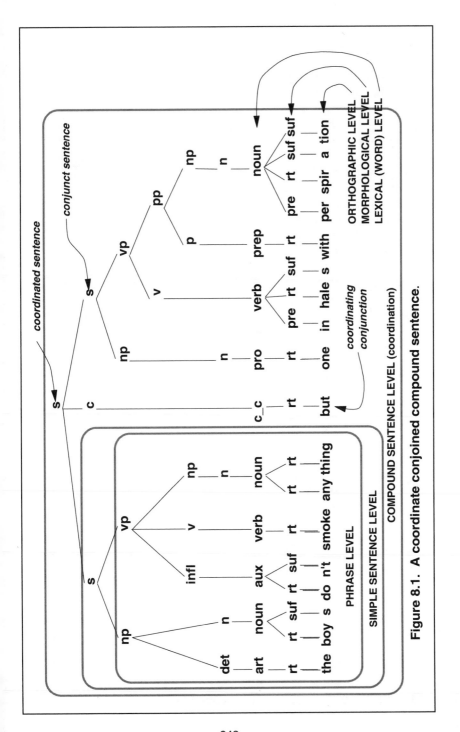

Figure 8.1. A coordinate conjoined compound sentence.

243

The E–language goal is to define "grammatical sentence in English." The I–language goal is to define the "sound–meaning pairings in English."

From the philosophical point of view, the differences are clear. The E–language model assumes that a human language, like English, is definable as an "external reality," like mathematics, that can exist independent of a human. The I–language model assumes that a human language is definable as a biological property of human beings. In a nutshell: In the I–Language perspective, if we knew everything there was to know about the human brain, neurological system, mind, and body, we would know everything there was to know about human language, but still not know everything there was to know about mathematics. In the E–language perspective, if we knew everything about the human mental and physiological capacities, we would still not know all there was to know about human language or mathematics.

I discuss the E–language position to facilitate reference to the linguistic literature. Most materials before 1990 have been written in this view. I champion the I–language view. This parser model may not offer a clear definition of grammatical sentence in English, but it does offer a mechanism to correlate a string with aspects of meaning.

E–LANGUAGE RESEARCH is based on these definitions. Here we use *sentence* in its conventional meaning: a free–standing proposition containing a subject and a predicate:

- A **sentence** of a human language is a string of elements, in which the elements (words, lexical items) are taken from a fixed list of elements.
- A **language**, L, is a set of sentences.
- The **goal of E–language research** on a language L is to construct a grammar that can separate the grammatical sequences, which are sentences of L, from the ungrammatical sequences, which are not sentences of L, and to study the nature of the grammatical sequences.
- The **grammar** of L is a device that separates the grammatical from the ungrammatical sequences and defines "grammatical in L."

In our Prolog terminology (see Figure 8.3), E–language research would consider the syntax parser to be one parser with all of the lexical definitions and combinatorial principles incorporated into one large Prolog grammar. If a string meets all of the definitions, it is grammatical and is assigned a phrase marker. If a string does not satisfy all of the Prolog definitions and goals, it is ungrammatical.

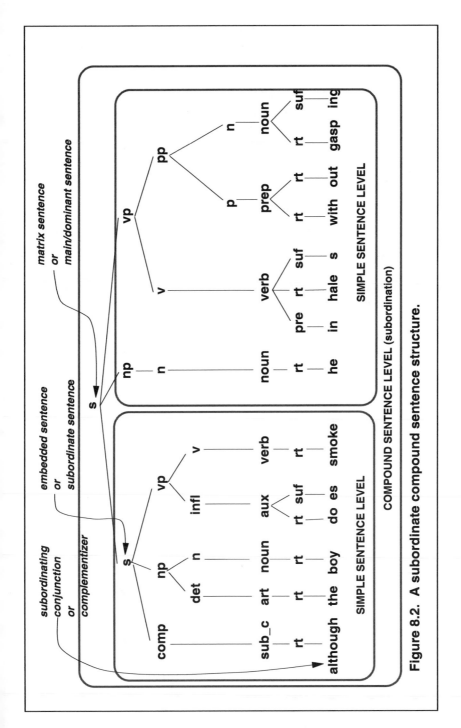

Figure 8.2. A subordinate compound sentence structure.

245

The alternative is I–LANGUAGE RESEARCH, following Chomsky (1986b), which offers these definitions:

- A **sentence** of a human language is:
  - ▸ at the orthographic (phonetic) level a string of elements, in which the elements (words, lexical items) are taken from a fixed list of elements.
  - ▸ a sound–meaning correspondence, or sound–meaning pair.
- A **language** consists of sound–meaning pairings.
- The **goal of I–language research** on a language L is to specify the sound–meaning correspondences that exist in L.
- The **grammar** of L is a device that defines the sound–meaning pairings of L.

An I–language model is not concerned to pass judgment on the grammaticality of a sentence and to identify it as a member of a set. An I–language model aims to specify sound–meaning pairings in a language and to correlate specific aspects of the string of symbols (sounds, orthography) with specific aspects of meaning. I do not discuss how to represent meanings. Instead, I indicate how a parser assigns the string of orthographic symbols a phrase structure that correlates with aspects of meaning. For instance, I show how the parser decides a string is ambiguous by assigning two different phrase markers to the string.

Converting this to Prolog terminology, as indicated in Figure 8.3, an I–language model can be factored into numerous small Prolog parsers, each of which assigns some aspect of structure to some aspect of the orthographic string. For discussion, suppose we have a compound sentence parser, a simple sentence parser, a phrase parser, and a morphological parser. Each of these is a self–contained system consisting of a set of Prolog statements defining a lexicon and rules of combination of the elements in that lexicon.

Such an I–language conception permits the possibility that for some string, each Prolog parser will succeed and assign that string a structure, for example, *The girl remembered that the boy forgot.* For some other string, each Prolog parser may fail, and the string will be assigned no structure, e.g., *Only but taked the if girl oxens not soup superstruction happen do.* For other strings, some parsers may succeed and others may fail, for example, *I wonder why to go, She loved himself, Mary explained me how to go.* For these strings, some parsers will assign some structure, and therefore, they can be partially interpreted.

Chomsky (1957) presented the following sentences:

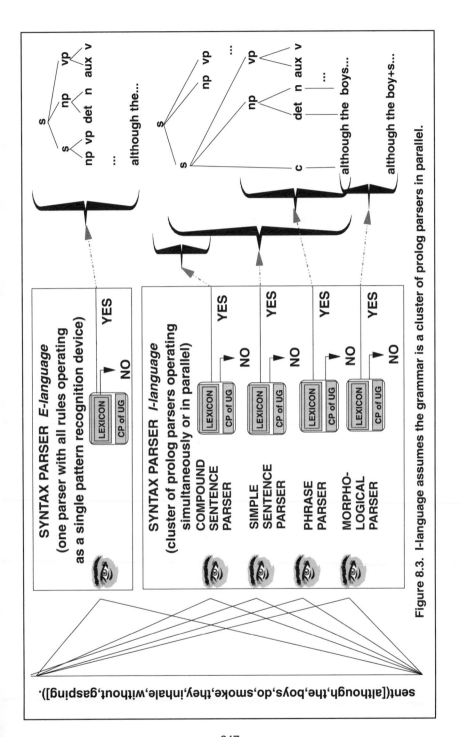

Figure 8.3. I-language assumes the grammar is a cluster of prolog parsers in parallel.

247

(1)   Sincerity frightened John.
(2)   John was frightened by sincerity.

(3)   John frightened sincerity.
(4)   Sincerity was frightened by John.

E–language research and I–language research see these sentences as defining two different problems.

- **E–LANGUAGE RESEARCH** considers each sentence on its own merits. Sentences (1) and (2) are grammatical. Sentences (3) and (4) are ungrammatical. E–language research succeeds if we define a grammar that assigns structures to (1) and (2), but not to (3) and (4).
- **I–LANGUAGE RESEARCH**, ignoring concerns about the grammaticality or ungrammaticality of any sentence, would focus on a more abstract concept, *the same level of informant acceptability* between two or more strings. Sentences (1) and (2) have the same level of informant acceptability: The Prolog parser must assign parse structures to (1) and (2) to indicate that they share a basic aspect of meaning. Similarly, the parser must assign structures to (3) and (4) indicating that they share a basic aspect of meaning.

In order to focus on concepts relating to "same level of informant acceptability," and to specify the sound–meaning pairings that define a language, we can consider the grammar of a language, for example, the parser of English, to be a set of independent parsers, as in Figure 8.4. (I presented a rudimentary morphological parser in Chapter 7.) In this chapter we present a phrase parser, a simple sentence parser, and compound sentence parsers for complement and adjunct subordinations.

More specifically, Figure 8.4 represents the parser of English as consisting of numerous, small, modular parsers. One advantage of factoring various aspects of linguistic description into individual independent parsers is that for sentences that do not define valid sound–meaning pairings, the parser can output its findings about which aspects of the string are valid and which do not meet the Prolog definitions of English structure. A. Arzan (1992) developed such a parser in order to analyze the English compositions of native Spanish–speaking undergraduates at the University of Puerto Rico who were learning English. The parser input the raw text from the undergraduate essays. The output of the parser was a listing of the structure of the grammatical sentences plus an indication of the Prolog module that failed for the sentences that did not define a valid sound–meaning correspondence.

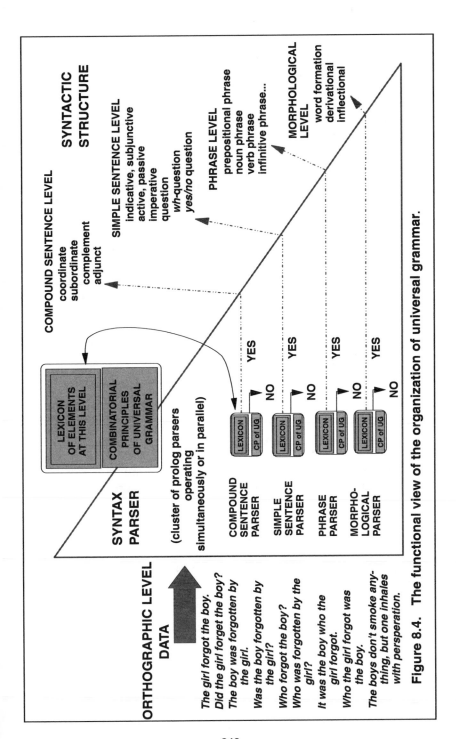

Figure 8.4. The functional view of the organization of universal grammar.

Figure 8.5 illustrates the type of description being offered. I continue to represent the *items which combine* as little boxes. The *rules of combination* will be expressed as *append* relations. I offer two representations for the structure of a sentence. One is the usual phrase marker, as in Figure 7.4. The other is a rectangular juxtaposition of boxes, which is often called a **chart** in computational linguistics books. The two notations are equivalent from a logical point of view. They express the same information. The fact that they are equivalent can be seen from a simple observation. The simplest way to produce one on a word processor is to define a table with each item centered in its cell. Use the word processor *cell–join* instruction to make the large cells (e.g., s, vp, np) which dominate smaller cells. Print with the cell walls to get the chart representation. Print without the cell walls to get the phrase marker.

Figure 8.6. indicates the various sources for sentences to be analyzed by the parser. A **corpus** is the set of sentences that is analyzed by the parser.

The linguistic researcher, whose goal is sketched in Figure 7.1, usually presents the parser with those sentences that linguistic theory shows to be complicated or to pose a challenge to the theory. A *crucial example* is a sentence that chooses between two alternative conceptions of grammar. In general, crucial examples fall into three classes. First, there are sentences that almost have the same orthographic (phonetic) string, but that have very different meanings:

(5)	John is easy to please.	Someone pleases John.
(6)	John is eager to please.	John pleases someone.

(7)	John appeared to Bill to like himself.	John likes himself.
(8)	John appealed to Bill to like himself.	Bill likes himself.

(9)	John is too clever to expect us to catch.	One expects
(10)	John is too clever to expect us to catch Bill.	John expects

Second, there are sentences that have very different structure, but that mean almost the same thing:

(11)	John is easy to please.
(12)	It is easy to please John.

(13)	John saw Mary.
(14)	Mary was seen by John.

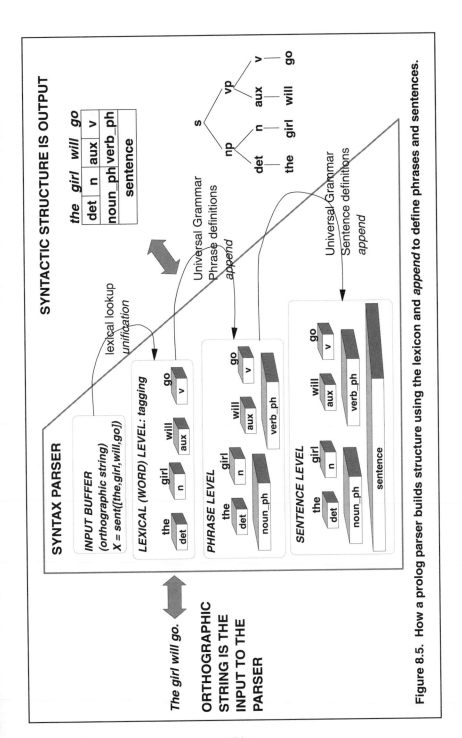

Figure 8.5. How a prolog parser builds structure using the lexicon and *append* to define phrases and sentences.

251

(15)   Each of the workers will respect the others.
(16)   The workers will respect each other.

Third, there are ambiguous sentences that simply challenge any parser and any speaker:

(17)   Buffalo buffalo buffalo buffalo.

Which can mean either that buffalo from Buffalo, N.Y. tend to confuse (i.e., buffalo) their fellow buffalo, or that buffalo tend to confuse buffalo from Buffalo.

(18)   Time flies like an arrow.

This has numerous ambiguities, some lexical and some structural. For instance, *Time flies like an arrow but fruit flies like a banana* requires us to analyze *time flies* as a compound noun. *Time flies* might be understood as occupants of Dr. Who's time capsule.

In the same sense that a TV repairperson has a *set of test patterns* that can test the limits of any TV set to input a signal and output a picture, so too, the linguist seeks a **set of test sentences** that would have the property that, if a parser correctly paired sound and meaning for these sentences, it will correctly pair sounds and meanings for any sentence or sentence fragments thrown at it.

If your TV set is out of adjustment and needs repairs, the TV repairperson does not perform the adjustments and evaluate the capacity of the TV set by playing Marlene Dietrich movies, newscasts, and cartoons. The capacity of the TV set to accurately analyze any signal can be judged by determining its ability to analyze certain highly specific, somewhat complex, signals – called test patterns. If a TV set can accurately analyze the test patterns, then one can assert that it will correctly analyze any signal.

The test patterns projected by the technician, which completely characterize the signal–to–picture_message correlations of the TV set, are usually an odd bunch of straight and wavy lines, some stationary and some of which jiggle their way across the screen. If in the course of normal TV watching a person saw one of these patterns, it might appear that the TV set was misbehaving. Of course, it would merely be showing off what it could do. There is no sense in which a TV test pattern is a "normal" picture, or a composite of "normal" pictures, and there is no sense in which it should be. A test pattern is to the signal–message system what Everest is to the mountain climber, a challenge of his or her maximum capacity.

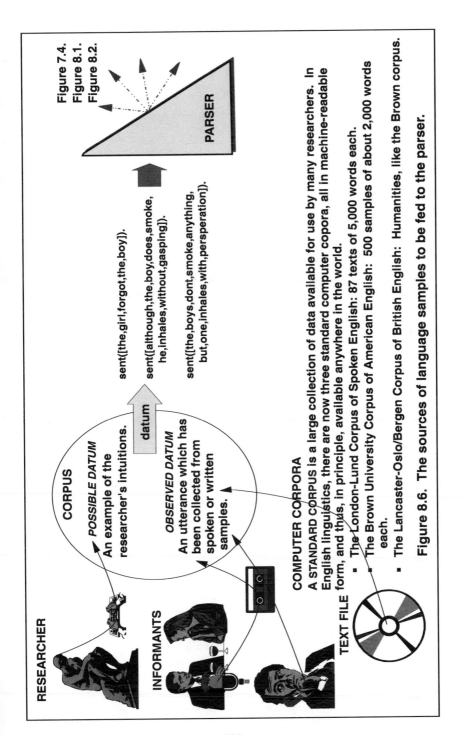

RESEARCHER

Figure 7.4.
Figure 8.1.
Figure 8.2.

PARSER

CORPUS

POSSIBLE DATUM
An example of the researcher's intuitions.

datum

sent([the,girl,forgot,the,boy]).

sent([although,the,boy,does,smoke,
he,inhales,without,gasping]).

sent([the,boys,dont,smoke,anything,
but,one,inhales,with,persperation]).

OBSERVED DATUM
An utterance which has been collected from spoken or written samples.

INFORMANTS

COMPUTER CORPORA
A STANDARD CORPUS is a large collection of data available for use by many researchers. In English linguistics, there are now three standard computer copora, all in machine-readable form, and thus, in principle, available anywhere in the world.

TEXT FILE
- The London-Lund Corpus of Spoken English: 87 texts of 5,000 words each.
- The Brown University Corpus of American English: 500 samples of about 2,000 words each.
- The Lancaster-Oslo/Bergen Corpus of British English: Humanities, like the Brown corpus.

Figure 8.6. The sources of language samples to be fed to the parser.

When a theoretical linguist presents the parser with a complex sentence that might be judged as a nonconversational sentence, the linguist is often testing the extremes of the signal–to–message pairing operations. The assumption is, if the parser works for the sentences that span the range of possible pairings, it will work for those sentences that are less challenging. Hence, theoretical linguists often challenge the parser with a **possible datum**, an example sentence designed by the linguist based on his or her understanding of lexical and grammatical processes to challenge the parser's ability to pair sounds and meanings. One goal of research is to find a set of sentences, the **test patterns of English**, such that if any parser can define accurate sound–meaning pairs for these, then it will define accurate pairings for any sentence.

Considering Figure 7.1, if we regard the goal of linguistic research to be the construction of a parser that matches the intuitions of a native speaker of English, then the linguist who presents example sentences to the parser is conducting an **experiment** with each sentence submitted. If the parser offers the same analysis as the informant, then the experiment succeeds. If the parser offers an analysis that differs from the informant, this indicates that the linguist's model is incorrect and needs to be modified.

Some linguists only query the parser using an **observed datum**, an utterance or written sample, that has been collected from spoken or written samples.

Some linguists work on the construction of a parser that will analyze the speech/writing of data collected in the field by linguists from informants engaged in normal conversation. These parsers aid in the classification of dialect information, gender–biased linguistic preferences, and so on.

An enormous literature is devoted to text linguistics, the analysis of corpora that are usually in written form. For instance, large text corpora that are readily available include: all the printed text of the *Wall Street Journal* for the past five years, all of Shakespeare's writings, the various versions of the Bible, the bilingual weather reports in Canada, the Congressional record, cases that have been settled in federal, state, and local courts, and the list goes on. Some of this material is available on compact disks, others are available over the internet via ftp. (See Edwards & Lampert, 1993, for a listing of available materials.)

8.2. Rule Governed Creativity: Derivations

Let us examine the principles involved in developing a Prolog grammar to generate simple sentences such as *The boy remembered the girl, A girl forgot the boy*. These are simple sentences that contain a subject noun phrase, a direct object noun phrase, and a transitive verb.

The Prolog program, consisting of g0801 and g0802, defines a set of sentences (see Session 8.1).

```
/*      Program:      g0801          lexicon_8a              */

/*      lexical entries:   the units to be combined         */
det([the]).
det([a]).
n([boy]).
n([girl]).
v([remembered]).
v([forgot]).
v([saw]).
v([knew]).
```

The Prolog statements in g0801, lexicon_8a, are read as follows:

det([the]).	*the* is a determiner.
n([boy]).	*boy* is a noun.
v([forgot]).	*forgot* is a verb.

More specifically, we should say: the list consisting of one element, [the], is a determiner. The list consisting of one element, [boy], is a noun. The one element list, [forgot], is a verb.

For the present, I will present a sentence as a multielement list, [the,girl,forgot,the,boy], and the lexical items as one–element lists n([girl]). The grammatical principles, g0802, indicate how the one–element lists can

```
/*      Program:      g0802          grammar1                */
/*                  This grammar defines a small set of sentences.   */

/*      syntactic rules of combination                       */
sent(X)      :-      np(A),vp(B),append(A,B,X).
vp(X)        :-      v(A),np(B),append(A,B,X).
np(X)        :-      det(A),n(B),append(A,B,X).

/*      general derivational mechanisms                      */
append([],L,L).
append([X|L1],L2,[X|L3]) :- append(L1,L2,L3).
```

be appended to yield the multielement list.

The items in g0801 are the constituents with which the grammar defines sentences. The principles of combination of these constituents, given in g0802, are read like this:

sent(X) :-   np(A),vp(B),append(A,B,X).

X is a sentence if A is a noun phrase and B is a verb phrase and A and B appended yield X.

vp(X)   :-   v(A),np(B),append(A,B,X).

X is a verb phrase if A is a verb and B is a noun phrase and A and B appended yield X.

np(X)   :-   det(A),n(B),append(A,B,X).

X is a noun phrase if A is a determiner and B is a noun and A and B appended yield X.

Figure 8.7 indicates how the body of the np(X) principle operates. In A, a *yes/no* question, the principle indicates that [the] and [girl] form a noun phrase. B, a *wh*–question synthesizing a larger construction from components, shows that the determiner [the] and the noun [girl] can append to form the noun phrase [the,girl]. C, a *wh*–query to find the noun, shows that np(X) defines a valid noun phrase, [the,girl], when we append the noun [girl] to the determiner [the]. D, a *wh*–query to find the determiner, shows that np(X) defines a noun phrase, [the,girl], when we append the determiner [the] to the noun [girl].

All the queries in Figure 8.7 require the Prolog interpreter to refer to the lexicon to determine the validity of the query. The interpreter must verify that det([the]) and n([girl]) are lexical items. Session 8.1 indicate the results of querying grammar1.

Referring to Figure 8.8, the Prolog query *sent(X)* asks: *For what values of X is it true that X is a sentence?* Prolog responds X = *[the,boy,remembered,the,boy].* We enter a semicolon to request another example. By entering a semicolon for each Prolog response, we cause Prolog to backtrack to see if there are any more possibilities that satisfy the relations in g0802. Eventually, we obtain all 32 of the sentences defined as grammatical by grammar1. There are 32 possible ways that the lexical items in g0801 can be combined by the principles in g0802. To say it in Prolog: There are 32 lists, given in Session 8.1, that are valid ways of combining the one–element lists in g0801 according to the principles of combination g0802.

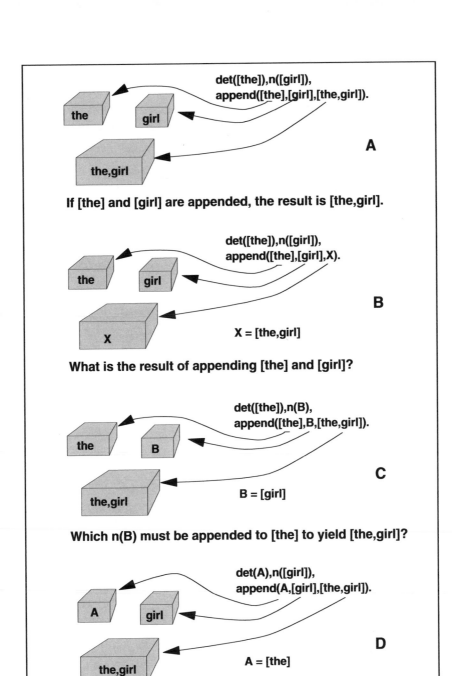

Figure 8.7. The relation: *np(X) :- det(A),n(B),append(A,B,X).*

```
% Prolog
C-Prolog version 1.5
| ?- [g0801].
| ?- [g0802].

| ?- sent(X).
X = [the,boy,remembered,the,boy] ;
X = [the,boy,remembered,the,girl] ;
X = [the,boy,remembered,a,boy] ;
X = [the,boy,remembered,a,girl] ;
X = [the,boy,forgot,the,boy] ;
X = [the,boy,forgot,the,girl] ;
X = [the,boy,forgot,a,boy] ;
X = [the,boy,forgot,a,girl] ;
X = [the,girl,remembered,the,boy] ;
X = [the,girl,remembered,the,girl] ;
X = [the,girl,remembered,a,boy] ;
X = [the,girl,remembered,a,girl] ;
X = [the,girl,forgot,the,boy] ;
X = [the,girl,forgot,the,girl] ;
X = [the,girl,forgot,a,boy] ;
X = [the,girl,forgot,a,girl] ;
X = [a,boy,remembered,the,boy] ;
X = [a,boy,remembered,the,girl] ;
X = [a,boy,remembered,a,boy] ;
X = [a,boy,remembered,a,girl] ;
X = [a,boy,forgot,the,boy] ;
X = [a,boy,forgot,the,girl] ;
X = [a,boy,forgot,a,boy] ;
X = [a,boy,forgot,a,girl] ;
X = [a,girl,remembered,the,boy] ;
X = [a,girl,remembered,the,girl] ;
X = [a,girl,remembered,a,boy] ;
X = [a,girl,remembered,a,girl] ;
X = [a,girl,forgot,the,boy] ;
X = [a,girl,forgot,the,girl] ;
X = [a,girl,forgot,a,boy] ;
X = [a,girl,forgot,a,girl] ;
no

| ?- sent([the,boy,remembered,the,girl]).
yes
| ?- sent([the,girl,forgot,the,boy]).
yes
| ?- sent([the,girl,boy,the,forgot]).
no

| ?- ^D
%
```

Session 8.1. A grammar defines a set of well-formed sentences.

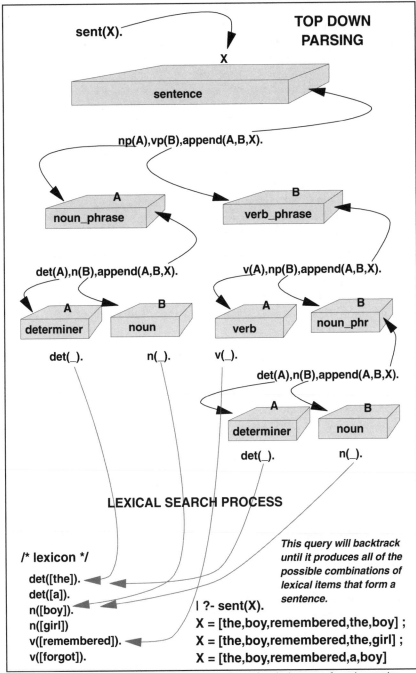

Figure 8.8. A top down parser searches for tokens of categories.

259

The query sent(X) is a **top–down query** because it requires the Prolog interpreter to refer to the rules of combination before it refers to the lexicon. The query sent([the,girl,forgot,the,boy]) (see Figure 8.9) is a **bottom–up query** because it requires the Prolog interpreter to refer to the lexicon before it refers to the rules of combination. The phrases "top–down" and "bottom–up" derive from the phrase–marker analysis. In a phrase marker, the lexical items are on the bottom and the phrase structure defined by the rules of combination is on top (see Figure 7.4).

- A TOP–DOWN PARSER is not given any words, but is presented with an X, for example, sent(X). The parser must first look at the rules of combination to try to analyze this X into smaller and smaller parts, eventually ending up with the lexical categories: n(_), v(_), det(_). At this point, using a LEXICAL SEARCH PROCESS, the parser enters the lexicon to search for tokens of each category type (see Figure 8.8).
- A BOTTOM–UP PARSER is given an ordered list of words, and the parser, using a process called TAGGING, must look them up in the lexicon to determine their category types. After tagging, the parser can start to try to build the phrase structure from the bottom up (see Figure 8.9).

Top–down and bottom–up refer to (a) how the parser operates procedurally and (b) the type of query posed to the parser. There is one lexicon and one set of principles of combination that define the constructions at a level. To some extent, one can look at a Prolog program and decide that the program is top–down or bottom–up. The query

np(X) :- det(A),n(B),append(A,B,X)

might be called bottom–up because it first selects lexical items and then verifies the combination. The query

np(X) :- append(A,B,X),det(A),n(B)

could be called top–down because it first selects the combination and then, using a lexical search process, verifies that A is a determiner and B is a noun in the lexicon. If the Prolog interpreter were implemented in a parallel processor, and all goals were tested simultaneously, then the order of goals would not affect the direction of the parse procedure.

Referring to Session 8.1, the Prolog query *sent([the,boy,remembered, the,girl])* asks: Is *the boy remembered the girl* a sentence?

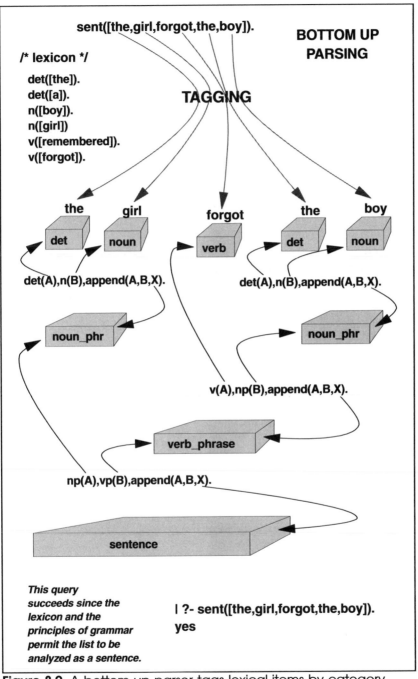

Figure 8.9. A bottom up parser tags lexical items by category.

Prolog must determine, for the given elements and the given rules of combination,whether *the boy remembered the girl* is a possible combination. Prolog answers *yes*. The Prolog query *sent([the,girl,boy, the,forgot])* asks whether *the girl boy the forgot* is a sentence. Because this string cannot be formed by combinatorial rules, g0802 operating on g0801, Prolog answers *no*.

Grammar1, consisting of g0801 and g0802, describes only a small fragment of English because it has only a few lexical items and only three syntactic rules of combination. We could increase the number of sentences defined as grammatical by adding lexical items: *det([this])...,* *n([woman])..,* *v([kiss])...* We could also add new rules of combination. For instance, grammar1 could define intransitive sentences by adding the rule: *vp(X) :- v(X)*. This would define as grammatical strings: *the girl remembered, the boy forgot.*

If we added a thousand words to the lexicon and a few dozen rules to the syntactic rules of combination, the grammar could define a large number of sentences as grammatical.

The syntactic definitions of g0803 are similar to those of g0802, but in g0803 *append* is first in the body of the statement, whereas in g0802 *append* occurs last.

```
/*      Program:        g0803           grammar2            */
/*              This grammar makes infinite use of finite means. */

/*      English definitions of combination of elements         */
s(X)    :-  append(A,B,X),np(A),vp(B).
vp(X)   :-  append(A,B,X),v(A),np(B).
vp(X)   :-  append(A,B,X),v(A),s(B).      /*  recursive definition  */
np(X)   :-  append(A,B,X),det(A),n(B).

/*      general derivational mechanisms                        */
append([],L,L).
append([X|L1],L2,[X|L3]) :- append(L1,L2,L3).
```

These are **logical conditions on syntactic combinations**, henceforth, **syntalogical conditions**, that define valid and invalid. The following six syntalogical conditions are logically equivalent and have the same truth conditions. Each statement is a set of goals that define a structure; they are not procedural statements about the order in which to build a structure:

```
s(X)    :-    append(A,B,X),np(A),vp(B).
s(X)    :-    np(A),append(A,B,X),vp(B).
s(X)    :-    vp(B),append(A,B,X),np(A).
s(X)    :-    append(A,B,X),vp(B),np(A).
s(X)    :-    vp(B),np(A),append(A,B,X).
s(X)    :-    np(A),vp(B),append(A,B,X).
```

The syntalogical conditions of g0802 and g0803 are presented in the order that first defines *sentence*, then *verb phrase*, and then *noun phrase*, like this:

```
s(X)    :-    np(A),vp(B),append(A,B,X).
vp(X)   :-    v(A),append(A,B,X),np(B).
np(X)   :-    append(A,B,X),np(B),det(A).
```

Because these are logical conditions and not procedural instructions, they can occur in any order and will produce the same definition of grammatical sentence. The grammar presented earlier is logically equivalent to these grammars:

```
vp(X)   :-    np(B),v(A),append(A,B,X).
s(X)    :-    np(A),vp(B),append(A,B,X).
np(X)   :-    append(A,B,X),np(B),det(A).

np(X)   :-    det(A),append(A,B,X),np(B).
vp(X)   :-    v(A),append(A,B,X),np(B).
s(X)    :-    np(A),append(A,B,X),vp(B).
```

We will consider **rule** as synonymous with *syntalogical condition*. If we were writing in pure Prolog, then we could (a) rearrange the Prolog syntalogical statements of the grammar in any order, and (b) reorder the goals of any syntalogical statement in any way without changing the definition of a *grammatical sentence*.

A RULE, or PRINCIPLE OF COMBINATION, is a nonprocedural definition of the logical conditions that a string must meet in order to be assigned a structure.

G0803 introduces a new rule,

```
vp(X)    :-    append(A,B,X),v(A),s(B).
```

which is read like this: X is a verb phrase if X is A and B appended and A is a verb and B is a sentence.

This logical statement introduces recursion into the grammar. A **recursive element** is a fact or relation defined either in terms of itself or as part of itself. In our grammar, s(X) is a recursive element since s(X) is defined in terms of an np and vp, but vp is defined in terms of s(X). G0803 is a recursive set of Prolog statements which defines the acceptable combinations of words.

Figure 8.10 indicates the values of the variables in vp(X) in the analysis of s([the,girl,forgot,the,boy,knew,the,girl,saw,the,boy]).

Recursive definitions provide lots of opportunity for program crashes and infinite loops (see Session 3.5). But on a more positive note, they also enable us to make infinite use of finite means.

In Session 8.2, the query *s([the,girl,forgot,the,boy,kissed,the,girl])* fails because the lexical entry *v([kissed])* is not in the lexicon. The query *s([the,girl,forgot,the,boy,the,forgot,girl])* fails because this string of constituents does not meet the logical definition of *sentence* offered by g0803.

The set of syntactic definitions in g0803 define an unbounded number of sentences as illustrated in Session 8.2.

```
% prolog
C-Prolog version 1.5
| ?- [0801].
| ?- [0803].
yes

| ?- s([the,girl,forgot,the,boy]).
yes

| ?- s([the,girl,forgot,the,boy,remembered,the,girl]).
yes

| ?- s([the,girl,forgot,the,boy,knew,the,girl,
            saw,the,boy]).   (See Figure 8.10.)
yes

| ?- s([the,girl,forgot,the,boy,kissed,the,girl]).
no

| ?- s([the,girl,forgot,the,boy,the,forgot,girl]).
no

| ?- ^D
[ Prolog execution halted ]
%
```

Session 8.2. Grammar2 defines an unbounded set.

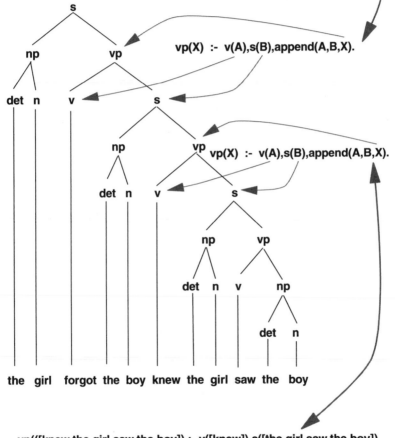

This phrase marker contains nested subordinate clauses. There is a sentence complement in the top two verb phrases. The recursive vp combinatorial principle which defines recursion is indicated at the points where the parser appeals to this principle to license the assignment of structure to the string.

vp([forgot,the,boy,knew,the,girl,saw,the,boy]) :- v([forgot),s([the,boy, knew,the,girl,saw,the,boy]),append([forgot],[the,boy,knew,the,girl, saw,the,boy],[forgot,the,boy,knew,the,girl,saw,the,boy]).

This is the value of the variables which are true for this phrase marker.

vp(X) :- v(A),s(B),append(A,B,X).

vp(X) :- v(A),s(B),append(A,B,X).

the girl forgot the boy knew the girl saw the boy

vp(([knew,the,girl,saw,the,boy]) :- v([knew]),s([the,girl,saw,the,boy]), append([knew],[the,girl,saw,the,boy],[knew,the,girl,saw,the,boy]).

This is the value of the variables which are true for this phrase marker.

Figure 8.10. The application of the recursion principle.

265

The set of synta-logical conditions – g0803 – and the lexicon – g0801 – illustrate two properties of a generative grammar in the E–language perspective: A grammar defines "grammatical sentence" and "bifurcates" grammatical from ungrammatical strings. Also, a grammar makes claims about an unbounded number of sentences. These were basic points stressed in Chomsky's earliest works.

8.3.   Parsers Assign Structure to an Ordered String

G0804 offers a partial definition of *noun phrase* in English (see Session 8.3). It is a tiny grammar to describe a fragment of the linguistic structures at the phrase level. It illustrates the principles by which a

```
/*       Program:        g0804                          */    1
/*               A grammar of a fragment of English.    */    2
/*               A definition which identifies and labels the  */  3
/*                       constituents of a simple noun phrase. */  4

/*       DATABASE OF ELEMENTS AT A LEVEL               */    5
/*       lexical entries for determiners and nouns     */    6
det([the]).                                                   7
det([a]).                                                     8
det([this]).                                                  9
det([that]).                                                 10
                                                             11
n([boy]).                                                    12
n([girl]).                                                   13
n([man]).                                                    14
n([woman]).                                                  15

/*       PRINCIPLES OF COMBINATION OF ELEMENTS    */        16
/*       definition to recognize and label        */        17
/*       constituents of a noun phrase            */        18
np(X)    :-      append(A,B,X),det(A),n(B),  /* pattern recog */  19
                 /*      format output                  */   20
                 nl,nl,write('det = '),write(A),  /* label determiner */  21
                 write(' n = '),write(B),       /* label noun  */  22
                 nl,write('np = '),write(X).    /* label noun phr */  23

/*       UNIVERSAL COMPUTATIONAL PRINCIPLES       */        24
/*       general derivational mechanisms          */        25
append([],L,L).                                              26
append([X|L1],L2,[X|L3]) :-      append(L1,L2,L3).          27
```

generative grammar can identify and label the constituents of a string and also the general organization of all of the grammars to be presented here.

G0804 consists of four sections:

- The **header**, lines 1–4, contains only comment statements indicating the name of the program, the purpose of the program, and sometimes information about how to load it and pose queries.
- The **lexical database**, lines 5–15, consists of the words and morphemes that are combined to construct linguistic structures. In later studies, the lexical database will be a separate file, and as usual, printed in a shaded double box.
- The **syntalogical rules**, line 16–23, are in two parts:
  - The **pattern recognition goals**, line 19, often labeled /* *pattern recognition* */ in later programs, define the conditions that must be met by constituents in a string to be called a *noun phrase*. The pattern recognition goals, line 19, say: *X is a noun phrase if A and B are appended and A is a determiner and B is a noun.*
  - The **format output goals**, which output the information about constituent structure, lines 20–23, are often preceded by a comment: /* *format output* */ or /* *construct labeled bracketing* */. In all our early grammars, the information about constituent structure output matches closely the definition of constituent structure offered by the pattern recognition goals. In later grammars, when the output includes empty categories, the information output might include elements not represented in the pattern recognition goals.
- The **general derivation mechanisms**, lines 24–27, will include only *append* in our early grammars. These fundamental computational processes of sentence construction remain the same for all languages.

In general, we will have the *format output goals* follow the pattern recognition goals. The grammar will only assign structure to sentences that satisfy the *pattern recognition goals*.

The output goals are read as follows:

nl,nl,write('det = '), write(A),   line 21

Skip a line and skip a line and write to the screen *det* = and write the

267

determiner found.

write(' n = '),write(B),   line 22

Write to the screen *n =* and write the noun found.

```
% Prolog
C-Prolog version 1.5
| ?- ['g0804'].
grammar3.prg consulted 868 bytes 0.05 sec.
yes

| ?- np(X).
det = [the]  n = [boy]
np = [the,boy]
X = [the,boy] ;

det = [the]  n = [girl]
np = [the,girl]
X = [the,girl] ;

det = [the]  n = [man]
np = [the,man]
X = [the,man] ;

det = [the]  n = [woman]
np = [the,woman]
X = [the,woman]
yes

| ?- np([the,woman]).
det = [the]  n = [woman]
np = [the,woman]
yes

| ?- np([that,woman]).
det = [that]  n = [woman]
np = [that,woman]
yes

| ?- np([the,boy]).

det = [the]  n = [boy]
np = [the,boy]
yes

| ?- ^D
[ Prolog execution halted ]
%
```

Session 8.3. Identify and label np constituents.

nl, write('np = '),write(X).   line 23

Skip a line, write to the screen *np =,* and write the value of the noun phrase.

Session 8.3 indicates the results of queries posed to g0804.

The first query is *np(X).*: *For what values of X is X a noun phrase?* The query *np(X)* outputs a newline and the values for the determiner and noun, then a newline and the value of the noun phrase, and then the value X that satisfies the query.

If we query *np([the,woman]).*: *Is* the woman *a noun phrase?*, then Prolog answers *yes*.

Sometimes we want to parse a string and obtain a simple *yes/no* as to whether the string satisfies the grammar or not. Other times we actually want to assign labels to the recognized constituents. G0805 permits us to choose if we want only a *yes/no* answer or structural information for the *yes* answers.

G0805 contains an item in the database *continue(X).*, where X can be *yes* or *no*. If X is *yes*, then the */* format output */* section will output the findings of the pattern recognition section to the screen and label the constituents as in g0804. In Session 8.4, the query *continue(X)* yields X = *yes*, which is the value loaded by g0805. The query *np([the,boy]).* produces an output with labels *det = the, n = boy,* and *np = the boy*.

The goals following the */*format output*/* comment comprise an *or–statement*. Either *continue(no)* is true – which it is if *continue(no)* is in the database and the Prolog statement is satisfied, or, if *continue(yes)* is in the database and the first half of the *or–statement* fails, Prolog writes constituent structure information to the screen.

The Prolog statement *no_structure* changes *continue(yes)* to *continue(no)*. With *continue(no)* true, the definition of *np(X)* will make *yes/no* judgments to indicate if X is a noun phrase or not, but it will not output the values found for the constituents if the query succeeds. The query *np([the,boy]).* yields *yes*, but no structure is output.

The statement *structure* converts *continue(no)* to *continue(yes)*. For the query *np([the,girl]).*, g0805 outputs the constituents identified.

The Prolog relation *assert(noun([dog]))* places *noun([dog]).* in the database. The relation *retract(noun([dog]))*. removes *noun([dog])* from the database. The normal way to load facts, like *noun([dog])*, into the database is to place them into a lexicon and load the lexicon. A second way to load a fact into the database is to use the relation *assert(..)*. In general, we will only use *assert* and *retract* to add dummy markers that affect input and output. *Assert* and *retract* make a Prolog program procedural and are not part of pure Prolog.

269

G0806 is a sentence grammar that indicates the phrasal constituents of sentences it defines. Session 8.5 indicates that when queried: *s([the,girl,forgot,the,boy])*. G0806 responds: *the* is a determiner, *girl* is a noun, *the girl* is a noun phrase, *the* is a determiner, *boy* is a noun, *the boy* is a noun phrase, *forgot the boy* is a verb phrase, and *the girl forgot the boy* is a sentence.

Session 8.5 indicates the constituent structure information about the string, *the girl forgot the boy*, in the order that the Prolog parser identifies the constituents using the definitions of the grammar. Most

```
/*        Program: g0805                                        */
/*        The definition of noun phrase of grammar3, but modified. */
/*        When continue(yes) is true, the structure of the np is   */
/*              output..                                           */
/*        When continue(no) is true, the structure of the np is    */
/*              not output.                                        */

/*        program to enable us to turn on/off output of structure  */
continue(yes).
structure          :-        retract(continue(_)),assert(continue(yes)).
no_structure       :-        retract(continue(_)),assert(continue(no)).

/*        lexicon of forms                                         */
det([the]).
det([a]).

n([boy]).
n([girl]).

/*  definition to identify and label constituents of a noun phrase */
np(X)    :-  append(A,B,X),det(A),n(B),   /*       pattern recog   */
             /*        format output                               */
             (                       /*       start either-or      */
                    continue(no)     /*       stop                 */
             ;                        /*       or                  */
                    (nl,nl,write('det = '),write(A),  /* otherwise */
                    write(' n = '), write(B),   /*       label      */
                    nl,write('np = '),write(X)) /*       label      */
             ).                       /*       end or              */

/*  general derivational mechanisms   */
append([],L,L).
append([X|L1],L2,[X|L3]) :-  append(L1,L2,L3).
```

270

linguistic analyses use some two–dimensional diagram, like a phrase marker, to show the parser's output.

A **phrase marker**, as in Figure 7.4, expresses three types of information:

- A sentence can be factored into constituents, where each constituent is a continuous string of elements (letters or sounds).
- The constituents form a hierarchy, that is, some constituents (sentence) dominate other constituents (noun

```
% prolog
C-Prolog version 1.5
| ?- ['g0805'].
grammar4.prg consulted 1092 bytes 0.0833333 sec.
yes

| ?- continue(X).
X = yes
yes

| ?- np([the,boy]).
det = [the]   n = [boy]
np = [the,boy]
yes

| ?- no_structure.
yes

| ?- continue(X).
X = no
yes

| ?- np([the,boy]).
yes

| ?- structure.
yes

| ?- np([the,girl]).
det = [the]   n = [girl]
np = [the,girl]
yes

| ?- ^D
[ Prolog execution halted ]
%
```

Session 8.4. Querying g0805 for *yes/no* and structure.

phrase, verb phrase).

■ Labels on the nodes in the PM indicate similarities and differences between the constituents and indicate there are types of constituents. Because *the boy* is dominated by *np*, and *the girl* is dominated by *np*, they are both the same kind of constituent: a *noun phrase*.

Figure 8.11 corresponds to Session 8.5.

```
/*      Program:      g0806                                    */
/*              This grammar defines a small set of sentences. */
/*              It identifies and labels the constituents of a */
/*                      sentence.                              */

/*      lexicon of elements which function in the grammar      */
det([the]).
det([a]).

n([boy]).
n([girl]).

v([remembered]).
v([forgot]).

/*      English rules of combination                          */
s(X)    :-      append(A,B,X),np(A),vp(B),
                nl,nl,write('np = '),write(A),
                write(' vp = '),write(B),
                nl,write('s = '),write(X).

vp(X)   :-      append(A,B,X),v(A),np(B),
                nl,nl,write('v = '),write(A),
                write(' np = '),write(B),
                nl,write('vp = '),write(X).

np(X)   :-      append(A,B,X),det(A),n(B),
                nl,nl,write('det = '),write(A),
                write(' n = '),write(B),
                nl,write('np = '),write(X).

/*      general derivational mechanisms                       */
append([],L,L).
append([X|L1],L2,[X|L3]) :-  append(L1,L2,L3).
```

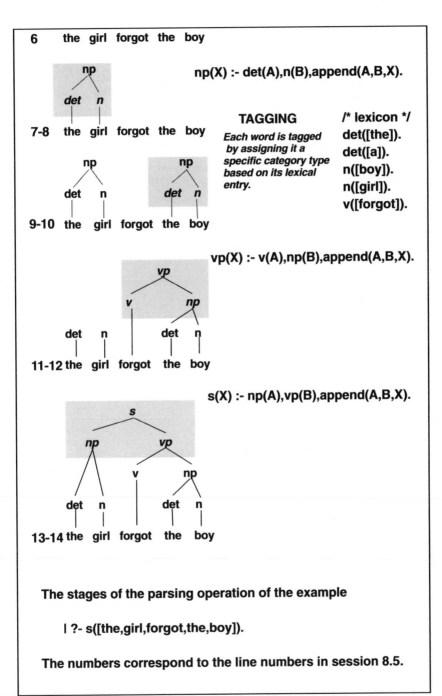

6   the girl forgot the boy

np(X) :- det(A),n(B),append(A,B,X).

7-8   the girl forgot the boy

TAGGING   /* lexicon */

*Each word is tagged
by assigning it a
specific category type
based on its lexical
entry.*

det([the]).
det([a]).
n([boy]).
n([girl]).
v([forgot]).

9-10 the girl forgot the boy

vp(X) :- v(A),np(B),append(A,B,X).

11-12 the girl forgot the boy

s(X) :- np(A),vp(B),append(A,B,X).

13-14 the girl forgot the boy

The stages of the parsing operation of the example

I ?- s([the,girl,forgot,the,boy]).

The numbers correspond to the line numbers in session 8.5.

Figure 8.11. How g0806 assigns structure in session 8.5.

273

A phrase marker contains no information about the order in which the constituents were added to the phrase marker. One cannot examine a phrase marker and decide if one np was added before another or if the PM was constructed bottom–up or top–down. Sessions 8.3–8.5 contain information about the order of assignment of structure to constituents. Figure 8.11 indicates how g0806 identifies the constituents in *The girl forgot the boy*. In general, in linguistics, the order of assignment of structure is irrelevant to the determination of the sound and meaning

```
% prolog                                              1
C-Prolog version 1.5                                  2
| ?- ['g0806'].                                       3
grammar5.prg consulted 1748 bytes 0.0833333 sec.      4
yes                                                   5

| ?- s([the,girl,forgot,the,boy]).              6

det = [the]   n = [girl]                        7
np = [the,girl]                                 8

det = [the]   n = [boy]                         9
np = [the,boy]                                  10

v = [forgot]   np = [the,boy]                   11
vp = [forgot,the,boy]                           12

np = [the,girl]   vp = [forgot,the,boy]         13
s = [the,girl,forgot,the,boy]                   14
yes                                             15

| ?- s([a,boy,remembered,a,girl]).              16

det = [a]   n = [boy]                           17
np = [a,boy]                                    18

det = [a]   n = [girl]                          19
np = [a,girl]                                   20

v = [remembered]   np = [a,girl]               21
vp = [remembered,a,girl]                        22

np = [a,boy]   vp = [remembered,a,girl]         23
s = [a,boy,remembered,a,girl]                   24
yes                                             25

| ?- ^D                                         26
[ Prolog execution halted ]                     27
%                                               28
```

Session 8.5. G0806 outputs the constituents of a sentence.

properties of a sentence.

G0806 provides in Session 8.5 all the information required to construct a phrase marker for *the girl forgot the boy*.

Each sentence in English has associated with it a syntactic structure that indicates the constituent structure of the sentence at each level. The precise nature of the syntactic structure has been the focus of linguistic research since Chomksy introduced the idea in his earliest publications. For example, Chomsky (1957) opened Chapter 4, *Phrase Structure*, with this line: "Customarily, linguistic description on the syntactic level is formulated in terms of constituent analysis (parsing). We now ask what form of grammar is presupposed by description of this sort." (p. 26). Chomsky (1992) opened his recent work, *A Minimalist Program for Linguistic Theory*, with these general considerations.

> Language and its use have been studied from varied points of view. One approach, assumed here, takes language to be part of the natural world. The human brain provides an array of capacities that enter into the use and understanding of language (the *language faculty*); these seem to be in good part specialized for that function and a common human endowment over a very wide range. One component of the language faculty is a generative procedure (an *I–language*, henceforth language) that generates structural descriptions (SD's), each a complex of properties, including those commonly called 'semantic' and 'phonetic.' These SD's are the expressions of the language. The theory of a particular language is its grammar. The theory of languages and the expressions they generate is universal grammar (UG); UG is a theory of the initial state S0 of the relevant component of the language faculty. We can distinguish the language from a conceptual system and a system of pragmatic competence. (p. 1)

Chomsky's first major work was called *Syntactic Structures* (1957), not *Generative Grammar*. The main focus of Chomsky's research is on the data structures that define the form and content of the expressions of language. The secondary focus is on the generative mechanisms that make infinite use of finite means to define the expressions. Assume that each sentence has associated with it at least one phrase marker. A **generative grammar** defines the sound–meaning pairs of a language and assigns to each sound–meaning pair a phrase marker indicating its constituent structure.

275

8.4.   Top–Down and Bottom–Up Parsing: Derivations

A **parser** is a device that pairs an ordered string of elements with a phrase marker. In all our examples, the **ordered string of elements** will be at the orthographic level: a string of letters, spaces, and punctuation using the elements found on a computer keyboard. The **phrase marker** will be in a notation which indicates the constituent structure of the string. We have presented a phrase marker as a tree. As will be shown, constituent structure can also be represented in a matrix, or chart.

Let us attempt to clarify a potential misunderstanding. A parser, as a **logical device**, offers a pairing of a string with a structure. As a logical device, there is no input and output, there exist only pairs: *(string1,structure1), (string2,structure2),... (stringN,structureN).* There is no logical sense in which one "starts" with a string and matches it to a structure, or starts with a structure and mates it with a string. A parser, as a **procedural device**, has to start somewhere on something. For purely heuristic reasons of computational practicality (and efficiency), most parsers that exist as computer programs start with the string and compute a structure for it. Consider an analogy.

Given the following equation, suppose we want to calculate pairs (X,Y) and fill in Table 8.1.

$$X*Sin(X)/arctan(1/X) = Y$$

Consider Figure 8.12. Because the equation defines pairs (X,Y) in a logically neutral way, it is irrelevant if we assume $X = 0, 1, 2...$ and calculate values of Y to fill in Table 8.2, or if we assume $Y = 0, 1, 2...$ and calculate values of X to fill in Table 8.3. From a procedural point of view, it is much easier to start with values of X and calculate values of Y, than to start with values of Y and calculate values of X.

The same type of biconditional relation obtains between the branching structures and the string of words that we call an English sentence.

Table 8.1.	
A bidirectional function.	
X*Sin(X)/arctan(1/X) = Y	
X	Y
?	?
?	?
?	?

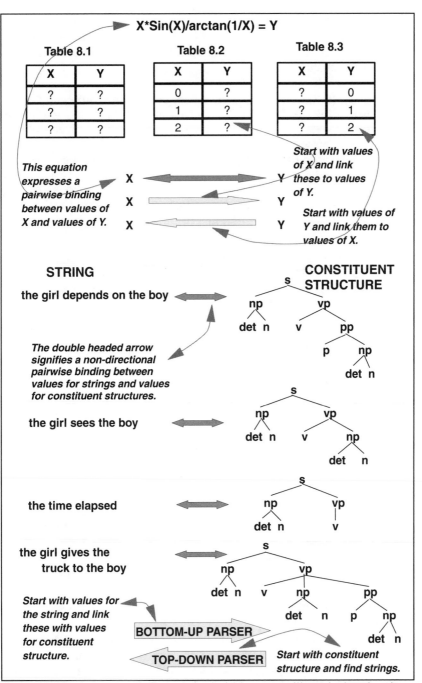

Figure 8.12. A parser defines a pair (string, constituent_structure).

Let us consider a **string** to be a string of words, for example, *The girl depends on the boy.* A **Constituent Structure (CS)** is a phrase marker without any words at the bottom. A parser defines a relation between a string and a constituent structure.

parser[S(X),CS(X)]	**The parser defines pairs S(X) and CS(X).**
parser[S(X) → CS(X)]	**The parser finds CS(X) for a given S(X).**
parser[CS(X) → S(X)]	**The parser finds S(X) for a given CS(X).**

Referring to the lower part of Figure 8.12, suppose we agree that constituent structure, CS(X), is the structural representation of the phrasal information we want the grammar to pair with the string: S(X). Logically, there is no order to the relationship between the string and CS(X). The grammar is a logical specification of valid matches: pair CS(X) and S(X) to yield PM(X). As indicated by the arrows at the bottom of the figure, a bottom–up parser procedurally links the string to a CS(X). A top–down parser links a CS(X) to a string.

The mechanisms and procedures by which a parser pairs a string and a constituent structure to yield a phrase marker are called **derivational processes** or **parsing strategies**. The question now is: How does the Prolog parser join CS(X) and S(X) to yield PM(X)?

To understand how a parser works on a sentence of any complexity, we will have to enrich our ideas about strategies. As long as we focus on queries such as s(X) and s([the,girl,forgot,the,boy]), our present understanding suffices. But how are we to understand the parsing procedure for the query: s([A,B,forgot,C,boy])? This is a mixture. Let us summarize and then enlarge on the definitions.

Prolog provides two basic derivational processes. **Top–down parsing** first produces the constituent structure CS(X) and all the labeled bracketing and then joins it with a string S(X). Virtually all research in generative grammar from 1957 until X–bar theory was developed in the 1980s used basically top–down derivational processes. All grammars based on phrase structure rules are essentially top–down. **Bottom–up parsing** starts with an ordered string S(X) and joins it with CS(X) to produce PM(X). **X–bar theory**, a concept of phrase structure introduced by Chomsky in the 1960s, introduced the idea that constituent structure was projected from the lexical heads in the string and, in this sense, was the beginning of bottom up parsing in generative grammar research (see Leacock, 1990, for discussion).

As suggested in Figure 8.13, the Prolog parser follows a strategy very similar to a game–playing machine or a code–cracking device. We can think of the Prolog parser as stacking up blocks, in which each block on the bottom corresponds to a word in the string.

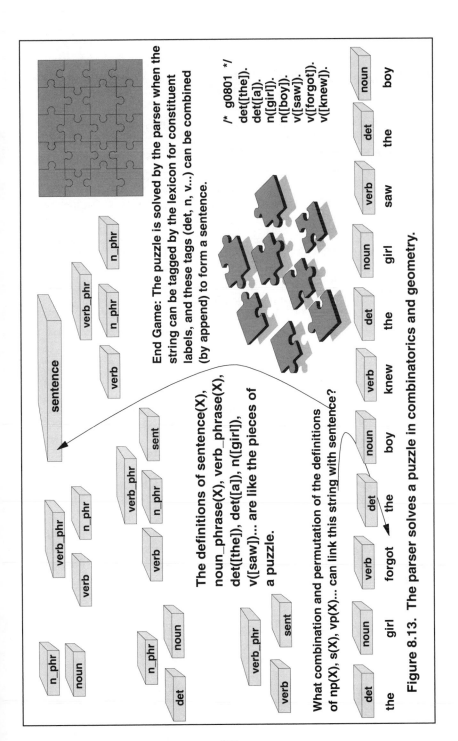

End Game: The puzzle is solved by the parser when the string can be tagged by the lexicon for constituent labels, and these tags (det, n, v...) can be combined (by append) to form a sentence.

```
/* g0801 */
det([the]).
det([a]).
n([girl]).
n([boy]).
v([saw]).
v([forgot]).
v([knew]).
```

The definitions of sentence(X), noun_phrase(X), verb_phrase(X), det([the]), det([a]), n([girl]), v([saw])... are like the pieces of a puzzle.

What combination and permutation of the definitions of np(X), s(X), vp(X)... can link this string with sentence?

Figure 8.13. The parser solves a puzzle in combinatorics and geometry.

279

The generative grammar, that is, the lexicon and rules of combination, define the blocks that can be piled on top of the bottom row. The goal is to apply the information in the lexicon and grammars so that the top block is one single block, *sentence*.

Figure 8.14 indicates that the parser's goal is to produce a two–dimensional geometric construction – a phrase marker – by solving a combinatorial problem defined by Prolog definitions of *lexical item* and *constituent*. Normally, we would represent a phrase marker, as in Figure 7.4, as a tree. In order to understand the parser's operation, however, it is often useful to think of the phrase marker as a matrix or a chart. The chart is constructed by stacking up boxes defined by the grammar on top of the boxes on the bottom row, each of which corresponds to a word in the string.

The grammar defines valid sets of blocks that can be piled up. A statement like

np(X)   :-   det(A),n(B),append(A,B,X).

says that we can place an *n_phrase* block on top of the two blocks: *det* and *noun*.

Each constituent in a phrase marker could be assigned four numbers:

P indicating how many constituents precede it.
F indicating how many constituents follow it.
O equal to the number over it.
U equal to the number of constituents under it.

We are not interested in the specific details (because the Prolog interpreter takes care of them for us), but one could sharpen these ideas and consider each sentence as a set of constituents, in which each constituent is defined by its type (np, vp) and by four numbers indicating its linear order and its hierarchical position. We return to this later, but for now we can appreciate that the Prolog interpreter keeps track of this information. In a more advanced grammar than we can present here, these four numbers could be considered as the memory address of the constituent in the parser's memory. In such a grammar, this indexing scheme would play a major role in the description of the empty categories (*e*) in sentences such as *Who will Tess think that Sean looked at e? Tess seemed e to like cheesecake. The apple was eaten e by Tracy.*

We could consider the sets of blocks defined by the simple facts and by the append relations to be like dominos, as sketched in Figure 8.15.

A PARSER produces a two dimensional geometric construction, a phrase marker, by solving a combinatorial problem defined by prolog definitions of *constituent*.

sentence						
noun_phrase		verb_phrase				
			prepositional_phrase			
					noun_phrase	
det	noun	verb	prep		det	noun
the	girl	depends	on		the	boy

GEOMETRIC CONSTRAINTS

The phrase marker of any sentence, S(X), is a doubly ordered set of constituents. Each constituent has a LINEAR ORDER with elements that precede it and others which follow it. Each constituent has a HIERARCHICAL ORDER with elements that dominate it and others that it dominates.

COMBINATORIAL CONSTRAINTS

Build a two dimensional structure (phrase marker) that has *sentence* at the top and *words* marked for category at the bottom by combining puzzle pieces, of which the following are a small subset.

```
det([the]).
np(X) :- det(A),n(B),append(A,B,X).
vp(X) :- v(A),pp(B),append(A,B,X).
pp(X) :- p(A),np(B),append(A,B,X).
```

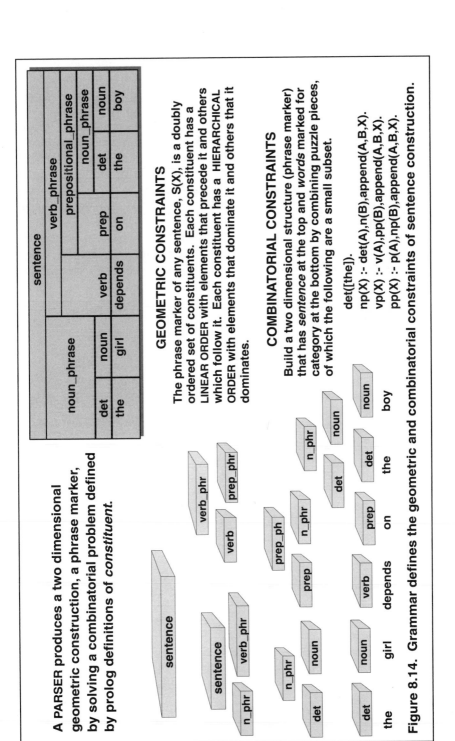

Figure 8.14. Grammar defines the geometric and combinatorial constraints of sentence construction.

281

Each SYNTAX DOMINO is a two–dimensional graphic analog of a Prolog definition of phrase or constituent given by universal grammar or by the English lexicon.

The parser, as a game–playing machine, assembles blocks on top of the bottommost string of blocks, each of which corresponds to one word in the string. The ENDGAME is well–defined: The game is over and the parse complete when there is a continuous solid set of boxes linking the topmost block – sentence – with the string of boxes on the bottom.

A top–down domino player will start filling in the dominos from the topmost sentence. A bottom–up player will start filling them in from the bottom boxes.

The process by which the parser links the syntax dominos corresponding to simple facts with the words in the orthographic string is called either **tagging,** by a bottom–up player, or **lexical searching,** by a top–down player.

Figure 8.16 illustrates the basic process by which the domino–playing Prolog machine tries to combine pieces on the playing field. To understand this figure we must remember:

- The set of **possible puzzle pieces** that exist are defined by the Prolog statements, that is, the simple facts and the definitions of phrase using the append relation. It is an empirical question to determine the category labels of the words and to define the types of phrases that exist in language.
- The **Prolog interpreter**, with no programming required on our part, plays the game of dominos. When we pose the query – s([the,girl,depends,on,the,boy]) – the Prolog interpreter will search the linguistic database for all possible combinations and permutations of phrase definitions that can make this statement true. We do not have to tell Prolog how to search or where to search.

Prolog will try alternative definitions of a phrase, that is, it will pull syntax dominos from the sack of dominos and try to find matches as it builds a structure for the string. If the definition fails, that is, the syntax domino does not fit, Prolog backtracks. When Prolog backtracks to find another definition, this is equivalent to clearing a domino from the playing field and replacing it into the domino sack.

Figure 8.17 aims to clarify the idea that there is no logical distinction between top–down and bottom–up parsing in the game–playing parser.

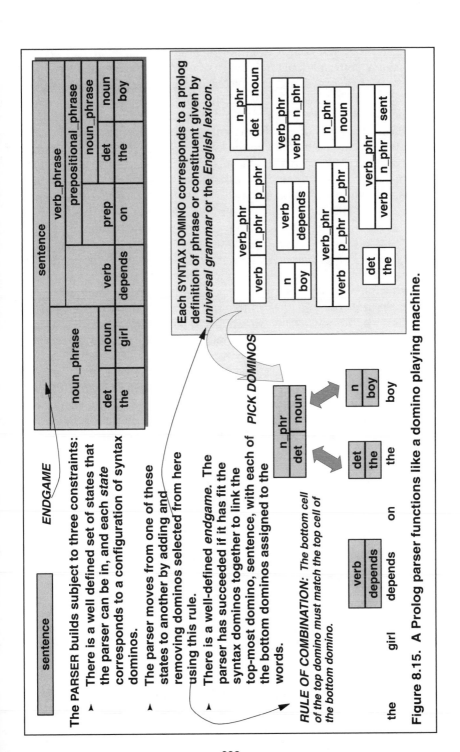

Figure 8.15. A Prolog parser functions like a domino playing machine.

We can imagine a domino–playing machine that has several independent computational units, each of which can examine the playing area and either add or remove pieces. It would be like four different people playing the same game of dominos, each one working on a different section of the playing field. One parser (A) might be working top–down and expanding sentence into n_phr and v_phr. Another (D) might be working bottom–up on the tail end of the string and be tagging *boy* as a noun. A third (C) might be assigning the category n_phr to a pattern perceived: det, noun. A fourth (B) might be trying to integrate the results of the top–down parser with the bottom up parser. This fourth parser is not reaching into the parts pile for another piece to add to the field. Rather, it is going to link the n_phr built by the bottom–up parser with the n_phr added by the top–down parser.

Figure 8.18 illustrates that each syntax–domino corresponds to a specific simple fact or phrase definition given in the Prolog grammars. The principles of universal grammar and the contents of the English lexicon fix the contents of the Prolog grammars. All of the illustrative examples we present lack the basic bugbear of parsing: *ambiguity*. At each level, there may be alternative definitions of the same token. Consider the problems involved in tagging. The word *yellow* can be a noun, a verb, or an adjective, hence, the grammar must contain these three syntax dominos: n([yellow]), v([yellow]), and adj([yellow]). The word *on* is a *preposition* in *The woman sat on the radio*, but a *particle* in *The woman turned on the radio*. There are two dominos: prep([on]). and particle([on]). At the phrase level most phrases have multiple definitions. There are many definitions of verb_phrase (see Section 8.5). A noun phrase can include a determiner or not: np(X) :- n(X), as in *(np (n john))* or np(X) :- det(A),n(B),append(A,B,X), as in *(np (det the)(n woman))*.

Figure 8.19 clarifies a division of labor. The **Prolog Machine**, or the Prolog interpreter, defines the game–playing strategy, and it obeys these three rules:

- Select a syntax domino from the valid moves.
- RULE OF COMBINATION: A bottom cell of the top domino must match the top cell of the bottom domino.
- ENDGAME: The interpreter succeeds when the word string is linked to the topmost sentence node with no words left over.

The **grammar**, the set of syntax dominos, which defines valid moves, are expressed as simple facts and as relations using *append* one or more times.

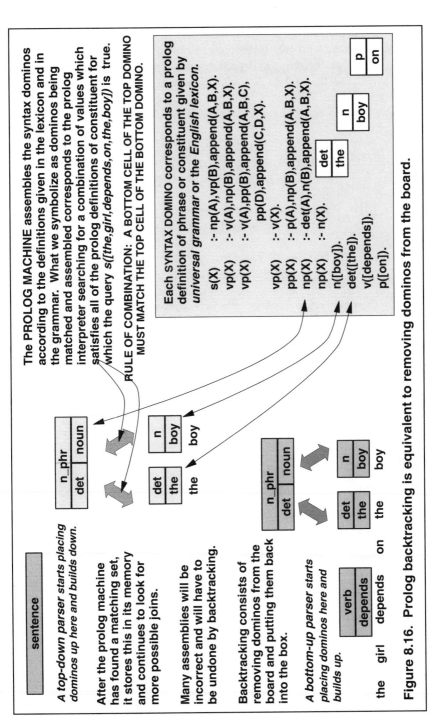

The PROLOG MACHINE assembles the syntax dominos according to the definitions given in the lexicon and in the grammar. What we symbolize as dominos being matched and assembled corresponds to the prolog interpreter searching for a combination of values which satisfies all of the prolog definitions of constituent for which the query *s([the,girl,depends,on,the,boy])* is true.

RULE OF COMBINATION: A BOTTOM CELL OF THE TOP DOMINO MUST MATCH THE TOP CELL OF THE BOTTOM DOMINO.

Each SYNTAX DOMINO corresponds to a prolog definition of phrase or constituent given by *universal grammar* or the *English lexicon.*

```
s(X)     :- np(A),vp(B),append(A,B,X).
vp(X)    :- v(A),np(B),append(A,B,X).
vp(X)    :- v(A),pp(B),append(A,B,C),
            pp(D),append(C,D,X).
vp(X)    :- v(X).
pp(X)    :- p(A),np(B),append(A,B,X).
np(X)    :- det(A),n(B),append(A,B,X).
np(X)    :- n(X).
n([boy]).
det([the]).
v([depends]).
p([on]).
```

A *top-down parser starts placing dominos up here and builds down.*

After the prolog machine has found a matching set, it stores this in its memory and continues to look for more possible joins.

Many assemblies will be incorrect and will have to be undone by backtracking.

Backtracking consists of removing dominos from the board and putting them back into the box.

A *bottom-up parser starts placing dominos here and builds up.*

Figure 8.16. Prolog backtracking is equivalent to removing dominos from the board.

Figure 8.20 indicates that the goals of research in computational linguistics cleave into two independent but interacting areas.

The **goal of computational research** on parsers is to develop a Prolog machine that achieves the endgame as rapidly as possible when playing dominos. Following Wiener, we might define a CYBERNETIC MACHINE as any device meeting these three conditions:

[A]   The device has a well–defined set of **possible internal states**, {S(a)...S(x)}, that may be finite or infinite. At any time, it is in one of these possible states, S(i).

[B]   The device has some process or **algorithm for moving** from one state to the next: S(i+1) = $F_{ADVANCE}$[S(i)...].

[C]   The device has some process or algorithm for deciding when it is in a **final state**, S(endgame).

Game–playing devices, like the domino player we suggest, are cybernetic machines. Shannon (1950/1971) offered one of the first proposals that indicated that a computing machine could be programmed to play chess. We mark his text with letters to show how his proposals constitute a cybernetic machine. Shannon stated:

> Some [interesting possibilities] can be illustrated by setting up a computer in such a way that it will play a fair game of chess. This problem, of course, is of no importance in itself, but it was undertaken with a serious purpose in mind. The investigation of the chess playing problem is intended to develop techniques that can be used for more practical applications.
>
> The chess machine is an ideal one to start with for several reasons. The problem is sharply defined, both [B] in the allowed operations (the moves of chess) and [C] in the ultimate goal (checkmate). It is neither so simple as to be trivial nor too difficult for satisfactory solution. And such a machine could be pitted against a human opponent, giving a clear measure of the machine's ability in this type of reasoning. ...
>
> The problem of setting up a computer for playing chess can be divided into three parts: [A] first, a code must be chosen so that chess positions and the chess pieces can be represented as numbers; [B] second, a strategy must be found for choosing the moves to be made; and third, this strategy must be translated into a sequence of elementary computer orders, or a program. (pp. 104–105)

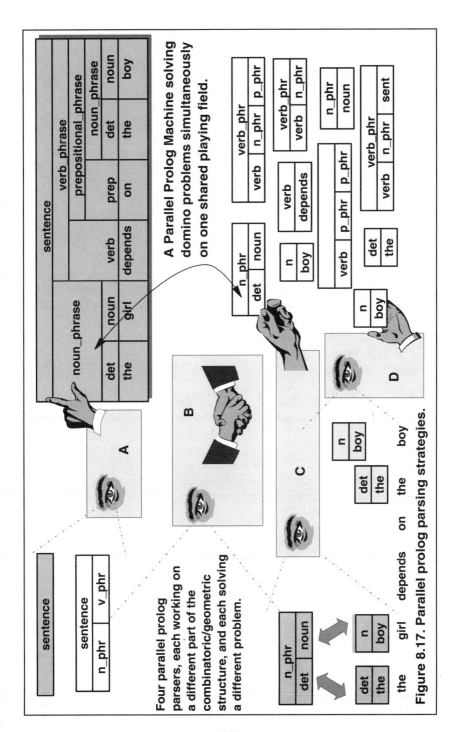

A Parallel Prolog Machine solving domino problems simultaneously on one shared playing field.

Four parallel prolog parsers, each working on a different part of the combinatoric/geometric structure, and each solving a different problem.

Figure 8.17. Parallel prolog parsing strategies.

287

Berenstein and de V. Roberts (1958) offer an analysis of computational procedures to play chess. They stated:

> In a chess game there are only two questions to which absolutely definite and unavoidable answers can be given: [B] 'Is this move legal?' and [C] 'Is the game over?' To all other questions there are various possible answers, though some may be more acceptable than others. The problem is to equip the machine with a system of evaluating the merits of the alternatives. This, as we have remarked, is what makes the tasks interesting. If cut–and–dried answers to all possible situations could be worked out by a computer, chess would immediately lose its fascinations. (pp. 110–111)

Some games can be solved more efficiently by parallel processors than by a single processor. A game of dominos, or a jigsaw puzzle, would reach the endgame faster if there were two, three, or more people manipulating pieces and assembling the constructions. Other games, like chess, might not achieve an endgame faster if all moves were made by a committee of two, three, or more.

In the goals of computational research in Figure 8.20, we can think of the optimal parser for English as a set of parallel processors working with a shared memory to solve problems in combinatorial geometry (as in Figure 8.17).

In placing the syntax dominos on the playing field in order to link the string of words with the topmost sentence, there is no special order in which the dominos must be positioned. A young child constructing a jigsaw puzzle might randomly select a piece from the puzzle box and build all structures around this one. The child could randomly select pieces from the puzzle box until it found one that joined the initial piece, then, by randomly selecting more pieces, build on the initial structure until the puzzle was completed. Eventually, through trial and error, the child would complete the puzzle. Similarly, any Prolog interpreter, by exhaustively backtracking through the grammar and lexicon, will find all the combinations that result in successful parses if any exist.

The **goal of linguistic research**, the main focus of this study, aims to determine what types of syntax dominos exist. What are the basic category types? What are the types of phrase categories defined by *append*?

The main focus of linguistic research is to define, and formulate as Prolog definitions, the constraints that define possible answers to the problems in combinatorial geometry posed by human languages.

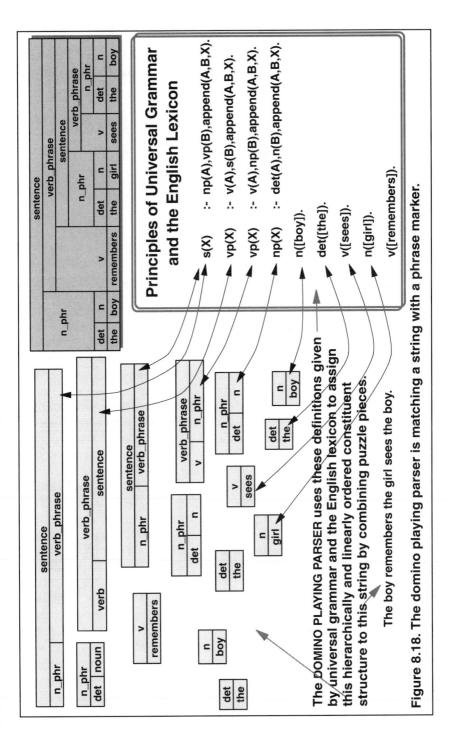

Principles of Universal Grammar and the English Lexicon

s(X)   :- np(A),vp(B),append(A,B,X).
vp(X)   :- v(A),s(B),append(A,B,X).
vp(X)   :- v(A),np(B),append(A,B,X).
np(X)   :- det(A),n(B),append(A,B,X).
n([boy]).
det([the]).
v([sees]).
n([girl]).
v([remembers]).

The DOMINO PLAYING PARSER uses these definitions given by universal grammar and the English lexicon to assign this hierarchically and linearly ordered constituent structure to this string by combining puzzle pieces.

The boy remembers the girl sees the boy.

Figure 8.18. The domino playing parser is matching a string with a phrase marker.

289

Linguistic research defines the individual puzzle pieces (simple facts and relations), the shape of the board (the bottom string is the word level and the top node is the sentence level), and the endgame (every word must be incorporated into the structure).

- **Linguistic research** defines the game and the valid moves.
- **Computational research** defines the optimal game–playing strategy.
- **Computational linguistic research** integrates the results to yield a parser that can link an orthographic string with its syntactic structure.

To a large extent linguistic research and computational research are orthogonal. The linguist's definitions of *possible constituent, possible phrase, possible sentence, possible compound sentence,* and *possible discourse* define complex puzzle pieces. If the linguist has a well–defined lexicon and grammar for English, and it provides correct answers on the most rudimentary inefficient trial–and–error Prolog machine, then this very same grammar will function and provide the same answers on the most elaborate efficient and speedy parallel Prolog computer ever to be built.

The general idea that a parser is a domino player and the grammar of a language is a definition of the dominos and their valid combinations holds for all human languages. Research in English determines the particular shape of puzzle pieces in English. Research on UNIVERSAL GRAMMAR defines the concept **possible puzzle piece**, that is, what are the limits on *possible lexical entries* and *possible rules of syntactic combination*? (See the discussion of **factoring**, pp. 167–169.)

Referring to Figure 7.1, the Prolog definitions, consisting of the simple facts and the append relations, express the linguist's representation of the knowledge of language that hopefully matches the knowledge of language of an English informant. The computational model we advance, the **domino model**, may represent no property – and may correlate with no property – in the knowledge or performance of any informant.

The domino model is a computational tool for the linguist to test definitions of lexical items and grammatical principles which play a role in the linguist's representation of the informant's competence. The game–playing model is a way for the linguist to access the Prolog database. Each sentence, for example, s([the,cow,jumped,over,the,moon]), is a query to the linguist's definitions of *lexical item, phrase, sentence,* and *morpheme.*

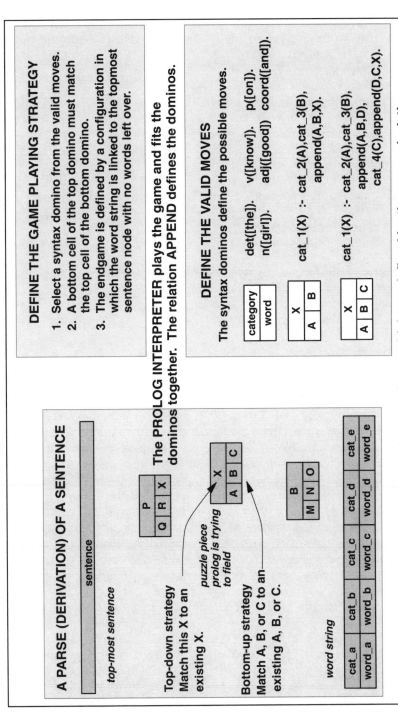

FIGURE 8.19. The prolog interpreter joins the pieces which are defined by the *append* relation.

The domino model is a convenient fiction, a nice aid to our thinking about how a Prolog interpreter proceeds to decide the truth value of our query.

Consider these queries:

s([the,girl,depends,on,the,boy]).

Is *The girl depends on the boy* a sentence?

s(X).

Return a list that is a sentence defined by the lexicon and grammar.

s([the,_,depends,on,the,_]).
s([the,X,depends,on,the,Y]).

Return two lexical items for which the list [the,_,depends,on,the,_] is a sentence defined by the linguist's grammar.

s([the,X,depends,on,the,X]).

Return one lexical item that can be placed in the two positions of the list to yield a sentence defined by the grammar.

Referring to Figure 7.6, one might think of the domino model as being a characterization of the performance of an informant. But the domino model does not appear to characterize either perception or production of a sentence by a human. The top–down query, s(X), would require the domino player to place the dominos from the topmost sentence to the bottom string, as in Figure 8.8. This would be a model of speaker sentence production only if people produced random sentences as their performance norm. One might argue that the domino model's response to the query s([the,girl,depends,on,the,boy]) is a perception model. But this is unlikely because people seem to understand a sentence from left to right, in other words, they seem to assign structure from left to right, and our computer model is plunking down dominos almost at random. And what type of performance is represented by queries containing variables?

The domino model does not appear to correlate with an informant's knowledge or performance. It is a tool with which the linguist can pose queries to the linguistic model in order to verify or refute the linguist's claims about lexical structure and grammatical processes.

292

GOALS OF COMPUTATIONAL RESEARCH

- Develop a prolog machine which plays dominos well.
  - ➤ It solves problems in combinatorial geometry.
  - ➤ Parallel processors solve simultaneous problems.
- Develop a game playing strategy
  - ➤ Top down strategy
  - ➤ Bottom up strategy
- Prolog, by definition, solves domino type problems.

GOALS OF LINGUISTIC RESEARCH

- The syntax dominos define the possible game pieces that can be fielded onto the playing area.
- Research on human language answers:
  - ➤ What are the basic category types of words? det, noun, verb, adjective, preposition, adverb...
  - ➤ What are the types of phrasal categories which are defined by *append*? noun_phrase, verb_phrase, prepositional_phrase, sentence...
  - ➤ What types of selectional properties can be given in a lexical entry? For instance, *put* requires a noun_phrase and a prep_phrase complement.
- Are the puzzle pieces defined by universal principles?

A PARSE (DERIVATION) OF A SENTENCE

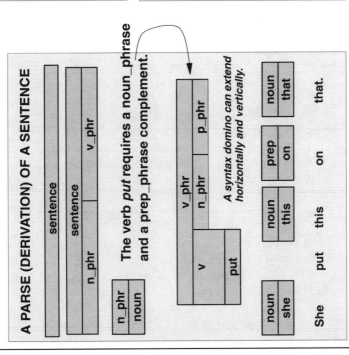

The verb *put* requires a noun_phrase and a prep_phrase complement.

A syntax domino can extend horizontally and vertically.

FIGURE 8.20. Linguistic research defines the possible complexity of puzzle pieces.

The domino model is a heuristic tool for a linguist to think about abstract linguistic processes in physical terms, just as electrical engineers think about the complexities of electron flow by comparing electricity in wires to water flowing through pipes. Voltage pushing current through a wire is like pressure forcing water through a pipe. Such heuristic models are to be judged for their pragmatic fruitfulness in suggesting further inquiry. Electricians wear rubber gloves, not water wings because they face the danger of electrocution, not death by drowning.

We have considered only the most basic types of simple facts and relations and, in particular, have considered only constituents that function independently of the constituents that precede and follow them. Some lexical items, such as *eke out*, would require a more complex structure than we have presented. The verb *put* requires a noun_phrase and a prepositional_phrase complement. *The girl put the book on the table.* *The girl put. *The girl put the book. *The girl put on the table.* Figure 8.20 indicates that the grammar must be formulated so that the syntax domino for *put* includes information about the configuration of nodes adjacent to *put.* (I discuss such examples in detail in section 8.5).

We will alternate between two equivalent notations. The domino notation functions mainly to enable us to understand the principles of derivation and parsing and to understand the memory structures and computational processes required to link an orthographic string with a structure. The tree notation, used extensively by linguists, is useful for understanding many of the constraints relating to the pairing of sound and meaning in languages.

In g0807, npl(X), with *append* last, and npf(X), with *append* first, both define noun phrase. They differ only in the order of goals. Logically, they are identical. Procedurally, they differ considerably. The following discussion aims to clarify some technical problems in procedural Prolog.

Session 8.6 indicates that if we query npl(X), *is X a noun phrase*, and npf(X), *is X a noun phrase*, we get the same answers. They both produce the same set of noun phrases in the same order.

Npl(X) terminates with a *no* after it has exhausted all possibilities for np. Npf(X) does not terminate at all. The append–first definition goes into an infinite loop after it outputs the last example. Let us look to see what is happening.

G0808 outputs the constituents that the grammars are trying to combine to find a noun phrase, *before* they have succeeded in finding any noun phrase. In most cases we will organize our grammars into two parts: a *pattern recognition* module that will test some string to see if it can be assigned a constituent structure, and a *format output* module that will only output the constituents *after* they have been identified in a successful

294

```
/*      Program:        g0807                                   */
/*                      Two different strategies to identify noun phrases */
/*                      npl assigns structure with append last  */
/*                      npf assigns structure with append first */


/*      LEXICON OF FORMS                                        */
det([the]).
det([a]).
det([this]).
det([that]).
n([boy]).
n([girl]).
n([man]).
n([woman]).


/*      DEFINITIONS TO IDENTIFY CONSTITUENTS                    */
npl(X)  :- det(A),n(B),append(A,B,X).    /*   append last parser  */
npf(X)  :- append(A,B,X),det(A),n(B).    /*   append first parser */


/*      GENERAL DERIVATIONAL MECHANISMS                         */
append([],L,L).
append([X|L1],L2,[X|L3])  :-  append(L1,L2,L3).
```

search. G0808, by placing output goals before some pattern recognition goals, outputs all of the possibilities that Prolog tries before it either succeeds or fails.

Session 8.7 indicates the output of g0808. Line 6, *npl([the,woman])*, asks: *Is the woman a noun phrase?* Npl searches the lexicon for a value A and binds A to *the*. Npl binds B to *boy*. Npl writes the values of A and B to the screen and then tests the goal *append([the],[boy],[the,woman])*, which fails. Npl backtracks and binds B to *girl*, the second noun in the lexicon. The values of A and B are written. The *append([the],[girl],[the, woman])* goal fails, and Prolog backtracks. Because *woman* is the fourth entry in the lexicon, Prolog finds it on the fourth try. The *append* goal succeeds and Prolog answers *yes*.

In Session 8.7, line 12, npf([the,woman]) asks: *Is the woman a noun phrase?* The first goal is *append(A,B,[the,woman])*. As a first guess, Prolog binds the A to the empty set *[]* and B to the element *[the,woman])*. This fails because there is no lexical entry *det([])* or *n([the,woman])*. As a second try, Prolog binds A to *[the]* and B to *[woman]*. Prolog looks up *det([the])* and *n([woman])* in the lexicon, and finding them both, succeeds.

```
% Prolog
C-Prolog version 1.5

| ?- [g0807].
g0807 consulted 836 bytes 0.05 sec.
yes

| ?- npl(X).
X = [the,boy] ;
X = [the,girl] ;
X = [the,man] ;
X = [the,woman] ;
X = [a,boy] ;
X = [a,girl] ;
X = [a,man] ;
X = [a,woman] ;
X = [this,boy] ;
X = [this,girl] ;
X = [this,man] ;
X = [this,woman] ;
X = [that,boy] ;
X = [that,girl] ;
X = [that,man] ;
X = [that,woman] ;
no

| ?- npf(X).
X = [the,boy] ;
X = [the,girl] ;
X = [the,man] ;
X = [the,woman] ;
X = [a,boy] ;
X = [a,girl] ;
X = [a,man] ;
X = [a,woman] ;
X = [this,boy] ;
X = [this,girl] ;
X = [this,man] ;
X = [this,woman] ;
X = [that,boy] ;
X = [that,girl] ;
X = [that,man] ;
X = [that,woman] ;

^C
Action (h for help): a
[ execution aborted ]
| ?- cntl-d
%
```

Session 8.6. Noun phrases defined by g0807.

Notice that (line 14) evaluating npf, Prolog found that *the woman* is an np on the second try.

Evaluating the query *npl([that,boy])*, Prolog tries several different bindings for A and B as it sequentially steps through the lexicon looking for possibilities. Prolog succeeds on the 13th try. Evaluating *npf([that,boy])*, Prolog first tests the *append* goal and sets A = [] and B = [that,boy]. This fails because there is no appropriate lexical entry. Prolog next binds A = *[that]* and B = *[boy]* and proceeds to search the lexicon for *det([that])* and *n([boy])*. In line 34, *yes* signals success.

This example illustrates four things:

Append–first parsing first selects the constituent structure for the noun phrase and then tries to find values for the determiner and noun by searching the lexicon, that is, it starts with the string and tries to segment it in such a way that segments match constituents defined in the

```
/*      Program:      g0808                                    */
/*              Two strategies for assigning structure to      */
/*              noun phrases.                                   */

/*      LEXICON OF FORMS                                        */
det([the]).
det([a]).
det([this]).
det([that]).
n([boy]).
n([girl]).
n([man]).
n([woman]).

/*      DEFINITIONS TO IDENTIFY AND LABEL CONSTITUENTS  */
npl(X) :-         det(A),n(B),                /* pattern recognition  */
                  nl,write('det = '),write(A),  /* format output      */
                  write(' n = '),write(B),    /* format output      */
                  append(A,B,X).              /* pattern recognition  */

npf(X) :-         append(A,B,X),              /* pattern recognition  */
                  nl,write('det = '),write(A),  /* format output      */
                  write(' n = '),write(B),    /* format output      */
                  det(A),n(B).                /* pattern recognition  */

/*      GENERAL DERIVATIONAL MECHANISMS                        */
append([],L,L).
append([X|L1],L2,[X|L3]) :- append(L1,L2,L3).
```

lexicon. Append–last parsing first searches the lexicon.

Second, in general, particularly for large lexicons, append–last parsing is much slower than append–first parsing. Append–last parsing will try every possible combination of constituents that one can construct from the lexicon before it arrives at the one that is successful. Append–first parsing will try to segment the input string in all possible

```
1.     % prolog
2.     C-Prolog version 1.5
3.     | ?- [g0808].
4.     g0808 consulted 1020 bytes 0.05 sec.
5.     yes

6.     | ?- npl([the,woman]).
7.     det = [the]   n = [boy]
8.     det = [the]   n = [girl]
9.     det = [the]   n = [man]
8.     det = [the]   n = [woman]
11.    yes

12.    | ?- npf([the,woman]).
13.    det = []   n = [the,woman]
14.    det = [the]   n = [woman]
15.    yes

16.    | ?- npl([that,boy]).
17.    det = [the]   n = [boy]
18.    det = [the]   n = [girl]
19.    det = [the]   n = [man]
20.    det = [the]   n = [woman]
21.    det = [a]   n = [boy]
22.    det = [a]   n = [girl]
23.    det = [a]   n = [man]
24.    det = [a]   n = [woman]
25.    det = [this]   n = [boy]
26.    det = [this]   n = [girl]
27.    det = [this]   n = [man]
28.    det = [this]   n = [woman]
29.    det = [that]   n = [boy]
30.    yes

31.    | ?- npf([that,boy]).
32.    det = []   n = [that,boy]
33.    det = [that]   n = [boy]
34.    yes

35.    | ?- ^D
36.    [ Prolog execution halted ]
37.    %
```

Session 8.7. The output of g0808.

298

ways and check each possible segmentation against the lexicon.

Third, the two parsing strategies exploit different aspects of the computer's resources. Apend–last parsing is computationally intensive in that it requires the generation of sentences until the appropriate sentence is found, but it does not place large demands on computer memory. Append–first parsing is not computationally intensive in that large numbers of sentences are not calculated. However, append–first parsing can be memory (stack space) intensive. In general, if *append* is early in a statement, the statement is memory intensive. If *append* is late in the statement, it is computationally intensive.

Fourth, append–last parsing uses the grammar to produce sentences that are then compared, one at a time, against the sentence to be parsed. At no point does the append–last parser ever consider any sentence structure that cannot be generated by the lexicon and rules of combination. The append–first parser regularly considers sentences which cannot be defined by the lexicon and rules of grammar. Insofar as the append–first parser offers an incorrect factoring of the string, e.g., *[the,woman]* as *A = []* and *B = [the woman]*, it is considering and ruling out ill–formed structures. (See the discussion of the *generate/filter strategy* and the *scan/recognize strategy* in Section 2.1.)

Session 8.8 indicates what happens for searches that are doomed to fail because the items (*one, two, three*) are not in the lexicon. No matter what query we ask npl, for example, *npl([one,two]), npl([one,two,three]),...,* it will in each case generate each noun phrase possible from its lexicon and compare it against the queried string. Not so with npf. Npf will behave differently for different strings. Npf will segment the input string every possible way into two parts, A and B, and check every possible segmentation against the lexical entries for *det(A)* and *n(B)*.

Referring to Figure 8.20, the issues relating to append–first and append–last parsing are technical questions about how best to attain the goals of computational research. Logically, but not procedurally, the following are identical. It is a technical question to decide which is best.

sent(X) :–	np(A),vp(B),append(A,B,X).
sent(X) :–	np(A),append(A,B,X),vp(B).
sent(X) :–	np(A),vp(B),append(A,B,X).

The issues of deciding *whether sentence is a constituent of language, whether a sentence can be factored into an np and a vp,* and *what constitute factorizations of an np and a vp* are conceptual questions internal to universal grammar that define the goals of linguistic research. Linguistic research must decide if a sentence is an np appended to a vp. Computational research decides how best to implement the decision.

299

```
% prolog
C-Prolog version 1.5
| ?- [g0808].
g0808 consulted 1020 bytes 0.0666667 sec.
yes

| ?- npl([one,two,three]).
det = [the]   n = [boy]
det = [the]   n = [girl]
det = [the]   n = [man]
det = [the]   n = [woman]
det = [a]   n = [boy]
det = [a]   n = [girl]
det = [a]   n = [man]
det = [a]   n = [woman]
det = [this]   n = [boy]
det = [this]   n = [girl]
det = [this]   n = [man]
det = [this]   n = [woman]
det = [that]   n = [boy]
det = [that]   n = [girl]
det = [that]   n = [man]
det = [that]   n = [woman]
no

| ?- npf([one,two]).
det = []   n = [one,two]
det = [one]   n = [two]
det = [one,two]   n = []
no

| ?- npf([one,two,three]).
det = []   n = [one,two,three]
det = [one]   n = [two,three]
det = [one,two]   n = [three]
det = [one,two,three]   n = []
no


| ?- npf([one,two,three,four]).
det = []   n = [one,two,three,four]
det = [one]   n = [two,three,four]
det = [one,two]   n = [three,four]
det = [one,two,three]   n = [four]
det = [one,two,three,four]   n = []
no

| ?- ^D
[ Prolog execution halted ]
%
```

Session 8.8. Different parsing strategies.

G0809 is an append–first version of g0801 and g0802. If we query g0809 with *yes/no* questions (see Session 8.9), it will give the same answers we get from g0801 and g0802 (see lines 6–13). If, however, we query g0809 with a *wh*–question: *sent(X)*, line 14, then it will give us all possible answers given its lexicon and rules of combination (lines 15–18 plus many not listed) and finally end in a loop.

```
/*      Program:        g0809                                    */
/*              An append-first version of grammar1              */
/*      LEXICON OF FORMS                                         */
det([the]).
det([a]).
n([boy]).
n([girl]).
v([remembered]).
v([forgot]).

/*      DEFINITIONS TO IDENTIFY CONSTITUENTS                     */
sent(X) :-      append(A,B,X),np(A),vp(B).
vp(X)   :-      append(A,B,X),v(A),np(B).
np(X)   :-      append(A,B,X),det(A),n(B).

/*      GENERAL DERIVATIONAL MECHANISMS                          */
append([],L,L).
append([X|L1],L2,[X|L3]) :-  append(L1,L2,L3).
```

To terminate the loop, we type **control–c** (line 19). We select the possible action, **a**, which causes the search to abort and returns us to the Prolog prompt (line 27).

Some confusion is to be expected anytime a formal deductive system (algebraic, geometric, combinatorial, or computational) is brought in to define the formal properties of a physical or biological system. One need only reflect on the confusion in the 17th century when Newton introduced the concept of *instantaneous velocity*: *How fast is an arrow moving when it is at point X?* It was obvious to anyone living then, that when the arrow is *at* point X, it is not moving. It is only moving when it is *between* point X and point Y. Since then, refinements in calculus have clarified notions about differences and limits, and everyone feels quite at home with the contradictions in *instantaneous velocity*. One can expect that technical concepts of *parsing, recursion,* and *complexity,* pulled from computer science to explicate processes and data structures in human language, may lead to apparent contradictions and, consequently, confusion. As a new data domain falls under a formal deductive system, the student must read with an eye to distinguish *temporary confusion*, arising from a new way of thinking about data, from *genuine muddledheadedness*, which has other sources, many of which are discussed by Peirce (1877/1965) in his essay, "How to Make our Ideas Clear."

We can see the difference between npl and npf if we imagine that we ask these questions of a human being and not of a Prolog parser. Imagine a nonstop chatterbox who mumbles his thoughts while cogitating. (See the discussion of the idiot–savant inventory clerk in Section 1.3.) We ask: *npl([that,boy])*, *Is that boy a noun phrase?* The mumbler starts: *The boy* is a noun phrase, but not the one you want.

```
1.     % prolog
2.     C-Prolog version 1.5
3.     | ?- [g0809].
4.     g0809 consulted 908 bytes 0.05 sec.
5.     yes

6.     | ?- sent([the,boy,remembered,the,girl]).
7.     yes
8.     | ?- sent([the,girl,forgot,the,boy]).
9.     yes
8.     | ?- sent([a,boy,forgot,the,boy]).
11.    yes
12.    | ?- sent([the,girl,boy,the,forgot]).
13.    no

14.    | ?- sent(X).
15.    X = [the,boy,remembered,the,boy] ;
16.    X = [the,boy,remembered,the,girl] ;
17.    X = [the,boy,remembered,a,boy] ;
18.    X = [the,boy,remembered,a,girl] ;

19.    ^C
20.    Action (h for help): h
21.    a          abort
22.    c          continue
23.    d          debug
24.    t          trace
25.    Action (h for help): a
26.    [ execution aborted ]

27.    | ?- ^D
28.    [ Prolog execution halted ]
29.    %
```

Session 8.9. The output of G0809.

302

The girl, the man, and *the woman* are noun phrases, but not the one you asked about. Prattle, prattle, prattle, until he succeeds: *That woman* is a noun phrase, and it is the one you asked about, so *yes* is the answer. Now suppose we ask our friend: *npf([that,boy])*. He starts: *[]* is not a determiner, and *[that,boy]* is not a noun; *[that]* is a determiner and *[boy]* is a noun, so *yes*, the string you inquired about can be segmented so that it contains constituents in the lexicon.

8.5.   Horizontal Appends: Complement Structures

One main goal of our research is to isolate and define the problem–solving skills, pattern–recognition abilities, and memory–storage capacities that would be required in a Prolog machine in order to program a generative grammar of English that could pair sounds and meanings in the same way as a native speaker of English. The aim of this section and the next is to indicate that the basic relational database concepts of pure Prolog, along with the binary relation append, suffice to characterize the data structures internal to the lexicon that are normally referred to by linguists by terms such as *complement structures, appositive constructions,* and *selectional restrictions.* I hope to show that the shape of the data structure of a lexical item in the lexicon can be characterized in terms of the number of append relations and the organization of append relations.

A main goal of linguistic research on English is to find the category types (which define the simple Prolog facts) and to find the definitions of phrase (which are expressed as append relations). Following our domino model, the goal is to design the puzzle pieces that can be combined to define the principles of sentence construction. I now present some data in a traditional grammatical notation – phrase markers – and then indicate how the lexicon must be structured to characterize these data. See Gross (1989a, 1989b, 1990, 1991, 1992, 1993).

The smallest sentences have only a subject and a verb. A verb that has only a subject is called an *intransitive* verb, for example, *die, elapse, dream, snow,* and *rain.*

(1)   The dog died.
(2)   It rained.

A *transitive* verb occurs in sentences that have a subject and an object, for example, *see* and *touch.*

(3)   Mary saw/touched/kissed/knows Bill.

Some verbs can be both transitive and intransitive: *read* and *eat*, for instance.

(4)   Mary read.   Mary read the book.
(5)   John ate.   John ate the donut.

Some verbs require a following prepositional phrase, for example, *depend on* and *look at*:

(6)   The boy depends on the girl.
(7) *   The boy depends.
(8) *   The boy depends the girl.

The constituents that follow the verb in a simple sentence comprise the verbal complement of the verb. Figures 8.21 and 8.22 give a partial listing of the diverse complement structures found in English. For the moment, let us define **complement** as the phrase(s) that are linked to the verb as objects, for example, *on the girl* is the complement of *depend* in *depend on the girl*; *the book to Mary* is the complement of *give* in *give the book to Mary*.

We assume that *complement*, as a technical term in our theory, is well–defined in terms of the computational processes that project structure onto a string based on the lexical information about items in that string. Heuristically, if a parser is considering a verb, the parser must have sufficient internal memory cells to hold each of the items that will eventually be placed under the verb phrase projected from that verb. Our definition of *complement* relates to the computational idea of *parser window* and is a technical term in the derivational processes of our theory. When we try to define *complement*, we are defining how many independent constituents the parser must be able to juggle, permute, and combine in its working memory before it locks onto the pattern it will accept as the representation. The term *complement* may or may not have some significance in the structural description assigned to a string by the parser. At the risk of befuddling those uninitiated into the terminology of current linguistic research, we might mention that in our view, *government* is a crucial notion in defining the *processes* by which a grammar produces structures which link a sound and a meaning, but government is not well defined on the structural descriptions assigned to a string as a *representation*.

The following sentences illustrate the complement types in Figures 8.21 and 8.22:

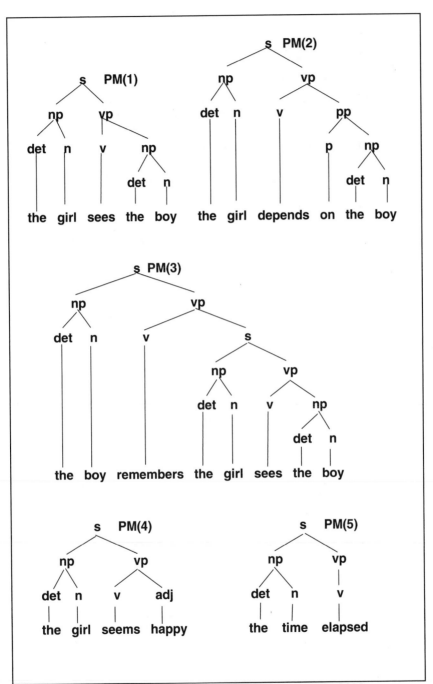

Figure 8.21. Phrase markers defined by g0810 and g0811.

(9) (a) PM(1), Verb + Complement: V NP
    (b) The girl sees the boy.
    (c) The girl (VP (V sees) (NP the boy))

(10) (a) PM(2), Verb + Complement: V PP
     (b) The girl depends on the boy.
     (c) The girl (VP (V depends) (PP on the boy))

(11) (a) PM(3), Verb + Complement: V S
     (b) The boy remembers the girl sees the boy.
     (c) The boy (VP (V remembers) (S the girl sees the boy))

(12) (a) PM(4), Verb + Complement: V ADJ
     (b) The girl seems happy.
     (c) The girl (VP (V seems) (ADJ happy))

(13) (a) PM(5), Verb + Complement: V
     (b) The time elapsed.
     (c) The time (VP (V elapsed))

(14) (a) PM(6), Verb + Complement: V NP PP
     (b) The girl gives the truck to the boy.
     (c) The girl (VP (V gives) (NP the truck) (PP to the boy))

(15) (a) PM(7), Verb + Complement: V PP PP
     (b) The boy goes from the truck to the girl.
     (c) The boy (VP (V goes) (PP from the truck) (PP to the girl))

(16) (a) PM(8), Verb + Complement: V NP S
     (b) The girl tells the boy the girl seems happy.
     (c) The girl (VP (V tells) (NP the boy) (S the girl seems
         happy))

(17) (a) PM(9), Verb + Complement: V PP S
     (b) The boy explains to the girl the time elapsed.
     (c) The boy (VP (V explains) (PP to the girl) (S the time
         elapsed))

The grammar must contain information about which complement structures are possible for each verb. The verb *put* requires both an NP and a PP and must occur in a phrase marker like PM(6):

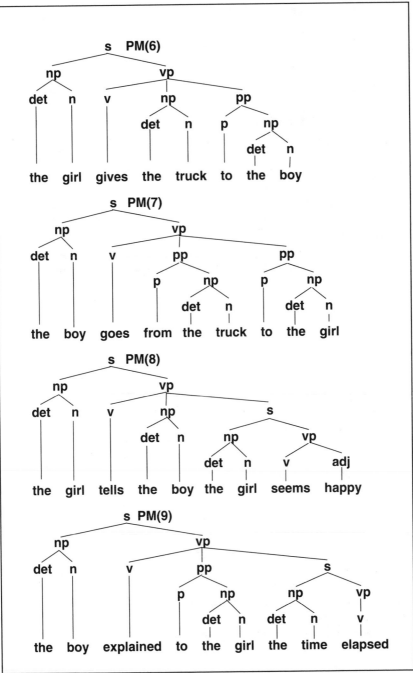

Figure 8.22. Phrase markers defined by g0810 and g0811.

(18)   (a)   Mary put the book on the table.
       (b) * Mary put the book.
       (c) * Mary put on the table.

The verb *explain* (*indicate, claim,* etc.) requires a PP S or S complement:

(19)   (a)   John explained to us that they had won.
       (b) * John explained us that they had won.
       (c) * John explained to us.
       (d)   John explained that they had won.

Our objective is to design a Prolog parser that will link each of these strings with the appropriate constituent structure to yield the structure information in Figures 8.21 and 8.22. To accomplish this, the parser must solve a problem in combinatorial geometry.

What are the shapes and sizes of the puzzle pieces that we must assign to the verbs *see, depend, remember, seem, elapse, give, go, tell,* and *explain*?

The dominos assigned to verbs and nouns are two–dimensional structures that are defined by append relations. A simple domino, corresponding to a simple fact, for example, verb([elapse]), det([the]), or n([mary]), contains no append relation. This is a **zero append entry**. Larger entries are defined by append relations in two possible ways: horizontally (linearly) and vertically (hierarchically). We will classify lexical entries according to the **horizontal append number** (**hap number**) and the **vertical append number** (**vap number**). Figure 8.23 indicates examples with hap numbers of 0, 1, and 2. Figure 8.24 indicates examples with vap numbers of 0, 1 and 2.

Basically, the issue is this: The syntax domino assigned to a verb consists of a certain number of rows and columns. If a verb requires specific complements, its domino will define several columns. If a verb requires (selects) a specific preposition (*depend on/*depend at*), then the syntax domino will define several rows.

The HAP NUMBER is exactly the number of arguments that are in the complement of a verb. Each argument must be placed into the syntax domino by an append relation, so the hap number is by definition the number of arguments in the complement. Roughly speaking, hap numbers correlate with what has been called subcategorization or s–selection by generative grammarians. A syntax domino expands in the horizontal direction (linearly) one cell for each hap number.

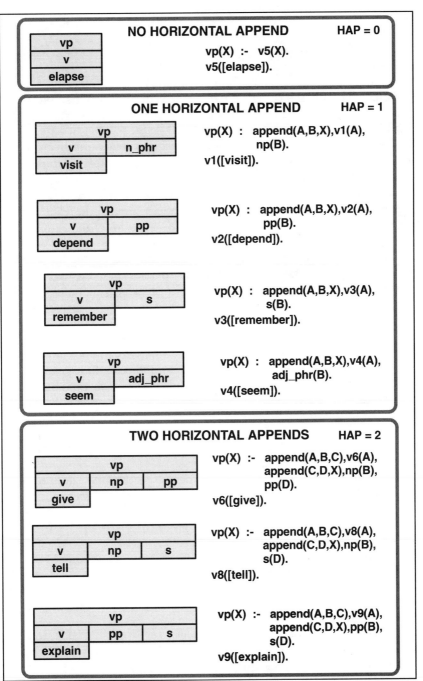

Figure 8.23. *Horizontal appends* define the head's arguments.

The **VAP NUMBER** indicates if the verb has selection or cooccurrence restrictions with the arguments in its complement. The vap number is 0 for a verb that has no selection restrictions on the items in its complement. A vap number of 1 or more indicates that there are selection restrictions. A syntax domino expands in the vertical dimension (hierarchically) by one cell for a vap number of 1, 2, 3, and so on.

From a linguistic point of view, one might ask: Do HAP and VAP numbers refer to: (a) the results of a parse or (b) the lexical entry? The answer is indirectly to the results of a parse (the structural descriptions assigned as a representation) and directly to the structure of the lexical entry. For those who like analogies, consider this. When some baseball players step to the plate, the outfield moves in. When Babe Ruth was batting, the outfield moved back and the infield spread out. Assume that the parser has a dynamically configured memory organization that allocates quantity and quality of memory as the parse proceeds. The HAP and VAP numbers of a lexical item indicate to the parser how much memory it will/may need. These numbers are relevant to the derivational processes that project structure from the lexical entries and construct the representations, and may or may not be relevant to the representations which relate a sound to a meaning. Big HAP/VAP numbers say: Open a big parse window and get ready to juggle several categories.

There are two ways that an append relation can expand a syntax domino. This definition uses *append* to expand the domino horizontally:

vp(X)   :-   **v(A),pp(B),append(A,B,X).**   **hap # = 1**
v([depend]).

This is read: X is a verb phrase if A is a verb, and B is a prepositional phrase, and X is A and B appended.

This definition uses two appends to expand the domino horizontally. Each *append* adds a prep_phrase to the complement:

vp(X)   :-   **v(A),pp(B),append(A,B,C),**   **hap # = 2**
                      pp(D),append(C,D,X).
v([go]).

This is read: X is a verb phrase if A is a verb, and B is a prepositional phrase, and A and B appended yield C, and D is a prepositional phrase, and C and D appended yield X.

This definition uses the first *append* to expand the domino horizontally to add the prep_phrase complement and the second *append* to indicate that the preposition must be the preposition in the lexical entry of the verb:

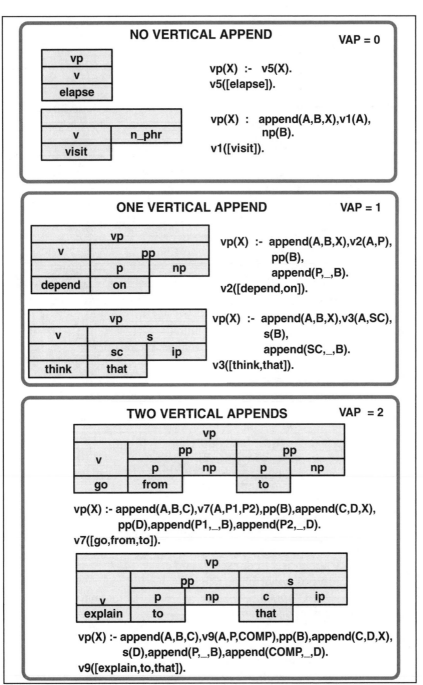

Figure 8.24. *Vertical appends* define the selection properties.

311

```
vp(X)    :-    v(A,P),pp(B),append(A,B,X),        hap # = 1
               append(P,_,B).                     vap # = 1
v([depend,on]).
v([look,at]).
v([rail,against]).
```

This is read: X is a verb phrase if v(A,P) is a lexical item, and B is a prepositional phrase, and A and B appended yield X, and P appended to anything is the prepositional phrase B.

The latter append, append(P,_,B), guarantees that the prepositional phrase begins with the preposition P given in the lexical entry for the verb. This second append does not add another argument to the complement of the verb; rather, it confirms that the item appended to form the argument of the verb starts with the correct element. *Selection restrictions*, sometimes called *cooccurrence restrictions*, are expressed by vertical appends as shown in the next section.

The hap number always correlates with an expansion of the domino in the horizontal direction. A vap number of 1 indicates that one of the arguments has selection restrictions and increases the size of the domino one unit in the vertical direction. A vap number of 2 or more indicates that there are 2 or more arguments with selection restrictions, but the size of the domino does not increase. Consider a verb like *go* which selects for two prepositional phrases – one with *from* and the other with *to*. This has a hap number of 2 and a vap number of 2. Verbs can have multiple entries, or perhaps one logically complex entry, that define various HAP/VAP structures:

```
vp(X)    :-    v(A,P1,P2),pp(B),append(A,B,C),
               append(P1,_,B),
               pp(D),append(C,D,X),
               append(P2,_,D).
```

This is read: X is a verb phrase if
    A is a verb, and B is a prepositional phrase, and
    C is A and B appended, and   hap
    B is P1 appended to anything, and   vap
    D is a prepositional phrase, and
    X is C and D appended, and   hap
    D is P2 appended to anything.   vap

Any lexical entry in any language can be expressed in terms of append relations. If we want to understand how a parser assigns a structure to a tree, we can think of these append relations as correlating with rectangular syntax dominos. Most linguistic work, however, does not represent the structure of a sentence as a rectangular block of dominos. Most linguists present their analyses of the sound–meaning correlations of language in terms of trees, like in Figures 8.21 and 8.22. There is no difference in the information content between the domino notation and the tree notation.

Referring to Figure 8.20, there are independent but interrelated directions to research in computational linguistics.

- We could further pursue computational research by developing the structural properties of the domino model. We could analyze the assignment of hap and vap numbers and classify lexical items in terms of them, or
- We could pursue linguistic research and investigate the information content of the syntax dominos.

We choose the latter. I do not develop the domino model any further. I present all examples in the form of trees and formulate all lexical and grammatical properties in terms of simple facts and append relations.

The Prolog definitions developed here are constraints on words, phrases, clauses, and sentences for English in particular and language in general. The results of this research will govern the operation of any Prolog interpreter, current or future, serial or parallel, big or small.

Lexicon_8b, g0810, contains information about nouns, adjectives, prepositions, and verbs (see Sessions 8.10 and 8.11). In this presentation, there are nine types of verbs, $v1(\_)$ to $v9(\_)$, each corresponding to a verb phrase structure in Figure 8.6. There is no significance to these numbers; they are only for reference. A more motivated classification would be in terms of hap and vap numbers. G0811 contains the Prolog mechanisms to project the necessary complement structure for the lexical items in g0810.

The lexical markings that indicate the possible range of complement structures for a verb are called by linguists the **subcategorization restrictions** for that verb. A verb such as *elapse* has only a single subcategorization restriction, which indicates that it defines only the verb complement structure in PM(5). A verb such as *put* has only a single subcategorization restriction, indicating that it defines only the verb complement structure in PM(6). Some verbs (*eat, read, give, explain*, etc.) have more than one subcategorization restriction. The verb *eat* defines both the complement structure in PM(1) and PM(5).

```
/*      Program:      g0810   lexicon_8b            */
/*              No complement or selections restrictions  */
/*                      indicated.                   */

/*          entries for nouns                       */
n([boy]).
n([girl]).
n([time]).
n([truck]).
n([hay]).
/*          entries for adjectives                  */
adj([happy]).
adj([kind]).
/*          entries for determiners                 */
det([the]).
det([a]).
/*          entries for prepositions                */
p([on]).
p([from]).
p([with]).
p([to]).
/*          entries for verbs                       */
v1([sees]).
v1([eats]).
v1([ate]).
v2([depends]).
v3([remembers]).
v4([seems]).
v4([appears]).
v5([elapses]).
v5([elapsed]).
v5([eats]).
v5([ate]).
v6([gives]).
v6([put]).
v6([handed]).
v7([goes]).
v8([tells]).
v8([reminded]).
v8([told]).
v9([explains]).
v9([describes]).
v9([shouted]).
```

In the present example, if a verb has only one subcategorization, such as *elapse*, then it occurs only once in lexicon_8b, as *v5([elapsed])*. If a verb has two subcategorizations, such as *eat*, it occurs twice: *v1([eats])* and *v5([eats])*. Lexicon_8b is only partially specified. Many of the verbs there only once should have multiple entries because they occur with more than one subcategorization.

It is possible to say a lexical item, such as *put*, in a Prolog lexicon *defines* the complement structure in PM(6) because the Prolog statements are logical definitions. The lexicon does not contain a phrase marker (or any tree structure); instead, the lexical entry of an item is a set of instructions (blueprints) for building structure. Normally, in linguistics, one says that the lexical item *put* **licenses** the complement structure in PM(6). Licensing is a complicated topic, but it boils down to this. If the

```
/*      Program:        g0811                                  */1
/*              A simple grammar to define sentences that      */2
/*              contain verbs with various complement structures.  */3
/*              You must load a lexicon to get results.        */4

s(X)    :-  append(A,B,X),np(A),vp(B).    /*      s            */5
np(X)   :-  append(A,B,X),det(A),n(B).    /*      np           */6
pp(X)   :-  append(A,B,X),p(A),np(B).     /*      pp           */7

vp(X)   :-  append(A,B,X),v1(A),np(B).    /*      v np         */8
vp(X)   :-  append(A,B,X),v2(A),pp(B).    /*      v pp         */9
vp(X)   :-  append(A,B,X),v3(A),s(B).     /*      v s          */10
vp(X)   :-  append(A,B,X),v4(A),adj(B).   /*      v adj        */11
vp(X)   :-  v5(X).                        /*      v            */12

vp(X)   :-  append(A,B,X),v6(A),          /*      v np pp      */13
            append(C,D,B),np(C),pp(D).

vp(X)   :-  append(A,B,X),v7(A),          /*      v pp pp      */14
            append(C,D,B),pp(C),pp(D).

vp(X)   :-  append(A,B,X),v8(A),          /*      v np s       */15
            append(C,D,B),np(C),s(D).

vp(X)   :-  append(A,B,X),v9(A),          /*      v pp s       */16
            append(C,D,B),pp(C),s(D).

append([],L,L).                                                17
append([X|L1],L2,[X|L3]) :- append(L1,L2,L3).                  18
```

grammar pairs a string with a constituent structure (see Figure 8.4), it should be possible to ask about any node or branching in the phrase marker: "What permitted – or licensed – the parser to construct this constituent structure and to assign it to the string?" The information in a lexical entry, and in particular its markings for subcategorization, **license** the possible complement structures that a parser can generate and assign to strings containing that lexical item.

Session 8.10 gives the results of g0811. Each of the sentences (lines 9–17) is defined as grammatical by g0811. The query *s([the,boy,gives, the,girl,the,truck]).* fails. Of course, *the boy gives the girl the truck* is in fact a well–formed sentence of English. Hence, this empirical claim of g0811 is incorrect.

We must increase the range of complement types defined by g0811 to include V NP NP. Verbs that permit NP NP complements include *give, tell,* and *bring*: *give the girl the book, tell the girl the story, bring us the money, elect Tracy president, consider Sean a genius,* and so on.

Session 8.11 indicates that g0811 defines sentences with subcategorization violations to be ill–formed: **the girl sees on the boy* is ill–formed because *see* does not license a prepositional phrase complement: **the girl depends the boy* is ill–formed because *depend* licenses only a prepositional complement.

A basic idea in linguistics is that constituent structure is projected from lexical heads. A **lexical head** is an item in the lexicon (a noun, verb, adjective, preposition, or adverb) that defines specific types of structure, usually through subcategorization restrictions. I only discuss verb heads, but noun heads can have restrictions, for example, *fact* permits a sentence complement: *The fact that he died caused great unhappiness.* Prepositions have subcategorization properties: *between* requires a coordination or a plural, for example, *between John and Mary, *between John.* Most prepositions precede the noun phrase in English, hence, they are called *pre*positions; however, some follow the noun phrase: *two days ago.* Some prepositions occur with more than one subcategorization. *Before* can take an NP complement: *Before you lies the Rubicon;* an S complement: *Before you cross it, watch out;* and can be intransitive: *He did it before.*

The term *government* relates to the idea of *licensing*. We will use government as follows. A *lexical head* (an item such as *put* or *elapse*) **governs** all those nodes in the tree whose production is licensed by the lexical entry and the Prolog mechanisms that use the blueprints in that entry to construct a labeled bracketing. In other words, a lexical item such as *put* governs all of the nodes in its domino and all of the dominos under the *put* domino.

In our view, government is defined in terms of the processes that

316

are actively constructing a tree/domino_puzzle and not in terms of an existing tree. That is, government is defined on nodes that are not yet attached and that are being juggled in the parser window. This is a subtle point, but confusion can be reduced by remembering that **government** is a crucial notion defining how much of the string the parser must consider

```
% Prolog
C-Prolog version 1.5
| ?- [g0810].
g0810 consulted 2944 bytes 0.15 sec.
yes
| ?- [g0811].
g0811 consulted 2944 bytes 0.15 sec.
yes

| ?- s([the,girl,sees,the,boy]).
yes

| ?- s([the,girl,depends,on,the,boy]).
yes

| ?- s([the,boy,remembers,the,girl,sees,the,boy]).
yes

| ?- s([the,girl,seems,happy]).
yes

| ?- s([the,time,elapsed]).
yes

| ?- s([the,girl,gives,the,truck,to,the,boy]).
yes

| ?- s([the,boy,goes,from,the,truck,to,the,girl]).
yes

| ?- s([the,girl,tells,the,boy,the,girl,seems,happy]).
yes

| ?- s([the,boy,explains,to,the,girl,the,time,
            elapsed]).
yes

| ?- s([the,boy,gives,the,girl,the,truck]).
no

| ?- ^D
[ Prolog execution halted ]
%
```

Session 8.10. Output of g0810 and g0811.

in order to assign structure (government fixes the size of the parser window) and is not defined in terms of a tree that has already been constructed.

Information in a lexical entry, and in particular a subcategorization restriction, constitutes a set of instructions to the derivational mechanisms that build structure. *Government* and *licensing* are computational ideas defined in terms of *derivational processes* (processing mechanisms, memory structures, and pattern recognition) that construct a labeled bracketing and assign it to a string. If the parser is **licensed** to insert a node or to construct a branching structure by the subcategorization information in the lexical entry, X, then X **governs** all of the nodes inserted and all of the structure created.

To summarize, we assume that **government** and **licensing** are specified in terms of **derivational considerations** defined by the processes that project structure from lexical heads. The mechanisms that use subcategorization information to project structure from a head are *X–bar theory* and the *parametrized principles of universal grammar*.

```
% prolog
C-Prolog version 1.5
| ?- [g0810].
g0810 consulted 2944 bytes 0.15 sec.
yes
| ?- [g0811].
g0811 consulted 2944 bytes 0.15 sec.
yes

| ?- s([the,girl,sees,on,the,boy]).
no

| ?- s([the,girl,depends,the,boy]).
no

| ?- s([the,girl,seems,the,boy]).
no

| ?- s([the,time,elapsed,the,girl]).
no

| ?- s([the,girl,gives,at,the,truck,to,the,boy]).
no

| ?- ^D
[ Prolog execution halted ]
%
```

Session 8.11. G0810 and g0811 subcategorization violations.

Conceivably, one might be able to put the cart before the horse and characterize *government* and *licensing* in terms of structural considerations defined on phrase markers, that is, in terms of *conditions defined on representations* that constitute the output of the parser. The issue concerns top–down versus bottom–up parsing.

If we formulate *government* and *licensing* as conditions defined on **representations** produced by the grammar, then we are developing a top–down parsing mechanism. The information in the lexicon does not constrain the production of structure or the pairing of structure with strings. If constraints are defined on representations, then the derivational processes will link strings and structures in various ways, and the constraints on representations will rule out the forms that are not licensed. This technique might be called the *generate and filter* technique.

If we define *government* and *licensing* in terms of the **derivational principles** that project structure from the lexical entries for the heads (nouns, verbs) in the string, then we are developing a bottom–up (parsing) mechanism. The derivational mechanism only builds the structures that are licensed by the subcategorization (HAP/VAP) information of the lexical heads in the string.

The organization of the grammar into lexicon_8b and program g0811 follows more from rhetorical principles than anything else. No linguist analyzing these data would assign numbers to verb classes *v1(...)*, *v2(...)*, and so on, and present such lists as a lexicon. G0811 places all of the principles that construct labeled bracketing away from the lexicon, but most linguists consider the mechanisms that build structure to be a part of, or an extension of, lexical principles. We placed the verbs in a lexicon in numbered classes so that the numbers would match the phrase markers listed in Figure 8.6. We placed the mechanisms which define the structure projected from lexical items in g0811 so that they could be more easily studied.

The Prolog statements in g0811 correlate directly with items in the lexicon. For instance, line 8 in g0811, defines the projection of *v1(...)* verbs. Line 9 defines the projection of *v2(...)* verbs.

Linguists often speak of *X–bar theory* and *universal grammar* as projecting the labeled bracketing from a lexical head. Each verb in the lexicon is a **head** of a verb phrase. In this presentation, lexicon_8b is a list of verbal heads. G0811 is a rude presentation of the X–bar principles that project structure from heads.

8.6.   Vertical Appends: Selection Restrictions.

I now focus on those verbs that take prepositional complements:

V PP, V NP PP, V PP PP, and V PP S. Some verbs require a specific preposition:

V PP

(1)   John depended on the boat.
(2) *   John depended in the boat.

(3)   John looked at the movie.
(4) *   John looked on the movie.

V PP PP

(5)   Mary went from New York to Los Angeles.
(6) *   Mary went at New York for Los Angeles.

V NP PP

(7)   Bill borrowed five dollars from Mary.
(8) *   Bill borrowed five dollars to Mary.
(9)   The sophists took Socrates for a fool.
(10) * The sophists took Socrates at a fool.

V PP S

(11)   John indicated to us that we had won.
(12) * John indicated at us that we had won.
(13)   John demanded from us that we move out by Friday.
(14) * John demanded to us that we move out by Friday.

A **lexicon** is the repository of all of the idiosyncratic information about the items at any level. If we wish to understand the computational mechanisms (in particular, the pattern–recognition devices, the memory structures, and the combinatorial devices) that underlie the internal structure of the lexicon and that utilize lexical information to link a list of words with a constituent structure, then we should describe lexical entries in terms of *hap* and *vap numbers* and consider them to be Prolog definitions of horizontal and vertical dependencies of heads with nearby constituents. Lexical entries are instruction to the parser.

We will represent the Prolog definitions as dominos, as in Figure 8.25, when we want to show how we structure a particular lexical entry to enable the parser to solve its problem in computational geometry. At other times, however, we use the terminology that exists in past and present linguistic literature. Some of this past terminology contains considerable intuitive insight, but is lacking in formalizable properties or in any view of the computational and memory capacities that might underlie the concept of the lexicon as containing instructions.

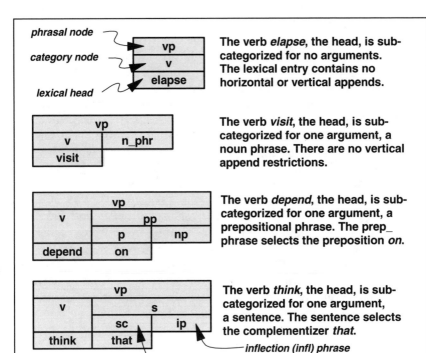

The verb *elapse*, the head, is sub-categorized for no arguments. The lexical entry contains no horizontal or vertical appends.

The verb *visit*, the head, is sub-categorized for one argument, a noun phrase. There are no vertical append restrictions.

The verb *depend*, the head, is sub-categorized for one argument, a prepositional phrase. The prep_ phrase selects the preposition *on*.

The verb *think*, the head, is sub-categorized for one argument, a sentence. The sentence selects the complementizer *that*.

The verb *go*, the head, is subcategorized for two arguments, a prep_phrase and a prep_phrase. The first prep_phrase selects the preposition *from*. The second prep_phrase selects the preposition *to*.

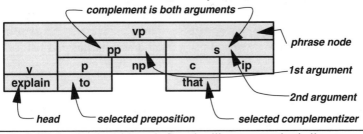

The verb *explain*, the head, is subcategorized for two arguments, a prep_phrase and a sentence. The prep_phrase selects the preposition *to*. The sentence selects the complementizer *that*.

Figure 8.25. Lexical entries defined with *append* relations.

No matter what notation we choose to represent the structure of a sentence, we will always assume that the structure assigned to a sentence results from a projection of the information in the lexicon and the constraints of universal grammar. Figure 8.26 indicates the type of phrase structure representation to be used.

Let us consider a **head** to be a word that is a lexical category (an adjective, a noun, or a verb). For each head, the lexicon contains **subcategorization restrictions**, which license the constituent structure of the complement of the head, and **selection restrictions**, which license specific properties of the constituents governed by the head. In examples (1–14), the ill–formed sentences satisfy all subcategorization restrictions, but they violate selection restrictions.

The technical terms *subcategorization restriction* and *selection restriction* have been replaced in current literature by concepts related to *s–selection*. For the purposes of that discussion, however, we can consider *subcategorization* and *selection* to refer to the external view of the lexicon. They represent the information that the parser requires from the lexicon to license the assembly of structure in the phrase marker.

Let us continue discussing verbs and phrases with verb heads, although all of the mechanisms we develop also apply to nouns, prepositions, adjectives, and adverbs, adjectives usually take prepositional complements. But the preposition must be lexically specified: *proud of/*at Tracy, amused at/*of the stories, happy about/*of the prize, pleased with/*from him, renowned for/*from its cheesecake*. The preposition *between* requires the coordinating conjunction *and* and not *or*: *between Tess and Tracy, *between Tess or Tracy*. Nouns can require specific prepositions: *the need for/*at love, the lack of/*from money*.

In the examples and diagrams, there is no significance to be assigned to the labels of verb types, for example, *v1, v2, v3*. These numbers are for reference only. Also, words that begin a subordinate clause, for example, *that, for, how, why, what*, have traditionally been called *subordinating conjunctions*. We will usually call them *complementizers* and label the sentence containing them the *subordinate sentence*. We consider a *sentence* to be a noun_phrase appended to a verb_phrase.

G0812, lexicon_8c, contains information about verb–preposition selection. The following entry pairs *depend* and *on*. The v2 lexical entry is read like this: *depend* is a verb of class *v2* and selects the preposition *on*:

v2([depend],[on]).

The entry for *go* contains two prepositions. This is read: *goes* is a verb of class *v7* and selects the preposition *from* and the preposition *to*:

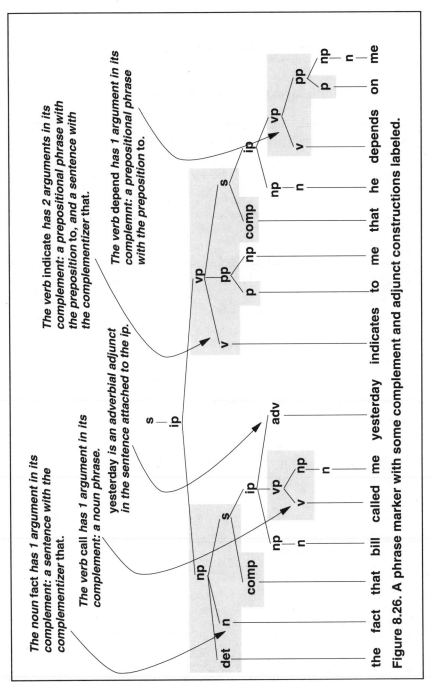

The noun *fact* has 1 argument in its complement: a sentence with the complementizer *that*.

The verb *call* has 1 argument in its complement: a noun phrase.

yesterday is an adverbial adjunct in the sentence attached to the *ip*.

The verb *indicate* has 2 arguments in its complement: a prepositional phrase with the preposition *to*, and a sentence with the complementizer *that*.

The verb *depend* has 1 argument in its complemnt: a prepositional phrase with the preposition *to*.

Figure 8.26. A phrase marker with some complement and adjunct constructions labeled.

Figure 8.26. Complement and adjunct constructions.

323

v7([goes],[from],[to]).

G0813 contains Prolog code to project the phrase markers for the lexical items. Consider this projection rule, line 2:

vp(X) :- append(A,B,X),v2(A,P),PP(B),append(P,_,B).

X is a verb phrase if A and B appended yield X, and A and P are a v2, and B is a prepositional phrase, and P appended with anything yields B.

```
/*        Program:        g0812        lexicon_8c        */
/*        Lexical entries with verbs marked for complements        */
/*                and preposition selection        */

/*                entries for nouns        */
n([boy]).
n([girl]).
n([truck]).
n([car]).
/*                entries for prepositions        */
p([on]).
p([to]).
p([at]).
p([from]).
/*                entries for determiners        */
det([the]).
det([a]).
/*                entries for verbs        */
v1([sees]).
v1([left]).
v2([depends],[on]).
v2([looks],[at]).
v3([remembers]).
v4([seems]).
v5([elapses]).
v5([left]).
v6([gives],[to]).
v6([takes],[from]).
v7([goes],[from],[to]).
v7([drives],[from],[to]).
v8([tells]).
v9([explains],[to]).
v9([shouts],[to]).
```

The goal *pp(B)* assures that *B* is a valid prepositional phrase. The goal *append(P,_,B)* assures that the prepositional phrase has the preposition *P* specified in *v2(A,P)* and that selection is satisfied; *append(P,_,B)* is true if *B* is preposition *P* appended to anything.

Session 8.12 indicates the results of querying g0812 and g0813. Sentences with *depend on* are well–formed, but the query *s([the,boy,depends, at,the,truck])*. yields *no* because a selection restriction of *depend* is not satisfied. The query *s([the,girl,explains,the,boy,the,truck,left])*. yields *no* because the subcategorization of *explain* licenses only *V PP S* and not *V NP S* complement structures. The query *s([the,girl,explains,at,the,boy, the,truck, left])*. yields *no* because the selection restriction of *explain* licenses the preposition *to* but not *at*.

The information about subcategorization and selection becomes very complicated very fast. Some verbs, such as *go*, permit some PP complements to be repeated:

(15)   Tess went from Paris to Rome.

```
/*      Program:        g0813                                   */

vp(X)   :-      v5(X).

vp(X)   :-      append(A,B,X),v2(A,P),pp(B),append(P,_,B).

vp(X)   :-      append(A,B,X),v6(A,P),append(C,D,B),
                np(C),pp(D),append(P,_,D).

vp(X)   :-      append(A,B,X),v7(A,P1,P2),
                append(C,D,B),pp(C),append(P1,_,C),
                pp(D),append(P2,_,D).

vp(X)   :-      append(A,B,X),v9(A,P),append(C,D,B),
                pp(C),append(P,_,C),s(D).

np(X)   :-      append(A,B,X),det(A),n(B).

s(X)    :-      append(A,B,X),np(A),vp(B).

pp(X)   :-      append(A,B,X),p(A),np(B).

append([],L,L).
append([X|L1],L2,[X|L3]) :-     append(L1,L2,L3).
```

(16)   Tess went from Paris to Rome to Berlin.
(17)   Tess went from Paris to Rome to Berlin to Moscow.
(18) *   Tess went from Rome from Paris to Berlin.

(19)   Tess went to Rome.
(20)   Tess went from Rome.

```
% Prolog
C-Prolog version 1.5
| ?- [g0812].
g0812 consulted 2980 bytes 0.166667 sec.
yes
| ?-[g0813].
g0813 consulted 2980 bytes 0.366667 sec.
yes

| ?- s([the,boy,looks,at,the,truck]).
yes

| ?- s([the,boy,depends,on,the,truck]).
yes

| ?- s([the,boy,depends,at,the,truck]).
no

| ?- s([the,girl,explains,to,the,boy,the,truck,left]).
yes

| ?- s([the,girl,explains,the,boy,the,truck,left]).
no

| ?- s([the,girl,explains,at,the,boy,the,truck,left]).
no

| ?- s([the,girl,goes,from,the,truck,to,the,car]).
yes

| ?- s([the,girl,gives,the,truck,to,the,boy]).
yes

| ?- s([the,girl,takes,the,truck,from,the,boy]).
yes

| ?- s([the,girl,takes,the,truck,at,the,boy]).
no

| ?- ^D
[ Prolog execution halted ]
%
```

Session 8.12. Selection information of g0812 and g0813.

(21) * Tess went to Paris to Rome.

In our grammars we regard prepositions to be subcategorized for complement structures. The preposition *before* can occur intransitively, as in (22). Intransitive prepositions are often called *adverbs*. *Before* can be transitive, as in (23). Transitive prepositions are called *prepositions*. And *before* can license a sentence complement, as in (24). Prepositions with sentence complements are often called *subordinating conjunctions*:

(22)	Mary left before.	before = adverb
(23)	Mary left before John.	before = preposition
(24)	Mary left before Susan arrived.	before = subordinating conjunction

The fact that there are three different names for *before* depending on its complement structure derives from the methods used by traditional linguists to isolate and define the elements that function at a level. In a generative model, there is no reason to consider *before* as defining three different syntactic categories. No one ever suggested that *know* was anything more than a verb, although it has the same subcategorizations as *before*: *Tess knows, Tess knows Sean*, and *Tess knows that Tracy left*. In some generative literature, the word *complementizer* is used where structuralist linguists used *subordinating conjunction*: *that, after, before, when*, and so on.

Some verbs require a prepositional phrase of a specific type (*locative, time, duration, manner*) but no specific preposition. *Put* requires a locative; *last* requires a durational phrase:

(25)   Tracy put the book on the table/near the window/between the shoes.
(26) * Tracy put the book at noon/for a hour.
(27)   The movie lasted for two hours/until dinner time.
(28) * The movie lasted yesterday/at noon/after lunch.

There are also verbs that require *on* or *in*, but do not permit *onto* or *into*: *John went on/onto the boat*, but *John decided on/*onto the boat. The money passed into/*in his account. He came into/*in his inheritance. The passage into/*in womanhood, John fell onto/on the floor. John rolled out of bed onto/*on the floor.*

Sentences (15–28) suggest that there exists considerable internal structure in the lexical specification of prepositional selection restrictions.

Appendix I. The Disk Included with this Book

The printed versions of the programs and session files in this book match C–Prolog, version 1.5, installed on an Ultrix Vax. With simple modifications, most of the programs will run on any IBM PC (8088 or better) and on a Macintosh using the supplied shareware Prolog language interpreters. Information about the IBM PC and Macintosh versions of shareware Prolog is in three places. First, this book. Second, in the README.TXT files on the disk. Third, on the Internet on the New York University Bulletin Board, called the *NYU Campus Wide Information Service* (*CWIS*), (see Appendix II).

> **TO INSTALL ON ANY IBM PC 8086, 286, 386, 486**
>
> 1) place disk in drive A:
> 2) type
> **A:INSTALL**
> 3) wait for response:
> *Prolog–2 and Programs Installed on C:*
> 4) type
> **PROLOG2**
> and you are ready to run any program in this book.

IBM   Prolog–2 and the programs have all been tested on several IBM PC compatibles. The version on the disk ran successfully on a generic brand IBM PC 386sx, 16mhz, 4 meg ram, 40 meg drive and on a 486DX66 with 32 meg ram, four 420 meg drives with an 8 meg memory intelligent VESA controller, which is specifically configured to do autocad. In both cases, a memory manager to free up the lower 640K dramatically improves performance. Prolog–2 ran most of the programs on an 8086, 4mhz, 640K ram, and a 20 meg drive, but some programs can take 2 minutes to run.

MAC   Open–Prolog and the programs have been tested on several different Macintoshes. *The disk is in IBM format and you need a Macintosh utility to read the files.* Or download them from CWIS@nyu.edu, see Appendix II.

C   The C–Prolog version of the programs contains comment lines indicating how to modify the files to run under Quintus Prolog. If you are using C–Prolog or Quintus, you are on a large computer that almost certainly is connected to the Internet. All programs can be obtained by e–mail, ftp, or by gopher from NYU. See Appendix II.

Contents of the Distribution Disk

eslpdpro.zip is the shareware copy of Prolog–2 from Expert Systems Ltd. See Sessions 2.3 and 2.4 for information about the source of this product.

install.bat is a batch file that will uncompress the relevant files and install Prolog–2 on your computer on hard disk drive C:. To automatically install Prolog–2 and the IBM version of the programs, place the disk into drive A:, and then type:

A:\INSTALL

TO INSTALL ON A MACINTOSH

You must have a utility to read disks in IBM format or download the files from CWIS@nyu.edu

Look at the files README.1st READMEM.TXT on the disk.

pkunzip.exe is a shareware copy of the decompression program to extract the operating files from the floppy disk.

pkzipfix.exe may be required on some computers (usually a 286) if the zip files cannot be extracted. This is discussed in the README.txt file.

progibm.zip contains all of the programs in the book formatted to run on an IBM PC.

progmac.sea contains all of the programs in the book formatted to run on a Macintosh.

programs.zip is all programs in the book, precisely as they look in the book, formatted to run in C–Prolog, version 1.5, on an Ultrix Vax. The most recent and updated versions of the programs are at the NYU CWIS gopher site.

open–pro.sea is the version of Prolog for the Macintosh. You will need a Macintosh utility to read the file that is on an IBM formatted disk.

The Format of the Distribution Disk

The disk is formatted for an IBM PC compatible 1.44 meg drive. All files, including those for the Macintosh, were written to the disk by an IBM PC.

The disk contains several README files. Everyone should study the README.1st file. It is formatted to print on a HPIII printer.

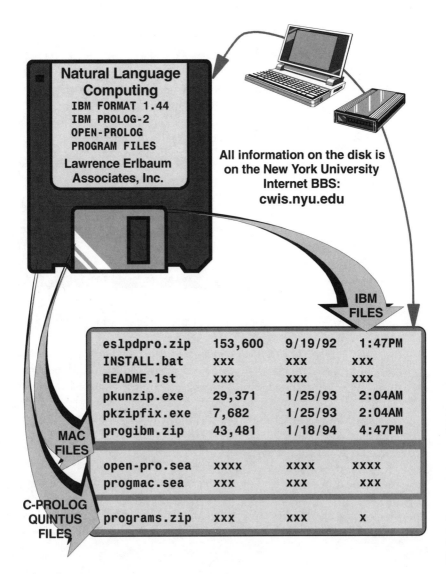

Natural Language Computing
IBM FORMAT 1.44
IBM PROLOG-2
OPEN-PROLOG
PROGRAM FILES
Lawrence Erlbaum Associates, Inc.

All information on the disk is on the New York University Internet BBS: cwis.nyu.edu

IBM FILES

eslpdpro.zip	153,600	9/19/92	1:47PM
INSTALL.bat	xxx	xxx	xxx
README.1st	xxx	xxx	xxx
pkunzip.exe	29,371	1/25/93	2:04AM
pkzipfix.exe	7,682	1/25/93	2:04AM
progibm.zip	43,481	1/18/94	4:47PM

MAC FILES

| open-pro.sea | xxxx | xxxx | xxxx |
| progmac.sea | xxx | xxx | xxx |

C-PROLOG QUINTUS FILES

| programs.zip | xxx | xxx | x |

Appendix II. How to access the NYU Bulletin Board CWIS

On the Internet, NYU is a Gopher Site. Move through your menus until you arrive at **cwis.nyu.edu**. Then select these items:

About NYU CWIS (Campus–Wide Information System)
Using NYU CWIS (A map of the NYU system)
New and Noteworthy (New additions to the NYU information base)

These listings show a directory for the **NYU Linguistics Department** containing the most recent freeware Prologs and programs.

Use **veronica** or **archie** to access this information and obtain your own copies. Program files are always ASCII and can be obtained by e–mail. Executable and compressed files must be obtained as binary transfers, usually via ftp.

All the ASCII README files contain detailed information about how to access several systems for information about languages like *lisp* and *Prolog*, about how to obtain free programs and information, and about how to install and run the free materials on the IBM PC and Apple Macintosh. The instructions on how to access materials from CWIS are contained in README.1st.

> **New York University**
> **Campus Wide Information Service**
> **CWIS**
>
> **cwis.nyu.edu**
>
> **gopher site for veronica and archie**
> *The source for all updates to*
> *shareware Prologs and programs.*

Essential reading on the resources of the Internet is this study:

Edwards, J. A. (1993). Survey of electronic corpora and related resources for language researchers. In J.A. Edwards & M.D. Lampert (Eds.) Talking data: Transcription and coding in discourse research (pp. 263-310). Hillsdale, NJ: Lawrence Erlbaum Associates.

The Internet permits the worldwide instantaneous interchange of information between the computers of universities and industry.

The resources of the Internet are easily understood. Imagine that all of the books in a huge library were shaken from the shelves by an earthquake. The books lie heaped on the floor in disarray. Hundreds of volunteers break into groups and start to sort them to place them back onto the shelves. Each group has a well–defined sorting/ordering strategy by which they can define *progress*. But if we step back and examine closer, we see that one group is ordering books according to the author's last name, the next according to the title, the next according to subject matter, and still others according to date of publication, the international book number, or the physical size of the books. The books carefully arranged by one group would be judged in total disarray the another group. But within each group's paradigm, defined by their ordering strategy and keywords, the books are neatly arrayed. There are local patterns of arrangement, but no global perspective that integrates them. The promise of the Internet lies in the fact that huge amounts of data reside on computers only a few keystrokes away from your screen. The frustration of the Internet follows from the fact that the data is fragmented into chunks, each of which may be coherently organized according to keywords, but may not tie in with any other chunk using different keywords. CWIS will contain a thesaurus of keywords.

CWIS@nyu.edu, the New York University Public Domain Bulletin Board, houses information about how to access data on the Internet to answer the following question under the stated assumptions.

> **How can we program a computer so that we can interact with it in a natural language (English, Chinese...) and not have to use an artificial language (Cobol, C, Fortran...)? What problems must we solve so that the tail will no longer wag the dog?**
>
> **We assume that the conceptual problems involved are answered by the theory of universal grammar of Noam Chomsky, and the technical problems are answered by nonprocedural logical constraint–based languages like Prolog.**

Except for the Prolog programs, little data will reside on CWIS. It will contain mostly information about how to find the data you want and suggestions about where you might look. CWIS will function like a table of contents, an abstract, or an index to information on the Internet relevant to answering the above question under the given assumptions.

332

Appendix III.   Flavor Files

Prolog is a generic term that refers to a variety of computer languages that more or less are nonprocedural and more or less backtrack. There are several "brand names" of Prolog: C–Prolog, Quintus, Prolog–2, Open–Prolog, Microlog, and Arity, to name those we have used at the NYU Academic Computing Facility. Within any given brand, there may be different versions, as older versions are replaced by newer ones. And there also may be different versions, each one matched to a particular type of computing machine (DEC, IBM, Apple) or a specific operating system (UNIX, VMS, DOS, Windows).

The various brands, versions, and implementations are called **flavors** of Prolog. C–Prolog, version 1.5, on a UNIX VAX is a different flavor than the same brand and version on a VMS machine. And Prolog–2 on an IBM PC is a different flavor than Quintus Prolog.

```
/*        p05bib.pro                    */
/*        This file has the dec10       */
/*        flavor on an IBM PC.          */
:- state(token_class,_,dec10).
/*        p0515                         */
/*        p0516                         */
/*        p0517                         */
/*        See Session 5.14.             */
```

A **flavor file** is a set of relations (or procedures) that you can load into Prolog of brand X version A on machine B and have it behave exactly like (or sort of like) Prolog of brand Y version P on machine Q. A flavor file makes one Prolog emulate another. If you have a program that runs perfectly on one Prolog configuration and you want to run it on another, you have two choices: (a) change the code of your program so that it runs in the new flavor of Prolog, or (b) load a flavor file into the new computer to make it behave like the old one.

Of course there are limits. There is no flavor file you can load into an IBM PC to make it emulate Quintus Prolog on a VAX cluster. But with some luck, you might succeed where the resources are not so far apart. Consider p05bib.pro, a flavor file that makes an IBM PC appear to be a DEC 10. Another example is in *edit.bat* on the included disk.

Session 5.14 produces a bibliography from database p0515 according to the format statements in p0516 using the search statements in p0517. If you try to load p0515, p0516, and p0517 as indicated in Session 5.14, the programs may not run as shown in the book. The example is run in C–Prolog on a DEC machine. To make the programs run on the IBM PC, you might do the following. First you place all of the individual program files, p0515–p0517 in one file, p05bib.pro. Second, you place the :-state(token_class,_,dec10). as the first statement of the file.

Now load this large program including the state relation:

```
>Prolog2
| ?-  [p05bib].
| ?-  search17.
| ?-  search18.
```

The program will work. How it works will depend on your machine. Your machine is only an IBM PC and not a DEC Vax. A flavor file can perform some conversions, but it cannot make a silk purse from a sow's ear. The relation :- **state(token_class,_,dec10)** is a flavor pill that gives the file its flavor. It must be the first statement, and essentially it converts Prolog–2 to a DEC 10 type Prolog before it processes the remaining statements in the file. If some of the programs do not run on your IBM PC, try to run them with this flavor file as the first statement.

There is not much one can do about the out–of–memory errors if you use shareware Prologs. You must move to a Prolog with a price tag to obtain an excellent memory manager. One "solution" that may work, but may distort the operation of the programs, exploits a side–effect of the cut, !, relation. The cut prohibits the Prolog interpreter from backtracking beyond the cut. This has a logical force, but in many computers this will have a pragmatic effect on memory management. From a practical point of view, if Prolog must backtrack it must use memory storage to keep track of where it must backtrack to and what range of variables remain to be tried for goals that are backtrack targets. But a cut blocks backtracking, so, if the Prolog interpreter has been written efficiently, when it passes a cut, it erases from memory all of the backtracking information about goals that can never be backtracking targets. Suppose we have this set of goals: *...goal1,goal2,!,goal3,goal4...* When Prolog is testing goal2, it has backtracking information about goal1. After the cut, Prolog is testing goal3. But because it can never go back to goal1 or goal2, Prolog can erase from memory all of the backtracking pointers. Hence, there is more "free memory" when Prolog is at goal3 than there is when Prolog is at goal2. Judicious placement of the cut can recover memory that is allocated, but will never be referred to.

334

Appendix IV. Looking into Prolog:
listing, trace and *breakpoint*

Prolog has two functions that enable a user to observe how the Prolog machine is coping with memory storage and with the assignment of values to variables: *listing* and *trace*. I provide no specific examples because these instructions have three properties. First, their behavior depends both on the flavor (brand, version) of Prolog you have and on your specific implementation (DOS, windows, UNIX...). Second, they produce a voluminous output even in simple cases. Third, it can be difficult to obtain a hardcopy printout (on paper) of the copious output. If you are invoking Prolog under the UNIX operating system, you can use the *script* command to obtain a file containing the reams of information. But with shareware on an IBM PC or Macintosh, you may have to stare unblinkingly at the screen as the information whizzes by. You get what you pay for. It is worth spending the time to learn to use these two commands. A third command, *breakpoint* or *spy*, is the most useful of all, but it is difficult to understand what it does without a thorough grasp of Prolog theory, hence, it is hard to use for beginning Prologers.

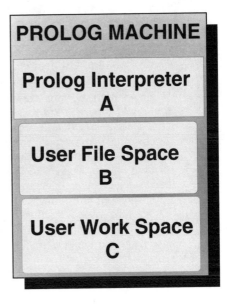

PROLOG MACHINE

Prolog Interpreter
A

User File Space
B

User Work Space
C

Referring to Figure 3.1 in the text, the Prolog machine has three work spaces in the memory: (**A**) the interpreter itself, (**B**) the user file space containing your loaded programs, and (**C**) the user work space where the Prolog interpreter searches for answers to your query.

listing. At any point during your session, you can type *listing*. This causes the interpreter to print to the screen all of the information stored in the various memory locations. In some Prologs, listing gives information from (A–C), in some only (B–C), and in others only (B). If listing includes (A–C), you may get a vast amount (10+ pages) of printout even before you have loaded your own program. If you have a variable, say NOUN, in your program, Prolog will store this in a memory location with a number, say _007. Listing usually forgets your variable names and outputs the number of the memory location. If you have loaded a simple fact, for example, noun([girl])., this will appear exactly as it is in your program. But any statement with a variable will have a number where your variable should be. The order of statements in your program seldom matches the order of items flushed to the screen by listing. Listing is useful for those who make forgetful blunders, for instance, it will let you know if you accidentally loaded your program two times or perhaps forgot to load it at all.

trace. At any point during your session, you can type *trace*. From that point on, Prolog will report to the screen all of the activity that goes on in the work space area. Often trace permits you to set the level of trace, with various titles: *creep, crawl, jump, fast,* and so on. The slowest speed reports every little detail of the work space every time Prolog makes even the slightest move. The fastest usually reports on the results every time Prolog executes a new relation in your program. Trace can produce a huge amount of information, most of it about the internal operations of the Prolog interpreter. But set to skip the lowest level of detail, it can be useful to show how your Prolog statements are being executed. Trace finds its greatest appeal among those people who are not easily bored.

breakpoint. This is the most useful of all of the debugging instructions. Each Prolog has its own way of executing breakpoint, but there are some general elements in common. If you include breakpoint as a goal in your statement, for example, ...goalx,breakpoint,goaly..., then when Prolog evaluates the breakpoint, it is neither true nor false, rather it stops and flashes a message on the screen waiting for you to tell it if breakpoint is true (and Prolog can go on to goaly) or is false (and should halt or backtrack). But before you tell Prolog to go on, halt, or backtrack, you can use a number of instructions (listing. among them) to examine the state of the Prolog machine. If you know that Prolog always makes a mistake when interpreting a goal, say goaly, of your relation, then you can place a breakpoint before goaly and find out what is the state of the Prolog machine (the value of all variables, the contents of the work space) when it is evaluating goaly. Often Prolog, even shareware, has facilities for printing the screen contents during a breakpoint so you can use hardcopy and not have to squint at numbers blazing by on the screen. The ability to use breakpoints effectively is the mark of a programmer who understands the organization and operation of the Prolog interpreter, and who has thought through the logical organization of their program.

References

Arnauld, A. (1964). *The art of thinking: Port–Royal logic* [*La Logique, ou L'Art de Penser*] (J. Dickoff & P. James, Trans.). New York: Bobbs–Merrill Company. (Original work published in 1662)

Arnauld, A. & Pierre, N. (1992). *La Logique ou L'Art de Penser* [Notes et postface de Charles Jourdain] (1992). Paris: Gallimard. (Original work published in 1662)

Aronoff, M. (1976). *Word formation in generative grammar.* Cambridge, MA: MIT Press.

Arzan, A. (1992). *Lodes of grammar: Syntactic error analysis for intelligent computer–assisted language instruction.* Unpublished doctoral dissertation, New York University, New York, N.Y.

Bains, G.S. (1994). *Complex structures in Hindi–Urdu: Explorations in government and binding theory.* New York: Peter Lang.

Baumol, W.J. & Wolff, E.N. (1992). Comparative U.S. productivity performance and the state of manufacturing: The latest data. *Center for Applied Economics Newsletter, 10*, 1–4.

Berenstein, A., & de V. Roberts, M. (1958). Computer versus chess player. In R.R. Fenichel & J. Weizenbaum (Eds.), *Computer and computation.* San Francisco: W.H. Freeman.

Berwick, R.C., & Weinberg, A.S. (1984). *The grammatical basis of linguistic performance: Language use and acquisition.* Cambridge, MA: MIT Press.

Bratko, I. (1990). *Prolog: Programming for artificial intelligence.* (2nd. ed.) New York: Addison–Wesley.

Chomsky, N. (1951). *The morpho–phonemics of modern Hebrew.* New York: Garland.

Chomsky, N. (1957). *Syntactic structures.* The Hague: Mouton.

Chomsky, N. (1964). *Current issues in linguistic theory.* The Hague: Mouton.

Chomsky, N. (1965). *Aspects of the theory of syntax.* Cambridge, MA: MIT Press.

Chomsky, N. (1966). *Cartesian linguistics: A chapter in the history of rationalist thought.* New York: Harper and Row.

Chomsky, N. (1968). *Language and mind.* New York: Harcourt Brace Jovanovich.

Chomsky, N. (1970). Remarks on nominalizations. In N. Chomsky (Ed.), *Studies on semantics in generative grammar.* (pp. 11–61) The Hague: Mouton.

Chomsky, N. (1971). *Problems of knowledge and freedom: The Russell lectures.* New York: Pantheon Books.

Chomsky, N. (1972). *Studies on semantics in generative grammar.* The Hague: Mouton.

Chomsky, N. (1975a). *Reflections on language.* New York: Pantheon Books.

Chomsky, N. (1975b). *The logical structure of linguistic theory* (drawn from an unpublished 1955–56 manuscript). New York: Plenum Press.

Chomsky, N. (1977). *Language and responsibility* (M. Ronat, Ed., J. Viertel, Trans.). New York: Pantheon Books.

Chomsky, N. (1980a). On binding. *Linguistic Inquiry, 11,* 14–46.

Chomsky, N. (1980b). On cognitive structures and their development. In M. Piattelli–Palmarini (Ed.), *Language and learning: The debate between Jean Piaget and Noam Chomsky.* Cambridge, MA: Harvard University Press.

Chomsky, N. (1980c). *Rules and representation.* New York: Columbia University Press.

Chomsky, N. (1981). *Lectures on government and binding.* Dordrecht, The Netherlands: Foris Publications.

Chomsky, N. (1982). *Some concepts and consequences of the theory of government and binding.* Cambridge, MA: MIT Press

Chomsky, N. (1986a). *Barriers.* Cambridge, MA: MIT Press.

Chomsky, N. (1986b). *Knowledge of language: Its nature, origin, and use.* New York: Praeger.

Chomsky, N. (1987). *Language in a psychological setting.* (Working Papers in Linguistics). Tokyo, Japan: Sophia Linguistica.

Chomsky, N. (1988). *Language and problems of knowledge: The Managua lectures.* Cambridge, MA: MIT Press.

Chomsky, N. (1990). On formalization and formal languages. *Natural language and linguistic theory, 8,* 143–147.

Chomsky, N. (1991a). Linguistics and cognitive science: Problems and Mysteries. In A. Kasher (ed.), *The Chomskyan turn.* Oxford: Blackwell.

Chomsky, N. (1991b). Some notes on economy of derivation and representation. In R. Freidin (Ed.), *Principles and parameters in comparative grammar.* Cambridge, MA: MIT Press.

Chomsky, N. (1992a). Language and interpretation: Philosophical reflections and empirical inquiry. In J. Earman (Ed.), *Inference, explanation, and other philosophical frustrations.* Berkeley: University of California Press.

Chomsky, N. (1992b). *A minimalist program for linguistic theory.* Cambridge, MA: MIT Working Papers in Linguistics.

Chomsky, N. (to appear). Explaining language use. *Philosophical Studies.*

Chomsky, N., & Lasnik, H. (1977). Filters and control. *Linguistic Inquiry, 8,* 425–504.

Clocksin, W., & Mellish, C. (1981). *Programming in Prolog.* Berlin: Springer Verlag.

Covington, M. (1993). *Natural language processing for Prolog programmers.* Englewood Cliffs, NJ: Prentice–Hall

Curme, G.O. (1931). *A grammar of the English language in three volumes. Vol. I: History of the English language, sounds and spellings, word–formation.* Boston: DC Heath.

Curme, G.O. (1931). *A grammar of the English language in three volumes. Vol. II: Parts of speech and accidence.* Boston: DC Heath.

Curme, G.O. 1931. *A grammar of the English language in three volumes. Vol III: Syntax.* Boston: DC Heath.

Darwin, C. (1962). *Origin of the species by means of natural selection.* New York: Touchstone Books. (Original work published in 1859)

Descartes, R. (1964). *The philosophical works of Descartes* (E.S. Haldane & G. Ross, Trans.). New York: Dover Press (Original work published 1911)

Dewey, J. (1969). *Experience and education.* London: Collier–Macmillan. (Original work published 1938)

Dodd, T. (1990). *Prolog: A logical approach.* Oxford: Oxford University Press.

Dougherty, R.C. (1970). A grammar of coordinate conjoined structures: I. *Language, 46,* 850–898.

Dougherty, R.C. (1971). A grammar of coordinate conjoined structures, II. *Language, 47,* 298–339.

Dougherty, R.C. (1975). Harris and Chomsky at the syntax–semantics boundary. In D. Hockney (Ed.), *Contemporary research in philosophical logic and linguistic semantics* (pp. 137–193). Dordrecht–Holland: D. Reidel.

Dougherty, R.C. (1976). Einstein and Chomsky on scientific methodology. *Linguistics, 167,* pp. 5–14.

Dougherty, R.C. (1979). An information theoretical model of grammar reproduction. Annual Summer Meeting of the Linguistic Society of America: Forum Lecture.

Dougherty, R. C. (1983). Current views of language and grammar. In F. Machlup & U. Mansfield (Eds.), *The study of information: Interdisciplinary messages.* New York: J. Wiley.

Dougherty, R. C. (1984). Theory and principles of digital signal processing. In W.D. Stanley, G.R. Dougherty, & R.C. Dougherty (Eds.), *Digital signal processing* (pp. 1–314) Englewood Cliffs, NJ: Prentice–Hall.

Dougherty, R.C. (1988). Language learning machines. *Semiotic Inquiry, 8,* 27–42.

Dougherty, R.C. (in preparation). *Universal grammar in Prolog: Structures between sound and meaning.*

Edwards, J. (1993). Survey of electronic corpora and related resources for language researchers. In J. Edwards & M.D. Lampert (Eds.), *Talking data: Transcription and coding in discourse research* (pp. 263–310). Hillsdale, NJ: Lawrence Erlbaum Associates.

Encyclopedia Britannica. (1983). Cryptography. In *The New Encyclopedia Britannica* (Vol V). Chicago: Encyclopedia Britannica.

Fixx, J. (1972). *Problems for the super intelligent.* Garden City, NY: Doubleday.

Fixx, J. (1976). *More problems for the super intelligent.* Garden City, NY: Doubleday.

Freidin, R. (Ed.) (1991). *Principles and parameters in comparative grammar.* Cambridge, MA: MIT Press.

Freidin, R. (1992). *Foundations of generative syntax.* Cambridge, MA: MIT Press.

Fromkin, V., & Rodman, R. (1993). *An introduction to language* (5th. ed.) New York: Harcourt, Brace, Jovanovich.

Gazdar, G, & Mellish, C. (1989). *Natural language processing in Prolog: An introduction to computational linguistics.* New York: Addison–Wesley.

Gross, M. (1986). *Les Adjectifs composes du Francais.* Paris: CNRS.

Gross, M. (1989a). The use of finite automata in the lexical representation of natural language. In M. Gross & D. Perrin (Eds.), *Electronic dictionaries and automata in computational linguistics.* New York: Springer Verlag.

Gross, M. (1989b). *Grammaire Transformationnelle du Francais: 3 Syntaxe de l'Adverbe.*

Paris: Cantilene.

Gross, M. (1990). Linguistics representation and text analysis. In *Proceedings of the 1990 Meeting of the Academic Europeae*. Strasbourg.

Gross, M. (1991). Constructing Lexicon–Grammars. In B. Atkins and A. Zampoli (Eds.), *Computational approaches to the lexicon*. London: Oxford University Press.

Gross, M. (1992). The lexicon–grammar of a language: Application to French. In K. Brown (Ed.), *Encyclopedia of language and linguistics. London*: Pergamon Press.

Gross, M. (1993). Lexicon based algorithms for the automatic analysis of natural language. In F. Beckmann & G. Heyer (Eds.), *Theory and practice of the lexicon*. Berlin: Walter de Gruyter.

Gross, M., & Perrin, D. (1989). *Electronic dictionaries and automata in computational linguistics*. New York: Springer Verlag.

Halitsky, D., & Dougherty, R.C. (in preparation). *The cognitive imperative*.

Harrap's New Collegiate French and English Dictionary (P. Collin, H. Knox, M. Ledesert, & R. Ledesert, Eds.) (1982). London: Harrap.

Harris, Z. (1951). *Methods in structural linguistics*. Chicago: University of Chicago Press.

Harris, Z. (1957). Co–occurrence and transformation in linguistic structure. *Language, 33*, 283–340.

Harris, Z. (1965). Transformational theory. *Language, 41*, 363–401.

Hodges, A. (1983). *Alan Turing: The enigma*. New York: Touchstone Books.

Jespersen, O. (1894). *Progress in language*. London: George Allen and Unwin.

Jespersen, O. (1961). *A modern English grammar on historical principles*. London: George Allen and Unwin. (Original work published 1913)

Jespersen, O. (1964). *Essential of English grammar*. Atlanta, A: University of Alabama Press. (Original work published 1931)

Johnson, M. (1988). *Attribute value logic and the theory of grammar*. Center for the Study of Language and Information.

Johnson, S. (1938). Preface to the English dictionary. In C.W. Elliott (Ed.), *Prefaces and prologues to famous books* (The Harvard Classics, pp. 182–207) New York: P.F. Colllier. (Original work published 1755)

Katz, B., & Levin, B. (1988). Exploiting lexical regularities in designing natural language systems. (Lexicon Project Working Papers, Vol. 22). Cambridge, MA: MIT Artificial Intelligence Laboratory.

Koskenniemi, K. (1983). *Two level morphology: a general computational model for word–form recognition and production*. Unpublished doctoral dissertation, University of Helsinki, Helsinki,Finland.

Lasnik, H., & Uriagereka, J. (1988). *A course in GB syntax; Lectures on binding and empty categories*. Cambridge, MA: MIT Press.

Leacock, C. (1990). *Lexically based parsing with application to infinitive control constructions in English*. Unpublished doctoral dissertation, City University of New York, New York, NY.

Leacock, C. (1991). *On the interpretation of PRO*. (IBM Watson Lab Research Reports)

Leacock, C., Towell, G., & Voorhees, E. (1993a). Corpus–based statistical sense resolution. In *Proceedings of the ARPA Workshop on Human Language Technology*. San Francisco: Morgan Kaufman.

Leacock, C., Towell, G, & Voorhees, E. (1993b). Towards building contextual representations of word senses using statistical models. In *Proceedings of the SIGLEX Workshop on the Acquisition of Lexical Models from Text*. (Also to appear in B. Boguraev & J. Pustejovsky (Eds.), *Corpus Processing for Lexical Acquisition*. Cambridge, MA: MIT Press.

Lightfoot, D. (1984). *The language lottery: Toward a biology of grammars*. Cambridge, MA: MIT Press.

Lightfoot, D. (1991). *How to set parameters: Arguments from language change*. Cambridge, MA: MIT Press.

Machlup, F., & Mansfield, U. (Eds.), (1983). *The study of information: Interdisciplinary messages*. New York: J. Wiley.

Malpas, J. (1987). *Prolog: A relational language and its applications*. Englewood Cliffs, NJ: Prentice–Hall.

Meyers, A. (1994). *A unification–based approach to government and binding theory*. Unpublished doctoral dissertation, New York University, New York: NY.

Miller, G.A. (1991). *The science of words* (Scientific American Library, Vol. 35) New York: W.H. Freeman.

Miller, G.A., Leacock, C., Tengi, R, & Bunker, R.T. (1993). A semantic concordance. In *Proceedings of the ARPA Workshop on Human Language Technology*. San Francisco: Morgan Kaufman.

Miller, G.A., Chodorow, M., Landes, S., Leacock, C., & Thomas. R.G. (1994). Using a semantic concordance for sense identification. In *Proceedings of the ARPA Workshop on Human Language Technology*. San Francisco: Morgan Kaufman.

Mueller, R., & Page, R. (1988). *Symbolic computing with Lisp and Prolog*. New York: J. Wiley.

O'Grady, W., Dobrovolsky, M., & Aronoff, M. (1993). *Contemporary linguistics: An introduction* (2nd. ed.). New York: St. Martin's Press.

Peirce, C.S. (1877). The fixation of belief. In C. Hartshorne & P. Weiss (Eds.), *Collected papers of Charles Sanders Peirce* (Vol. V, pp. 223–247). Cambridge, MA: Harvard University Press.

Peirce, C.S. (1965). *Collected papers of Charles Sanders Peirce. Vol. V: Pragmatism and pragmaticism* (C. Hartshorne & P. Weiss, Eds.). Cambridge, MA: Harvard University Press.

Pereira, F.C. & Warren, D. (1980). Definite clause grammars for language analysis: A survey of the formalism and a comparison with augmented transition networks. *Artificial Intelligence, 13*, 231–278.

Perrin, D. (1989). *Automates et Allgorithmes sur let Mot*. Paris: CNET.

Piattelli–Palmarini, M. (Ed.). (1980). *Language and learning: The debate between Jean Piaget and Noam Chomsky*. Cambridge, MA: Harvard University Press.

Plato. (1952). Meno (B. Jowett, Trans.). In *The dialogues of Plato* (*Great Books of the Western World, Vol. 7*, pp. 174–191). Chicago: Encyclopedia Britannica.

Pollard, C. & Sag, I.A. (1987). *Information–based syntax and semantics*. Chicago:

Center for the Study of Language and Information. University of Chicago Press.

Radford, A. (1985). *Transformational syntax: A student's guide to Chomsky's extended standard theory*. Cambridge, UK: Cambridge University Press.

Russell, B. (1974). *The art of philosophizing, and other essays*. Totowa, NJ: Littlefield, Adams.

Sapir, E. (1921). *Language: An introduction to the study of speech*. New York: Harcourt, Brace and World.

Searle, J. (1984). *Minds, brains, and science*. Cambridge, MA: Harvard University Press.

Shannon, C. (1949). The mathematical theory nf communication. In C. E. Shannon & W. Weaver (Eds.), *The mathematical theory of communication* (pp. 1–54). Urbana: The University of Illinois.

Shannon, C. (1956). *Automata studies*. Princeton: NJ: Princeton University Press.

Shannon, C. (1971). A chess–playing machine. In R.R. Fenichel & J. Weizenbaum (Eds.), *Computers and computation*. San Francisco: W.H. Freeman. (Original work published in 1950)

Shannon, C. & Weaver, W. (1949). *The mathematical theory of communication*. Urbana: The University of Chicago Press.

Shieber, S. (1986). *An introduction to unification based approaches to grammar*. Chicago: Chicago University Press.

Shieber, S. (1992). *Constraint–based grammar formalisms: Parsing and type inference for natural and computer languages*. Cambridge, MA: MIT Press.

Silberztein, M. (1989). The lexical analysis of French. In M. Gross & D. Perrin (Eds.), *Electronic dictionaries and automata in computational linguistics*. New York: Springer Verlag.

Sowa, J. (1987). A Prolog to Prolog. In A. Walker, M. McCord, J.F. Sowa, & W.G. Wilson (eds.), *Knowledge systems and Prolog: A logical approach to expert systems and natural language processing*. New York: Addison–Wesley.

Sproat, R. (1992). *Morphology and computation*. Cambridge, MA: MIT Press.

Stabler, E.P. (1993). *The logical approach to syntax*. Cambridge, MA: MIT Press.

Stanlex, W.D., Dougherty, G.R., and Dougherty, R.C. (1984). *Digital signal processing* (2nd. ed.). Englewood Cliffs, NJ: Prentice–Hall.

Stein, G. (1935). Parts of speech and punctuation. In *Lectures in America* (pp. 79–90). New York: The Modern Library, Inc.

Sterling, L., & Shapiro, E. (1987). *The art of Prolog: Advanced programming techniques*. Cambridge, MA: MIT Press.

Susman, L.S. (1990). *Pragmatic performance and reflections of competence*. Unpublished doctoral dissertation, New York University, New York, NY.

Turing, A. (1950). Computing machinery and intelligence. In *Mind*.

Tzoukerman, E., & Liberman, M. (1990). A finite state morphological processor for Spanish. *COLING, 3*.

van Riemsdijk, H., & Williams, E. (1986). *Introduction to the theory of grammar*. Cambridge, MA: MIT Press.

Walker, A., McCord, M., Sowa, J.F., & Wilson, W.G. (1987). *Knowledge systems and Prolog: A logical approach to expert systems and natural language processing*.

New York: Addison–Wesley.

Weizenbaum, J. (1976). *Computer power and human reason: From judgment to calculation*. San Francisco: W.H. Freeman.

Wiener, N. (1948). *Cybernetics: or control and communication in the animal and the machine*. New York: J Wiley.

Wiener, N. (1954). *The human use of human beings: Cybernetics and society*. Garden City, NY: Doubleday.

Index of Names

Index

345